Women and Epilepsy

Women and Epilepsy

Edited by

M.R. TRIMBLE

Reader in Behavioural Neurology,
Department of Neurology,
Institute of Neurology,
Queen Square

and

Consultant Physician in Psychological Medicine,
The National Hospital for Neurology and Neurosurgery,
Queen Square,
London, UK

JOHN WILEY & SONS
Chichester · New York · Brisbane · Toronto · Singapore

Other Wiley Editorial Offices

John Wiley & Sons, Inc., 605 Third Avenue,
New York, NY 10158-0012, USA

Jacaranda Wiley Ltd, G.P.O. Box 859, Brisbane,
Queensland 4001, Australia

John Wiley & Sons (Canada) Ltd, 22 Worcester Road,
Rexdale, Ontario M9W 1L1, Canada

John Wiley & Sons (SEA) Pte Ltd, 37 Jalan Pemimpin   05-04,
Block B, Union Industrial Building, Singapore 2057

Library of Congress Cataloging-in-Publication Data

Women and epilepsy / edited by M.R. Trimble.
     p.   cm.
   Includes bibliographical references and index.
   ISBN 0 471 92998 0
   1. Epilepsy. 2. Women—Diseases. I. Trimble, Michael R.
   [DNLM: 1. Anticonvulsants—pharmacology. 2. Depression.
3. Epilepsy. 4. Menstruation Disorders. 5. Pregnancy
Complications. 6. Sex Characteristics. 7. Sex Factors. 8. Women.
WL 385 W872]
   RC372.W66   1991
   616.8'530082—dc20
   DLC
   for Library of Congress   91-8460
                                                            CIP

A catalogue record for this book is
available from the British Library

Typeset by Inforum Typesetting, Portsmouth
Printed in Great Britain by Biddles Ltd, Guildford

Contents

Section IV

Contributors

D. Back, *Department of Pharmacology and Therapeutics, New Medical School, Ashton Street, Liverpool L69 3BX, UK*

Tim Betts, *Neuropsychiatry Clinic, Department of Psychiatry, Queen Elizabeth Hospital, Birmingham B15, 2TH, UK*

Sarah Boden, *Neuropsychiatry Clinic, Department of Psychiatry, Queen Elizabeth Hospital, Birmingham B15 2TH, UK*

R. Corcoran, *Chalfont Centre for Epilepsy, Chalfont St Peter, Gerrards Cross, Buckinghamshire SL9 0RJ, UK*

P. Crawford, *Regional Neurosciences Unit, Walton Hospital, Liverpool 9, UK* (present address: *Bootham Park Hospital, York YO3 7BY, UK*)

Hanneke M. de Boer, *Institute for Epilepsy, Heemstede, The Netherlands*

Zarrina Kurtz, *Department of Paediatric Epidemiology, Institute of Child Health, 30 Guilford Street, London WC1N 1EH, UK*

A.M. McGuire, *Department of Neuropsychiatry, Institute of Neurology, Queen Square, London WC1N 3BG, UK*

M. Orme, *Department of Pharmacology and Therapeutics, New Medical School, Ashton Street, Liverpool L69 3BX, UK*

Philip N. Patsalos, *University Department of Clinical Neurology, Institute of Neurology, Queen Square, London WC1N 3BG, UK*

John M. Pellock, *Division of Child Neurology, Medical College of Virginia, Virginia Commonwealth University, Richmond, Virginia 23298, USA*

Mary M. Robertson, *Academic Department of Psychiatry, Middlesex Hospital, Mortimer Street, London W1N 8AA, UK*

David C. Taylor, *Royal Manchester Children's Hospital, Jesson House, Manchester Road, Swinton, Manchester, M27 1FG, UK*

P. Thompson, *Chalfont Centre for Epilepsy, Chalfont St Peter, Gerrards Cross, Buckinghamshire SL9 0RJ, UK*

B. Toone, *King's College Hospital, Denmark Hill, London SE5 9RS, UK*

Michael R. Trimble, *Department of Neurology, Institute of Neurology, Queen Square, London WC1N 3BG, UK*

D. Upton, *Chalfont Centre for Epilepsy, Chalfont St Peter, Gerrards Cross, Buckinghamshire SL9 0RJ, UK*

Susan C. Usiskin, *The National Hospital for Neurology and Neurosurgery, Maida Vale, London W9 1TL, UK*

Sheila J. Wallace, *University Hospital of Wales, Heath Park, Cardiff, Wales CF4 4XW, UK*

Mark S. Yerby, *Oregon University Health Service, 1040 NW 22nd Avenue, Portland, Oregon 97210, USA*

Preface

In editing this book, it has not been my intention, as reviewers are inclined to say, to produce another book on epilepsy. Further, although the book emerged from a meeting of the same title, and some discussions from that meeting are included in the text, it is not intended to be merely the proceedings of a conference. Rather, the theme emerged after discussions with colleagues as an important topic, not covered by any existing text, which deserved a publication in its own right.

One of the interesting challenges of preparing the list of contributors was the multidisciplinary nature of the theme, and, of course, the necessity to achieve a balance between the sexes. The latter was the easier task to achieve, while the former remains a formidable obstacle in terms of amalgamating the different needs of the subject and the requirements of potential readers.

The first section deals with some psychosocial issues. A highly personal account of experiences of living with epilepsy by Sue Usiskin, is followed by chapters on quality of life and its assessment by Anna McGuire, and a description of some of the counselling techniques adopted by the Epilepsy Institute at Heemstede by Hanneke de Boer. These contributions are followed by chapters on epidemiology (Zarrina Kurtz), developmental differences between the sexes (David Taylor), and the problems of adolescence and its associated epilepsy syndromes, some of which appear to be sex related (Jack Pellock and Sheila Wallace).

The next section deals with sex hormones, seizure threshold, and contraception (Philip Patsalos, and Michael Orme and his colleagues), while Pamela Crawford discusses the controversial issue of catamenial epilepsy. In the next chapter, Mark Yerby has reviewed a considerable amount of published work relating to pregnancy and the very important subject of teratogenesis and congenital malformations. Practical advice is given about management of pregnant women with epilepsy.

In the final section affective disorder (Mary Robertson) and cognitive problems (Pamela Thompson and colleagues) are discussed, and Brian Toone reviews the limited, but interesting, literature on sexual auras and seizures, noting some potential male/female differences. Tim Betts has provided a thought-provoking chapter on pseudo-, or non-epileptic, seizures and raises the timely issue of sexual abuse in relationship to at least some forms of the condition. The book finishes with my own review of famous women who have, or may have, suffered from a seizure disorder, and a collection of women who are real or fictional whose epilepsy is described in literature.

It is hoped that this book will reveal some of the very special problems of women with epilepsy, and stimulate among readers ideas both for their own management of patients, and for rewarding research proposals.

MICHAEL TRIMBLE
London 1990

Section I

1

The woman with epilepsy

Susan C. Usiskin
The National Hospital for Neurology and Neurosurgery, London, UK

> The important thing is not to be cured but to learn to live with your illness
> (S. Freud)

INTRODUCTION

The aim of this chapter is to explore the impact of epilepsy on the social and vocational aspects of a woman's life. A number of areas will be considered: childhood, adolescence (psychological factors, compliance and leisure), the menstrual cycle, contraception, sexual relationships, marriage, pregnancy, childbirth and child care, employment, later life and old age.

BEING A CHILD

The impact of having a child with epilepsy can be significant medically, socially and psychologically. It affects family equilibrium and can be a frustrating disorder for everyone. Parents may be confused as to what to expect or demand of their 'afflicted' child and be nervous about letting her out of their sight. They will want to know whether she will outgrow the condition and certainly no guarantees can be given. The way they perceive the disorder to be, irrespective of whether their perception is accurate, will be a key factor in the way they are able to cope. The family's adjustment has a profound impact on how the child reacts.

The strange symptoms the child experiences may create an acutely stressful situation. If siblings are stand-offish and peers rejecting, she will have nowhere to turn for support and confirmation of worth. If parents are able to contain their anxiety, the child will stand a good chance of overcoming these difficulties in time. Where this is not the case, social slights and cruel remarks may cause long-term and sometimes fundamental damage. The very

Women and Epilepsy. Edited by M.R. Trimble
© 1991 John Wiley & Sons Ltd

vulnerable may downgrade ambition, avoid competition and withdraw from society, whilst the overprotected become irritable, angry and manipulative. Dependency may be a problem for some. Parents often foster this and may later regret the pattern they have established. Where this begins early and continues into adulthood, it is sometimes irreversible.

A seizure disorder may be used to manipulate both the home and school situation. Growth to independence—the most important task of parenthood—may be compromised by epilepsy, leading to illness behaviour and increased dependency, with resulting difficulties in assuming adult roles in work and marriage.

ADOLESCENCE

Adolescence is a time of acute self-consciousness and emotional turmoil. Long before adolescents have any certainty about themselves, they are forced to make various choices about their future, which result in undesirable pressures and anxiety about failure.

Impact of epilepsy

Puberty heralds physical and hormonal changes in preparation for the reproductive role. Where the onset of epilepsy coincides with puberty, the adolescent girl may question her fitness for this potential role. At the same time, when she should normally be moving towards greater independence, her parents may very well respond by overprotecting her. If they allow themselves to be brainwashed into believing the common misconceptions about epilepsy (see Table 1) and its implications for her, or treat her as if she had a serious illness, their attitudes will be transmitted to the child. They may have a difficult task deciding what is best for her and require expert guidance and information.

Overprotection should be avoided. This applies equally at home and at school. The girl's teachers must be persuaded not to be unduly lenient, as this may encourage in her a feeling that she deserves special consideration which is not realistic. Having epilepsy should not be used as an excuse for

Table 1.   Common misconceptions concerning epilepsy

Association of epilepsy with mental illness and mental handicap

Assumption that seizures themselves (i.e. single seizures) cause damage

Presumed inheritance (i.e. regardless of aetiology, etc.)

Epilepsy is for life (no remission is possible)

Seizures are 100% controllable by medication (and if they do occur you are under-medicated!)

non-achievement or low goals—such a philosophy is very unconstructive and may have serious implications psychologically, namely lack of self-worth and inferiority.

It is important that the young girl and her family are able to discuss the issues that will form a basis from which she is able to grow in confidence. Her physician should introduce key issues, such as fear, anger, denial and confusion, and ensure continuity of care as far as possible. Good communication will encourage a feeling of trust, so that a therapeutic relationship may develop and grow. This may only happen, if she feels that the physician is not only interested in her condition from an academic viewpoint. It is worth noting that, in my experience as an epilepsy counsellor, precise seizure frequency has little impact on how well some patients adjust in psychological terms. Whether a person has two, three or four seizures per month is very rarely the crucial factor. There are many other more influential issues involved here. These include acute anxiety, loss of dignity, social isolation and low self-esteem.

The adolescent girl and her parents may have a variety of misconceptions about epilepsy, which they need to share. A prime example of this is the association of epilepsy with mental illness and mental handicap. There is also quite a widespread assumption that seizures themselves cause damage. Ideas concerning presumed inheritance may often be found. This can be a source of considerable anxiety and should be raised by the physician and appropriate advice given. Self-stigmatization, so detrimental to successful adjustment, may occur if these 'taboo subjects' are left unaired. The process of obtaining proper information is a crucial one, without which the girl may ultimately see herself as the victim of a vindictive world, a perspective to be avoided.

Compliance

Adolescence is often a time of rebellion and good advice is seldom welcome, especially if it comes from parents or their chosen professionals. This may be a factor in problems with compliance, the regularity with which the adolescent girl takes her medication or, indeed, if she takes it at all. Other factors involved may be anger and denial. Quite often there is a great deal of resentment attached to a diagnosis of epilepsy with its associated stigma. Non-compliance may be viewed as an indication of the subject's difficulty in coming to terms with the fact of her epilepsy. By avoiding her antiepileptic medication she is, in fact, denying her need for this treatment. She is pretending that her epilepsy does not exist.

Non-compliance may be used as a stick with which to beat her parents and her physician, whom she indirectly holds responsible for her dilemma. There may also be social reasons for non-compliance. An adolescent girl may fear that regular consumption of medication will mark her out from the rest of her peer group and provoke some unwelcome enquiries.

The ideal antiepileptic drug would have solely an antiepileptic effect, but some drugs also produce unwanted side effects. These may range from cognitive impairment and mild sedation to gum disorders, hair loss and weight gain. If any of these factors are a problem they may act as a further disincentive to the adolescent girl with epilepsy.

Leisure and travel

There are surprisingly few leisure pursuits that may not be enjoyed by people with epilepsy. There are no hard and fast rules but, in general, climbing, canoeing and scuba-diving are best avoided (the risks presented, for example, in having an atonic drop attack on a rock-face, a complex partial attack in a canoe or a tonic–clonic seizure whilst scuba diving are good reasons not to participate in them). Common sense should prevail at all times. Activities such as swimming and horse riding are best when accompanied by someone who is aware of first aid for seizures. This also applies to travel and recreational pursuits where long distances are involved.

It would be sensible for an adolescent girl with epilepsy to have a friend with her when she goes away. She must, of course, ensure that she has adequate supplies of antiepileptic medication and an 'I have epilepsy' card giving details of her identity, type of epilepsy, where she is staying and which drugs she takes. This information should be carried by the girl on her person, at all times, for the duration of her stay. In so doing, unnecessary risks are curtailed and less is left to chance. Such strategies are to be encouraged; living with epilepsy is a risky business and any precautions which minimize further risk are good practice.

The menstrual cycle

Some women have menstrual or pre-menstrual epilepsy (catamenial epilepsy), in which seizures occur just before menstruation or during it. Although some doctors are sceptical about this, there is no doubt that this condition exists (see Chapter 10). Little is understood about why pre-menstrual seizures, or indeed the pre-menstrual syndrome, occur, and why treatments advocated for the latter work for some women and not for others.

In Western Europe and the USA until as recently as the last century, it was not uncommon for a woman with epilepsy to have her ovaries removed. Doctors were most likely to operate on girls whose seizures seemed to worsen just before or during menstruation. Few, if any, long-term cures were effected by such drastic procedures, and the whole process evoked much criticism. It was not unusual for women with epilepsy to find themselves in an institution, asylum or epileptic colony, where like lepers they could be expected to live out their lives in isolation. Epilepsy was regarded as a strongly inherited disease, and eugenic laws were passed in order to prevent the birth of 'tainted offspring'. Today we understand that inheritance plays a relatively small part in the causation of seizures.

Sexual relationships

It is not uncommon for some women with epilepsy to be concerned about the possibility of a seizure during sexual activity. There are a number of reasons why this should be so. A woman may feel very vulnerable and fear that a seizure during sex will spoil her partner's feelings for her and that she will cease to be attractive to him. She herself may have mixed feelings about 'letting go' during intercourse and there may be a link here between her feelings about being 'out of control' per se and her epilepsy. Having epilepsy means having to come to terms with the inevitability of being 'out of control' during seizures. This is *not* easily achieved.

In my experience as an epilepsy counsellor, women sometimes confuse the physically similar features of a convulsive seizure and those of orgasm. Once this tendency has been identified and openly discussed, it may be pointed out that the former is to be endured and the latter enjoyed. With time, patience and reassurance, the problems may be overcome.

The woman with epilepsy should have no special difficulty using contraception, and the advice of a doctor or family-planning clinic will ensure that an appropriate method is used. Knowledge of the influence of anticonvulsant drugs on the effectiveness of oral contraception will be essential if this is the preferred method (see Chapter 9).

MARRIAGE

Marriage is one of the central goals of life for many people. However, in some countries the odds are still stacked against its realization for the woman with epilepsy. In India even today, a woman known to have the condition has virtually no chance of an arranged marriage. People with epilepsy are thought to be uneducable, unemployable, and a danger to the community. This view is quite widely held in Third World countries but clearly not restricted to them. Fundamentalist groups in most religious cultures, who follow ancient laws to the letter, still adhere to the view that epilepsy is always an inherited disease. Such laws were originally intended to prevent its spread, but now that it is understood that inheritance plays a relatively small part in the causation of seizures these outdated laws are quite irrelevant.

The existence of such laws and their dismissive view of the woman with epilepsy as a marriageable commodity may partly explain why some women are loath to reveal the fact of their condition to their future husband and his family. The fear of rejection may be very daunting to them. With this in mind, they must balance the relative advantages and disadvantages of concealing or revealing their epilepsy. Some decide to say nothing and no doubt live in fear that a seizure before the wedding day will prevent the marriage entirely, or that one after the event could be seen as grounds for divorce. Such women are likely to suffer from acute anxiety and feelings of guilt which may be difficult to resolve.

PREGNANCY

These days, happily, many women with epilepsy, including myself, marry and have children. The majority have straightforward pregnancies and healthy babies. A common and legitimate concern is that the drug they are taking may harm their baby. Unfortunately none of the antiepileptic drugs are entirely safe in pregnancy, although carbamazepine is generally thought to be the least harmful (see Chapter 11).

Twenty years ago, when I embarked on my first pregnancy, I was not warned of the effects my antiepileptic medication could have on my baby. My son, happily, was unaffected but the birth of our daughter marked the beginning of an intensely traumatic few years for us. My daughter showed clear signs of maternal phenytoin ingestion, with congenital heart defects and excessive hair growth on both her body and face. No indication could be given about her future and at this stage she looked terribly ill. The first two years were critical but fortunately she attained near-normal development for her age by the time she was three. From then on she went from strength to strength.

Medication may need to be reviewed before a pregnancy begins and during it. This is not unusual. A woman should be sure to inform her antenatal clinic of the following at her first visit:

— that she has epilepsy;
— what her seizures are like (their nature, length, pattern and frequency);
— what medication she takes;
— whether her husband/partner has epilepsy.

With appropriate guidance, the majority of women will encounter few difficulties. This equally applies during the delivery and after the birth.

BABY CARE

The pros and cons of breast and bottle feeding are for the individual to decide. Where active epilepsy is a problem, bottle feeding may be more appropriate.

It means that feeding can be shared with the male partner if seizures occur, or if lack of sleep is a trigger factor. Where there is a risk of dropping the baby during a seizure, it is good practice to sit on floor cushions whilst feeding. This minimizes risk to the mother as well. It is preferable to wash and change the baby on a waterproof mat placed on the floor, rather than on a bed from which the child may fall. I made it a rule never to bath my babies when I was alone with them, and I advise other mothers with epilepsy to adhere to this simple rule. Once common sense and practical precautions are put into practice, there is no reason why women with epilepsy should not enjoy parenthood.

HELPING YOUNG CHILDREN TO COPE

'Does mother often do this?'

It is no doubt a very distressing experience for young children to make sense of their mother's seizures. In my experience a coping strategy is essential if children are to handle this dilemma positively. If they see an adult responding calmly, this is an important and influential first step. Children learn best by example.

Coping with a traumatic experience such as a seizure presents a dilemma to the child. It constitutes a role reversal, if only a temporary one, where the mother is helpless and dependent and the child becomes the 'carer'. If this is to work in practice, it will be necessary for the child to have a small practical role to perform. This should be a simple task. My own son would run and get a cloth to place under my face to protect it from abrasions, and to absorb excess saliva. At the same time my small daughter would sit stroking my face, offering words of comfort. I believe that to deny a child a role in such situations would only serve to exacerbate their fears and make matters worse. Similarly, it is important that their questions are addressed in a positive and simple manner as and when they arise. My own children were very relieved to learn that, despite my groaning sounds, I was not in fact in physical pain during a seizure.

Although at home we were united in attitude and strategy, difficulties arose when my seizures occurred on the street. Widespread ignorance concerning epilepsy still abounds in the community. My son was asked: 'Does mother often do this?' by an indignant customer at the local butcher, as he tended to me on the floor of the shop. The fact is that members of the public find it incredible that a small child should be seen to cope with a situation better than they could themselves.

It is not unusual to meet with a certain amount of hostility. I have been asked whether I thought it was fair to have had children at all and have at times been refused help by employees of various high street businesses. One wet and windy afternoon I was passing the local building society when I recognized the first signs of a seizure. Wasting no time I entered, beckoning for help as I crumpled to the floor. The seizure gained momentum. I felt very conspicuous as, apart from myself, the shop was empty. The staff stayed exactly where they were behind the counter. None of them came to my aid as I shook and groaned.

Eventually the seizure subsided and I lay wondering how I might get one of the staff to ring my husband at his office nearby. As soon as I was able, I crawled across the floor to the counter, clutching my epilepsy card. I indicated my husband's work number on it and fortunately he appeared in minutes. The manager, who was still behind the counter, explained that he thought I was the diversion for a robbery and had he come to my aid there would have been a chance for an accomplice to get behind the counter. I remember hearing this in complete disbelief. My husband explained that my condition was entirely genuine but the manager was quite adamant that he could not afford to take any risks.

I make a special point of going back to see people where I have had a seizure. When someone has been helpful they may appreciate seeing me well and have questions to ask about the condition. Those who have not been helpful benefit from basic education about epilepsy in the form of a simple leaflet covering first aid for fits.

EMPLOYMENT

Is the woman with epilepsy employable?

Finding and keeping work is increasingly difficult for everyone. In the face of this competition, a woman with epilepsy may feel that her chances of getting employment are slim. She may not be immediately successful in getting the job of her choice but the temptation to blame her epilepsy should be resisted.

The first essential when competing in the job market is to have educational or technical qualifications or skills to offer, appropriate to the type of employment sought. Other important factors are age, experience and good references. The woman's attitude and enthusiasm, together with her ability to sell herself at interview, are also vitally important. In order to be realistic about her employment prospects she should consider whether the presence of her epilepsy is relevant to the type of work she seeks. Much will depend on the nature and severity of her condition and whether there are any additional disabilities. If her seizures are completely controlled and she has appropriate skills to offer, her chances should not be adversely affected. There may, however, be other factors which influence successful employment: the adverse effects of drugs, the incidence and severity of seizures, lack of social skills and low self-esteem. On balance, an individual with skills and talents is much more employable, despite a few seizures, than someone else with no seizures and no appropriate skills.

THE WOMAN WITH EPILEPSY 11

There are some jobs which are barred to people with epilepsy. These include working in the armed services, the police and fire services. The driving of heavy goods or public service vehicles of all kinds is prohibited. Any job where driving is essential will be closed to a woman with epilepsy unless she has been completely seizure free for two years or she has only had seizures during sleep for a period of three years. It may be difficult to gain admission to schools of nursing and medicine, though each case is rightly considered on its merits. The teaching of most subjects is possible but there may be restrictions placed on teaching physical education and swimming.

To conceal or reveal

How much should an employer be told about epilepsy? Many people feel that revealing their epilepsy will deter employers. In general terms more problems may arise from concealing epilepsy than from revealing it. This should be done in the right way at the right time. It should not, however, be over-emphasized. The danger here is that the problems may eclipse the qualities that attract the employer to the candidate. It is an advantage to know how to present epilepsy to an employer with knowledge and skills to correct misinformation. Sometimes an individual medical account written in lay terms can be useful as back-up. Many employers feel that the woman with epilepsy will be likely to take time off work and be generally unreliable. Concern is also expressed over liability to accidents. Research has shown that, in fact, they take less time off work, are reliable and have fewer accidents than other employees (Burden, 1981). These facts, together with the right kind of skills and qualifications, are positive selling points to an employer.

Unfortunately, some women use their epilepsy as an excuse for getting out of responsibilities at work. In so doing they are acting in an irresponsible manner, both to themselves and their employers. Their behaviour may confirm the suspicion that epilepsy in itself makes an employee incompetent and unreliable and in this way make employment for others with this condition more difficult to obtain. Employers with no previous experience of epilepsy will be inclined to judge the condition by the behaviour of those who live with it. Much of the stigma associated with epilepsy will be dispelled by the positive attitudes of those who have the condition than by any other means.

LATER LIFE

The menopause

The average age of women when the periods stop and pregnancy is no longer possible is in the early fifties. Some of the unpleasant characteristics associated with the menopause occur in a small number of women, and hormone replacement therapy may help if symptoms such as mood changes and hot flushes are severe. Supplementary oestrogen may help prevent excessive loss of calcium and osteoporosis. The latter renders bones increasingly brittle and more liable to break. If seizures are a problem, osteoporosis may present a real hazard.

Old age

The incidence of epilepsy falls in middle life but rises steeply in later life. About 20% of new cases begin after menopausal age. There are few studies of the effects of the disorder in such an age group but the elderly may be particularly sensitive to side effects of antiepileptic drugs, such as unsteadiness, drowsiness and confusion.

CONCLUSION

My personal and professional experience of epilepsy in the lives of women has revealed much about their primary concerns. In order that there may be a chance of gradual change, it is important to establish how various underlying tensions affect their daily lives.

Self-stigma, perceived stigma, lack of confidence and of social skills may devastate the chance of a reasonable social and working life. In my view there is a clear conflict between the way epilepsy is seen by the public and the way it feels to those who live with it. To the unaffected, the person with epilepsy is 'normal' between seizures. However reasonable this view might seem, the dilemma lies in the fact that to the individual with epilepsy life between seizures is rather like walking on a series of trap-doors, any one of which may throw you to the ground without a moment's notice. They live with an ever-present threat, never knowing when the next seizure will strike.

There is little doubt that normal issues are magnified for the woman with epilepsy, but with determination, a positive attitude, appropriate guidance and information most difficulties may be overcome.

REFERENCE

Burden, G. (1981) Social aspects. In: *Epilepsy and Psychiatry* (ed. E.H. Reynolds and M.R. Trimble), pp. 296–235. Churchill Livingstone, Edinburgh.

2

Quality of life in women with epilepsy

A.M. McGuire
Institute of Neurology, London, UK

INTRODUCTION

The concept of quality of life

Quality of life (QOL) is a much used yet ill-defined term. The concept has come to prominence in recent years in the health care field due to an increasing prevalence of patients with chronic disease, advances in medical knowledge and an associated decline in the relevance of traditional health status indicators such as mortality and morbidity. Such indicators, while of undoubted value in acute conditions, are of lesser relevance in chronic conditions in which treatment is not curative and may bring with it unwanted side effects.

The definition of QOL is a problematic area. Everyone has their own idea as to what QOL is, and therein lies the problem; what is of extreme importance to one individual may be of no relevance to another. Reaching a consensus as to what specific items are important to QOL has yet to be achieved, if indeed this is feasible or desired. There is, however, a growing acceptance among workers in this field as to the general life domains which contribute to feelings of satisfaction with life. In 1980 the World Health Organization (WHO), in recognition of the increasing need to monitor the consequences of disease and treatment on patients' lives, published a set of guidelines entitled 'International Classification of Impairments, Disabilities and Handicaps'. They propose three levels at which disease can impact on an individual: impairment, disability and handicap. Impairments refer to abnormalities of body structure and organ/system functioning and thus relate to the impact of disease at the physiological level. Disability is seen as the impact of illness on the person's functional ability and activity level. It is the definition of handicap which most closely relates to QOL issues. Handicap is defined in societal

Women and Epilepsy. Edited by M.R. Trimble
© 1991 John Wiley & Sons Ltd

terms and attempts to define the disadvantage (due to disease or treatment) in which an individual finds themselves in relation to their peers when viewed from the norms of society. Thus handicap in terms of employment would differ for the patient who is beyond retiring age and would not normally be expected to be working, and for the younger patient who cannot work due to illness, but would be expected to do so if in good health. The link between degree of disability and handicap is complex. It is possible to be disabled and not be handicapped. The person with a severe disability may well be able to perform all their normal social roles with the use of physical aids and/or support from professionals, work colleagues, family and friends. Conversely, a minor disability may result in severe handicap dependent upon the situation in which the individuals finds themselves. Many factors will influence the degree to which a particular disability will be seen as a handicap, including age, sex, attitudes, support and type of society.

Six areas of importance to adequate social functioning are proposed by the WHO: orientation, physical independence, mobility, occupation, social integration and economic self-sufficiency. These are viewed as minimal survival roles; thus it is stated 'one can identify certain fundamental accomplishments that are related to the existence and survival of man as a social being and are expected of the individual in virtually every culture' (WHO, 1980).

This theme of a core of life domains essential to determining QOL can be seen throughout the literature relating to this topic, with general agreement being evident (see Table 1). The theoretical approach to defining general areas of importance to QOL has been confirmed by a recent factor analytic study on 536 patients with cardiovascular disease (Jenkins et al., 1990). Five dimensions emerged—low morale, symptoms, neuropsychological function, interpersonal relationships and economic/employment.

While a consensus appears to exist as to the key life domains pertinent to QOL, the way in which a person arrives at a determination of their QOL

Table 1. Examples of core domains important to QOL proposed by selected authors

	Hornquist (1982)	Wenger et al. (1984)	WHO (1980)	Spitzer (1987)	Ware (1987)	Fallowfield (1990)
Physical	+	+	+	+	+	+
Psychological[a]	+	+	+	+	+	+
Social	+	+	+	+	+	+
Occupation	+	+	+			+
Economic status	+	+	+			
Structural	+					
Role functioning					+	
Perceptions		+			+	
Symptoms		+				

[a] Includes cognitive/intellectual and emotional factors.

remains a subject for debate. A number of attempts have been made to conceptualize QOL and these fall into three main categories: needs satisfaction; satisfaction and situation-expectation discrepancy; attainment of life goals.

Hornquist (1982) proposed that QOL is the 'degree of need satisfaction' within six specific areas (see Table 1). Once basic survival needs have been met, the determination of needs is an individual phenomenon. A complex relationship between the six areas of need is suggested with, assuming that all needs cannot be met, the individual having to make choices (conscious or unconscious) as to which needs to fulfil. This idea contrasts with the needs hierarchy proposed by Maslow (1970). Maslow proposed that man is motivated to satisfy needs in a pre-determined order, the higher needs being ignored until the more basic needs are met. The hierarchy suggested is: physiological needs, safety needs, social needs, ego needs, status recognition and self-fulfilment. Hornquist (1982) also distinguishes extrinsic (type of housing, signs of appreciation) and intrinsic (satisfaction with housing, experienced self-esteem) needs. Intrinsic satisfaction is influenced by desires as well as extrinsic satisfaction.

The suggestion of the role of desires/expectations is expanded in the suggestion of Staats and Stassen (1987) that future expectations are a major component of present perceived QOL. Thus, actual abilities or life situation are not as important as the discrepancy between actual situation and expected situation. In line with this, Campbell et al. (1976) define satisfaction as 'the discrepancy perceived between aspiration and achievement' and advocate the use of this term in defining QOL. Satisfaction is seen as a cognitive process in which a comparison with some external criteria (including expectations) is made. In addition, it is suggested that a differentiation be made between 'satisfaction of success' in which rising expectations and goals are achieved, and that associated with declining expectations (Campbell et al., 1976).

A slightly different approach is outlined by Cohen (1982), who suggests a theory of life quality based on the capacity of an individual to realize his own life plans. This theory is based on the work of the American philosopher Josiah Royce, who held that 'a human person is a life lived according to a human plan'. It is this life plan that gives us our individuality and a purpose to life; thus when we describe what we have done, what we are doing and what we intend to do with our lives, we are giving an account of ourselves, justifying our existence. Illness impacts on QOL by preventing us from following this plan.

In summary, a number of life domains important to QOL can be defined. These include physical, psychological, social, occupational and economic aspects of life. Satisfaction within these domains is related to need fulfilment, the discrepancy between achievements and aspirations, and societal and individual expectations of 'normative' functioning.

Sex differences in quality of life research

There appear to be surprisingly few gender differences in relation to either life domains important to QOL or overall satisfaction with life. Diener (1984), in a review of factors influencing subjective well-being, including gender, concludes that 'although women report more negative affect, they also seem to experience greater joys, so that little difference in global happiness or satisfaction is usually found between the sexes'. There are, however, a number of studies in which gender differences have been found. Hall (1976), in a British survey of subjective measures of QOL, observed that women regarded health as an important component of the quality of their lives more often than men. Okun *et al.* (1984) conducted a meta-analysis of studies investigating the relationship between subjective health and overall well-being and found a stronger relationship for females than for males. However, a study by Willits and Crider (1988) found no effect of gender on this relationship. Briscoe (1982), in a review of sex differences in well-being, noted that women are more likely to report psychiatric and physical problems than men. This finding is supported by the work of Campbell (1981) who, in a large survey of the American population between 1957 and 1978, found women were more likely to describe experiences of negative affect. It has been suggested that women report more symptoms because illness is less stigmatizing for women: 'the ethic of health is masculine' (Phillips, 1964). Alternatively, the increased concern about health seen in women may heighten their perception of symptoms (Briscoe, 1982).

With regard to other domains, Krupinski (1980) used a specifically designed questionnaire in which respondents were asked to rate how important different aspects of life were to them. A randomly selected population of 3105 people (977 households) was surveyed and it was found that women placed higher importance on family, being free of worries, material security and personal relations, being in useful work and freedom from pressure at work than did men. In contrast, men placed higher importance on recreation and housing. Hall (1976) reported that women regarded family life as important while men were more concerned with their standard of living, work and political freedom.

Self-image is another area in which gender differences have been seen. Campbell (1981), in a study of well-being in the American population, found that women were less willing to express satisfaction with themselves as a person and also felt less in control of their lives. In the same study, dissatisfaction with self emerged as more predictive of general well-being than dissatisfaction with any other area studied (including health, relationships, marriage, society, work and education).

Quality of life and the woman with epilepsy

Epilepsy is a chronic condition, affecting approximately one in 200 people (Duncan, 1989), in which QOL issues are indeed pertinent. The diagnosis of epilepsy can bring with it many problems over and above that of experiencing recurrent seizures. Stigmatization, social isolation, psychological problems, educational and employment difficulties have all been documented in people with epilepsy (Dodrill *et al.*, 1984; Scambler and Hopkins, 1986; Thompson and Oxley, 1988; Levin *et al.*, 1988). There are various medical (Duncan, 1990), social (Thompson and Oxley, 1988; Scambler, 1990) and psychological factors (Vining, 1987; Trimble, 1988; McGuire and Trimble, 1990) which may influence the QOL of the person with epilepsy (see Table 2).

Where difficulties exist in the patient with epilepsy these may be attributed to a number of causes. First, the disease process itself and any resultant brain damage or dysfunction may impact on the individual's abilities. Secondly, treatment may also play a role in producing impairments or disabilities which impact on the patient's QOL. Side effects of anticonvulsant medication, such as tiredness, double vision, cognitive deficits or the sequelae of surgery, for example, hemiplegia, memory disturbance or personality change, may affect the patient's QOL to as great or greater an extent than the occurrence of seizures. Thirdly, societal attitudes may also play a major role in the determination of the QOL of a patient with epilepsy. Discrimination, stigmatization and non-acceptance of the individual with epilepsy are all too common (Bagley, 1972; Scambler and Hopkins, 1986) and likely to affect the QOL of the person experiencing them. Collings (1990), in a study of factors related to general well-being in a group of patients with epilepsy, found that while epilepsy-related variables were more predictive than sociodemographic variables, it was people's perceptions of themselves (self-image) and their epilepsy that were most predictive of overall well-being. Infrequent seizures, short time since diagnosis, having absence seizures, having confidence in the diagnosis and being employed also emerged as important variables in producing feelings of general well-being.

The woman with epilepsy faces additional burdens to those common to all

Table 2. Contributory factors to impaired QOL in people with epilepsy

Factor	Specific items
Medical	Seizure occurrence (frequency, severity) Medication (intrusion, side effects) Hospitalization (in-patient/out-patient)
Social	Stigmatization (felt/enacted) Family dynamics (overprotection) Employment difficulties Legal restrictions (driving)
Psychological	Cognitive deficits (memory, concentration) Intellectual decline Psychiatric (depression, anxiety, behaviour disturbance)

patients with epilepsy. Seizures may be increased due to hormonal changes during the menstrual cycle (catamenial seizures). Problems may occur with contraception due to interaction between oral contraceptives and some anti-convulsant medications, notably phenytoin, phenobarbitone, primidone and carbamazepine (ILAE, 1989). Epilepsy-related difficulties during pregnancy include fluctuating anticonvulsant levels, an increased risk of seizures, poss-ible teratogenicity of medication and fear of the child inheriting epilepsy (Yerby, 1987). Drug-related effects on appearance, for example the coarsen-ing of facial features and gingival hypertrophy seen with phenytoin and al-opecia and weight gain due to valproate therapy (Duncan, 1990), may be of particular relevance to the woman with epilepsy. Women may also be at increased risk for the development of psychiatric problems including depres-sion and anxiety (for discussion see Chapter 14).

The findings in healthy populations that health is more strongly associated with QOL in women than men, and that self-image—an important predictor of well-being—is lower in women, may mean that epilepsy (and its associated health and self-image problems) may impact more on the QOL of women than that of men.

NATIONAL HOSPITAL STUDIES

Background

At the National Hospital for Neurology and Neurosurgery, we have been interested in how epilepsy and its treatment impacts on the everyday lives of people with epilepsy and their perception of QOL (McGuire et al., 1990, in preparation). To aid this work we have developed a method for assessing the QOL of patients with epilepsy. Four major concepts underpin the metho-dology. First, it is proposed that, in general terms, five areas important to QOL can be defined. These are physical functioning, cognitive abilities, emo-tional status, social functioning and economic/employment status (WHO, 1980). Secondly, it is recognized that within these general areas specific items of importance will vary from individual to individual. These individual dif-ferences may be related to a wide range of factors, including age, sex, illness, personality and other sociodemographic variables. Thirdly, it is hypothesized that QOL is a function of levels of expectation. Thus, it is the discrepancy between current life situation and expectations that is important in determin-ing an individual's QOL, not simply how they are at present. Following on from this, QOL can be improved in two ways, either by increasing actual abilities or by decreasing the expectations that an individual holds. Fourthly, it is suggested that QOL is a relational phenomenon. In judging their QOL, an individual makes comparisons of their current life situation in relation to other times and people in their lives.

The method we have been developing (QOLAS) is based on repertory grid technique (Fransella and Bannister, 1977). This methodology provides a practical, standardized and objective way of assessing people's perceptions of QOL. There are three components to the technique: elements, constructs and the repertory grid. 'Elements' refers to the areas under study. In relation to QOL (and based on concepts 3 and 4 outlined above), ten 'elements' were chosen to represent various situations and people in the patient's life: as you are now (NOW), as you were before having epilepsy (BEFORE), as you would like to be (LIKE), as you expect to be (EXPECT), your mother (MOTHER), your father (FATHER), as other people see you (OTHERS), a close friend (FRIEND), the best possible life (BEST), the worst possible life (WORST). 'Constructs' is the term given to the ways in which the individual differentiates between the 'elements'. For example, in comparing the elements 'as you are now', 'your mother' and 'your father' a patient may respond 'My mother and father do not have epilepsy and I do.' 'Having epilepsy' is a way in which that patient differentiates those three 'elements' and would therefore be termed a 'construct'. Alternatively, the patient may have responded by saying 'My mother and I are alike as we both make friends easily, while my father is a loner and finds it difficult to form friendships.' In this case 'making friends' would be the 'construct'. By making multiple comparisons of the elements, a number of constructs can be elicited, individual for each patient. The repertory grid is a rating that the patient gives to each construct for each element (see Figure 1).

Quality of life assessment schedule (QOLAS)

Patients are interviewed to determine specific areas of importance (constructs) to their QOL, within the general framework of the five main areas outlined previously (physical functioning, cognitive abilities, emotional status, social functioning, economic/employment status). During the interview, the elements are presented in groups of three and the patient is asked to 'think of a way in which two of these are alike and different from the third in terms of their quality of life'. This procedure is repeated until ten 'constructs' have been elicited (two for each of the five main areas). They are then asked to rate on a five-point scale, ranging from 'Not a problem' to 'It could not be worse', how much of a problem each construct is for each element. This forms the repertory grid.

Two types of measures are calculated. First, a global measure is computed, QOL6. This is the absolute distance between the elements 'as you are now (NOW)' and 'as you would like to be (LIKE)' ranked against the following element to LIKE distances: BEFORE–LIKE; EXPECT–LIKE, FRIEND–LIKE; BEST–LIKE; WORST–LIKE. This measure takes into consideration the role of expectations (NOW–LIKE distance) and the relational properties

	E1	E2	E3	E4	E5	E6	E7	E8	E9	E10
CONSTRUCT 1 (PHYSICAL)	3 *	2	1	2	1	2	2	2	1	4
CONSTRUCT 2 (PHYSICAL)	4	2	1	3	1	2	4	2	1	4
CONSTRUCT 3 (COGNITIVE)	2	2	2	1	1	2	4	2	2	4
CONSTRUCT 4 (COGNITIVE)	2	1	2	1	1	3	3	4	2	5
CONSTRUCT 5 (EMOTIONAL)	3	4	1	2	1	3	3	2	2	5
CONSTRUCT 6 (EMOTIONAL)	4	3	2	4	1	3	2	2	1	5
CONSTRUCT 7 (SOCIAL)	5	3	1	3	1	2	3	2	1	5
CONSTRUCT 8 (SOCIAL)	1	2	2	1	1	2	3	1	1	3
CONSTRUCT 9 (EC/EMPL)	3	2	1	2	1	3	4	1	2	2
CONSTRUCT 10 (EC/EMPL)	4	2	3	3	1	2	2	1	3	4

Figure 1. Example of repertory grid.

E1 to E10 = elements: E1, 'NOW'; E2, 'BEFORE'; E3, 'LIKE'; E4, 'EXPECT'; E5, 'MOTHER'; E6, 'FATHER'; E7, 'OTHERS'; E8, 'FRIEND'; E9, 'BEST LIFE'; E10, 'WORST LIFE'.
EC/EMPL, Economic/employment status.
* Rating on 1–5 scale 1 = Not a problem, 5 = It could not be worse.

of QOL (comparison to other element–LIKE distances). A high rank indicates a poor perception of QOL, in that the higher the rank the farther away from the ideal 'LIKE' the person sees themselves. The lowest rank possible is 1 and the highest is 6. In addition, scores for the five general areas or subscales (PHYSICAL FUNCTIONING, COGNITIVE ABILITIES, EMOTIONAL STATUS, SOCIAL FUNCTIONING, ECONOMIC/EMPLOYMENT STATUS) are computed to describe a profile for each patient (see Figure 2). Each subscale score is calculated as the absolute NOW–LIKE discrepancy score for the two specific items within that subscale. For example, the combined score for constructs 'having epilepsy' and 'tiredness' would give a score for the scale PHYSICAL FUNCTIONING.

Psychometric properties of QOL6

The procedure has been administered to 50 patients with chronic epilepsy, on four occasions over a period of six months to provide data relating to sensitivity and reliability. The global measure (QOL6) successfully discriminated a group of patients who had experienced one or more significant life events during the study period from those reporting no life events (one-way ANOVA, $F = 6.98$, $p < 0.023$) (McGuire *et al.*, 1991, in preparation). In addition, this measure demonstrated significant pre- and post-operative changes in a group of patients who sucessfully underwent surgery for the relief of facial pain (trigeminal neuralgia) ($t = 3.36$, $p < 0.015$, $n = 7$) (McGuire *et al.*, 1991, in

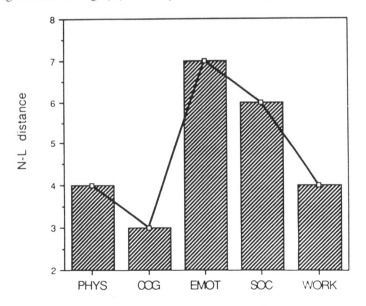

Figure 2. Example of QOL profile

preparation). These findings relate to the sensitivity of the measure. With regard to reliability, the test–retest reliability coefficients for various time intervals is given in Table 3.

It is of interest that the measure appears to be more reliable over longer time intervals. This may reflect the stable nature of QOL or could be due to short-term changes in feelings about QOL due to participation in the study (increased attention being paid to the individual, seeing a psychologist and thinking about the issues relating to QOL). Alternatively, this finding may be a result of evanescent changes based on short-term life event changes which do not impact irrevocably on QOL.

Table 3. Test–retest reliability coefficients for QOL6

Session comparison	Interval	r^a	p
S1–S2	1 month	–0.10	0.96
S2–S3	2 months	0.11	0.67
S1–S3	3 months	0.45	0.08
S3–S4	3 months	0.53	0.04
S2–S4	5 months	0.17	0.53
S1–S4	6 months	0.73	0.001

[a] Spearman's correlation coefficient; 50 patients.

STUDY OF SEX DIFFERENCES

Procedures

A subgroup of patients from the main QOL study were analysed to investigate sex differences related to QOL. Nine female and nine male patients were matched on age and level of intellect (IQ). The demographic details of these groups are given in Table 4.

The two groups were well matched with respect to seizure type. With regard to medication, carbamazepine was the most commonly prescribed anticonvulsant, being taken by 6/9 in the female group and 5/9 in the male group. The majority of patients were receiving a combination of drugs (polytherapy); seven patients were on monotherapy with either carbamazepine ($n = 4$), primidone ($n = 2$) or phenytoin ($n = 1$). Full details of study entry medications for both groups can be found in Table 5.

Patients completed the QOL assessment on four occasions: baseline (S1), 1 month (S2), 3 months (S3) and 6 months (S4). Details of seizure rate, medication change and the occurrence of any significant life events were recorded at each visit.

Table 4.   Demographic details of male and female groups

Variable	Female	Male
Age: mean (SD)	46.9 (15.2)	45.3 (11.8)
IQ: mean (SD)	91.8 (11.0)	90.2 (7.6)
Qualifications:		
None	7	6
CSEs/'O' levels	0	1
Vocational	2	2
Occupation:		
Unemployed	1	0
Open employment	0	0
Sheltered employment	7	9
Retired	1	0
Age of onset (years)		
Mean (SD)	7.7 (5.3)	11.7 (9.0)
Aetiology:		
Known	4	5
Not known	5	4
Seizure types:		
Simple partial	0	2
Complex partial	8	7
Secondary generalized	6	8
Primary generalized	0	0
Unclassified	1	1

Table 5.   Medication details of the two groups: median and (range)

	Female group	N	Male group	N
PHT	–	0	362.5 (350–450)	4
CBZ	1400 (600–1800)	6	1000 (800–1600)	5
VPA	3000	1	2000 (1000–2500)	5
CLB	20	1	10 (10–30)	4
PRIM	750	2	–	0
PHB	–	0	120	1

N, number of patients; PHT, phenytoin; CBZ, carbamazepine;
VPA, valproate; PHB, phenobarbitone; PRIM, primidone; CLB, clobazam.

Results

Statistics

Data were analysed using the Statistical Package for the Social Sciences (Norusis, 1983). Non-parametric statistics were used throughout due to non-normality of the QOL variables (QOL6, PHYS, COG, EMOT, SOC,

WORK). Mann–Whitney U tests were used to investigate group differences on these variables at all occasions (S1, S2, S3, S4). In addition, session 1 scores were subtracted from session 4 scores (S4 – S1) and Mann–Whitney U test applied to this difference measure (D14) to determine any group-related differences in changes in QOL scores during the study period.

Weekly seizure rates were calculated as:

$$\frac{\text{number of seizures since last visit}}{\text{number of days since last visit}} \times 7$$

Mann–Whitney U tests were used to identify group differences on weekly seizure variables.

Life events data were coded '1' if a life event, judged to be of importance by the patient, was reported at any stage of the study, and '0' if no life event was recorded for the six months of the study. Chi-square analysis was performed to investigate group differences in the reporting of life events. Dunn–Bonferroni (Dunn, 1961) corrections for multiple comparisons were used throughout the analysis.

Areas of importance chosen

Table 6 lists the constructs elicited for both groups. It appears that men and women with epilepsy are similar in the areas they view as important to QOL, both placing high importance on epilepsy, fits, memory, making friends, independence and financial security. There are a few differences between the sexes: females list anxiety and keeping in touch with friends more frequently than males, while males list anger, having a partner and lack of social life more often than females.

QOLAS

No significant group differences were seen on any of the QOL variables (QOL6, PHYS, COG, EMOT, SOC, WORK) on any occasion and, in addition, the groups did not differ with regard to change in QOL scores during the six months of the study (D14) (see Figures 3 and 4).

Life events

Analysis indicates that the groups did not differ in the reporting of life events during the study period.

Table 6. Areas of importance (constructs) elicited

Dimension	Construct/area of importance	Females	Males
Physical	Fits	5	4
	Epilepsy	5	4
	Physical ability (being active, able to walk)	3	5
	Tiredness/fatigue	3	3
	Incontinence	2	1
	Miscellaneous (catarrh, back pains, handicap)	2	2
Cognitive	Memory	6	5
	Concentration	3	2
	Mental speed	2	3
	Qualifications	2	1
	Learning/use of past experiences	2	1
	Intelligence	2	0
	Literacy skills	0	1
	Organizational skills	2	0
	Ambitions/goals	1	1
Emotional	*Anxiety/nervousness	<u>5</u>	<u>2</u>
	*Anger/temper/arguments	<u>3</u>	<u>7</u>
	Depression	3	3
	Being moody/bossy/even temperament	<u>4</u>	<u>0</u>
	Frustration	2	2
	Confidence	2	3
	Feeling happy	2	4
	Being understanding/caring/helpful/doing duty	2	2
	Being in control	1	1
	Living in past	1	0
	Making best of things/persevering	1	1
	Being pitied	1	0
	Being courageous	0	1
Social	Independence/self-care/own home	6	7
	Making friends/communicating/having close friends	6	8
	*Contact with friends/visiting people	<u>5</u>	<u>0</u>
	Being close to family/happy home life	4	3
	Loneliness	2	4
	*Having partner/being married	<u>2</u>	<u>5</u>
	Holidays/travel	2	1
	Relationship with partner	1	0
	Able to have children	1	0
	*Social life/going on outings	<u>0</u>	<u>4</u>
	Having shared interests with others	0	1
	Sexual relationships	0	1
Economic/ employment	Financial independence/money to spend	9	9
	Being in work/lack of job	3	5
	Job satisfaction	2	2
	Keeping in fashion	1	0
	Fear of losing job/job security	1	0
	Keeping busy/occupied during day	1	0
	Being successful/sense of achievement	0	2

* Constructs in which sex differences were seen.

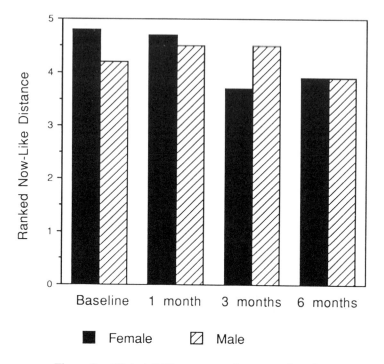

Figure 3. Global QOL scores, males versus females

Seizures

Table 7 contains the data relating to weekly seizure rates. The female group had significantly higher rates of complex partial seizures on all visits (Session 1: $Z = -1.99$, $p < 0.046$; Session 2: $Z = -1.84$, $p < 0.066$; Session 3: $Z = -2.64$, $p < 0.008$; Session 4: $Z = -2.1$, $p < 0.035$). Investigation of change in seizure rate during the study period (six months) revealed no group differences.

Conclusions

The results of this study indicate that women with epilepsy do not differ greatly from men in their perceptions of QOL. Some small differences emerged. The group of women with epilepsy placed more importance on being free of worries/anxiety and keeping in touch with friends than did the men. These findings are in keeping with previous reports in the literature which suggest that women place family and personal relations and being free of worries higher in importance to life quality than men (Hall, 1976; Krupinski, 1980) and that women report psychiatric symptoms (anxiety) more readily than men (Briscoe, 1982).

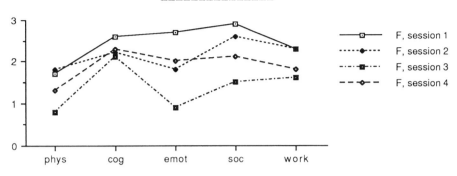

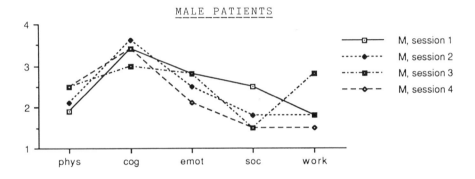

Session 1, Baseline; Session 2, 1 month; Session 3, 3 months; Session 4, 6 months

Figure 4.   QOL profile scores, males versus females

Table 7.   Weekly seizure rates

		Females				Males			
		S1	S2	S3	S4	S1	S2	S3	S4
SPS	Mean	–	–	–	–	0.1	0.2	0.2	0.1
	SD	–	–	–	–	0.1	0.3	0.1	0.1
CPS	Mean	2.0	1.1	2.5	1.6	0.1	0.1	0.0	0.1
	SD	2.2	1.0	3.2	2.0	0.1	0.3	0.0	0.1
2GEN	Mean	0.2	0.1	0.1	0.1	0.1	0.1	0.2	0.1
	SD	0.2	0.1	0.1	0.1	0.2	0.1	0.2	0.3

SPS, simple partial; CPS, complex partial; 2GEN, secondary generalized.

The men in this study placed more importance on being in control of their tempers, having a partner or being married and social life than did the women. Krupinski (1980) reported that men place more importance than women do on recreation, which is in keeping with the finding of this study that men view social life as important. The finding that men report being married as important more often than women do is of interest. There are no studies in the literature to support this finding; however, studies have demonstrated that women with epilepsy are more likely to marry than men with epilepsy. Ounsted and Lindsay (1981) in a 13-year, prospective, follow-up of 100 children diagnosed as having temporal lobe epilepsy between 1948 and 1964 found that, of those considered marriageable, 41% of men and 92% of women were married. This difference was significant at the 0.001 level. Similarly, Pierzcha and Grudzinska (1987) report that, in a group of 243 patients with epilepsy, 50.6% of men were married—a lower rate than both women with epilepsy and the general population. In healthy populations some differences relating to perceptions of marriage have been found. Campbell (1981) found young married women with no children to report higher levels of satisfaction than any other group, while Willits and Crider (1988) found males to report more satisfaction with marriage than females. Campbell (1981) does, however, comment that the traditional idea that marriage is the indispensable core of a woman's life and less important to men has been challenged in recent years, with an increasing number of women entering the workforce.

In general, very small sex differences were seen in this study and the objective assessment of QOL (QOLAS) showed no significant differences between sexes over a six-month period. This seems to be in line with the majority of the literature, which reports few differences between the sexes in many important life domains (Campbell, 1981; Briscoe, 1982; Diener, 1984; Collings, 1990). It may be that the impact of epilepsy on a patient's life is so great that it predominates over any minor differences due to gender.

In summary, quality of life is a multi-faceted phenomenon in which sociodemographic variables, including age, sex and race, have a role to play. Assessment procedures in which the individuality of this concept is recognized have obvious advantages over those that neglect this aspect. Individual differences in items important to QOL, whether a function of age, sex or illness, will thus be incorporated into the QOL asessment and not overlooked. In this way one is more certain that areas of importance to the patient are being addressed and the influence of treatment on these important factors in the patient's life can be monitored.

REFERENCES

Bagley, C. (1972) Social prejudice and the adjustment of people with epilepsy. *Epilepsia*, **13**, 33–45.

Briscoe, M. (1982) Sex differences in psychological well-being. *Psychol. Med. Monogr.*, Suppl. 1.

Campbell, A. (1981) *The Sense of Well-being in America: Recent Patterns and Trends.* McGraw-Hill, New York.

Campbell, A., Converse, P. and Rodgers, W. (1976) *The Quality of American Life.* Russell Sage Foundation, New York.

Cohen, C. (1982) On the quality of life: some philosophical reflections. *Circulation*, **66** (5 part 2), III29–33.

Collings, J.A. (1990) Epilepsy and well-being. *Soc. Sci. Med.*, **31**, 165–170.

Diener, E. (1984) Subjective well-being. *Psychol. Bull.*, **95**, 542–575.

Dodrill, C.B., Breyer, D.N., Diamond, M.B., Dubinsky, B.L. and Geary, B.B. (1984) Psychosocial problems among adults with epilepsy. *Epilepsia*, **25**, 168–175.

Duncan, J.S. (1989) Strategies of antiepileptic drug treatment in patients with chronic epilepsy. In: *Chronic Epilepsy: Its Prognosis and Management* (ed. M.R. Trimble), pp. 143–149. Wiley, Chichester.

Duncan, J.S. (1990) Medical factors affecting quality of life in patients with epilepsy. In: *Quality of Life and Quality of Care in Epilepsy* (ed. D. Chadwick), pp. 80–87. Royal Society of Medicine Round Table Series 23, Alden Press, Oxford.

Dunn, O.J. (1961) Multiple comparisons among means. *J. Am. Stat. Assoc.*, **56**, 52–64.

Fallowfield, L. (1990) *The Quality of Life: The Missing Measurement in Health Care.* Souvenir Press, London.

Fransella, F. and Bannister, D. (1977) *A Manual for Repertory Grid Technique.* Academic Press, London.

Hall, J. (1976) Subjective measures of quality of life in Britain: 1971–1975. Some developments and trends. *Soc. Trends*, **7**, 47–60.

Hornquist, J.O. (1982) The concept of quality of life. *Scand. J. Soc. Med.*, **10**, 57–61.

International League Against Epilepsy. Commission on Genetics, Pregnancy and the Child (1989) Guidelines for the care of epileptic women of childbearing age. *Epilepsia*, **30**, 409–410.

Jenkins, C.D., Jono, R.T., Stanton, B.A. and Stoup-Benham, C.A. (1990) The measurement of health-related quality of life: Major dimensions identified by factor analysis. *Soc. Sci. Med.*, **31**, 925–931.

Krupinski, J. (1980) Health and quality of life. *Soc. Sci. Med.*, **14a**, 203–211.

Levin, R., Banks, S. and Berg, B. (1988) Psychological dimensions of epilepsy: A review of the literature. *Epilepsia*, **29**, 805–816.

Maslow, A.H. (1970) *Motivation and Personality.* Harper and Row, New York.

McGuire, A.M. and Trimble, M.R. (1990) Quality of life in patients with epilepsy: The role of cognitive factors. In: *Quality of Life and Quality of Care in Epilepsy* (ed. D. Chadwick), pp. 69–77. Royal Society of Medicine Round Table Series 23, Alden Press, Oxford.

McGuire, A.M., Joyce, C.R.B. and Trimble, M.R. (1991) Quality of life in patients with epilepsy: the role of life events. (In preparation)

Norusis, M.J. (1983) *SPSS-X Users Guide.* McGraw-Hill, New York.

Okun, M.A., Stock, W.A., Haring, M.J. and Witter, R.A. (1984) Health and subjective well-being: A meta-analysis. *Int. J. Aging Hum. Dev.*, **19**, 111–113.

Ounsted, C. and Lindsay, J. (1981) The long-term outcome of temporal lobe epilepsy in childhood. In: *Epilepsy and Psychiatry* (eds E.H. Reynolds and M.R. Trimble), pp. 185–215. Churchill Livingstone, Edinburgh.

Phillips, D.L. (1964) Rejection of the mentally ill: The influence of behaviour and sex. *Amer. Sociol. Rev.,* **29**, 679–687.

Pierzcha, K. and Grudzinska, B. (1987) The number of children and marriage among men with epilepsy. *Neurol. Neurochir. Pol.,* **21**, 19–23.

Scambler, G. (1990) Social factors and quality of life and quality of care in epilepsy. In: *Quality of Life and Quality of Care in Epilepsy* (ed. D. Chadwick), pp. 63–69. Royal Society of Medicine Round Table Series 23.

Scambler, G. and Hopkins, A. (1986) Being epileptic: Coming to terms with stigma. *Sociol. Health and Illness,* **8**, 26–43.

Spitzer, W.O. (1987) State of science 1986: Quality of life and functional status as target variables for research. *J. Chronic Disease,* **40**, 465–471.

Staats, S.R. and Stassen M.A. (1987) Age and present and future perceived quality of life. *Int. J. Aging Hum. Devel.,* **25**, 167–176.

Thompson, P. and Oxley, J. (1988) Socioeconomic accompaniments of severe epilepsy. *Epilepsia,* **29** (Suppl. 1), S9–S18.

Trimble, M.R. (1988) *Biological Psychiatry,* pp. 283–314. Wiley, Chichester.

Vining, E.P.G. (1987) Cognitive dysfunction associated with antiepleptic drug therapy. *Epilepsia,* **28** (Suppl. 2), S18–S22.

Ware, J.E., Jr (1987) Standards for validating health measures: Definition and content. *J. Chronic Disease,* **40**, 473–480.

Wenger, N.K., Mattson, M.E., Fuberg, C.D. and Elinson, J. (eds) (1984) *Assessment of Quality of Life in Clinical Trials of Cardiovascular Therapies.* Le Jacq, New York.

Willits, F.K. and Crider, D.M. (1988) Health rating and life satisfaction in the later middle years. *J. Gerontol.,* **43**, S172–S176.

World Health Organization (1980) *International Classification of Impairments, Disabilities and Handicaps.* WHO, Geneva.

Yerby, M.S. (1987) Problems and management of the pregnant woman with epilepsy. *Epilepsia,* **28** (Suppl. 3), S29–S36.

3

Counselling women towards independence

HANNEKE M. DE BOER
Institute for Epilepsy, Heemstede, The Netherlands

INTRODUCTION

I have been working in epilepsy since 1966, when I first started as a vocational therapist in a sheltered workshop connected with the Instituut voor Epilepsiebestrijding in Heemstede, the Netherlands. This chapter therefore involves only a certain category of women, namely those who have been admitted to the institute.

The centre has two main sections: one of 130 beds mainly for assessment and rehabilitation, and one of 530 beds for medium and long stay. An average of 400 patients are admitted annually, of whom 50 are referred for rehabilitation. It is patients in the latter category who are especially referred to the vocational training centre of the sheltered workshop.

HISTORY

Before 1957 there were hardly any vocational facilities for people with epilepsy within the institute. It was felt that it was better not to offer work to the patients staying there, as it would provoke aggression and mutual rivalry. There were, however, a number of workshops where patients worked, growing vegetables and repairing shoes, in order to help and support the institute but without payment.

In 1957 this situation changed when the management of the centre for epilepsy hired a vocational therapist, who was invited to establish a modern workshop for rehabilitation of people with epilepsy. However, his task encompassed more than just offering an occupation. Striving towards reintegration into society was another objective.

Women and Epilepsy. Edited by M.R. Trimble
© 1991 John Wiley & Sons Ltd

On 1st July 1958 the workshop became an official sheltered workshop, operating under the Ministry of Social Affairs. This allowed people with epilepsy to be properly employed and to be paid a wage.

Originally only men were employed, but later, in 1959, female employees were admitted, and according to the annual report the choice of words and behaviour of the men had improved.

PRESENT SITUATION

Some 500 people now work in the workshop under a sheltered employment scheme. The vocational training centre is part of the workshop, and is totally integrated with it. Thus we have people being assessed and trained working alongside people who are employed.

At present some 70 people, varying in age from 17 to 50 years, are placed in the vocational training centre. The majority are younger than 30 years and half of them are women. When the reason for admission to the institute is strictly medical, they may stay from six weeks to three months. When rehabilitation is also involved their stay at the centre may last for one to two years. The greater part of this group has an average or just below average intelligence.

If young people are still of school age when admited, they will go to school in order to try and finish their education during their stay.

The aims of the workshop are:

Assessment: The starting point of the assessment is the indication for admission given by the referring doctor. In general, attention is paid to the following aspects: work performance, social behaviour, future possibilities and seizures.

Rehabilitation: When it becomes clear from the assessment reports that a person lacks the abilities to function optimally in society, training programmes can be offered to enhance reintegration into society.

Permanent employment: Paid employment, under a sheltered employment scheme, is offered to people who cannot cope with work in open society because of a handicap. This caters for people with a severe epilepsy and/or multiple handicaps besides epilepsy.

WOMEN WITH AND WITHOUT EPILEPSY

The workforce in the UK, the USA and the Netherlands is compared in Table 1; it can be seen that, comparatively, the Netherlands lags behind. In Holland it is still customary for a married woman to stay at home, especially when the children are small.

The group of women with epilepsy whom we see in our centre form only a

Table 1. Percentage of the workforce who are women, compared in the UK, the USA, and the Netherlands (NL)

Year	UK	USA	NL
1980	33.3	42.5	31.2
1990	48.4	45.8	36.5

small proportion of those with epilepsy in the whole of the country. The rest we never see and know nothing about. Checking libraries, both in the Netherlands and the USA, to try and get an idea of the position of the woman with epilepsy in a larger perspective, failed as no literature seems to be available on this topic. In epilepsy research involving the emancipation and achievement of independence of people with epilepsy, no distinction is made between men and women.

Women who are referred to our centre have often had a limited opportunity to develop socially; they lack self-confidence, the will to succeed and a realistic perspective. They are often highly dependent on their parents in making up their minds about almost anything. They have ideas, dreams of what and who they want to be, and are just waiting for it to happen. They are mostly unhappy with their present situation but seem unable to change. Their aspirations are above their abilities and cannot be attained.

PROBLEM AREAS

When people come to our centre, there is usually a serious problem that cannot be solved by regional workers in the field of epilepsy in the home environment. Quite often women have seen many doctors and other professionals and have failed in many aspects of daily life, and still live at home.

It is the case that usually these women *suffer* from their epilepsy directly or indirectly, rightly or wrongly. Seizures in fact may not play an important role at this stage. The habit of relying on someone else for almost everything is much more of a problem and at the same time they resent it while being unable to change their situation. We see a great dependence on the parents (and vice versa), who are still very protective towards their daughter, all three of them often blaming the outside world and the epilepsy for every problem.

When such a person is admitted to the centre, attention is paid to the following aspects: diminishing the supposed influence of epilepsy on somebody's life, which involves medical assessment, treatment and counselling; improving the level of self-confidence.

WORK AS A MEANS OF TREATMENT

It is important to explain why we choose to use work, among other techniques, as a means of treatment, when counselling people with epilepsy. In our society, having a job is connected with an income, worthy social contacts, participation, personal development, social identity and status. In the treatment of epilepsy, work then offers a regular daily programme, demanding a clear structure. Stress, the making and keeping of contacts, fatigue, pleasure, etc., are all inherent in work, so that it provides realistic opportunities for assessment and training. In short, work is an important part of daily life. This also applies to women who, without having asked for it, sometimes have seizures.

In the vocational training centre various activities are being performed. These include: industrial packing and assembly; administration; printing; gardening; domestic science; creative therapy; and book-keeping.

THE SETTING

When a woman first comes to the training centre, usually after being admitted to the special epilepsy centre, she is shown round by a placement coordinator.

During the interview that follows the coordinator tries to obtain information concerning her background, her living circumstances, work, possibilities and problems, intelligence level and possible social problems. Quite often this interview is the first time that the woman has talked with a therapist alone, without her relatives or her husband. Often new information comes up during these interviews.

The coordinator decides, together with the client, where she is going to work and for how many hours a week. It may be obvious that in this discussion the choice of activities will be linked to background and future possibilities. This placement is then evaluated after two to three weeks.

In the training centre, there are men and women from very many different backgrounds and of various intelligence levels. Although it is not possible to offer everybody the precise activities they are used to, it is possible to offer a work situation comparable to that at home, with co-workers having similar communal problems and backgrounds.

We have one department where people who come from sheltered workshops or day care centres elsewhere are placed. Here the general intelligence level and the level of work performance are below average. In another department the population has, in addition to possible seizure problems, psychosocial and psychological problems. Most of them are not able to structure their lives themselves and need much help to do so. The approach of the vocational therapist is direct and authoritative, using techniques of behaviour therapy in order to teach patients how to behave within the structure of a work situation.

There is one packing department and an assembly department, where the workers are mainly of an average or just below average intelligence level, and from which most of them will be expected to return to their former occupation or will be trained to start a new job, their first either in open industry or in a sheltered workshop. The approach of the therapists here will be more or less like that of any ordinary employer.

At the domestic science department, we have a fully equipped kitchen, where housewives are assessed and trained in domestic skills.

This is also used on a part-time basis for youngsters to gain practical domestic training to enable them to live independently at a later stage. At our creative therapy unit techniques are offered to help all women to gain a hobby.

Thus, although we have several different departments in the workshop and therapists of varying attitudes, there is one basic rule which applies to each individual. She is expected to work to the best of her abilities. This means different demands on different people, although the whole of the programme, assessment and training takes place in a demanding environment—demands that everybody needs to be able to respond to, in order to be able to exist in society.

WORKING METHODS

During the first six to eight weeks after admission the 'patient' will be assessed, not only in the workshop but also in the house she lives in. All involved—the neurologist, the psychologist, the social worker, the nursing staff and the vocational therapist—assess within their own fields of expertise.

All these professionals meet at least once a fortnight to discuss findings, progress and courses of treatment. If it is found that the woman's medical treatment is as good as possible but that she lacks certain social skills or has psychosocial or psychological problems which prevent her from living an independent life, she may be advised to participate in programmes aimed at these aspects. This usually involves a longer stay at the centre and a move to another department, either for the rehabilitation of teenagers and adolescents or to a rehabilitation department for adults, depending on her age.

Additional therapies such as group therapy, individual psychotherapy and assertive therapy will be offered to enable the woman to get a clearer insight of herself, her environment and where her problems lie.

In the vocational training centre the programmes that are offered enhance the social and practical abilities the woman needs to be able to integrate independently in society, and provide a training ground for newly learned skills to be experienced within a realistic, demanding environment. The methods used in the training centre, aside from work itself, are individual training programmes which include such aspects as:

— coping with seizures in such a way that they do not interfere with performance either at work or in social contacts;

— coping with colleagues and friends, which includes training of social abilities, being able to keep a certain discipline in life, e.g. in the working situation, being responsible for herself and her own performance in any situation;
— educating colleagues and friends about epilepsy. There are four basic rules here:
    1. The woman with epilepsy should limit herself to her own epilepsy and her own seizures. If people want to know more they will ask;
    2. Not to scare others with alarming stories about what might happen, but has never happened;
    3. To explain only what happens when she has a seizure;
    4. To explain what people can do to help.

TARGETS TO BE ACHIEVED

All these methods are applied to individual women and aim at diminishing the supposed importance of epilepsy on her life, and improving her level of self-confidence.

Diminishing the role of epilepsy

We often find that women experience more restrictions in daily life by having seizures than seems necessary. A good example for this is the following:

A girl, aged 21, confessed that she had been to a party the night before and although she realized at some point that she should have gone home, she stayed and even had another glass of wine. 'Of course', she said, 'that resulted in a seizure the next morning—but only a small one', she added quickly, as if she were apologizing. During the following conversation it became clear that she had been taught by her parents, and in fact by every adult around her, that she should not go out alone and certainly not get involved in activities that might provoke seizures. She could not go out at night, to meet friends, for she would have to be accompanied by one of her parents and she could certainly not go to parties, as having late nights might cause seizures. This restricted her in gaining experience in developing social contacts and consequently in establishing social abilities.

Thus, her epilepsy was not her biggest handicap at all, but being unable to cope in life on her own, to stand on her own two feet, make her own decisions and accept her own responsibility. These inadequacies showed up in her work performance.

She had to be taught that everybody, as well as performing daily chores, is entitled to have fun; that she should set her own limitations and responsibilities. It was explained to her that any person who goes to a party reaches a point where he or she has to decide whether to go home or stay and have that other drink. The decision is usually based on whether or not you are having fun. Yes, and the next day there may be consequences—whether you have epilepsy or not. Such an approach brings the whole situation into a broader perspective—something everybody has to cope with, irrespective of having epilepsy.

We often find that epilepsy is blamed for every failure and at the same time is an excuse for not doing anything about them.

Improving the level of self-confidence

The programme of the vocational training centre is set up in such a way that the woman can only succeed, every step of the way. One of the methods often used here is the step-by-step training plan. In this, the vocational therapist, together with the client, stipulates which abilities she should attain to achieve her goal. The formulation of this goal is very important as it should motivate her to start the training in the first place. If employment is involved in her outlook on the future, feasible choices have to be made in order to formulate a realistic goal. Sometimes this is difficult at this stage, as the woman has an impossible dream—for instance, when she wants to become a pilot. If she realizes that this is not possible, she may lapse into inactivity from sheer frustration.

We do not take this dream away at this stage, especially as we cannot give her another one in return. So we will leave her dream intact and formulate a rather general but realistic goal which is acceptable and may even correspond to her dream. For instance: 'The step-by-step training plan will aim at your becoming a good worker'—simple but acceptable.

Now the necessary skills which are still to be obtained can be considered and are written down and taken step by step. Needless to say, the first few items are those which are considered not to be too difficult for the trainee. Each step may take one or two weeks, depending on the expected time the trainee may need to learn a new skill. Sometimes steps are broken down, as in the case of one young woman who had great difficulties with time-keeping. We would negotiate with her how many times she would succeed in one week and then set a number below this estimation. This way, each week, there were successes and hardly any failures.

The basic idea behind this training scheme is to help the trainee enjoy her work, which is work she can do, with colleagues who give her positive feed-back, as they also enjoy that. Slowly but surely she develops into a co-worker, a colleague they can count on. In this situation we usually see the former, impossible dream fade away and more realistic wishes become topics of discussion.

The role of the vocational therapist is of course important in this process; a positive response to the trainee's successes is vital. The vocational therapist prepares the training but also draws up a contract in which therapist and trainee agree to work at the training. Both sign the contract.

The therapist also evaluates the situation once a week with the trainee, during which they decide together whether the trainee will move on to the next step. It is obvious that such a training can only take place in a real working environment where demands are being made and realistic confrontations met.

When the training is completed, the therapist and the trainee discuss what should happen next. If they both feel that the trainee is not yet ready to work in open industry, there is the possibility of applying for a job in the workshop under the sheltered employment scheme. This happens quite regularly with our group. This placement may be either within our own sheltered workshop or in a workshop in the region where the woman originally came from. If it is felt that the trainee should try her luck outside the workshop, training in interview techniques may be provided. She will also be helped to make a choice of occupation using psychological tests followed by verbal counselling. If further education is necessary before moving on, this will be organized. An example will clarify how this can be done.

Wilma was a 19-year-old girl who was admitted to the epilepsy centre for assessment and rehabilitation. She was placed in the vocational training centre originally just to be assessed. We found that she was a bright young girl, unable to make contacts with others, as she decided that they were not bright enough to make contact with her anyway. At home she had lapsed into total inactivity after she had been told she could not become a nurse because of her epilepsy. She had lost contact with schoolfriends and hardly went out of the house. She had many physical complaints, varying from headaches and stomachaches to seizures, which in fact during the assessment period did not appear to have an epileptic origin. She had lost any self-confidence she might have had.

At first she hated the training centre. The work offered and her co-workers were too simple for her, and she did not want to have anything to do with them. We started a step-by-step training plan after long verbal counselling aimed at trying to get her on the move, pick up her life more or less regardless of the outcome, which we should decide upon at a later stage.

During the training she regained confidence in herself and learned to deal with any restrictions the epilepsy might put upon her in an acceptable way. She also learned how to cope with her environment and wanted to become a nurse more than ever. However, she knew she needed some further education to be admitted to the nursing college. At this point she was still living in the teenage rehabilitation department of the epilepsy centre.

A total plan, lasting for two years, was drawn up, involving a psychologist, nursing staff, vocational therapist and, most importantly, Wilma herself. This plan consisted of the organization of the living, working and education possibilities during this period. She would leave the centre and start living independently nearby, so as to enable her to continue working in the sheltered workshop for four days a week. This way the gap between the institutionalized situation and the situation in which she would be looking after herself would not be too large. Also she could make up for her lack in education by taking an additional course. She thus used the sheltered employment training as a stepping stone towards full reintegration into society. After two years she applied for and got a job as a student nurse in a nursing home.

CONCLUSION

All approaches discussed in this chapter have only one aim, namely enhancing independence. Being independent means being able to cope in society—coping both within the living situation, the home environment, and in the outside world. This means that a woman with epilepsy needs to possess practical abilities, but also feel confident enough to use them.

Coping in the outside world often involves having work which is used both as a means to boost self-confidence and as an end in itself. By providing the opportunity for women to obtain these abilities their independence will be enhanced to its utmost and provide them with a little of optimal fulfilment.

Discussion session 1

Dr R. Newton: I wanted to open up a general discussion on the language we use when we talk about the people we see in our clinics. One important factor in the success of a person's life who has a tendency to have seizures is how they view themselves. Doctors, in general, probably both overestimate and underestimate their own importance in people's lives, people with epilepsy. One of the most important encounters is the first or the second when people hear the news that they may have epilepsy for the first time. It is a time of grief for them and we need to concentrate on the way they *feel* about the problem as opposed to what they do about it and what we do about it. The problem with the terms 'epileptic' or 'epileptic patient' is that they infer a stereotype. They reflect on a certain level a doctor's view, a prejudiced view, of people with epilepsy. In striking contrast was the way Sue Usiskin referred to herself, which was as a woman with epilepsy and she referred to 'people with epilepsy' and 'women with epilepsy' throughout her talk.

I think physicians in general can only begin to start helping people with epilepsy when, through a process of self-knowledge, they address their own prejudices about it, their own fears about it and their own revulsion of handicap. When they have done that they might start thinking of and seeing people who have epilepsy and then when they have done that they will start saying 'people with epilepsy' without having to think to about it.

S. Usiskin: I agree with the substance and style of what you have just said. It is often said to me 'Well, what is wrong with being called epileptic? After all, we refer to people with diabetes as diabetics, so what is the difference?' Well, the difference is how you feel about it. I would rather see the word epileptic, as a noun, eradicated. It may be used as an adjective, an epileptic seizure, as big or small or fat or thin, but I would rather that as a noun it was no longer used.

Philip Patsalos: There is an additional term that we currently use at the Chalfont Centre and that is clients. Epilepsy has been eliminated.

Dr Trimble: 'Clients' has become a popular term. It is an American term and it implies a monetary relationship.

Dr D. Taylor: The utterance is not responsible for the negative stereotype. It would not be any more or less prejudicial to think of people with syphilis as syphilitic. If the stereotype is a negative one, the language merely enshrines this. What one needs to do is to face the phenomenon head on and drive the prejudice as far as one can out of one's mind. But that is not an easy thing to do. What has happened to people with impairment in their mental functioning such that they do not think quite as fast as people who have not got such impairment of their mental functioning, over the years, has been that the negative stereotype has dirtied up the language. That is to say, the original classification of mongol, imbecile and idiot in the French language have all trafficked into the language of abuse.

Dr Trimble: One or two of the lay organizations, like Epilepsy International and the British Epilepsy Association, have views on this. People in the States feel strongly about this issue.

Dr Mark Yerby: The term epileptic is discouraged in American medical schools and by American physicians because of its derogatory nature. It is also thought, in America, that 'fits' is considered rather offensive and it is not in general use amongst medical personnel.

Frank Besag: I think the terminology does change thinking, certainly in the medical profession. It is all too easy for a medical student to be taught 'known epileptic'—it is an easy way of writing off someone with epilepsy. It encourages people not to take histories, not listen to patients and, as a consequence, they fail to manage people with epilepsy properly.

Dr Green: One of the problems, of course, is that epilepsy is an umbrella term. I like very much the title of Niall O'Donohoe's book, which is *The Epilepsies of Childhood*. There is a wide variety of different epilepsies, so when you see a child with epilepsy you can say to the parent 'Well look, you know there are many different types and your child has such and such, etc.' We explain to the family about the type of epilepsy and what the prognosis is. The problem with an umbrella term is that if a person is labelled as 'epilepsy' or 'epileptic' then somebody will say to them 'Ah yes, but I had an uncle who had epilepsy and this happened to him'. Then the person will think they come into this same category.

Dr Reed: It is interesting how consciousness raising varies from disease to disease. Comparing epilepsy with other long-term neurological diseases, for example Parkinson's Disease or motor neurone disease, these are now associated in the public's mind with famous people who have had them. They have spoken out and helped to raise money. With epilepsy, that is not the case at all. We need a famous spokesperson.

Dr Betts: I have got several patients with active epilepsy who climb mountains and who canoe, and it is perfectly safe providing they know what they are doing and the people they are with know that they may suddenly drop off mountains. One of my patients actually does have atonic seizures, and she climbs mountains. I said 'Don't you fall off?', and she said 'We all fall off all the time, that's what the ropes are for.'

The other point is that fear of having a seizure during intercourse is one of the commonest reasons for women and men with epilepsy having a degree of sexual inhibition. One of our students actually did some research with young women with epilepsy and made a film called 'Letting Go'. She found their commonest fear was the fear of what happens when they have intercourse.

Dr I. McKinley: Ms de Boer, how much work do you have to do preparing employers for receiving the people who have been training?

Dr H. de Boer: We do not. In fact, I am rather opposed to that. I feel that if a person is ready to go out and try and get a job, that is what he or she should do. I do not think we should act as mother, and I do not think you can ask an employer to have specific requirements for this particular woman because she has epilepsy. He wants an employee, he wants to make money and that is fair. So we try and prepare the patients for a proper occupation.

Dr McKinley: Some employers have work in industry which is not 100% safe for all employees. We certainly get asked by them for advice about whether or not a job is suitable, if they want to employ a potential employee who has epilepsy.

Dr H. de Boer: It is slightly different in my country. Usually there is a company doctor involved. If not, I feel you can never give general advice. You have to know what the person's seizures are like, when she has them, day or night, when they are working or when they are having a rest—if the job involves working at a machine, and the person always falls backwards, no extra danger involved. Actually, when people are working—concentrating—we do not see many seizures.

Dr Trimble: There is a growing trend for temporal lobe epilepsy surgery. When you review the follow-up studies, you find patients are often relieved of their seizures, or virtually so, but the social rehabilitation of those patients does not occur. So, the same number of patients are out of work or living independently as before operation. Now, in psychiatric practice, if you carry out a leucotomy it is part and parcel of doing the operation that a full re-habilitation programme is organized for that patient before the operation can be done. I think one of the failures of the temporal lobe epilepsy surgery programmes is that they do not pay attention to rehabilitation.

Dr H. de Boer: I could not agree more; rehabilitation is needed. At our centre, if somebody does go for an operation that person will come back after the operation is done and the rehabilitation will just continue.

Dr Hugo: I was very glad to hear that you are able to employ a lot of women with epilepsy as nurses. Here in the UK the health service is the biggest single employer. It is an awful employer of people with epilepsy; all sorts of hurdles are put up against them.

Dr Yerby: Ms McGuire, does your method have any utility when one wants to develop therapeutic interventions?

A. McGuire: I think that is a very important application. Our method brings out things that would normally be overlooked. By looking at patients on an individual basis, they may reveal to you areas that you have not thought about. By their profiles you could determine what areas they are dissatisfied with and how the intervention is doing.

Dr Yerby: How much variability was there in the scores when the same person repeated them within a short period of time?

A. McGuire: The retest liability that we have looked at ranged from about 0.1 at one month to 0.7 at six months. We did separate out patients who had some major life event during the study, and the measures did actually differentiate; they were able to detect changes in quality of life related to some major life events. We have also used it in a study of patients having surgery for trigemi-nal neuralgia, and it is a sensitive measure in picking up changes due to surgery.

Section II

4

Sex differences in epilepsy: epidemiological aspects

ZARRINA KURTZ
Institute of Child Health, London, UK

INTRODUCTION

From the earliest times epilepsy was regarded as evidence of something special, associated with either special gifts or special affliction. That great men such as Alexander the Great, Mohammed, Julius Caesar and Dostoevsky had seizures has always been used to reinforce the positive image of epilepsy (Ounsted, 1974). The condition was described in women but was thought to occur less frequently. Epilepsy may have been hidden in women, to a considerable extent because of their less prominent position in society. Simulated seizures, however, were described almost exclusively in women and were regarded as a somewhat underhand means of gaining advantage through illness (Temkin, 1945).

The relative importance of epilepsy in women and men can truly be understood only through population-based epidemiological study. Information gathered by these methods can tell us whether there are differences between men and women in the frequency and seriousness of epilepsy—in prevalence, incidence, morbidity and mortality. We can also determine whether different epileptic syndromes tend to occur among men and women, whether the disease tends to take a different course and have different consequences, and whether the risks and risk factors are different. Finally, we can determine whether there are differing possibilities for the prevention and management of epilepsy in men and women.

PREVALENCE

Virtually all studies of the prevalence of epilepsy, however cases are defined and ascertained, whatever the sample used and in whatever country they are

Women and Epilepsy. Edited by M.R. Trimble
© 1991 John Wiley & Sons Ltd

carried out, agree in finding a higher prevalence in men than in women. The difference, however, is usually a small one. The early population studies based on general practice in the UK found 61% of males and 59% of females with chronic epilepsy and an overall prevalence of 4.2 per thousand (Crombie *et al.*, 1960); and 3.5 per 1000 males and 3.1 per thousand females (Pond *et al.*, 1960). More recently, among equal numbers of men and women (3000 of each) in a single practice in Tonbridge, 41 men and 81 women were found to have a history of at least one non-febrile convulsion (Goodridge and Shorvon, 1983). In the USA in the large population follow-up carried out in Rochester, Minnesota, 6 per 1000 males and 5.6 per 1000 females with epilepsy were found—a non-significant difference (Hauser and Kurland, 1975).

The preponderance of males over females with epilepsy is more clearly seen in childhood. A large study of epilepsy occurring from birth up until the age of 20 among children and adolescents in two counties in central Oklahoma showed a slightly higher prevalence in boys in each age group until after 14 years, when the rates were approximately equal; the highest male/female ratio (M:F = 1.5) was observed in children aged under 1 year (Table 1) (Cowan *et al.*, 1989).

In the UK, epilepsy has been studied in three nationally representative cohorts of children followed up from birth (Cooper, 1965; Verity and Ross, 1985). For people born in 1946 followed to the age of 36, a male excess of those with a history of epilepsy was found (with men forming 56% of those with epilepsy compared with 52% of men in the whole cohort) (Britten *et al.*, 1986); and there were slightly more boys than girls suffering febrile convulsions among the cohort born in 1970 (Verity and Ross, 1985). However, for those born in 1958, 35 boys and 29 girls had a history of epilepsy when information was gathered at the age of 11 (Ross *et al.*, 1980). The sex difference in cumulative incidence was found to be the same by the age of 23, when 66 young men and 58 young women with a history of epilepsy were identified (Kurtz, unpublished data).

Table 1. Prevalence of epilepsy by sex and age in Oklahoma and Cleveland counties, 1983 (from Cowan *et al.*, 1989, with permission)

Age (years)	Male		Female		Total	
	No.	Rate[a]	No.	Rate[a]	No.	Rate[a]
<1	33	4.95	22	3.29	55	4.11
1–4	144	5.92	115	5.01	259	5.48
5–9	174	5.80	138	4.77	312	5.30
10–14	139	4.86	123	4.45	262	4.66
15–19	136	3.87	135	3.85	271	3.86
Total	626	5.02	533	4.40	1159	4.71

[a] Rate per 1000.

If proxy measures for the prevalence of epilepsy are taken, such as children in school known to have the condition, or discharges and deaths of people with epilepsy from hospital, the preponderance of males is much greater than that found in representative population-based studies. For example, the number of discharges and deaths of people with epilepsy from NHS hospitals in 1966 (showing large sex differences) were among the sparse data on prevalence available to the Reid Committee (Department of Health and Social Services and the Welsh Office, 1969) (Table 2). The proportions of boys and girls resident in special schools for epilepsy in England and Wales in 1977 were 64% and 36%, respectively (Morgan and Kurtz, 1987). These data do not describe either epilepsy defined rigorously or its distribution in the population, and are likely to reflect factors that influence admission to hospital or residential care but not the true prevalence (Kurtz *et al.*, 1987).

In countries very different from the UK, male/female differences in the prevalence of epilepsy are likely to be due to different relative contributions of causal factors such as parasitic and other infections, trauma, and the abuse of alcohol. However, the findings cannot be simply interpreted in this way as a higher rate is usually found in females. For example, in a town of approximately 20 000 in Nigeria, the prevalence of active epilepsy among people aged over 7 years was 5.1 per 1000 males and 6.5 per 1000 females (Osuntokun *et al.*, 1987). Using the same study protocol, a female excess has also been found in several Latin American countries (Cruz *et al.*, 1986) and elsewhere.

INCIDENCE

Incidence rates are higher in males than females also. Hauser and Kurland reported in 1975 that over the 30-odd years of their population study of epilepsy in Rochester, Minnesota, the mean annual incidence of epilepsy in

Table 2. Estimated number of discharges and deaths of people with epilepsy from National Health Service hospitals in England and Wales during 1966; by age and sex (DHSS, 1969, reproduced with permission of HMSO)

Age group	Persons	Male	Female
All ages	15 300	8800	6500
0–4	1400	900	500
5–14	2300	1300	1000
15–19	1600	900	700
20–24	1300	800	500
25–34	1800	1000	800
35–44	2000	1000	900
45–64	3300	2000	1300
65 and over	1600	800	800

males was 51.8 per 100000 and 46.2 per 100000 in females (Hauser and Kurland, 1975). The difference in sex-specific rates was not significant at any time over the entire period, however. The yearly incidence of all types of epilepsy (excluding febrile convulsions) was investigated between 1967 and 1977 in a population of nearly 250000 in Denmark (Juul-Jensen and Foldspang, 1983). The rates for males and females are shown in Table 3. The highest incidence of epilepsy is found in children and it rises again in old age. This was found by Pond in 1960 and also in a recent study in the UK, in which newly diagnosed or suspected cases of epilepsy were reported from 275 general practices from June 1984 to October 1987 (Sander *et al.*, 1990). Among these there were 607 males and 588 females; males had a higher incidence of febrile convulsions (M:F = 134:86), and a higher rate of definite epilepsy (M:F = 289:275). There were more females among those thought possibly to have epilepsy and among those found not to have epilepsy. The criteria used to define epilepsy will clearly affect the relative proportions of male and female cases found in any particular population. The excess of females found in the Tonbridge general practice study (Goodridge and Shorvon, 1983) may be because all those with a single seizure were included.

Greater sex differences in incidence are found among children and old people when the incidence of the condition itself is at its highest, than in epilepsy arising in middle life. In addition, a greater *tendency* to seizures is seen consistently in males who have, for example, a higher rate of febrile convulsions (Wallace, 1987). It was found in the National Child Development Study based on the 1958 British birth cohort that 2.4% of all children at the age of 7 had a history of febrile convulsions (Ross and Peckham, 1983). Of these 366 children, 56% were boys and 44% were girls, a difference that is not significant at the 5% level. There was also no significant difference in the

Table 3.   Yearly incidence of all types of epilepsy by gender and age in men and women (excluding febrile convulsions) (from Juul-Jensen and Foldspang, 1983, with permission)

Age at onset of epilepsy	New cases in the years 1967–1977		Yearly incidence 100 000	
	Male	Female	Male	Female
0–4	151	108	149	111
5–9	47	37	49	40
10–14	30	35	39	46
15–19	33	24	39	27
20–29	63	49	22	18
30–39	50	25	33	17
40–49	32	26	26	19
50–	58	49	20	13
Total	464	353	39	28

pattern of onset (age at which the first febrile convulsion occurred), but it is interesting to note that equal numbers of the boys were treated at home or in hospital, while half as many girls went to hospital as were treated at home (Table 4). Hospital-treated cases were likely to be the most severe, as 12% went on to develop non-febrile epilepsy by the age of 13 compared with 0.5% of those who were treated entirely at home.

Table 4. Febrile convulsions and place of treatment (Ross and Peckham, 1983)

	At home		In hospital (at least once)		Total	
	Number	%	Number	%	Number	%
Boys	104	50.7	101	49.3	205	100
Girls	98	60.1	63	39.1	161	100
Total	202	55.2	164	44.8	366	100

In the elderly, a significantly higher incidence in males is consistently found. This may be illustrated by the findings of a study carried out over a five-year period in an urban population in Denmark; 77 new cases of epilepsy were found per 100 000 people aged over 60. Although there were more women with epilepsy in this population because there were more women in the age group, incidence rates for epilepsy were significantly higher in men (Lühdorf et al., 1986) (Table 5).

Table 5. Epilepsy in the elderly. Distribution according to age and sex among 251 patients (Reproduced from Luhdorf et al., 1986, with permission)

Age	Patients not previously treated		Patients with established epilepsy		Population (1.1.82)	
	Male	Female	Male	Female	Male	Female
60–64	20[b]	9	12	15	2625	3724
65–69	22[a]	16	9[b]	2	2487	3812
70–74	13	31	5	13	2167	3954
75–79	13	17	6	14	1466	3413
>80	12[b]	10	5	7	1343	4187
Total	80[c]	83	37	51	10 088	19 090

Significant overweight of male patients:
[a] $p < 0.05$; [b] $p < 0.005$; [c] $p < 0.0005$.

The prevalence of those with a history of epilepsy will reflect the higher incidence in males and the death rate. The prevalence of current or active epilepsy will be determined by incidence and rates of remission of seizures and death rates.

NATURAL HISTORY

The risk of recurrence of seizures after a first unprovoked seizure was reported among patients presenting at four major hospitals serving the population of Minneapolis St Paul, in the USA (Hauser *et al.*, 1982) and in the UK (Hopkins *et al.*, 1988). The risk of recurrence was not found to be different in males or females in either study.

Little difference in the prospect of remission between males and females was found by Annegers *et al.* (1979). Females had slightly higher rates of remission of seizures in the early years following diagnosis, but the probabilities of remission became similar by 20 years after diagnosis, and remained small when discontinuation of medication was included as a criterion (Figure 1).

However, a higher relapse rate in those with established seizures is usually found amongst girls and women. In a Dutch follow-up of 146 children with

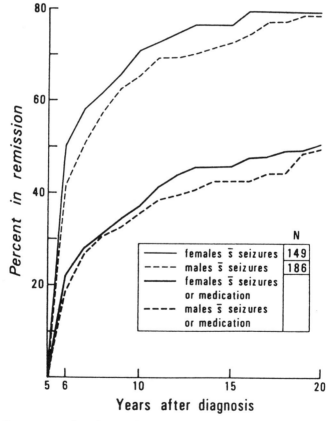

Figure 1. Percentage of patients with idiopathic epilepsy in remission, by sex and medication status. (from Annegers *et al.*, 1979, with permission)

epilepsy, the relapse rate was significantly higher in girls on withdrawal of antiepileptic therapy after a seizure-free period of at least two years and normalization of the EEG (Arts *et al.*, 1988) (Figure 2). It was found that in primary generalized epilepsy no factor significantly increased the likelihood of recurrence. But in partial epilepsy, significant factors predictive of recurrence were the presence of a neurological deficit (focal neurological signs and/or mental retardation), female sex, a positive family history, and the number of drugs necessary for control of the seizures.

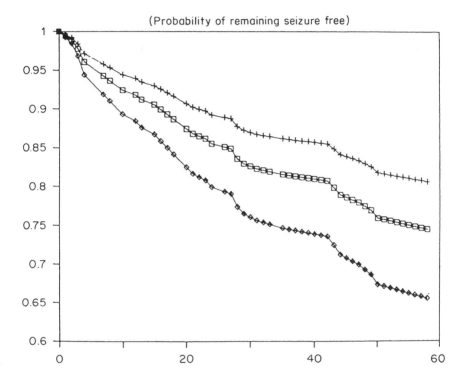

Figure 2. Probability of remaining seizure free after withdrawal of anticonvulsant medication by sex. Cumulative remission rate for all cases ($\square$) and for males (+) and females ($\diamond$). If the remission rate for all cases at any moment after withdrawal of AED equals $\hat{S}$, then the remission rate for males at that moment will equal $\hat{S}^{0.73}$ and for females $\hat{S}^{1.43}$. The argument is as follows: if the baseline recurrence function equals $\hat{S}$ ($t;\bar{x}$), then the recurrence function for the covariates found to be significant equals $\hat{S}$ ($t;x$) = $\hat{S}$ ($t;\bar{x}$)^r, where $r = \exp [0.67(x_1 - 1.47) + 1.52(x_2 - 1.08]$ (x_1 = covariate for sex; x_2 = covariate for symptomatic seizures). If x_2 equals its average, then for males $r = \exp [0.67(1 - 1.47] = 0.73$, so $\hat{S}$ ($t;1,\bar{x}_2$) = $\hat{S}$ ($t;\bar{x}$)$^{0.73}$. For females, $x_1 = 2$, so their recurrence function equals $\hat{S}$ ($t;2,\bar{x}_2$) = $\hat{S}$ ($t;\bar{x}$)$^{1.43}$. (Reproduced from Arts *et al.*, 1988, by permission of International League Against Epilepsy)

Among 23 year-olds with a history of epilepsy in the 1958 British birth cohort, the rate of active epilepsy in young men (59%) was virtually no different from the rate in young women (57%) (Kurtz, unpublished data). Again, in the Tonbridge general practice study, no significant differences were found when the probability rates for active epilepsy and the proportion of patients in remission were calculated separately for males and females (Goodridge and Shorvon, 1983).

The death rate in epilepsy is markedly higher in men than women. Hauser reported that the 30-year cumulative standardized mortality ratio (SMR) for males with idiopathic epilepsy was 2.1 and for females it was 1.6. The sex difference in mortality was greatest during the first five years following diagnosis (Hauser et al., 1980). A detailed analysis of mortality data in the USA between 1959 and 1961, for epilepsy as the underlying cause of death, also showed that males have a higher rate than females (Kurtzke, 1972). In Warsaw, Poland, the mortality rate in people with epilepsy was 1.8 times that in the general population, although it was 3.5 times higher under the age of 50 (Zielinski, 1974). The rate was about the same in males and females until the fourth decade of life, but thererafter it was more than twice as high in males. The reasons for the gender differences in mortality risk are not clear.

CLINICAL MANIFESTATIONS

It is well recognized that epilepsy is not a homogeneous condition. Certain syndromes are found chiefly or only in girls or in boys. This is discussed in detail in Chapter 7. In spite of careful clinical examination and history-taking, distinction between syndromes is possible in probably no more than 60% of all cases presenting to the clinician. In population-based studies different clinical manifestations and syndromes of epilepsy do not show marked sex differences, as indicated by the studies carried out by Juul-Jensen (1983) (Table 6). Temporal lobe epilepsy, however, is found universally significantly more commonly in boys than girls. In Ounsted and Lindsay's series in Oxford there were 63 boys and 37 girls (Lindsay et al., 1979).

CAUSES

In the Rochester, Minnesota studies, a higher proportion of males than females with epilepsy had an ascertained cause for their convulsive disorder (Hauser and Kurland, 1975). It is, however, difficult to find clear-cut sex differences related to cause of epilepsy, mainly because exact attribution of cause is often not possible and because a number of factors are likely to be involved in causation in a single individual.

The influence of sex and heredity was studied by Pedersen and Krogh

Table 6.   All types of seizures excluding febrile convulsions (when possible placed in the different types of epilepsy) (from Juul-Jensen and Foldspang, 1983, with permission)

Type of epilepsy	Males	Females
Unclassifiable epilepsies	8	10
Primary generalized grand mal	184	201
Petit mal	29	29
Juvenile myoclonic epilepsy	8	17
Myoclonic astatic epilepsy	1	1
West's syndrome	6	10
Partial epilepsy with elementary symptomatology	123	146
Partial epilepsy with complex symptomatology	123	146
Partial epilepsy with secondary generalization	114	103
Rolandic epilepsy	0	4
Unverricht–Lundberg	3	1
Seizures provoked by alcohol	75	19
Seizures provoked by stress	71	50
Seizures provoked by medicine	4	16
Isolated seizures (unprovoked)	110	92
Total	778	727

Population in Greaer Aarhus in 1977: 244 800.

(1971). They also found more men in the symptomatic group of epilepsies and more women in the cryptogenic group. In addition, they found that patients with a family history of epilepsy in the cryptogenic group had a poorer prognosis than those without. The prognosis was worse for women than for men.

In children there is a largely unexplained excess of males with neurological disease such as cerebral palsy (Nelson and Ellenberg, 1978), and epilepsy occurs commonly in association with many of these conditions (Corbett, 1985). Aside from the 60–70% of cryptogenic epilepsies, for which there is no clear cause, post-traumatic epilepsy which accounts for about 20% and alcohol-related epilepsies accounting for about 6% probably do give rise to more epilepsy in men. Epilepsy due to cerebrovascular disease (15%) will be more common in men as these conditions are themselves more common in men, especially in later life (Bamford *et al.*, 1988). Cerebral tumours as a cause of epilepsy (6%) show no difference in rates between women and men.

The reproductive cycle in women

In girls, the onset of menarche is associated with the start of seizures in some cases. In an extensive review by Rosciszewska, a number of studies are described showing that epilepsy tends to begin during puberty (Rosciszewska, 1987). Lennox and Lennox (1960) found an association between the first seizure and menarche in 25% of 387 women whose onset of seizures was between the ages of 18 and 20. Hopkins has recorded that the age-specific annual incidence rate for epilepsy is approximately constant at 40–50 per 100 000 throughout the child-bearing period, and therefore pregnancy and the onset of non-eclamptic seizures will coincide in a number of women; there is no study which provides statistical evidence that pregnancy is likely to start epilepsy (Hopkins, 1987).

CONSEQUENCES

Puberty, menstruation, fertility, pregnancy, menopause

In women with epilepsy, the effects of menstruation, pregnancy and the menopause are both part of the natural history of the condition—which differs from the natural history in men—and part of the consequences of having epilepsy, which will again be unique to women.

Rosciszewska (1987) reports:

> There is little information on the effect of puberty in girls with already established epilepsy. However, in a study of 115 girls, whose epilepsy had begun at a mean age of 5.1 years, the course of the illness remained unchanged in only one-third of patients. In two-thirds of the remaining girls, seizure frequency increased, or a new type of seizure occurred; in one-third the seizure frequency decreased, or seizures stopped altogether. Generalized tonic–clonic seizures tended to increase, or join other seizure types, as did partial complex seizures. In contrast, absences rarely increased, and sometimes stopped. Exacerbation of epilepsy was more likely in girls whose epilepsy had begun at an earlier age, was of known aetiology, who had had numerous tonic–clonic seizures, and who had neurological or psychological abnormalities on examination, or abnormalities in the EEG. If menarche was later than that of a control population, then the frequency of seizures was likely to be greater during puberty. It is clear, therefore, that clinical features reflecting organic damage to the nervous system predict the likely cause of epilepsy during puberty.

The course of epilepsy in women during puberty and the relationship between seizures and menstruation is influenced by ovarian, pituitary and other hormones, and is largely dependent upon their interrelationship with serum anticonvulsant levels. Findings in this complex area and their interpretation are discussed in Chapters 8 and 10.

Fertility rates are reduced in both women and men with epilepsy, and women with complex partial seizures have been shown to be selectively disadvantaged (Webber et al., 1986).

It has been estimated that in the USA one of every 200 pregnancies occurs in women with epilepsy (Yerby, 1987). Their pregnancies are considered to be high risk because of increased risk of seizures during pregnancy, labour and delivery, and because of complications of pregnancy and adverse pregnancy outcomes. The known risks may lead to obstetric interventions such as induction and instrumental delivery which are often unnecessary and possibly harmful (Hopkins, 1987).

One-third of epileptic women have more seizures during gestation than they had prior to conception; a proportion have less (Yerby, 1987). It is difficult to predict which women will suffer from increased seizures, as the increased incidence is not related to seizure type, duration of epilepsy, or even the experience in a previous pregnancy. Management of anti-convulsant therapy is an important related factor, as discussed in Chapter 11.

The rate of congenital malformations in infants of epileptic mothers is 2.4 times higher than in the general population (Yerby, 1987). Annegers *et al.* (1976) found that children of *men* with epilepsy did not have an increased rate of congenital malformations of specific types compared to the general population.

Most mothers on anticonvulsant medication may safely breast feed their infants as only moderate quantities of these drugs pass into the milk (Hopkins, 1987).

The risk of seizures in the offspring of women with epilepsy was found by Annegers *et al.* to be significantly raised although this was not the case in children of men with epilepsy (Annegers *et al.*, 1976).

The effect of the menopause on epilepsy is reviewed by Rosciszewska (1974). Different authors report different effects of the menopause on seizure frequency: no effect, an increase in seizures, a recurrence of seizures at the time of the menopause, and finally, a remission of seizures during the menopause. In her own study it was found that seizures were more likely to improve during the menopause if they had previously been related to menstruation (Rosciszewska, 1974). Furthermore, epilepsy was more likely to improve during the menopause if the seizures had begun later in life, and had always been infrequent. On the other hand, women who had always suffered frequent generalized tonic–clonic or complex partial seizures were more likely to have an exacerbation during the menopause. It appeared that those whose seizures declined in frequency during the menopause had an age of menopause similar to that of the general population, whilst in those with an earlier menopause the seizure frequency remained either unchanged or, in a few cases, increased.

Learning and behaviour

A great deal of attention has been given to the effect of epilepsy on learning and behaviour. Boys are among the subgroups of children with epilepsy attending ordinary schools found to perform poorly on measures of attention (Stores *et al.*, 1978). The performance of 71 children with epilepsy in ordinary schools was compared with 35 non-epileptic controls, and epileptic boys were found to be significantly less attentive than non-epileptic boys—but *no* comparable differences were found among the girls (Stores *et al.*, 1978). Boys have also been found to be more retarded in reading than girls, and specific reading disability is seen, particularly in boys with focal seizures (Stores and Hart, 1976). However, in contrast to previously reported sex differences in academic performance of epileptic children, Jennekens-Schinkel *et al.* (1987) found both epileptic *and* control boys more vulnerable than girls. These authors note that it is well documented that boys have more learning problems than girls, whatever the aetiology, and girls show an advantage in the acquisition of specific language-related skills. They suggest, accordingly, that male sex rather than epilepsy is the decisive factor in causing the particular vulnerability in reading and spelling of epileptic boys.

In a paper published in 1974, Ounsted teased out the evidence to date for the relationship between seizures occurring in very young children and the causation of lesions which in turn give rise to attention deficit. The resulting effects on the child's intelligence—both overall and in specific performance of linguistic skills—will depend on the exact age at which the damage occurs and the *sex* of the child, as the two sexes develop their verbal and their performance skills at different paces. Taylor showed more than 20 years ago that the likelihood of psychosis intervening in a child with epilepsy as well as the timing of its onset is dependent on gender as well as on the laterality of the discharging focus (Taylor, 1969). In a review of cognitive function and behaviour in children with epilepsy, Cull points out that no significant difference between the number of boys and girls exhibiting behaviour disturbance has been reported in some studies, but that there are also reports of a greater number of disturbed boys relative to girls with epilepsy (Cull, 1988). It has been suggested that any gender bias depends upon the type of behaviour disturbance, with aggressive, antisocial behaviours associated with boys and neurotic disturbances found more frequently in girls.

It is interesting that Ounsted and Lindsay found no gender differences in grave handicap after 20 years' follow-up of childen with temporal lobe epilepsy (Ounsted and Lindsay, 1981). They comment that 'the handicaps that had rendered the young people totally dependent seemed to have over-ruled the operation of gender differences'.

Psychosocial aspects

The follow-up studies on people with epilepsy in the 1946 British birth cohort have shown that there was little difference between both uncomplicated and complicated cases and their controls at the age of 26 with regard to marriage, children, education or vocational qualifications, and a paid job (Britten *et al.*, 1986). But at 36 years, cohort members with epilepsy were significantly less likely than controls to be in paid work and to think life had been good to them, and were more likely to have previous experience of unemployment. There were no significant differences in life events, psychiatric morbidity, marital state, and home ownership.

Most studies, however, agree in showing that people with epilepsy have a lower rate of marriage than people without the condition. Lechtenberg in 1984 estimated that 56% of men with epilepsy and 69% of women are unmarried (Lechtenberg, 1984). However, among the sample of young people with temporal lobe epilepsy followed up by Lindsay and Ounsted, the prognosis for marriage is good for girls, provided they survive and are not grossly handicapped. Men, even though not heavily handicapped, more often than not do not marry (Ounsted and Lindsay, 1981) (Table 7).

The socio-economic consequences of epilepsy are included in a review of the literature on psychosocial dimensions published in 1988 (Levin *et al.*, 1988) and are also discussed by Masland (1985). Comment is made on gender differences only in relation to marriage and sexual life, as in other areas these are likely to arise in direct relation to differing roles and expectations that men and women have in our society. For example, if it is not necessary for a woman to have a paid job, factors affecting sufferers of epilepsy that relate to obtaining and keeping employment will not be important. Driving a car can be seen to be important to men and women for some of the same as well as different reasons; risk of accidents is the main reason that driving is restricted in people with epilepsy. An interesting study carried out in Washington has shown that the overall accident rate of drivers with epilepsy is twice that of the average driver. However, women with epilepsy have a lower accident rate than teenage men without epilepsy (Crancer *et al.*, 1968) (Figure 3).

PREVENTION AND MANAGEMENT

Differences between males and females with epilepsy are found in two main areas: firstly, in relation to the well-known increased vulnerability of the infant male brain in comparison with the female brain, leading to overall increased risk of damage from neurological insult giving rise to greater

Table 7. Comparison of married and single in 66 marriageable males and females (Reproduced from Ounsted and Lindsay, 1981, with permission)

		1977 Codes		
		Married	Single	Total
1964	Males	17	24	41
codes	Females	23	2	25
	Total	40	26	66

χ^2 (Yates modified) = 14.6; $p < 0.001$.

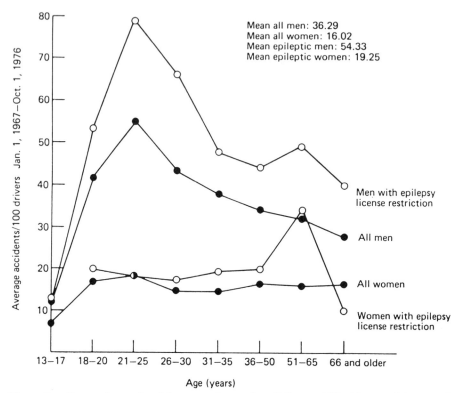

Figure 3.   Comparison of accident rates by sex for all licensed Washington drivers and drivers with an epilepsy licence restriction. (Reproduced from Masland (1985) by permission of Butterworth-Heinemann)

likelihood of seizures as well as problems of learning and behaviour. Males have higher incidence of and higher death rates in epilepsy, in common with their experience in many disease conditions. Secondly, a woman with epilepsy is more likely than a man to experience relapse of her seizures, and will certainly experience significant problems in relation to reproduction and bringing up children, with increased risks to her own and her children's health. However, women may still in our society be to some extent protected from problems with epilepsy related to earning a living.

In the prevention and management of epilepsy, we must await better fundamental understanding of the biology of brain development and of genetic mechanisms of seizure causation before it will be possible to reduce the occurrence of the majority of epilepsies. But prevention of accidental injury, abuse of alcohol, and of cerebrovascular disease would have a major effect in the primary prevention of symptomatic epilepsy.

The secondary prevention of learning and behavioural difficulties in childhood is particularly important in boys; in our current state of knowledge, this depends to a great extent upon close and careful management of anticonvulsant therapy. In women with epilepsy, the careful management of contraception throughout reproductive life—and during pregnancy, childbirth and the puerperium, protection of the mother from seizures and the fetus from unnecessary exposure to anticonvulsant medication—can do much to lessen the risks for her and for her offspring. In children and both men and women, expert and sensitive balanced control of seizures and anticonvulsant medication is the key to management; expert and sensitive advice and help about practical and psychological issues related to employment and type of job, and to relationships and making a home are equally important.

REFERENCES

Annegers, J.F., Hauser, W.A., Elvebach, L.R., Andersen, V.E. and Kurland, L.T. (1976) Seizure disorders in offspring of parents with a history of seizures: A maternal–paternal difference?' *Epilepsia,* **17**, 1–9.

Annegers, J.F., Hauser, W.A. and Elveback, L.R. (1979) Remission of seizures and relapse in patients with epilepsy. *Epilepsia,* **20**, 729–737.

Arts, W.F.M., Visser, L.H., Loonen, M.C.B., Tjiam, A.T., Stroink, H.,. Stuurman, P.M. and Poortvliet, D.C.J. (1988) Follow-up of 146 children with epilepsy after withdrawal of antiepileptic therapy, *Epilepsia,* **29**, 244–250.

Bamford, J., Sandercock, P., Dennis, M. *et al.* (1988) A prospective study of acute cerebrovascular disease in the community: The Oxfordshire community stroke project 1981–1986 (1) Methodology, demography and incident cases of first stroke. *J. Neurol. Neurosurg. Psychiatry,* **51**, 1373–1380.

Britten, N., Morgan, K., Fenwick, P.B.C. and Britten, H. (1986) Epilepsy and handicap from birth to age 36. *Dev. Med. Child Neurol.,* **28**, 719–728.

Cooper, J.E. (1965) Epilepsy in a longitudinal survey of 5000 children. *Br. Med. J.,* **1**, 1020–1022.

Corbett, J. (1985) Epilepsy as part of a handicapping condition. In: *Paediatric Perspectives on Epilepsy* (eds E. Ross and E. Reynolds), pp. 79–89. Wiley, Chichester.

Cowan, L.D., Bodensteiner, J.B., Leviton, A. and Doherty, L. (1989) Prevalence of the epilepsies in children and adolescents. *Epilepsia,* **30**, 94–106.

Crancer, A. , Jr, and McMurray, L. (1968). Accident and violation rates of Washington's medically restricted drivers. *JAMA,* **205**, 272–276.

Crombie, D.L., Cross, K.W., Fry, J., Pinsent, R.J.F.H. and Watts, C.A.H. (1960) A survey of the epilepsies in general practice. *Br. Med. J.,* **2**, 416–422.

Cruz, M.E., Barberis, P. and Schoenberg, B.S. (1986) Epidemiology of epilepsy. In: *Neurology: Proceedings of the XIII World Congress of Neurology* (eds K. Poeck, H.J. Freund and H. Ganshirt), pp. 229–239. Springer-Verlag, Berlin.

Cull, C.A. (1988) Cognitive function and behaviour in children. In: *Epilepsy, Behaviour and Cognitive Function* (eds M.R. Trimble and E.H. Reynolds), pp. 97–111. Wiley, Chichester.

Department of Health and Social Services and the Welsh Office Central Health Services Council (1969) *People with Epilepsy: Report of the Advisory Committee on the Health and Welfare of Handicapped Persons* (Chair: J.J.A. Reid). HMSO, London.

Goodridge, D.M.G. and Shorvon, S.D. (1983) Epileptic seizures in a population of 6000. I: Demography, diagnosis and classification, and role of the hospital services. *Br. Med. J.,* **287**, 641–644.

Hauser, W.A. and Kurland, L.T. (1975) The epidemiology of epilepsy in Rochester, Minnesota, 1935 through 1967. *Epilepsia,* **16**, 1–66.

Hauser, W.A., Annegers, J.F. and Elveback, L.R. (1980) Mortality in patients with epilepsy. *Epilepsia,* **21**, 399–412.

Hauser, W.A., Andersen, V.E., Loewenson, R.B. and McRoberts, M. (1982) Seizure recurrence after a first unprovoked seizure. *N. Eng. J. Med.,* **307**, 522–528.

Hopkins, A. (ed.) (1987) Epilepsy and pregnancy. In *Epilepsy,* pp. 381–388. Chapman and Hall Medical, London.

Hopkins, A., Garman, A. and Clarke, C. (1988) The first seizure in adult life: Value of clinical features, electroencephalography, and computed tomographic scanning in production of seizure recurrence. *Lancet,* **i**, 721–726.

Jennekens-Schinkel, A., Linschoofen-Duikersloot, E.M.E.M, Bouma, P.A.D., Peters, A.C.B. and Stijnera, Th. (1987) Spelling errors made by children with mild epilepsy: Writing to dictation. *Epilepsia,* **28**, 555–563.

Juul-Jensen, P. and Foldspang, A. (1983) Natural history of epileptic seizures. *Epilepsia,* **24**, 297–312.

Kurtz, Z., Tookey, P. and Ross, E. (1987) The epidemiology of epilepsy in childhood. In *Epilepsy in Young People* (eds E. Ross, D. Chadwick and R. Crawford), pp. 13–21, Wiley, Chichester.

Kurtzke, J.R. (1972) Mortality and morbidity data on epilepsy. In *The Epidemiology of Epilepsy: A workshop, DHEW (NIH)* (eds A. Alter and W.A. Hauser), pp. 21–36. NINCDS Monograph 14, Washington, DC.

Lechtenberg, R. (1984) *Epilepsy and the Family*. Harvard University Press, Boston.

Lennox, W.G. and Lennox, M.A. (1960) *Epilepsy and Related Disorders*, Vol. 2, pp. 645–650. Little Brown, Boston.

Levin, R., Banks, S. and Berg, B. (1988) Psychosocial dimensions of epilepsy: A review of the literature. *Epilepsia,* **29**, 805–816.

Lindsay, J., Ounsted, C. and Richards, P. (1979) Long-term outcome in children with temporal lobe seizures. I: Social outcome and childhood factors. *Dev. Med. Child. Neurol.,* **21**, 285–298.

Luhdorf, K., Jensen, L.K. and Plesner, A.M. (1986) Epilepsy in the elderly: incidence, social function, and disability. *Epilepsia,* **27**, 135–141.

Masland, R.L. (1985) Psychosocial aspects of epilepsy. In: *The Epilepsies* (eds R. Porter and P.L. Morselli), pp. 356–380. Butterworths.

Morgan, J. and Kurtz, Z. (1987) *Special Services for People with Epilepsy in the 1970s.* HMSO, London.

Nelson, K.B. and Ellenberg, J.H. (1978) Epidemiology of cerebral palsy. *Ann. Neurol.,* **19**, 421–435.

Osuntokun, B.O., Adeuja, A.O.G., Nottidge, V.A., Bademosi, O., Olumide, A., Ige, O., Yaria, F., Bolis, C.L. and Schoenberg, B.S. (1987) Prevalence of the epilepsies in Nigerian Africans: A community-based study. *Epilepsia,* **28**, 272–279.

Ounsted, C. (1974) Attention, intelligence and seizures of the immature brain. In: *Epilepsy: Proceedings of the Hans Berger Centenary Symposium* (eds P. Harris and C. Mawdsley), pp. 140–144. Churchill Livingstone, Edinburgh.

Ounsted, C. and Lindsay, J. (1981) The long-term outcome of temporal lobe epilepsy in childhood. In *Epilepsy and Psychiatry* (eds E.H. Reynolds and M.R. Trimble), pp. 185–215. Churchill Livingstone, Edinburgh.

Pedersen, H.E. and Krogh, E. (1971) The prognostic consequences of familial predisposition and sex in epilepsy. *Acta. Neurol. Scand.*, **47**, 106–116.

Pond, D.A., Bidwell, B.H. and Stein, L. (1960) A survey of epilepsy in fourteen general practices. I: Demographic and medical data. *Psychiatr. Neurol. Neurochir.*, **63**, 217–236.

Rosciszewska, D. (1974) *Clinical Course of Epilepsy during Puberty, Maturity and Climacterium.* Dissertation, Katowice, Poland.

Rosciszewska, D. (1987) Epilepsy and menstruation. In: *Epilepsy* (ed. A. Hopkins), pp. 373–381, Chapman and Hall Medical, London.

Ross, E.M., Peckham, C.S., West, P.B. and Butler, N.R. (1980) Epilepsy in childhood: Findings from the National Child Development Study. *Br. Med. J.*, **1**, 207–210.

Ross, E.M. and Peckham, C.S. (1983) Seizure disorder in the National Child Development Study. In *Research Progress in Epilepsy* (ed. F.C. Rose), pp. 46–59, Pitman, London.

Sander, J.W.A.S., Hart, Y.M., Johnson, A.L. and Shorvon, S.D. (1990) National general practice study of epilepsy: Newly diagnosed epileptic seizures in a general population. *Lancet*, **336**, 1267–1271.

Stores, G. and Hart, J. (1976) Reading skills of children with generalised or focal epilepsy attending ordinary school. *Dev. Med. Child. Neurol.*, **18**, 705–716.

Stores, G., Hart, J. and Piran, N. (1978) Inattentiveness in schoolchildren with epilepsy. *Epilepsia*, **19**, 169–175.

Taylor, D.C. (1969) Some psychiatric aspects of epilepsy. In: Current problems in neuropsychiatry: Schizophrenia, epilepsy and the temporal lobe. *Br. J. Psychiatry*, **114**, 106–109.

Temkin, O. (1945) *The Falling Sickness: A History of Epilepsy from the Greeks to the Beginnings of Modern Neurology.* Johns Hopkins Press, Baltimore.

Verity, C.M. and Ross, E.M. (1985) Longitudinal studies of children's epilepsy. In: *Paediatric Perspectives on Epilepsy* (eds E. Ross and E. Reynolds), pp. 133–140, Wiley, Chichester.

Wallace, S.J. (1987) Febrile convulsions. In: *Epilepsy* (ed. A. Hopkins), pp. 443–467. Chapman and Hall Medical, London.

Webber, M.P., Hauser, W.A., Ottman, R. and Annegers, J.F. (1986) Fertility in persons with epilepsy: 1935–1974. *Epilepsia*, **27**, 746–752.

Yerby, M.S. (1987) Problems and management of the pregnant woman with epilepsy. *Epilepsia*, **28**, S29–S36.

Zielinski, J.J. (1974) Epilepsy and mortality rate and cause of death. *Epilepsia*, **15**, 191–199.

5

Developmental and behavioural differences between males and females with special reference to epilepsy

DAVID C. TAYLOR
University of Manchester, UK

INTRODUCTION

In 1968, during the analysis of 100 cases of temporal lobe epilepsy operated upon by Falconer, I observed that in cases which proved to show mesial temporal sclerosis (MTS), the first epileptic fit ever had occurred before the age of 2 years where left-sided lobectomies were performed, whereas the first attack was distributed from 2 to 10 years where MTS had proved to be present in right-sided lobectomies. There were no such differences observable for any other lesion (Figure 1).

It had been argued (Cavanagh and Meyer, 1956; Ounsted *et al.*, 1966) that there was a causal connection between the first fit, which was usually a prolonged febrile seizure, and the MTS. This newly discovered difference between the hemispheres was suggestive of an effect of vulnerability in relation to a phase of development which differed between the hemispheres. But the numbers were too small for statistical proof. Later, working on Ounsted's large series of children with febrile convulsions, some of whom went on to develop temporal lobe epilepsy, it was possible to expand the material, based on the laterality of EEG foci, to show a precisely similar effect and to confirm the suspicion that females were vulnerable for a shorter time than males.

The diagram shown in Figure 2 is created from 65 patients with MTS drawn from the first 147 patients operated upon by Murray Falconer. To these 65 patients are added a further 65 patients from Ounsted's series of patients with temporal lobe epilepsy (Ounsted *et al.*, 1966) who had largely or exclusively lateralized foci in their EEG; and 58 males and 35 females who had an age of onset of epilepsy under 10 years were also considered. The patterns of age of

Women and Epilepsy. Edited by M.R. Trimble
© 1991 John Wiley & Sons Ltd

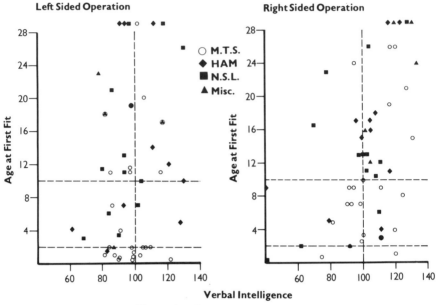

Figure 1. (From Taylor, 1981)

onset by side and by sex were entirely similar to those in the Guy's series and so the figures were combined in this analysis. MTS will be by far the most common lesion in the combined series and cases not of MTS will tend to run against the argument. Looking at the histogram as an indication of 'risk', the figures show that the risk to the left hemisphere falls steeply and exponentially while the risk to the right hemisphere has a peak at the age of 2 years. In the lower half of the diagram the risk for males declines smoothly over the first 4 years whereas the risk for females declines very rapidly in the second year of life. In all the conditions the effect ceases by the fifth year of life.

In other words it looked as though febrile convulsions would lead to MTS, not in a random manner but in relation to some window of opportunity in development, perhaps in relation to the maturation of a system or the degree of functional activity in that region of brain. A contemporary model for that was provided by the precise effect that the sort of motor effort made during the prodrome had on the part of the body later paralysed by poliomyelitis. Subsequently it has been shown, in the thalidomide catastrophe, just how precisely the timing of the intoxification is related to the nature and location of the resultant limb deformities.

THEORY OF SEX DETERMINATION AND DIFFERENTIATION

In 1969 the suggestion that males and females, and right and left brains, developed according to different schedules was regarded by the *Lancet* as a

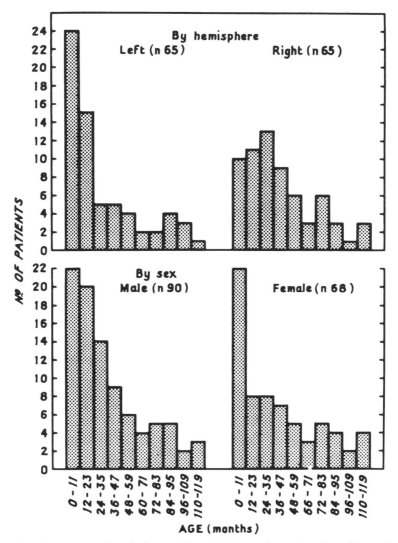

Figure 2.   Age at onset in relation to side of lesion and sex of patient (From Taylor, 1969)

'hypothesis' and it was published under that rubric. Such a hypothesis was, however, useful in addressing certain problems in human epilepsy, in particular the increased vulnerability of males. But any such theory touching on differential rates of maturation between the sexes would need to be shown to be broadly true across a variety of data and would need to be consistent with what was then known about the mechanisms of sex determination and differentiation.

At the time it had relatively recently been shown that, in the absence of a Y chromosome, mammals would proceed towards female morphology and psychological development. It followed, in our view, that the Y chromosome 'evoked' male characteristics out of the genome. What *was* recognized, particularly in sex determination, was the mechanism by which the indifferent gonad became determined as a testis so that fetal testosterone would circulate and produce general changes towards male morphology. Over subsequent years the location on the Y chromosome of the testis-determining factor Tdf has been reduced, currently, to a region of 35 kilobases (McLaren, 1990), but the question remains as to whether the whole of sex differentiation depends upon a cascade effect stemming from the formation of fetal testis, or whether the Y chromosome has a more persistent and enduring effect on development by modulating the *pace* of development.

At meetings in 1970 and 1971 and in our book (Ounsted and Taylor, 1972) we proposed that:

1. Differences in the development of the two sexes normally depend entirely on the Y chromosome.
2. The Y chromosome codes no specific structural information.
3. Rather it permits the genomic expression in males to occur more slowly over development.
4. This would allow more genomic information to be transcribed in males.
5. Thus a difference in the *pace* of development between the sexes would become a continuing modulator of further sex differences.

These propositions were advanced then and are maintained still because they are congruent with a wide variety of facts in terms of differential morbidity and mortality between the sexes. Their different developmental schedules are made evident in the timing of puberty, the menopause, and several aspects of the ageing process such as apocrine gland shutdown, bone demineralization, and possibly even the rate of fall-out of neurones in the brain (Hubbard and Anderson, 1983). Our interpretation of birthweight data and pre-natal hazard led us to suggest that females were born with a two to three-week maturity advantage, which extended until about two years at puberty, and about five years in mid-adult life.

The relative immaturity of males was a major risk factor in their mortality such that, starting with about 105 males born for every 100 females, the increased mortality of males brought equal numbers of males and females in the population by about the age of 45, and subsequently females survive such as to greatly exceed males in elderly populations.

REVIEW OF EPILEPSY STUDIES IN THE CONTEXT OF SEX DIFFERENCES

In this chapter I will concentrate on an overview of the various ways in which sex-related effects have emerged in various of our own studies of people with epilepsy over the last 20 years. Then I will return again to the contribution those studies have made to the evidence of differential cerebral maturation and development and sexually differentiated cerebral organization.

The differential overall attack rate of the epilepsies between the sexes is universally recognized. For example, Alstrom (1950), in a series of 492 males and 405 females (122:100), drawn from all ages of onset from childhood to aged 70, showed that 50% of the risk was past in females by 19 years but by males not until their 24th year. The wide age gap reflects the wide age spread.

What is less generally recognized is that in consequence, in any subset of patients with epilepsy, the appearance of equal numbers of male and females is evidence of a bias risk relative to the risk overall. In effect, equal numbers means an excess of females beyond expectation. In the preamble to a paper reporting the reanalysis of Slater *et al.*'s (1963) original and well-known study of epileptic psychosis, (Taylor, 1971) I showed the most concurrent large-scale data on people with epilepsy, namely the discharges and deaths from National Health Service hospitals during 1966 (quoted in Appendix 9 of the document 'People with Epilepsy') (Table 1).

This reveals excess rates in males in virtually every age group, giving an overall figure of 135 males per 100 females (135:100), which was very close to the rate in the populations we had studied. However, Slater *et al.*'s studies were based on 69 patients comprising 36 males and 32 females, and I was able to show that in the same source (Appendix 9) the sex ratio nationally for epileptic psychosis ($N = 2354$) was 97:100 and that the secondary diagnosis of epilepsy or epileptic psychosis was 93:100 for 1766 patients in mental hospitals and reduced to 114:100 for 5211 patients in mental handicap hospitals. The overall figures were 128:100 for epilepsy and 97:100 for epileptic

Table 1. Sex ratios in epilepsy

Age group	Males	Females	Males per 100 females
0–4	1400	900	180
5–14	2300	1300	130
(0–14)	(3700)	(2200)	(146)
15–19	1600	900	129
20–24	1300	800	160
25–34	1800	1000	125
35–44	2000	1100	122
45–64	3300	2000	153
65+	1600	800	100
All ages	15 300	8800	135

Source: *People with Epilepsy* (Appendix 9). Estimated number of discharges and deaths of people with epilepsy from National Health Service hospitals during 1966.

Table 2. Sex ratios in epileptic psychosis

	Mental illness hospitals			Mental subnormality hospitals		
	Male	Female	Males per 100 females	Male	Female	Males per 100 females
Primary diagnosis:						
Epilepsy	884	699	126	92	61	151
Epileptic psychosis	1159	1195	97	11	15	73
Secondary diagnosis:						
Epilepsy or epileptic psychosis	849	917	93	2776	2435	114

Both groups together	
	Males per 100 females
Primary diagnosis:	
Epilepsy	128
Epileptic psychosis	97
Secondary diagnosis:	
Epilepsy or epileptic psychosis	108

Source: *People with Epilepsy* (Appendix 9). Patients resident in psychiatric hospitals and units at 31 December 1963, with a primary or secondary diagnosis of epilepsy or epileptic psychosis.

psychosis (Table 2). Thus it seems that Slater *et al.*'s data was a proper subset and that, given epilepsy, female risk to psychosis was importantly increased, but that no one thought it worthy of comment or had any idea why it might be.

However, by identifying each of Slater's cases on a scattergram of age of onset of epilepsy versus age of onset of psychosis, startling new perspectives came to light (Figure 3).

First, the tautology of Slater's notion of 'interval' between onset of epilepsy and psychosis became evident, and the statistical error becomes clear because half the matrix is empty due to his case definition that the epilepsy must precede the psychosis. Slater and Moran (1969) had already published a note on this. But there are large, crucial, sex effects.

Up to the age of 20, 30 females and 24 males have had the onset of epilepsy. Beyond that age of onset 12 more men but only 3 more women in the series started their epilepsy. But psychosis has had its onset in 12 females but only 2 males before the age of 20 and the balance then becomes equal in the next quinquennium, then tips towards males in the next. This pattern must be seen in direct contrast to the age of onset pattern of schizophrenia. That disorder is an outstanding example *against* the general rule of earlier onset of any sickness in females as opposed to males (Angermeyer and Kuhn, 1988).

The age of onset histogram for epilepsy in Slater's series had a radically different profile from that of the Guy's/Maudsley series overall but was

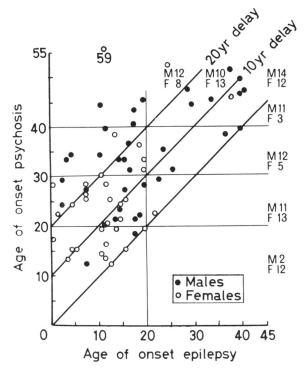

Figure 3.   Relationship between age of onset of epilepsy (recurrent seizures) and age of onset of epileptic psychosis. (From Taylor, 1971, with permission of Cambridge University Press)

similar to that of Flor-Henry's (1969) psychotic series and the subset of psychotics in the Guy's Maudsley series (Figure 4).

Slater *et al.*'s patients showed a peak age of onset of epilepsy at 10–14 for females and 15–19 for males, and the onset of psychosis in females started 5–10 years ahead of the males.

These findings revealed that patients with schizophrenia-like psychosis with epilepsy are not straightforward subsets, either of people with schizophrenia or people with temporal lobe epilepsy: femaleness, puberty and pace of development are all factors, and clearly age at first fit would largely preclude MTS as a pathological basis for their epilepsy.

The facts were also adumbrated in the correlation analysis in my thesis (1969) based on the analysis on 100 consecutive patients from Falconer's series (the second two fifties of his operative group), despite the low frequency of psychosis and the fact that only a proportion of those psychotic patients were schizophrenic (Taylor, 1972). So a contrast study was made between all the available patients with hamartomas ($N = 47$) and all the patients with MTS from the previous study of 100 consecutive patients ($N = 41$). This provided 88 patients

72

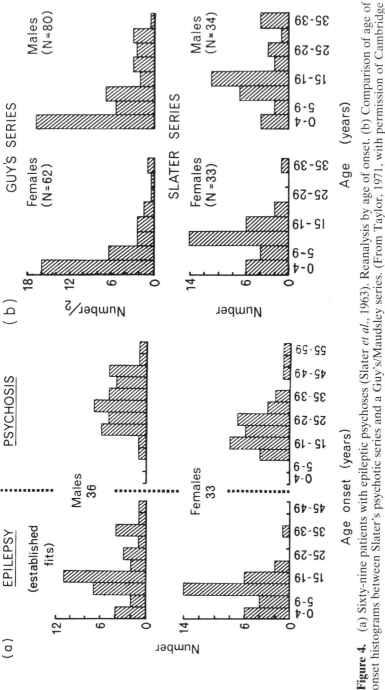

Figure 4. (a) Sixty-nine patients with epileptic psychoses (Slater *et al.*, 1963). Reanalysis by age of onset. (b) Comparison of age of onset histograms between Slater's psychotic series and a Guy's/Maudsley series. (From Taylor, 1971, with permission of Cambridge University Press)

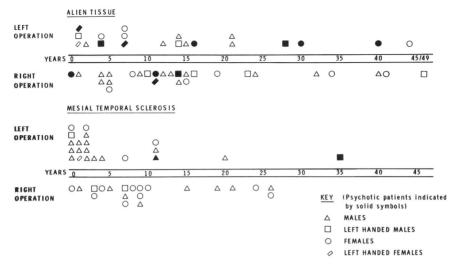

Figure 5. Age of onset of epilepsy in two groups of patients with temporal lobe epilepsy by side, sex and psychosis. (From Taylor, 1975, with permission of Cambridge University Press)

for whom there were very precise data available and who had been seen personally since the operation and again to complete the new study (Taylor, 1975).

The essence of that study is contained in Figure 5, which is another 'visual statistic' allowing a realization of the dispersal of the relevant variables over time. It emerged that the risk of epileptic psychosis is increased by five factors: femaleness, left-handedness, left brain location of lesion, alien tissue lesion, and late childhood/puberty onset of epilepsy. I have calculated the chance coincidence as one in 40 million, and I suggest that this implies a causal association between the factors. I have been shown cases with four or five of these factors many times when giving clinical seminars abroad to groups who are unacquainted with that particular aspect of my work. The study cannot be entirely replicated because no surgery is undertaken now in patients with schizophrenia-like psychosis of epilepsy, but it could be partially replicated with high-resolution scanning in the appropriate populations. Occasionally too, schizophrenia will still supervene where a left-handed female has had an alien tissue lesion removed from her left temporal lobe.

I am arguing that a psychosis is a developmental event in a brain that has come to be organized in an unusual way because of both damage and compensation effects. Sometimes, further development provides another alternative strategy and a psychosis can retreat; sometimes it does not and it cannot retreat. Early-onset 'schizophrenia' is atypical for women, hence women with schizophrenia-like psychosis with epilepsy are those precipitated into it by the closest combinations of the risk factors. The pattern of onset in males is nearer to that seen in 'schizophrenia', and hence the factors associated with the epilepsy may need to add quite little to their generally increased vulnerability.

In order to address the issue of unusual cerebral organization further in these 88 patients, in 1976 (Taylor, 1976) I examined their Wechsler IQ scale scores to see how these might vary between the various groups that could be composed by considering sex, side operated, and nature of lesion (alien tissue (AT) or MTS). These several subdivisions reduced the size of groups to levels that limited conventional statistical analysis, so that the technique was again based on retaining individual scores and manipulating small group scores in search of unusual effects. The resulting paper has been regarded even by friends as somewhat impenetrable and, located in a book on learning problems, has kept a low profile in the cumulative index. However, it is an important analysis of unique data and it provided several important pieces of evidence, including some differences between sexes.

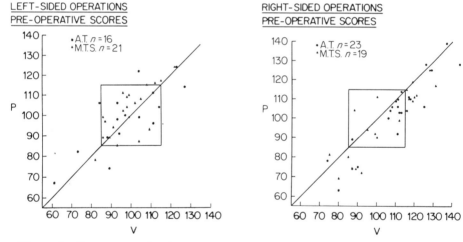

Figure 6. Scattergram showing performance and verbal scale score of each patient before operation. This diagram is a visual correlation of P and V. (a) Left operations; (b) right operations. (From Taylor, 1976)

First, the scattergrams (see Figure 6) and their statistical analysis provided clear evidence of the bias of effects on verbal and performance scores of left and right cerebral lesions, respectively, and this effect was increased by the temporal lobectomy. Secondly, the distribution of intelligence scores on the scattergram revealed that variance is increased in patients with right-sided lesions whereas most of the scores with patients' left-sided lesions are contained within a one-SD box. This suggests that left-sided lesions have constrained 'IQ' overall and that patients were more likely to be acceptable for operation with lower IQs if they had right brain lesions. Thirdly the effect of lobectomy on scores was generally to improve them in nearly all groups. Fourthly, in the analysis of those patients whose IQ score changed, on one scale at least, by 10 points at least, it could be shown that removal of AT lesions from the left temporal lobe produced an effect rarely seen in any condition, namely increased performance score associated with a decreased verbal score (Table 3).

Table 3. Eighty-seven patients with temporal lobe epilepsy. The number of patients making gains or losses of verbal (V) and performance (P) IQ scores of 10 or more points on Wechsler tests following temporal lobectomy for epilepsy (Taylor and Lochery, 1987)

Group		P+ V+	P– V–	P+ V–	P– V+	Total
MTS	Left	5	2	0	1	8
	Right	4	1	0	3	8
AT	Left	1	1	7	0	9
	Right	4	4	1	0	9
Total		14	8	8	4	34
Both groups	Left	6	3	7	1	17
	Right	8	5	1	3	17

After operation the circumstance V+P+ (considering *any* change of score) occurred 28 times; loss of both, (V–P–), occurred 13 times; P–V+ occurred 8 times; and the circumstance P+V– occurred 15 times, where 12 times it was in AT lesions, 11 times left operation, and 10 times in males.

Finally, intelligence was related to MTS such that it appears to have been relatively much reduced in women as compared with men where the left temporal lobe was affected. The smallest group was also that composed of operations on the left brain in women which revealed MTS (Table 4).

Table 4. The interaction between side operated, sex and pathological findings in the resected temporal lobe (Taylor and Lochery, 1987)

	Alien tissue		Mesial temporal sclerosis	
	Male	Female	Male	Female
Left operation	10	10	16	5
Right operation	18	9	10	10

$\chi^2 = 3.68$; $p < 0.1$.

On the other hand, the IQ of females with MTS in the right temporal lobe was higher than that of men in that group. My argument was that the relationship between cerebral lesions and intelligence was rule-governed although the rules were made complex by developmental considerations, including differential development as between the sexes, resulting in different sorts of functional organization. This would imply that similar lesions in similar loci might prove to have different effects on behaviour, or performance of skills, as between the sexes.

This is illustrated with Figures 7, 8, 9 and 10. Figure 7 is the summary of the projections by Inglis and Lawson (1982) from a meta-analysis of 16 studies of unilateral brain disease. In Figures 8, 9 and 10 the data of Taylor (1976) are arranged using similar techniques. Figure 8 shows a post-operative effect increasing left and right P and V differences. Figure 9 shows the sex and lesion effects of pre-operative verbal scores and Figure 10 the effects on P scores. The effect of lesion difference, AT or MTS, reverses the male versus female effects.

Thus it proved again later (Taylor and Lochery, 1987) that in a detailed analysis of the auras reported by these 88 patients, certain phenomena were related to verbal intelligence but only for males. The number of auras reported per patient varied precisely with verbal IQ for males but not for females (Table 5).

Table 5. Number of auras and verbal IQ (Taylor and Lochery, 1987)

No. of Auras	Mean pre-op verbal IQ	
	Males	Females
0	91.2	108.5
1	99.1	96.2
2	105.3	105.4
3	107.9	105.5
4+	116.1	96.8

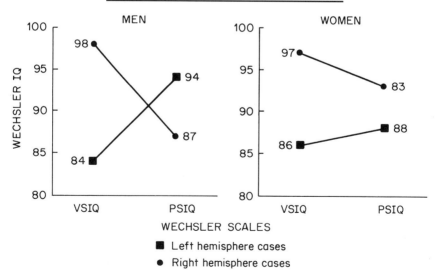

Figure 7. Scores on the verbal and performance scales of Wechsler's tests for male and female patients separately, as predicted from the linear regression analyses of 16 studies of unilateral brain damage. (From Inglis and Lawson, 1982. Copyright 1982. Canadian Psychological Association. Reprinted with permission)

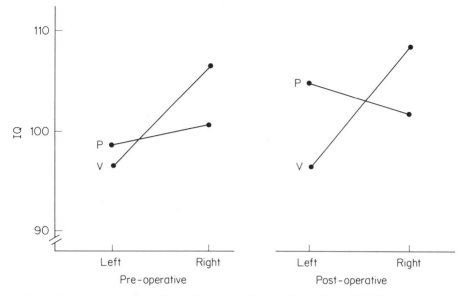

Figure 8.   Post-operative effect of increased left and right P and V differences

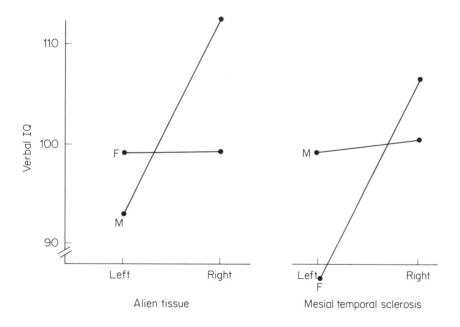

Figure 9.   Sex and lesion effects on verbal IQ

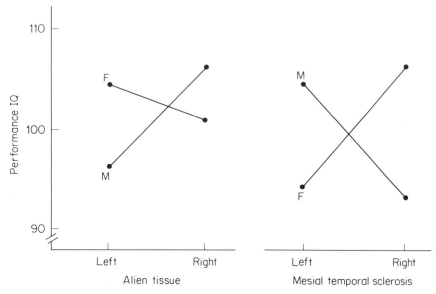

Figure 10.   Sex and lesion effects on performance scores

Auras that were exclusively 'intellectual' were confined to males. Or again, starting with the group of males with highest verbal IQ (AT, right operation) who averaged 3.1 auras each, every subsequent group had precisely less auras as compared with verbal IQ. No such effect was seen in female groups. 'Simple primitive' or vegetative auras were a function of early-onset epilepsy and lower intelligence (Table 6).

Table 6.   Mean number of auras and verbal IQ (Taylor and Lochery, 1987)

Aura count per person	Pre-op. verbal IQ	Lesion and side group
Males		
3.1	113.8	ATR
2.3	102.4	MTSL
1.8	101.3	MTSR
1.2	94.8	ATL
Mean verbal IQ for males = 104.7		
Females		
3.0	108.1	MTSR
2.4	101.4	ATR
2.3	101.0	ATL
3.6	87.8	MTSL
Mean verbal IQ for females = 101.0		
Total n = 79		
Mean verbal IQ = 103.3		

The study of aura could be repeated now and with advantages in several of the neurosurgical departments involved in the treatment of epilepsy. It needs to be known whether females are just more generally prepared to vouchsafe experiences which the duller men conceal. It seems more probable that the effects are not mediated by social process but that the result of aura studies confirms the association between early onset, MTS, simple vegetative auras, lower intelligence, and male sex which evidently run together in an understandable manner, relating to the timing of the original damage and the concurrent state and function of that part of the brain.

Flowing directly from these associations, an early study of 'aggression' and 'psychopathy' in the 100 patients of my thesis (Taylor, 1969) showed how male sex, left operation, early onset, lower full-scale IQ, lower social class of achievement, and lower social class of origin, came together as factors which identified psychopathy and aggression. However, it was clear that aggressiveness had little to do with agonistic displays but rather refers to interpersonal problems— rudeness, outspokenness or disagreeable traits. No direct association with MTS could be described, but the degree of psychosocial recovery of that group after surgery was similar to that seen in MTS patients in so far as the degree of recovery. Indeed the recovery of these 'psychopaths' after surgery should give pause to psychiatrists whose nomenclature rather presupposes that the traits are fixed into the formation of character and are unlikely to change.

Further evidence of sex-different effects in psychological functioning came from a small study (Taylor and Marsh, 1979) of 31 patients out of a group of 47 patients with alien tissue lesions who were able to complete Eysenck's inventory (then called the PQ), which contained scales for psychoticism, extroversion, neuroticism and lie (PENL) scores.

The study revealed significant differences of extroversion between left and right-operated males but not females and a gross excess in the lie scale result of left-operated females. This was the group most prone to schizophrenia-like psychosis (Table 7).

Table 7. Mean PENL scores by sex and side operated (from Taylor and Marsh, 1979, with permission of Elsevier Science Publishers)

	Mean age	P	E	N	L
Males, $N = 19$					
Left operations	34.6 ± 10.7	4.4 ± 2.7	7.6 ± 2.6	7.5 ± 5.9	9.4 ± 5.8
Right operations	36.0 ± 10.9	3.8 ± 2.5	12.9 ± 4.8	9.5 ± 6.3	10.0 ± 5.1
All males	35.4 ± 10.6	4.0 ± 2.5	10.7 ± 4.8	8.6 ± 6.0	9.7 ± 5.2
Females, $N = 12$					
Left operations	50.6 ± 15.4	1.8 ± 0.7	11.3 ± 3.7	12.9 ± 6.1	14.8 ± 2.6
Right operations	$30.8 \pm\ \ 6.7$	4.5 ± 4.5	10.0 ± 2.2	10.5 ± 4.8	9.0 ± 5.7
All females	44.0 ± 16.1	2.1 ± 2.8	10.8 ± 3.2	12.1 ± 5.6	12.8 ± 4.6
Normal comparison					
Males	27.5	3.8 ± 3.1	13.2 ± 4.9	9.8 ± 5.2	6.8 ± 4.1
Females	27.0	2.6 ± 2.4	12.6 ± 4.8	12.7 ± 5.2	7.7 ± 4.2

Sex differences were prominent when we took the precaution of correlating age with the P and L scale scores. On the N and L scales correlations moved in directly contrary directions with female scores increasing with age on those scales but with male scores decreasing. Thus overall correlations would have been confounded or else confusing.

Now I shall return to the earlier studies on febrile convulsions and other childhood epilepsies and differential pace of development. Between 1948 and 1953 Ounsted collected a personal series of over 1000 children in the Oxford region who had suffered any form of epileptic fit. The data were collected and coded by him personally, and 438 children were coded as having a first seizure associated with fever. No presumptions about the nature of the process were entertained. On later follow-up the seizure was coded as 'benign' if it remained a single episode, while 'severe' covered all other eventualities. The series was also divided, recording whether there was a history of fits with fever in first-degree relations (Taylor and Ounsted, 1971).

The age of onset histograms in six-month epochs are shown in Figure 11, which is divided by sex, family history and severity.

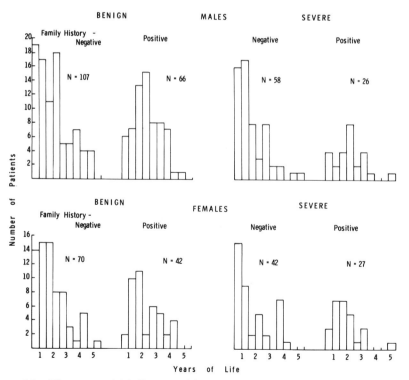

Figure 11.   The onset of febrile convulsions by age and sex and severity of outcome. (From Taylor and Ounsted, 1971, with permission)

The essential fact for present purposes is the difference in every analysis of the persistence of 'risk' in males beyond that to females. This fact is associated with a *relatively worse* prognosis for females when considering an outcome of 'chronic epilepsy'. Our figures compared closely with those of Lennox (1949) (Table 8).

Table 8. Relative excess female risk of severe outcome (From Lennox, 1949)

	Febrile convulsions	Chronic epilepsy	Original total
Male	149	36	185
Female	91	41	132
Total	240	77	317

$\chi^2 = 5.6$.

We interpreted these data as showing gender-dependent risk such that, although males were more at risk overall, the early period of risk for females was somehow associated with greater relative morbidity. In the epidemiological study by Sillanpaa (1973) the prevalence for males was 3.6 per 1000 and for females 2.8. Chevrie and Aicardi (1979) showed the relatively poorer progress of females who suffered onset of epilepsy in the first year of life. Of 166 males but only 127 females in the original study, 81 of each sex were left with persistent epilepsy.

It seemed to us that females were recruited to a disorder to which they are relatively less prone by more severe circumstances than afflict males. Indeed, throughout childhood there emerge certain 'epoch-related' epilepsies which seem to be tied to the developmental/maturational schedule. In a way, they provide suggestive evidence to support the existence of such epochs, though they may parallel the easily observable process of the precocity of female psychological development. I refer to the sorts of phenomenon which created such a problem for Wechsler in devising a test which would, to some extent, iron them out. Against psychological precocity with no real evidence of lack of efficiency in female brains (Hutt, 1972) is the greater growth and volume of male brain, both intra-uterine and post-natal, both absolute and relative to their increased body size (Skullerud, 1985). How can the paradox of greater size and greater immaturity be explained? One seems to be a function of the other. Male and female development are not on the same schedule. Brain sizes become similar at around 100 years of age (Miller *et al.*, 1980, 1984), when they have both atrophied to about the same degree. Although there is no unanimity about the rate at which they do so, there is some suggestion that females lead in the process (Hubbard and Anderson, 1983). Indeed, the increased growth of brain which males require to make (Moore *et al.*, 1988) might be the source of their increased propensity to dysfunction. Females required greater insults to deflect them; males are derailed by lesser problems. This is equally true of their somatic growth, where males reveal their tendency to fail to meet *their* expected growth norms more than females do to meet theirs.

In an unpublished personal study of the heights and weights of 1295 epileptic children, there was an excess of small-grown girls and boys (Table 9). More detailed analysis, however, confirmed the presence of a group of small-grown epileptic boys whose IQs were in the dull normal range, whereas the excess of small girls was associated with much reduced IQ and with lower birthweights (Table 10).

Table 9. Distribution of heights and weights of 1295 children by percentile rank

	+ 97	+ 90	+ 75	+ 50	− 50	− 25	− 10	− 3	N
Girls weight	3.2	6.5	16.8	22.9	22.3	15.2	9.3	3.8	475
Boys weight	3.9	9.9	15.6	24.0	23.9	14.1	5.7	2.8	820
Girls height	4.2	5.3	12.2	23.8	23.8	13.5	9.1	8.2	475
Boys height	2.8	5.7	12.7	23.8	22.3	17.6	10.6	4.5	820
Expected values	3	7	15	25	25	15	7	3	

The sorts of children recruited to these studies at the Park Hospital and at Lingfield during the 1970s were the casualties of the epoch-related epilepsies. Jeavons and Bower (1964) had shown in their study of infantile spasms a sex ratio of 210:100 and of 120:100 in their residual population of children with epilepsy. But the Lennox–Gastaut syndrome, early onset epileptic encephalopathy (EOEE or Ohtahara's syndrome) and neonatal seizures all appear to me as windows of opportunity for things to go wrong in development which are open longer for males. Females seem disproportionately exposed early in each epoch where, combined with better survival, they seem to come out with disproportionate levels of severe morbidity. Of course, the immune system is more effective too but even that may be vitally orchestrated by brain.

These direct effects are among the more superficial of the sex-differentiated influences. Since 1970 it has been accepted that structural differentiation takes place in brain. We have seen that developmental schedules unfold at different rates between the sexes; even as crude an anatomical division as that drawn between the hemispheres' different agendas and the direct impact and compensation strategies of lesions in brain will differ according to their nature and timing in development (Taylor and Marsh, 1979). When we come to think in terms of 'the effects of an event' it is perhaps less surprising that we find them complex. Perhaps we have discovered, from past mistakes that, unless our analyses take consideration of these factors, they will remain sterile or banal.

83

Table 10. Stature of 72 inpatients with epilepsy

	N	Age at admission	Percentage below school age	Percentage epilepsy in growth group	Median age onset epilepsy	IQ median	Percentage with IQ < 70	Birth weight	Percentage twins
Boys									
Small	21	7.6	14.0	70.0	18.0	68	50.0	7.9	0
Medium	15	10.6	13.0	48.4	36.0	81	38.0	7.12	6.0
Tall	7	11.10	28.0	43.8	96.0	105	28.0	7.10	14.0
Girls									
Small	13	7.3	45.0	61.9	15.0	46	70.0	6.4	8.0
Medium	10	11.2	10.0	52.6	24.0	86	40.0	7.4	10.0
Tall	6	10.9	0	66.6	83.0	100	17.0	8.3	0

Sex is defined as the differences in characteristics between males and females. Such characteristics need not be structural, nor even if they are, need they be regarded as immutable. Certain aspects of sex determination clearly reveal how environmental conditions, including social signals, act to alter morphology and change the sex of organisms, thus disposing of nature/ nurture, genes/environment dichotomies (Taylor and Ounsted, 1972).

Studying sex difference in disease reveals something about the process of sex determination and differentiation and about possible mechanisms of disease. (Classically, the relationship between smoking and lung cancer was illustrated in differential rates of cancer in relation to differential exposure. Subsequent habit changes by women have only served to re-enforce the message as their rates are now moving towards male rates). One clear-cut sex difference is their different morbidity and mortality for most diseases most of the time (Taylor, 1985).

In part, these differences are attributed to the fact that the genes concerned are on the X chromosome (sex-linked disorder). Part is due to absolute sex limitation such as is seen in the epilepsy-related syndromes of Aicardi and of Rett. Part is due to disease of somatic structures which do not exist in the other sex (cancer of the uterus). But the role of sex-differentiated structures, i.e. differences in cerebral organization and its consequences, is usually overlooked.

Ounsted and I have argued that the pace difference in development speaks of a more rapid female schedule from the moment of her intra-uterine growth deceleration. We believe that the evidence of continuity of Y chromosome influence is evident in that pace difference and is highlighted by individuals with Y replication (XYY, etc.) who are parodies of maleness—over-tall, over-dull, over-immature. This is contested by others (Deeming and Ferguson, 1988) who see fast male embryonal growth as evidence of quick pace of development.

We have seen evidence of the triviality of the Y chromosome message as a structural message in the fact that crocodilians and the turtles differentiate sexually only according to the temperature of their incubation (Deeming and Ferguson, 1988). There are varieties of animals that change sex according to ambient social signals in the make-up of the group (cleaner-fish). Such creatures make it plain that the animal possesses the entire genome but deploys it now this way, now that, by orchestrating its 'sex syndrome' from the autosomes.

The advantages of sexual reproduction have been said to be those provided by outbreeding vigour, and the increase in selection of potential new forms. Modern biologists (Bernstein *et al.*, 1987) argue that it is a good way to repair DNA. I suggest that in sexual reproduction we have a mechanism to possess a genome at a 'split-risk' in the form of the more conserving female, or in the form of the male who explores the potential of that genome for better or for worse with greater vigour.

The effects of this might be, in part, what is being called 'genomic imprinting' (Hall, 1990), a phrase used to recognize the fact that the effect of a genetic disorder in progeny can be varied as between which parent possesses the trait.

REFERENCES

Alstrom, C.H. (1950) A study of epilepsy in its clinical, social and genetic aspects. *Acta Psychiatr. Neurol. Scand.*, Suppl. 63.

Angermeyer, M.C. and Kuhn, L. (1988) Gender differences in age at onset of schizophrenia. *Eur. Arch. Psychiatr. Neurol. Sci.*, **237**, 351–364.

Bernstein, H., Hopf, F.A. and Michod, R.E. (1987) The molecular basis of the evolution of sex, *Adv. Genet.*, **24**, 323–370.

Cavanagh, J.B. and Meyer, A. (1956) Aetiological aspects of Ammons horn sclerosis associated with temporal epilepsy. *Br. Med. J.*, **2**, 1403.

Chevrie, J.J. and Aicardi, J. (1979) Convulsive disorders in the first year of life: Persistence of epileptic seizures. *Epilepsia*, **20**, 643–649.

Deeming, D.C. and Ferguson, M.W. (1988) Environmental regulation of sex determination in reptiles. *Philos. Trans. R. Soc. Lond.*, **322**, 19–39.

Flor-Henry, P. (1969) Psychosis and temporal lobe epilepsy: A controlled investigation. *Epilepsia*, **10**, 365–395.

Hall, J.G. (1990) Genomic imprinting: Review and relevance to human diseases. *Am. J. Hum. Genet.*, **46**, 103–123.

Hubbard, B.M. and Anderson, J.B. (1983) Sex differences in age-related brain atrophy. *Lancet*, **i**, 1447–1448.

Hutt, C. (1972) Neuroendocrinological, behavioural and intellectual aspects of sexual differentiation in human development. In: *Gender Differences: Their Ontogeny and Significance* (eds C. Ounsted and D.C. Taylor), pp. 73–121, Churchill Livingstone, Edinburgh.

Inglis, J. and Lawson, J.S. (1982) *Can J. Psychol.*, **36**, 670–683.

Jeavons, P.M. and Bower, B.D. (1964) Infantile spasms. *Clin. Dev. Med.*

Lennox, M. (1949) Febrile convulsions in childhood: Their relationship to adult epilepsy. *J. Pediatr.*, **35**, 427.

McLaren, A. (1990) What makes a man a man? *Nature*, **346**, 216–217.

Miller, A.K.H., Alston, R.L. and Corsellis, A.N. (1980) Variation with age in the volumes of grey and white matter in the cerebral hemispheres of man: Measurements with an image analyser. *Neuropathol. Appl. Neurobiol.*, **6**, 119–132.

Miller, A.K.H., Alston, R.L., Mountjoy, C.Q. and Corsellis, J.A.N. (1984) Automated differential cell counting on a sector of the normal human hippocampus: The influence of age. *Neuropathol. Appl. Neurobiol.*, **10**, 123–141.

Moore, W.M.O., Ward, B.S., Jones, V.P. and Bamford, F.N. (1988) Sex difference in fetal head growth. *Br. J. Obstet. Gynaecol.*, **95**, 238–242.

Ounsted, C. and Taylor, D. (eds) (1972) *Gender Differences: Their Ontogeny and Significance.* Churchill-Livingstone, Edinburgh.

Ounsted, C., Lindsay, J. and Norman, R. (1966) Biological factors in temporal lobe epilepsy. *Clin. Dev. Med.*, **22**, 135.

Sillanpaa, M. (1973) Medico-social prognosis of children with epilepsy: Epidemiological study and analysis of 245 patients. *Acta Paediatr. Scand. Suppl.* **237**, 3–104.

Skullerud, K. (1985) Variations in the size of the human brain: Influence of age, sex, body length, body mass index, alcoholism, Alzheimer changes, and cerebral atherosclerosis. *Acta Neurol. Scand.,* **102**, 71.

Slater, E. and Moran, P.A.P. (1969) The schizophrenia-like psychoses of epilepsy: Relation between ages of onset. *Br. J. Psych.,* **115**, 599–600.

Slater, E., Beard, A.W. and Glithero, E. (1963) The schizophrenia-like psychoses of epilepsy. *Br. J. Psych.,* **109**, 95–150.

Taylor, D.C. (1968) The outcome of temporal lobectomy for epilepsy. MD Thesis, University of London.

Taylor, D.C. (1969) Differential rates of cerebral maturation between sexes and between hemispheres: Evidence from epilepsy. *Lancet,* **ii**, 140–142.

Taylor, D.C. (1971) Ontogenisis of chronic epileptic pychoses: A reanalysis. *Pyschol. Med.,* **1**, 247–255.

Taylor, D.C. (1972) Mental state and temporal lobe epilepsy: A correlative account of 100 patients treated surgically. *Epilepsia,* **13**, 727–765.

Taylor, D.C. (1975) Factors influencing the occurrence of schizophrenia-like psychosis in patients with temporal lobe epilepsy. *Psychol. Med.,* **5**, 249–254.

Taylor, D.C. (1976) Develomental stratagems organizing intellectual skills: Evidence from studies of temporal lobectomy for epilepsy. In: *The Neuropsychology of Learning Disorders: Theoretical Approaches* (eds R.M. Knight and D.J. Bakker), pp. 149–171, University Park Press, Baltimore.

Taylor, D.C. (1981) Brain lesions, surgery, seizures and mental symptoms. In: *Epilepsy and Psychiatry* (eds E.H. Reynolds and M. Trimble), pp. 227–241, Churchill Livingstone, Edinburgh.

Taylor, D.C. (1985) Mechanisms of sex differentiation: Evidence from disease. In: *Human Sexual Dimorphism* (eds J. Ghesquiere, R.D. Martin and F. Newcombe), pp. 169–189, Taylor & Francis, Basingstoke.

Taylor, D.C. and Lochery, M. (1987) Temporal lobe epilepsy: Origin and significance of simple and complex auras. *J. Neurol. Neurosurg. Psychiatry,* **50**, 673–681.

Taylor, D.C. and Marsh, S. (1979) The influence of sex and side of operation on personality questionnaire responses after temporal loboetomy. In: *Hemisphere Asymmetries of Function in Psychopathology* (eds J. Gruzelier and P. Flor-Henry), Elsevier, Amsterdam.

Taylor, D.C. and Ounsted, C. (1971) Biological mechanisms influencing the outcome of seizures in response to fever. *Epilepsia,* **12**, 806–809.

Taylor, D.C. and Ounsted, C. (1972) The Y chromosome message: A point of view. In: *Gender Differences: Their Ontogeny and Significance* (eds C. Ounsted and D.C. Taylor). Churchill Livingstone, Edinburgh.

6

The adolescent female with epilepsy

JOHN M. PELLOCK
Medical College of Virginia, Richmond, Virginia, USA

INTRODUCTION

Adolescence is a difficult development stage between childhood and adulthood. It can be particularly difficult for a teenager with epilepsy because this disability creates further stress during a period already filled with very significant and frequently difficult adjustments. The adolescent experiences rapid physical development, a quest for independence, rebelliousness, inconsistent behaviour, and experiments with many ideas. These years are not only challenging for the adolescent but for all who deal with her/him. Some have termed these teenage years 'the normal schizophrenia of life' because of the cycling behavioural manifestations. The female adolescent, while struggling with her behaviour and body image changes, questions how epilepsy will affect her sexual, social and emotional development, including pregnancy and raising a family. This chapter will explore problems that the adolescent female must face, and what her physician should consider when treating her epilepsy.

ADOLESCENCE

The definition of adolescence is somewhat difficult. Some authors refer to specific ages, while others refer to stages of development surrounding puberty. It is the latter which serves best because of marked chronological variation in sexual and psychosocial development. Many refer to early, middle and late adolescence in terms of pubertal development (Hoffman, 1982). Tanner's sex maturity rating (SMR) scale is widely used for assignment of various stages (Tanner, 1962).

In girls, Stages 1 and 2 are defined as pre-adolescence, with sparse pubic hair and breast development. Mid-adolescence is defined by Tanner Stages 3 and 4, when pubic hair becomes more abundant and breast development

Women and Epilepsy. Edited by M.R. Trimble
© 1991 John Wiley & Sons Ltd

Table 1.   Classification of sex maturity stages in girls

SMR stage	Pubic hair	Breasts
1	Pre-adolescent	Pre-adolescent
2	Sparse, lightly pigmented, straight, medial border of labia	Breast and papilla elevated as small mound; areolar diameter increased
3	Darker, beginning to curl, increased amount	Breast and areola enlarged, no contour separation
4	Coarse, curly, abundant but amount less than in adult	Areola and papilla form secondary mound
5	Adult feminine triangle, spread to medial surface of thighs	Mature; nipple projects, areola part of general breast contour

Adapted from Tanner (1962).

proceeds to an areola and papilla forming a secondary mound. Full sexual maturity of breasts and pubic hair defines late adolescence, with adult feminine triangle and mature breasts (see Table 1). Onset of adolescence occurs between age 9 and 12, and lasts for 6–12 months. Middle adolescence occurs from ages 11 to 14 and lasts for an average of two to three years. Most girls reach late adolescence between the ages of 13 and 17. The chronology of these stages is dependent upon genetic, environmental and general health determinants, and does not necessarily correlate with behavioural changes.

The mean age of menarche in the USA and most industrialized countries is at present approximately 12½ years (Soules, 1987, Zacharias and Wurtman, 1970). This age varies with genetics, geography and time in history. Delayed menarche or primary amenorrhea is considered when girls have not had menstrual flow by four to five years after onset of puberty (Soules, 1987).

Adolescent psychosocial development produces large, erratic behavioural swings as the adolescent female is emancipated and establishes self and sexual identities. She also plans and prepares for her future adult role (Table 2) (Brookman and Bright, 1983). During early adolescence, there is a struggle between breaking away from childhood and parents, while often returning to adult protection. She is narcissistic and pre-occupied with physical changes while tending to exaggerate physical complaints. Hero worship is not

Table 2.   Adolescent psychosocial development

Emancipation from parents/adults
Establish self-identity
Establish sexual identity
Prepare for adult role in society—career, self-support

uncommon. During this time, both concrete and abstract maturation of cognition occurs. Magical thinking and feelings of omnipotence are not atypical. Sexual exploration usually begins in this period.

During middle adolescence, typically during ages 14–18, the independence/ dependence struggle continues and is characterized by rebellion, rejection of adults, autonomy and extreme importance of the peer group. Dress, language, behaviour and experimentation are all led by the peer group. Typical behaviour includes experimenting with substances of abuse such as alcohol and drugs, sexual and social behaviours, sports and jobs. For some reason antisocial behaviour becomes prominent. Risk taking is frequent; idealistic thinking and avid devotion to causes may be simultaneously present.

In late adolescence, adult status evolves. Marriage, parenthood and fulltime employment occur during or soon after this period. Further education or career preparation helps to prolong this transition for some. Only now does a fairly clear and realistic career, family and community evolve. Sexual identity and appropriate behaviour with intimacy and mutuality become a reality.

Physical maturation is usually completed a number of years prior to reaching psychosocial maturity. The struggle between being treated like a child by the family and sometimes needing this dependence versus being an adult and truly relating to the family as an adult is in constant evolution. Full participation as an adult in the parents' home is a constant struggle. Too often the adolescent is blamed for a lack of responsibility as she demands adult roles whilst continuing to show a mixed picture of independent–dependent adolescent psychosocial development.

EPILEPSY DURING ADOLESCENCE

Although there is a decline in the incidence of epilepsy during late childhood and adolescence, the prevalence increases from 3.0 to 5.2 per 1000 during the first decade of life to between 4.2 and 13.9 per 1000 during the second decade (Hauser and Hersdoffer, 1990). Thus, cumulatively more adolescents are affected than younger children. Epilepsy is the most common neurological disorder affecting adolescents.

Optimal treatment depends on classification of the seizure type and on the epilepsy syndrome (Pellock, 1989). The syndromes divide partial and generalized epilepsies into symptomatic (proven cause), cryptogenic (presumptive aetiology) and idiopathic (genetic) types according to the seizure type(s), EEG findings, associated neurological conditions, prognosis and response to antiepileptic drugs (Pellock, 1990b; Commission on Classification and Terminology of the International League Against Epilepsy, 1989; Dreifuss, 1991). Although benign epilepsies continue to present during the teenage years, symptomatic epilepsy becomes more common as adolescence progresses. The so-called encephalopathic epilepsies are much less likely to occur during the second decade than in earlier childhood (Hauser and Hersdoffer, 1990). Therefore, appropriate investigations such as computed tomography (CT) or magnetic resonance imaging (MRI) are indicated as part of the complete evaluation of new onset epilepsy in the adolescent to demonstrate possible structural lesions such as strokes and neoplasia (Pellock and Low, 1984).

Drug and alcohol-related seizures are common and an initial seizure may be the presenting symptom of a much more global disorder. In the adolescent with new onset seizures or exacerbation of epilepsy, a drug and substance abuse evaluation are necessary for a complete evaluation. However, a few relatively benign syndromes do present and will be discussed. Also, non-epileptic events and pseudoseizures are more likely to emerge during adolescence rather than childhood (Fenton et al., 1990). During later childhood and adolescence, the following specific syndromes may be identified: juvenile absence epilepsy, juvenile myoclonic epilepsy (JME), generalized tonic–clonic seizures (GTCS) upon awakening, Kojewnikow's syndrome and progressive myoclonic epilepsy (Pellock, 1990b; Roger et al., 1985).

ADOLESCENCE EPILEPSY SYNDROMES

Juvenile absence epilepsy

This syndrome is related to classic petit mal as an idiopathic generalized epilepsy with an age-related onset, more benign prognosis, and good therapeutic response to appropriate medications (Wolf, 1985b). The typical absences of this syndrome are similar to those seen in childhood petit mal but have fewer retropulsive movements. The seizure frequency is less with absences not occurring every day, but more commonly in a sporadic and seemingly clustered fashion. Onset is typically at or near puberty and the sex distribution is equal, whereas that in childhood absence is more frequent in girls. There is a higher association with GTCS, nearly 80%, and often this may precede the recognition of absence. GTCS frequently occur on awakening. Myoclonic seizures may also coexist. The typical EEG shows a more rapid spike and wave discharge at a frequency greater than 3 Hz.

Valproate therapy is preferred because of its control of both absence and GTCS usually with excellent response. Juvenile absence epilepsy appears as an intermediate syndrome between childhood absence and juvenile myoclonic epilepsy which it resembles in regard to age of onset, seizure frequency, and more rapid generalized polyspike and wave abnormality. Photosensitivity is less common in juvenile absence than in juvenile myoclonic epilepsy (Roger et al., 1985; Dreifuss, 1985). Table 3 illustrates the characteristics of the absence syndromes.

Table 3. Comparison of childhood absence, juvenile absence and juvenile myoclonic epilepsy (JME)

	Childhood	Juvenile	JME
Age of onset	3–12 years	Puberty	Puberty
Frequency	Multiple daily	Rarely daily clustered	Variable
EEG epileptiform activity	3 Hz spike wave	3.5–4 Hz spike wave	3.5–6 Hz spike wave
Generalized tonic–clonic	30–60% (during adolescence)	80% (before adolescence)	80–85%
Medications	Ethosuximide Valproic acid	Valproic acid Ethosuximide	Valproic acid
Prognosis	Favourable	Favourable	Favourable

Juvenile myoclonic epilepsy

Janz's syndrome or impulsive petit mal (Janz and Christian, 1957), now referred to as juvenile myoclonic epilepsy (JME), typically presents during puberty with patients experiencing their first 'grand mal' or clonic–tonic seizure or repeated myoclonic jerks on awakening (Asconape and Penry, 1984; Clement and Wallace, 1988; Delgado-Escueta and Enrile Bacsal, 1984; Tsuboi, 1977). Only with repeated questioning is the full syndrome realized, because patients and families do not associate the seizures with bilateral single or repetitive arrhythmic irregular myoclonic jerks or absences (Clement and Wallace, 1988; Delgado-Escueta and Enrile Bacsal, 1984).

Although some report a low incidence of absence in adolescents with JME (Clement and Wallace, 1988), others have shown numerous subclinical events during video-EEG monitoring (Panayiotopoulos et al., 1989). Sudden falls may be caused by the jerks, and both myoclonic and GTCS are more common in the morning. No disturbance of consciousness is noticed with myoclonic jerks. Seizures are precipitated by sleep deprivation or use of alcohol. Ictal and interictal EEGs show variable types of generalized spike and wave activity, often rapid irregular spikes and waves and polyspikes, and frequent photosensitivity. Sex distribution is equal.

The disorder has been linked to a locus on the short arm of chromosome 6 (Greenberg et al., 1988). Treatment with valproate is very successful (Clement and Wallace, 1988) but in rare uncontrolled cases benzodiazepines, primidone or polytherapy may be necessary. Although JME is referred to as a benign syndrome, its chronicity and relapsing nature upon discontinuation of medication are significant (Asconape and Penry, 1984).

Epilepsy with GTCS on awakening

Overlapping the syndromes of absence and JME, this epilepsy typically has its onset during adolescence, with GTCS occurring predominantly (over 90%) shortly after awakening or while relaxing in the evening (Wolf, 1985a). If other seizures are present, they are typically absence or myoclonic as in JME. The EEG shows a generalized dysrhythmia with photosensitivity, and there is a genetic predisposition. Further description is given in Chapter 7.

Kojewnikow's syndrome

Two distinct types of this syndrome are recognised (Dreifuss, 1989; Kojewnikow, 1895; Rasmussen *et al.*, 1958). The first represents a form of Rolandic partial epilepsy in both adults and children, associated with variable lesions of the motor cortex. Diagnostic features include partial motor seizures, myoclonia originating from the same cortical focus, EEG with normal background and focal paroxysmal abnormality (spikes and slow waves), with demonstrable aetiology and no progression except that of the cerebral lesion.

The second, more specific childhood disorder is suspected to be of viral aetiology. Typical onset is between 2 and 10 years, with a peak at 6 years, but adolescent cases are known. Partial motor seizures progress to other seizure types, progressive motor deficit, and ultimately mental retardation. The EEG background shows asymmetric slow diffuse delta waves and numerous ictal and interictal spike and sharp wave discharges not strictly limited to the Rolandic area. Early surgery including hemispherectomy is an increasing consideration in these patients. This is also referred to as Rasmussen's syndrome (Rasmussen *et al.*, 1958; Rasmussen, 1983).

Progressive myoclonic epilepsy

This syndrome combines numerous specific diseases, each with their own distinctive clinical course and pathology (Aicardi, 1986; Berkovic *et al.*, 1986; Roger *et al.*, 1985). It includes a variety of biochemical and infectious aetiologies as noted in Table 4. Myoclonus is prominent in these progressive conditions. The onset is in childhood or adolescence and neurological deficits involve cerebellar, pyramidal and extrapyramidal systems. Mental retardation although not invariable is common.

TREATMENT OF ADOLESCENT EPILEPSY

Seizure type is usually the first consideration in choosing the correct antiepileptic drug (Fenton *et al.*, 1990). One must carefully exclude symptomatic seizures, e.g. those following alcohol or drug use, or those closely related to

Table 4.   Selected disorders associated with progressive myoclonic epilepsy

Baltic myoclonus (Unverricht–Lundborg)

Lafora body disease

Dyssynergia cerebellaris myoclonia (Ramsey–Hunt)

Myoclonic epilepsy with ragged red fibres (MERRF)

Huntington's chorea

Wilson's disease

Hallevorden–Spatz disease

Infections
    Subacute sclerosing panencephalitis (SSPE)
    Creutzfeld–Jakob disease

Cerebral lipidoses
    GM1 gangliosidosis
    Juvenile Gaucher's disease
    Juvenile GM2 gangliosidosis
    Neuronal ceroid lipofuscinosis
    Sialidosis Type I and II
    Mucolipidosis Type I

Other metabolic disorders
    Hyperglycinaemia, non-ketolic
    Poliodystrophy with lactic acidosis
    D-Glycaemic aciduria
    Hexosaminidase deficiency (Tay-Sachs/Sandhoff)
    Biopterin deficiency

Variable PME degenerative syndromes

head trauma, as these do not usually require continuous and prolonged anti-convulsant therapy. The goal is to completely control seizures without producing undue side effects.

Monotherapy with carbamezepine or valproate has become popular in the treatment of epilepsy because of their seeming less deleterious acute and chronic effects on cognition and lack of cosmetic side effects (Pellock, 1990a). Cosmetic side effects of antiepileptic drugs are particularly important to the adolescent as body image is a primary concern. Any possible negative effects will promote non-compliance (Friedman *et al.*, 1986). Gingival hypertrophy and hirsutism are extremely embarrassing and are most commonly associated with the use of phenytoin (Pellock, 1990b; Schmidt, 1982). Alopecia has been reported with trimethadione, valproate and perhaps carbamazepine (Schmidt, 1982). Valproate associated hair loss is typically self-limited, with recovery of darker, more wavy hair without change in therapy and may be related to zinc chelation during valproate metabolism (Pellock, 1990a). Hirsutism may be the result of phenytoin treatment, endocrine dysfunction or a natural result of pubertal development (Bailey-Pridham and Sanfilippo, 1989). Weight gain is of major concern to the adolescent girl and has been reported in up to 50% of patients receiving valproate (Ramsey *et al.*, 1989; Dreifuss and Langer, 1988). Dietary counselling is somewhat helpful in controlling this adverse effect.

A second major concern is whether medications can safely be stopped during puberty or early adolescence. Early studies suggested that puberty tended to exacerbate seizure recurrence when medications were discontinued (Holowach *et al.*, 1972). However, additional investigations by several groups suggest that medication may be safely removed after a two to four-year seizure-free interval without exacerbation of epilepsy (Thurston *et al.*, 1982; Emerson *et al.*, 1981; Reynolds, 1989; Diamantopoulos and Crumrine, 1986). In uncontrolled patients, complex partial seizures decrease while GTCS increase in frequency (Nijima and Wallace, 1989). Normal neurological and intellectual status, fewer overall convulsions, generalized rather than partial epilepsy, earlier onset and normal EEG favourably predict successful withdrawal from medicine in 75% of patients who are seizure free for two to four years. Those with mental retardation or cerebral palsy have less chance of remission (Dreifuss and Langer, 1988; Thurston *et al.*, 1982; Emerson *et al.*, 1981; Reynolds, 1989).

PSEUDOSEIZURES

Pseudoseizures do not represent epilepsy and are thought to be either conversion symptoms or factitious events contrived for secondary gain. They have been variously called hysterical seizures, psychogenic seizures, or non-epileptic attacks. They may occur in both those with epilepsy and those who have no history or evidence of epilepsy. Pseudoseizures become more common as patients evolve from childhood through adolescence (Golden *et al.*, 1985). Epilepsy monitoring units with video/EEG have made the diagnosis of these events easier (Wyllie *et al.*, 1990a). It must be stressed, however, that patients may have both epileptic and non-epileptic attacks concurrently, and a full history of all spells should be clarified in detail before making a unifying diagnosis.

Pseudoseizures can also frequently be provoked by various types of suggestion (Cohen and Suter, 1982). We have even had pseudoseizures present as status epilepticus with the patient having not responded to multiple medications. The EEG clearly differentiates attacks from organic epilepsy (Pellock, 1991).

Sometimes following successful treatment of epilepsy during adolescence, excessive expectations of parents lead to stress resulting in the psychogenic seizures appearing as a relapse of epilepsy (Groh *et al.*, 1987). However, adolescent psychogenic seizures are usually independent of epilepsy. Headache and chronic pain are frequently reported as auras or initiating symptoms. Frequent associated factors include parental separation and divorce, sexual abuse or incest (Goodwin *et al.*, 1979; Gross, 1979; Chapter 15), physical abuse, parental substance abuse and adolescent depression. Treatment of patients with pseudoseizures must involve discovering the cause and be followed by appropriate psychological counselling for the individual and family. This frequently involves a special education setting as the symptoms are commonly associated with school failure (Groh *et al.*, 1987). Overall, the prognosis of pseudoseizures in adolescents is more favourable than in adults, probably because adolescents less frequently have true underlying personality disorders (Wyllie *et al.*, 1990b).

THE EFFECT OF EPILEPSY ON THE ADOLESCENT

Adolescents with uncontrolled epilepsy experience delays in physical and/or emotional maturation that complicate their adolescent development (Heisler and Friedman, 1981). They are often socially stigmatized (Viberg *et al.*, 1987). Dependence/independence struggles are magnified and may lead to aggression and rebellion. While trying to cope with medical disorders, adolescents may show exaggerations of normal behaviour which almost appear psychopathological at times. Whenever possible, normal development and positive coping mechanisms should be stressed and supported (Holmes, 1987).

The stress of chronic illness may not only retard growth and puberty, but also emotional development and emancipation from the family. Epilepsy produces interference with her education and socialization and is a barrier to some future career choices. It may also produce additional confusion with sexual identity.

Physicians and medical professionals may inadvertently add additional stressors through treatment of the patient (Brookman and Bright, 1983). Extreme embarrassment, threats to privacy and restricted mobility accompany investigations and treatment, resulting in a forced dependence and a tendency for the patient to regress. This may lead to ambivalence to the family and medical staff.

When additional physical or mental handicaps are associated with epilepsy, all stresses are further magnified. The handicapped adolescent is usually treated as a younger child. She frequently performs below her mental and/or physical capability. There may be a great disparity between biological, emotional and cognitive development. Over-protection by parents and medical staff impedes development of social and emotional maturation and further emphasizes poor self-esteem, frustration and fears. Although the adolescent is physically and emotionally handicapped, contraception must be considered. A good outcome is seen when additional physician and health professional time is spent in appropriate listening and counselling.

A number of coping mechanisms are typically used by the adolescent for increased stress. The ideal and hoped for mechanisms are insight and acceptance, but this is optimistic and frequently unlikely. Denial is common and may be of a constructive nature, leading to further development and planning for the future. However, denial may also be destructive. Other coping mechanisms used by the adolescent with epilepsy are outlined in Table 5.

It is important that family and treating physicians identify the coping mechanisms used by a particular adolescent. Pathological mechanisms should be identified as they may lead to further difficulties. Denial of epilepsy helps protect the young woman from peers who are likely to question or ridicule her epilepsy or medication use. However, it may promote non-compliance. When epilepsy is controlled it is frequently easier to deny its existence than explain it to friends. When chronic or refractory, despite antiepileptic medication, resentment toward authority figures may escalate.

Educational programmes directed toward the enlightenment of the public about epilepsy have apparently been successful, as judged by a survey of adolescent attitudes towards epilepsy in the same age group (Breger, 1976a,b). Fear of having to cope with a seizure and concern regarding genetic transmission were the main reasons for not accepting epilepsy in adolescents. In a retrospective study a general trend toward fewer seizures during puberty was observed, especially significant for females after menarche (Diamantopoulos and Crumrine, 1986).

Approximately 60% of adolescents with epilepsy attend normal school and are in regular classrooms (Freeman *et al.*, 1984). Seizures may not appreciably affect their activities but may have a greater effect on their learning. A survey

Table 5. Adolescent epilepsy coping mechanisms

Insight/acceptance—ideal, but unlikely

Denial—common
    Constructive—allows development, planning
    Destructive—increases non-compliance

Intellectualization—permits mastery

Rationalization—uncommon, fatalistic

Regression—common in early adolescent

Reaction formation—mastery

Projection—anger, frustration, alienation

Withdrawal—poor, promotes non-compliance

Panic—outbursts, diffuse hysteria

Acting out
    Temper outbursts, aggression
    Manipulation, non-compliance
    Running away, verbal abuse
    Flirting, suicide gestures
    Drug abuse

of adolescents with epilepsy by Clement and Wallace (1990) revealed more difficult behaviour in class, poorer reading comprehension and fewer than ex-pected participating in competitive sports or anticipating ever driving an auto-mobile. Others have also reported poorer arithmetic skills. The intellectual function of children and adolescents with epilepsy has a distribution similar to the general population but learning disabilities are more common (Hauser and Hersdoffer, 1990). Thus, school placement and vocational planning are of para-mount importance when treating the adolescent female with epilepsy.

SPECIAL ISSUES AFFECTING ADOLESCENTS WITH EPILEPSY

Drug abuse

As the adolescent rapidly evolves through various stages of psychosocial de-velopment, experimenting with various substances is to be expected. Tobacco, alcohol, marijuana, cocaine, inhalants, stimulants, hallucinogens, phen-cyclidine (PCP), opiates, sedative-hypnotics, tranquillizers and designer drugs such as modifications of meperidine and fentanyl are all reported to be used for recreation (Schonberg, 1988). The effect on the adolescent with epilepsy depends upon the amount and type of substance used during each session and the regularity of abuse. Alcohol, cocaine, amphetamines, heroin and PCP have all been associated with seizures (Alldredge et al., 1989).

Alcohol

Except for caffeine, alcohol is used by more people, in larger quantities, than any psychoactive substance. Despite efforts to regulate teenage drinkers, in 1986 91% of American high school seniors had tried alcohol, 65% had con-sumed it within the past month and 5% drank alcohol daily. It was once presumed that men drank more than women, but in the adolescent population differences are lessening, such that 69% of males and 61% of females re-ported alcohol use in the past month in 1986, but only 3% of females reported using alcohol daily. Surveys of American high school and university students estimate that about 10% of teenagers currently engage in heavy drinking (Hauser, 1990). While popular opinion may seem otherwise, among high school and college students fewer black than white children and young adults drink. However, blacks seem more likely to suffer social consequences from drinking (Hauser, 1990).

Clinical studies correlate alcohol abuse with poor seizure control. Hypo-thetical mechanisms include a stimulant effect, withdrawal effects associated with a fall in blood alcohol levels, enhancement of anticonvulsant metabolism, altered absorption of antiepileptic drugs and non-compliance in epileptic patients who drink. A recent international conference on alcohol and seizures suggested that both alcohol withdrawal and other factors are important in the cause of seizures (Porter *et al.*, 1990). Many patients with epilepsy tolerate small amounts of alcohol, but increased amounts may either lead to more seizures, increased antiepileptic drug toxicity, or even be part of a total non-compliance pattern. The association of alcohol use with head injury as a cause of epilepsy is well known (Porter *et al.*, 1990). Few patients with seizures associated only with ethanol use require chronic antiepileptic drug therapy.

Marijuana

Marijuana is said to be the substance chosen most often by young people for regular use, with 4% of American high school students using it daily. A survey in Canada revealed 70% of adolescents between the ages of 12 and 19 had used marijuana within the past year, and 1% used it daily. The major effects of marijuana are on behaviour. The extent of behavioural effects is directly related to the concentration of marijuana (tetrahydrocannabinol) used. At low doses, euphoria, a sense of relaxation, and increased visual, auditory and taste perceptions are reported. At higher doses, dysphoric reactions ranging from mild fear to distortions of body image, depersonalization, disorientation, and even paranoia and acute panic reactions may occur. As marijuana has a major effect on co-ordination tasks, its effect is likely to exacerbate the neurotoxicity of antiepileptic drugs. It has a major effect on learning and memory. A clinical withdrawal syndrome occurs on discontinuation, with symptoms of irritability, agitation, insomnia and electroencephalographic changes. Conjunctival injection is an objective sign of marijuana intoxication.

The literature concerning marijuana and its effects on epilepsy is complex, anecdotal and contradictory. Some reports suggest that there is actually a beneficial effect of marijuana, whereas others indicate an increase in seizures. Because of the impurity of drugs used and variations in types and amounts reportedly used by patients with epilepsy, no clear conclusion can be made. It would appear that no specific deleterious effect is noted, but when sleep cycle alterations are present, or there is non-compliance because of marijuana use, epilepsy is likely to become less well controlled.

Cocaine

Cocaine use by adolescents has increased dramatically throughout the world in recent years. A US survey of high school seniors shows that cocaine use increased from 9% to 17.3% from 1975 to 1986 (Schonberg,1988).

Cocaine produces intense feelings of euphoria, energy and confidence, and is particularly appealing to adolescents. They become more talkative, sociable, adventurous and sexual. The bashful adolescent girl instantly overcomes shyness, awkwardness, boredom, stress, sexual inhibitions and low self-esteem. This high, however, can be followed by a rebound crash that leaves the user feeling uncomfortable and desiring a return to her euphoric state. Tolerance and dependence occur with chronic cocaine use.

As with other illicit substances, exacerbation of epilepsy may be through a primary or secondary mechanism. Stimulation from cocaine has been reported to increase seizures in some users, while having no effects in others. Case reports describe exacerbation of seizures from cocaine (Alldredge *et al.*, 1989; Lechtenberg, 1984), but this is sometimes thought to be secondary to impurities within the cocaine (Kieburtz and Schiffer, 1989). Furthermore, adolescents with epilepsy may sell their medication to afford the more pleasurable cocaine. New onset seizures have been reported with cocaine use, as have cardiac arrhythmias, associated with either toxic levels of cocaine or impurities administered during intravenous use.

Stimulants

Stimulants cause a rush of euphoria similar to that experienced with cocaine. They are sometimes used by adolescents, not only for the sustained euphoria, but greater ability to concentrate, wakefulness, self-confidence, excitement and to depress appetite. The neurological side effects of amphetamine include seizures, and thus in the evaluation of new onset seizures in the adolescent one must clearly screen for amphetamines. Amphetamine abuse may cause an increase in seizure frequency; however, use of standard and regular doses of amphetamines as therapy sometimes helps decrease the effect of sedative anticonvulsants and can be used to treat epilepsy by altering sleep cycles (Holmes, 1987).

Other agents

Sedatives have similar effects to alcohol and seem to produce increased seizures during their withdrawal stage. Opiates also increase seizure frequency. Hallucinogens and PCP have variable effects, but very high doses of PCP have produced coma, cardiac arrhythmias, muscle rigidity, dysphagia and opisthotonic posturing and rhabdomyolysis, leading to acute renal failure, seizures and death. For other agents, their ability to exacerbate epilepsy is unknown.

Although drugs of abuse are highly discouraged, most patients with epilepsy can safely enjoy a glass of wine at dinner without causing undue alarm. Substance *abuse* is the main factor incriminated in exacerbation of epilepsy.

Driving

As part of adolescent development, driving an automobile is a much desired milestone of independence for most teenagers. Most people with epilepsy can obtain a driving licence, provided seizures are under control. Some may have difficulty obtaining a driving licence, which to many is the most serious social constraint of epilepsy (Lechtenberg, 1984; Engel, 1989). Many physicians feel that the right to drive can be a powerful incentive to compliance with medication, clinic visits and behavioural compliance with the family.

The seizure-free interval required by numerous countries and states varies from jurisdiction to jurisdiction (Gumnit, 1990). The basic rule is that the patient must be seizure free for a certain time before a driver's licence is granted. Fourteen countries, however, prohibit those with epilepsy from ever obtaining a driver's licence (Engel, 1989). In others, seizure-free intervals of 6–36 months are required. In the USA, each state has its own requirement, varying from a seizure-free waiting period of 6–24 months. In the UK it is two years. The types of reports to government agencies vary, with some having physician reports, while others put total responsibility on the patient.

Another limitation to receiving a driver's licence is medication toxicity. Drowsiness, diplopia and slowing in reaction time are all important considerations in the safe operation of a motor vehicle. The physician needs to consider the total neurological condition of the patient, along with medication effects, as sometimes being more important than a seizure-free interval when discussing driving.

Clinical issues of sexuality

Adolescents with epilepsy may have the same sexual drive as other teenagers. Over the last 15 years there has been increased public concern and research concerning adolescent sexuality, pregnancy and childbearing.

Since the sexual revolution that occurred in the late 1960s and 1970s, there has been a steady increase in the number of teenage women having premarital sexual intercourse (Davis, 1989). Also, adolescents below the age of 15 years continue to engage in premarital intercourse in increasing numbers. A clear explanation of sexual behaviour should be given to adolescents by those caring for them early in their teenage years or as puberty occurs. The meaning of safe sex and contraception must be explained as also must risks of teenage pregnancy in adolescents on antiepileptic drugs. We have personally experienced young teenage girls who were over-zealously counselled and have requested tubal ligation because of their fears of bearing malformed children. On the other hand, some adolescents completely deny any difficulties and continue to have children or abortions and do not use birth control.

The oral contraceptive pill is the most popular among adolescents who use effective contraception in many countries in the world (Shearin, 1989). The necessity for strict compliance, and certain interactions with antiepileptic drugs, must be understood by both physician and patient before its use is prescribed.

Common side effects of the oral contraceptive pill include nausea and vomiting, abdominal pain, headache, weight gain, acne, breast discomfort or tenderness, breakthrough bleeding, absence of or withdrawal bleeding and depression. Progestin-related side effects are hirsutism, oedema, weight gain and alterations in liver functions. The most discussed issue regarding epilepsy and oral contraceptives is drug interactions which render them ineffective. Barbiturates, carbamazepine, phenytoin and ethosuximide can induce liver microsomal enzymes, causing rapid metabolism of steroids (Shearin, 1989; Diamond *et al.*, 1985; Mattson *et al.*, 1986). Use of another method, another drug or higher dose of oral contraceptive is recommended. Valproate does not induce liver microsomal enzymes when used as monotherapy and may be used if appropriate for the seizure type.

One can appreciate the confusion when a young woman with epilepsy complains of hirsutism, weight gain, cognitive or behavioural side effects, amenorrhoea or other endocrine changes. The physician must decide whether oral contraceptive, antiepileptic drug or chronic illness is the culprit. Frequently, it is extremely difficult to identify the exact agent, for example, in deciding on the cause of hirsutism in the adolescent female. It can be peripheral, gonadotropic, exogenous or even part of a congenital anomaly such as trisomy 18, Cornelia de Lange syndrome, Hurler's syndrome or juvenile hypothyroidism (Bailey-Pridham and Sanfilippo, 1989). Phenytoin would certainly be one leading cause to consider. However, amoxicillin, cyclosporin, anabolic steroids, acetazolamide, penicillamine, danazol, endogenic steroids, diazide and phenothiazines may all be implicated as causes of hirsutism (Bailey-Pridham and Sanfilippo, 1989). A careful examination of the patient along with a history of onset and drug history may best indicate which agent, if any, is responsible.

Aristotle stated: 'of all bodily desires, it is the sexual to which they (adolescents) are most disposed to give way and in regard to sexual desire, they exercise no restraint.' Adolescent females with epilepsy, like others, are most fearful of being rejected. Counselling about sexuality, birth control and sexually transmitted diseases are best done as a matter-of-fact part of physician counselling during early and mid-adolescence. Prevention of the unwanted teenage pregnancy is paramount.

COMPLIANCE

Compliance to most physicians means that the patient takes medication and comes to clinic appointments as directed. It implies social responsibility, and an appropriate lifestyle, that produces good control of epilepsy. For example, sleep deprivation, alcohol abuse and emotional stress are said to exacerbate seizures and may be more deleterious than to the adolescent without epilepsy. Patients on antiepileptic drugs may experience lethargy, and school and work performance may require extra diligence.

Compliance-enhancing strategies include first establishing a good relationship with the adolescent, who must feel that the physician is fair, knowledgeable, authoritative and her champion. Non-compliance must be considered in discussion with the patient. Drug abuse and sexual behaviour must be discussed in privacy. Barriers keeping the adolescent from openly talking to the physician must be reduced. Be sure to see the patient alone and with her parents so that both are comfortable talking (Levin, 1990).

When medication or other instructions are given, they should be emphatic, structured and written (Brookman and Bright, 1983). A prescription should be provided with justification, explanations and a schedule that is simple enough for the patient to understand. When ordering a medication schedule at regular intervals, school work should be taken into consideration. Make the schedule easy to accomplish without embarrassment, with meals, in the morning, or at bedtime when possible. Also, regulating administration at the time of certain activities helps to remind the patient. Besides scolding non-compliant patients, they should be rewarded when successful with compliance. The physician must also reinforce the importance of following instructions. Psychosocial issues correspond highly to the presence or absence of non-compliance (Friedman *et al.*, 1986).

CONCLUSION

The adolescent female has a complex personality. Constant changes occur throughout these teenage years. Epilepsy poses additional problems as these young girls develop into women. Only through an understanding of adolescent health concerns and psychosocial issues can one fully treat the adolescent female with epilspey.

Lennox (1960) wrote that 'Epilepsy is not a continuously rough sea, but a recurrent tidal wave.' Certainly adding all the changes present in the adolescent girl to this tidal wave will produce what seems to be chaos one moment and joyful celebration the next. Psychosocial and adaptive support is mandatory (Vining 1989). Expect to be surprised and challenged!

REFERENCES

Aicardi, J. (1986) *Epilepsy in Children*. Raven Press, New York.

Alldredge, B.K., Lowenstein, D.H. and Simon, R.P. (1989) Seizures associated with recreational drug abuse. *Neurology, 39*, 1037–1039.

Asconape, J. and Penry, J.K. (1984) Some clinical and EEG aspects of benign juvenile myoclonic epilepsy. *Epilepsia, 25*, 108–114.

Bailey-Pridham, D.D. and Sanfilippo, J.S. (1989) Hirsutism in the adolescent female. *Pediatr. Clin. North Am., 36*, 581–600.

Belman, A.L. (1990) AIDS and pediatric neurology. *Neurol. Clin., 8*, 571–602.

Berkovic, S.F., Andermann, F. and Carpenter, S. (1986) Progressive myoclonus epilepsies: Specific cases and diagnosis. *New Engl. J. Med., 315*, 296–305.

Breger, E. (1976a) Attitudinal survey of adolescents towards epileptics of the same age group, Part 2: Social acceptance. *Maryland State Med. J.*, **25**, 41–46.

Breger, E. (1976b) Attitudinal survey of adolescents towards epileptics of the same age group, Part 1: Awareness and knowledgeability of the epileptic condition. *Maryland State Med. J.*, **25**, 61–67.

Brookman, R.R. and Bright, G.M. (1983) Adolescent health care. In: *Pediatrics* (ed. H.M. Maurer), pp. 99–123. Churchill Livingstone, Edinburgh.

Clement, M.J. and Wallace, S.J. (1988) Juvenile myoclonic epilepsy. *Arch. Dis. Child.*, **63**, 1049–1053.

Clement, M.J. and Wallace, S.J. (1990) A survey of adolescents with epilepsy. *Dev. Med. Child. Neurol.*, **32**, 849–857.

Cohen, R.J. and Suter, C. (1982) Hysterical seizures: Suggestions as a provocative EEG test. *Ann. Neurol.*, **11**, 391.

Commission on Classification and Terminology of the International League Against Epilepsy (1989) Proposal for revised classification of epilepsies and epileptic syndromes. *Epilepsia*, **30**, 389–399.

Davis, S. (1989) Pregnancy in adolescents. *Pediatr. Clin. North Am.*, **36**, 665–680.

Delgado-Escueta, A.V. and Enrile Bacsal, F. (1984) Juvenile myoclonic epilepsy of Janz. *Neurology*, **34**, 285–294.

Diamantopoulos, N. and Crumrine, P.K. (1986) The effect of puberty on the course of epilepsy. *Arch. Neurol.*, **43**, 873–876.

Diamond, M.L., Greene, J.W. and Thompson, J.M. (1985) Interaction of anticonvulsants and oral contraceptives in epileptic adolescents. *Contraception*, **31**, 623–633.

Dreifuss, F.E. (1985) Discussion of absence and photosensitive epilepsies. In: *Epileptic Syndromes in Infancy, Childhood and Adolescence* (eds J. Roger, C.C. Dravet, M. Bureau *et al.*), pp. 237–241, John Libbey, London.

Dreifuss, F.E. (1989) Pediatric epilepsy syndromes: An overview. *Cleve. Clin. J. Med.*, **56**, S166–S170.

Dreifuss, F.E. (1991) Classification of epilepsies in childhood. In: *Pediatric Epilepsy: Diagnosis and Therapy* (eds W.E. Dodson and J.M. Pellock), Demos, New York (in press).

Dreifuss, F.E. and Langer, D.H. (1988) Side effects of valproate. *Am. J. Med.*, **84**, 34–41.

Emerson, R., D'Souza, B.J., Vining, E.P. *et al.* (1981) Stopping medications in children with epilepsy: Predictors of outcome. *N. Engl. J. Med.*, **304**, 1125.

Engel, J. (1989) *Seizures and epilepsy*. Davis, Philadelphia.

Fenton, G.A., Gibbons, V.P., Pratt, G.D. *et al.* (1990) Characteristics and outcome of psychogenic seizures in children. *Ann. Neurol.*, **28**, 471.

Freeman, J.M., Jacobs, H. and Vining, E.P. (1984) Epilepsy and inner city schools: A school-based program that makes a difference. *Epilepsia*, **25**, 438–442.

Friedman, I.M., Litt, I.F. and King, D.R. (1986) Compliance with anticonvulsant therapy by epileptic youth: Relationship to psychosocial aspects of adolescent development. *Adolesc. Health Care*, **7**, 12–17.

Golden, N.H., Bennett, H.S. and Pollack, M.A. (1985) Seizures in adolescence: a review of patients admitted in an adolescent service. *J. Adolesc. Health Care*, **6**, 25–27.

Goodwin, J., Simms, M. and Bergman, R. (1979) Hysterical seizures: A sequel to incest. *Am. J. Orthopsy.*, **49**, 698–703.

Greenberg, D.A., Delgado-Escueta, A.V., Widelitz, H. *et al.* (1988) Juvenile myoclonic epilepsy (JME) may be linked to the BF and HLA Loci on human chromosome 6. *Am. J. Med. Genet.,* **31**, 185–192.

Groh, C., Tatzer, E. and Schubert, M.T. (1987) Psychogenic relapses in childhood epilepsy in puberty and adolescence. *J. Neurol.,* **234**, 97–99.

Gross, M. (1979) Incestuous rape: A cause for hysterical seizures in four adolescent girls. *Am. J. Orthopsy,* **49**, 704–708.

Gumnit, R.J. (1990) *Living Well with Epilepsy.* Demos, New York.

Hauser, W.A. (1990) Epidemiology of alcohol use and epilepsy: The magnitude of the problem. In: *Alcohol and Seizures: Basic Mechanisms and Clinical Concepts* (eds R.J. Poter, R.H. Mattson, J.A. Cramer and I. Diamond), Davis, Philadelphia.

Hauser, W.H. and Hersdoffer, D.C. (1990) *Epilepsy: Frequency, Causes and Consequences.* Demos, New York.

Heisler, A.B. and Friedman, S.B. (1981) Social and Psychological considerations in chronic disease: With particular reference to the management of seizure disorders. *J. Pediatr. Psychol.,* **6**, 239–250.

Hoffmann, A.D. (1982) *Adolescent Medicine.* Addison-Wesley, California.

Holmes, G.L. (1987) *Diagnosis and Management of Seizures in Children.* Saunders, Philadelphia.

Halowach, J., Thurston, D.L. and O'Leary, J. (1972) Prognosis in childhood epilepsy. *N. Engl. J. Med.,* **286**, 169.

Janz, D. and Christian, W. (1957) Impulsive petit-mal. *Dtsch. Z. Nervenheilk,* **176**, 346–386.

Kieburtz, K. and Schiffer, R.B. (1989) Neurologic manifestations of human immunodeficiency virus infections. *Neurol. Clin.,* **7**, 447–448.

Kojewnikow, L. (1895) Eine besondere Form von corticaler Epilepsie. *Neurol. Centralb.,* 1447–1448.

Lechtenberg, R. (1984) *Epilepsy and the Family.* Harvard University Press, Cambridge, MA.

Lennox, W.G. (1960) Social–emotional problems that impinge. In: *Epilepsy and Related Disorders* (ed. W.G. Lennox), pp. 919–999. Little Brown, Boston.

Levin, J. (1990) When doctors question kids. *N. Engl. J. Med.,* **323**, 1569.

Mattson, R.H., Cramer, J.A. and Darney, P.D. (1986) Use of oral contraceptives by women with epilepsy. *JAMA,* **256**, 238–240.

Nijima, S.I. and Wallace, S.J. (1989) Effects of puberty on seizure frequency. *Dev. Med. Child Neurol.,* **31**, 174–180.

Panayiotopoulos, C.P., Obeid, T. and Waheed, G. (1989) Absences in juvenile myoclonic epilepsy: A clinical and video electro-encephalographic study. *Ann. Neurol.,* **25**, 391–397.

Pellock, J.M. (1989) Efficacy and adverse effects of antiepileptic drugs. *Pediatr. Clin. North Am.,* **36**, 435–438.

Pellock, J.M. (1990a) Risks versus benefits of antiepileptic drug therapy. *Int. Pediatr.,* **5**, 176–180.

Pellock, J.M. (1990b) The classification of childhood seizures and epilepsy syndromes. *Neurol. Clin.,* **8**, 619–632.

Pellock, J.M. (1991) Status epilepticus. In: *Neurological Emergencies in Infancy and Childhood* (eds E.C. Myer and J.M. Pellock), Raven Press, New York (in press).

Pellock, J.M. and Low, N.L. (1984) Seizure disorders. In: *Practice of Pediatrics* (ed. V.C. Kelly), Harper & Row, New York.

Porter, R.J., Mattson, R.H., Cramer, J.A. and Diamond, I. (1990) *Alcohol and Seizures: Basic Mechanisms and Clinical Concepts.* Davis, Philadelphia.

Ramsay, R.E., Wilder, B.J., Pellock, J.M. *et al.* (1989) Conversion of polytherapy to valproate monotherapy in patients with tonic–clonic seizures. *Epilepsia*, **30**.

Rasmussen, T.B. (1983) Surgical treatment of complex partial seizures: Results, lessons and problems. *Epilepsia*, **24**, S65–S76.

Rasmussen, T.E., Olszewsik, J. and Lloyd-Smith, D. (1958) Focal cortical seizures due to chronic localized encephalitides. *Neurology*, **8**, 435–445.

Reynolds, E.H. (1989) The prognosis of epilepsy: Is chronic epilepsy preventable? In: *Chronic Epilepsy: Its Prognosis and Management* (ed. M.R. Trimble), pp. 13–20. Wiley, Chichester.

Roger, J. (1985) Progressive myoclonic epilepsy in childhood and adolescence. In: *Epileptic Syndromes in Infancy, Childhood and Adolescence* (eds J. Roger, C.C. Dravet, M. Bureau *et al.*), pp. 302–310, John Libbey, London.

Roger, J., Dravet, C.C., Bureau, M. *et al.* (1985) *Epileptic Syndromes in Infancy, Childhood and Adolescence*. John Libbey, London.

Schmidt, D. (1982) *Adverse Effects of Antiepileptic Drugs*. Raven Press, New York.

Schonberg, S.K. (1988) *Substance Abuse: A Guide for Health Professionals*. American Academy of Pediatrics.

Shearin, R.B. (1989) Bochlke: Hormonal contraception. *Pediatr. Clin. North Am.*, **36**, 697–716.

Shinnar, S., Berg, E.T. and Moshe, S.L. (1990) The risk of seizure recurrence following the first unprovoked seizure in childhood: A prospective study. *Pediatrics*, **85**, 1076–1085.

Soules, M.R. (1987) Adolescent amenorrhea. *Pediatr. Clin. North Am.*, **34**, 1083–1103.

Tanner, J.M. (1962) *Growth at Adolescence* (2nd edn). Scientific Publications, Oxford.

Thurston, J.H., Thurston, D.L., Dixon, B.B. *et al.* (1982) Prognosis of childhood epilepsy. *N. Engl. J. Med.*, **306**, 831–835.

Tsuboi, T. (1977) *Generalized Epilepsy with Sporadic Myoclonias of Myoclonic Petit Mal Type*, pp. 19–35. Thieme, Stuttgart.

Viberg, M., Blennow, G. and Polski, B. (1987) Epilepsy in adolescence: Implications for the development of personality. *Epilepsia*, **28**, 542–546.

Vining, E.P.G. (1989) Educational, social, and life-long effects of epilepsy. *Pediatr. Clin. North Am.*, **36**, 449–461.

Welldon, J. (1986) *The Rhetoric of Aristotle*. Macmillan, London.

Willmore, L.J., Triggs, W.J. and Pellock, J.M. (1991) Valproate toxicity: Risk screening strategies. *J. Child Neurol.*, **6**, 3–6.

Wolf, P. (1985a) Epilepsy with grand mal on awakening. In: *Epileptic Syndromes in Infancy, Childhood and Adolescence* (eds J. Roger, C. Dravet, M. Bureau *et al.*), pp. 259–270, John Libbey, London.

Wolf, P. (1985b). Juvenile absence epilepsy. In: *Epileptic Syndromes in Infancy, Childhood and Adolescence*, (eds. J. Roger, C.C. Dravet, and M. Bureau *et al.*), pp. 242–246, John Libbey, London.

Wyllie, E., Friedman, D. and Rothner, A.D. (1990a) Psychogenic seizures in children and adolescents: Outcome after diagnosis by ictal video and electroencephalographic recording. *Pediatrics*, **85**, 480–484.

Wyllie, E., Friedman, D., Luders, H. *et al.* (1990b) Comparison of outcome after video-electroencephalographic diagnosis of psychogenic seizures in children and adults. *Ann. Neurol.*, **28**, 471.

Zacharias, L. and Wurtman, R.J. (1970) Sexual maturation in contemporary American girls. *Am. J. Obstet. Gynecol.*, **108**, 833.

7

Epileptic syndromes of childhood and adolescence

SHEILA J. WALLACE
University Hospital of Wales, Cardiff, UK

INTRODUCTION

It is instructive to consider epileptic syndromes of childhood and adolescence in relation to their preponderance, or otherwise, in the female sex. This approach can lead to better understanding of the input of messages related either to sex chromosomes or sex hormones or both. Since, from the neonatal period onwards, there are differences between the incidence of epileptic syndromes, whether associated or not with major recognizable structural brain abnormalities, the input from sex chromosomes and thence hormones must be important. At present it is not clear whether this might act in a negative or positive sense. The main epileptic syndromes of childhood and adolescence are listed in Tables 1–3 by frequency or otherwise in female sex.

The finer points of brain development are different in male and females. This difference has been explored in particular by behavioural scientists (Buffery, 1976) but also by those interested in the age specificity of both generalized and lateralized seizures in response to fever and the latter's sequel of temporal lobe epilepsy (Taylor, 1969; Chapter 5). Taylor (1969)

Table 1.   Epileptic syndromes more common in females

Childhood absence epilepsy
Epilepsy with photosensitivity
Epilepsy in association with:
Rett syndrome[a]
Aicardi syndrome[a]

[a] Exclusively present in females.

Women and Epilepsy. Edited by M.R. Trimble
© 1991 John Wiley & Sons Ltd

Table 2. Syndromes which occur equally in males and females

Benign familial neonatal convulsions
Early myoclonic encephalopathy
Benign epilepsy with occipital paroxysms
Benign partial epilepsy with affective symptoms
Epilepsy with continuous spikes and waves during slow sleep (ESES)
Epilepsy with generalized convulsive seizures
Juvenile myoclonic epilepsy
Epilepsies associated with conditions in which there is autosomal dominant or recessive inheritance

Table 3. Syndromes commoner or exclusively present in males

Benign idiopathic neonatal convulsions ('fifth day fits')
Febrile seizures
Ohtahara syndrome
West syndrome (especially if symptomatic)
Benign myoclonic epilepsy in infants
Severe myoclonic epilepsy in infants
Myoclonic astatic epilepsy
Lennox–Gastaut syndrome
Epilepsy with myoclonic absences
Benign partial epilepsy with centrotemporal spikes
Benign partial epilepsy with extreme somatosensory evoked potentials
Juvenile absence epilepsy
Epilepsy with grand mal on awakening
Benign partial seizures of adolescence
Complex partial seizures with temporal or frontal foci
Landau–Kleffner syndrome
Epilepsies associated with X-linked disorders, e.g. fragile X, Menkes' disease

concluded that cerebral maturation proceeds more slowly in the male than in the female and that the right hemisphere matures more rapidly than the left. Thus the left brain of males is the area exposed for the longest period to risk of damage during basic development. On the other hand, it is suggested that should a female suffer an insult to the left brain this would be likely to have severe consequences, since the female left brain would be undergoing critical development when the whole organism is very young and thus particularly vulnerable.

There are, however, good reasons for considering possible male–female differences in cerebral development which occur in fetal life and could produce circumstances in which seizures are likely to occur. In particular, neuronal proliferation, migration and assembly may be modified by circulating sex hormones already evident prenatally (Geschwind and Galaburda, 1985). In animal studies oestrogens have been shown to enhance cortical maturation and myelogenesis, whereas androgens interfere with the oestrogen effect. Increasing sophistication in neuroradiological and neuropathological techniques has demonstrated that disorders of neuronal migration are recognizable in a wide variety of clinical types of epilepsy (Annotation, 1990). It is not yet clear whether sex hormones can influence the type or extent of migrational disorders which might later be associated with specific epileptic syndromes.

SYNDROMES COMMONER IN FEMALES

Childhood absence epilepsy

Approximately 8% of all children with epilepsy have typical absence seizures (Cavazzutti, 1980). Those affected are usually neurologically and intellectually within normal limits. This type of epilepsy has the clearest female predominance. In cohorts of children with absences, at least 60% are girls (Loiseau, 1985; Fois et al., 1987; Panayiotopoulos et al., 1989). Childhood absence epilepsy is characterized by the sudden onset and offset of loss of awareness accompanied by 3-Hz spike and wave on the EEG. As the result of careful simultaneous video and EEG studies, Penry et al. (1975) were able to show that in only 9.4% of cases could the absences be deemed simple, i.e, unassociated with any alteration in tone or movement. In the other 90.6% mild clonic components, increase or decrease in postural tone or automatisms were noted. The presence of automatisms may be particularly misleading, and a diagnosis of complex partial seizures of temporal lobe origin can be erroneously made. It is important to appreciate that automatisms were seen in 63% of the absences recorded by Penry et al. (1975), and were in particular related to duration. Absences occur very frequently, often more than 100 times per day. Children who present with absences have an overall risk of generalized tonic–clonic seizures (GTCS) of 40% (Loiseau, 1985). If GTCS occur they tend to be infrequent, but may commence up to ten years after the onset of absences.

Although considered one of the generalized epilepsies, careful stereo-electroencephalographic work has shown that the convulsive discharges in absences originate in the mesio-orbital gyrus of the frontal lobe and are synchronized in the reticular system. Abnormal neuronal migration has been identified in patients with absences, but all had also had GTCS (Meencke, 1987). Described in general terms as microdysgenesis, a diffuse increase in neurones in the stratum moleculare of the neocortex and in the white matter, dystopia of the Purkinje cells in the cerebellar cortex and dystopic neurones in the hippocampus were reported. Any possible role of sex hormones in determining the density of neurones in the stratum moleculare is not clear. There is a strong genetic component in the predisposition to absences. A positive family history of epilepsy is obtained in up to 44% of affected children (Aicardi, 1986). Microdysgenetic areas are found in other types of epilepsy in which genetic aspects appear important, but in which the clinical expression is as common or commoner in males. It seems possible that some influence of gender could determine whether absences or other types of seizure present.

The long-term outlook for childhood absence epilepsy is to some extent sex related. Absences tend to disappear round about puberty, even in untreated patients, though treatment with either ethosuximide or valproate or both is usually effective and produces rapid remission. GTCS, which can be more persistent than absences, have been reported as more likely to develop in males (Oller-Daurella and Sanchez, 1981). On the other hand, using multivariate analysis, male sex, normal intelligence and neurological examination and failure to induce spike and wave by hyperventilation have been found to be significantly associated with cessation of all types of seizures (Sato *et al.*, 1983). Further investigation of the reason why childhood absence epilepsy is commoner in girls seems indicated.

Epilepsy with photosensitivity

Although seizures induced by photic or pattern stimuli are by no means confined to childhood, photosensitivity usually presents between the ages of 6 and 12 years, and is commonest below the age of 16 years (Jeavons and Harding, 1975). The commonest precipitants are television viewed at close quarters or when the set is malfunctioning, and sunlight reflected off wet surfaces or through the leaves of trees. Black and white or sharply contrasted linear patterns can also cause seizures in susceptible people. Photosensitivity is a component of several epileptic syndromes rather than a syndrome in its own right. In particular, GTCS are likely to be precipitated, but absences or myoclonic jerks may occur. The ratio of females to males in patients with photosensitivity is at least 1.5:1 (Jeavons and Harding, 1975), with those in whom absences or myoclonic seizures are induced by intermittent photic stimulation being female three to four times more often than male. Photoconvulsive myoclonic jerking is also commoner in females. In long-term follow-up studies of those who have had absences or juvenile myoclonic epilepsy (Wolf and Gooses, 1986), the presence or absence of photosensitivity has not been explored as a prognostic factor, and this would seem worth investigation. An explanation for the greater incidence of photosensitivity in girls has yet to be unravelled, but hormonal factors have been suggested (Jeavons and Harding, 1975).

Increases in female sex hormones round about puberty might explain an increase in clinical expression at this time, but photosensitivity can be found as early as the second year in benign and severe myoclonic epilepsies in infancy and well before puberty in childhood absence epilepsy, suggesting that a simple relationship cannot exist.

Epilepsy in association with syndromes which occur only in females

Rett syndrome

Rett syndrome was first described in 1966 (Rett, 1966). It is presumed that the condition is lethal to males. Affected girls have normal cognitive and neurological development in the first six months or so of life, then cease to make appropriate progress and later lose previously acquired skills. Typically the girls have no dysmorphic features and initially formal neurological signs are unimpressive. The most characteristic early feature is loss of purposeful use of the hands associated with continuous hand-wringing, hand-patting and other repetitive stereotyped movements of the hands. Pyramidal and extrapyramidal tract signs, scoliosis and hyperventilation are associated with very poor intellectual abilities as the disorder progresses. Epilepsy occurs in approximately 75% of girls with Rett syndrome. In the individual the seizures are often of several different types. Atypical absences and partial seizures with or without secondary generalization are most usual. EEGs show an excess of slow frequencies with spike, polyspike or spike and wave activity (Bader et al., 1989). The spikes may appear most prominant in recordings from the middle third of the head and are enhanced by light sleep (Robb et al., 1989; Niedermeyer and Naidu, 1990). Resistance to antiepileptic therapy is common.

Aicardi syndrome

Aicardi syndrome was first reported in 1965, and a more complete description appeared four years later (Aicardi et al., 1969). The four main features are female sex (or the presence of XX chromosomes), infantile spasms, agenesis of the corpus callosum and lesions in the optic fundus referred to as lacunae (Chevrie and Aicardi, 1986; Donnenfeld et al., 1989). The lacunae have not been reported in any other condition, and are always multiple, tending to cluster round the optic discs. They are more or less rounded, white, yellowish or pinkish in colour and may be shiny. Faint pigmentation may be present round the edges but the central areas are always unpigmented. The lesions are at the same level as the retina and normal vessels are seen to cross them.

The seizures in Aicardi syndrome start early, often in the first days or weeks of life. In about 40% of cases, in addition to infantile spasms, other seizure types, usually unilateral or focal with fixed or variable locations, occur. The inter-ictal EEG is always abnormal. Although the clinical presentation is with infantile spasms, hypsarrhythmia was recorded in only 18% of 146 infants reviewed by Chevrie and Aicardi (1986), and the commonest abnormality was pseudoperiodic discharges which occurred asynchronously over both hemispheres. Asynchrony between bursts of activity in a suppression–burst type of EEG is considered highly suggestive of this condition.

Neurologically the girls have either gross hypotonia or unilateral or bilateral spasticity. Severe mental retardation is the rule. Costovertebral abnormalities are present in about 75% and non-specific facial dysmorphism has been reported occasionally.

There is no known case with a family history of the Aicardi syndrome, and it is postulated that the physical characteristics are secondary to a de novo mutation in an X chromosome. Recent investigation into possible X chromosome inactivation in Aicardi syndrome has shown that girls with particularly severe psychomotor retardation and very poor seizure control were likely to have skewed X-inactivation, whereas those with less severe symptomatology had random X-inactivation, suggesting that in some affected girls non-random X-inactivation may reflect heterogeneity of underlying molecular lesions (Neidich et al., 1990). Further identification of the abnormality might lead to a better understanding of how an X chromosome might influence neuronal migration and consequently propensities to seizures.

EPILEPSIES OCCURRING EQUALLY COMMONLY IN MALE AND FEMALE CHILDREN

Benign familial neonatal convulsions

Benign familial neonatal convulsions are inherited in an autosomal dominant manner. The gene has been mapped to the long arm of chromosome 20 (Leppert et al., 1989). The pre- and intranatal and immediate post-natal periods of affected infants are normal. Seizures commence on the second or third day, are clonic, brief, and repeated frequently for up to seven days (Plouin, 1985). Other seizure types may present later in childhood, but the neurological and intellectual status remains normal. There are no specific EEG changes during the neonatal period or later.

Early myoclonic encephalopathy

Aicardi (1985a) has emphasized that a high proportion of the reported cases of early myoclonic encephalopathy are definitely or presumed secondary to autosomally recessive inheritance. Thus equal numbers of affected females and males would be anticipated. In particular, patients with non-ketotic hyperglycinaemia and D-glutaric acidaemia present with this syndrome. Other associated conditions which have been described are poliodystrophy, progressive cerebral atrophy, hyperproprionic acidaemia, and multifocal spongy changes in the cerebral white matter.

The seizures start in the neonatal period or soon thereafter with erratic partial myoclonias which can be restricted to one part of a limb or may be generalized. They are eventually constantly repetitive throughout waking and sleep. Partial seizures appear almost immediately and tonic infantile spasms present at 3–4 months of age. The infants are hypotonic initially with spasticity, and sometimes opisthotonus, supervening later. There is minimal, if any, cognitive development.

In the early stages, the EEG is distinctive. There is no normal background activity. In both the awake and sleeping states, there are complex bursts of spikes, sharp waves and slow waves, irregularly intermingled, of 1–5 seconds duration, and separated by periods of almost complete suppression of 3–10 seconds duration. The bursts of activity never show bilateral synchrony in their individual components, but may occur synchronously or asynchronously over both hemispheres. When partial seizures commence, spike discharges may be seen localized to part of one hemisphere while the suppression–burst pattern persists unchanged. Atypical hypsarrhythmia may appear later in the first year.

The life expectancy for infants with early myoclonic encephalopathy is severely curtailed, with many dying in the first 2 years of life.

Benign epilepsy with occipital paroxysms

This syndrome is characterized by seizures with strong visual components which are followed in one-third of cases by a migraine-like headache (Gastaut, 1985; Panayiotopoulos, 1989). A family history of epilepsy was reported in one-third by Gastaut (1985), but this is recorded as much less frequent by Newton and Aicardi (1983) and Panayiotopoulos (1989). A personal history of febrile seizures is about five times as common as that in the general population. Thus this syndrome is one of the spectrum of genetic epilepsies with a variety of expressions. As such, equal presentation in males and females might be predicted, but since there are other epilepsies with strong genetic input and a bias to one or other sex there is no ready explanation for equal male and female representation in this syndrome.

The visual ictal symptoms have been described by Gastaut (1985). Most frequently there is amaurosis, which may be preceded by hemianopsia. Other patients have, in decreasing order of frequency, elementary visual hallucinations (phosphenes), complex visual hallucinations, visual illusions and combinations of the individual symptoms. These visual symptoms may be followed by hemiclonic seizures, complex partial seizures with automatisms,

GTCS or less often other seizure types. The attack terminates in a severe headache, with nausea and vomiting in one-third of cases. In some patients the attacks are precipitated by moving from a well-lit to a dark environment or vice versa. The EEG is a very characteristic feature of this syndrome. On a normal interictal background, trains of spike–waves appear uni- or bilaterally in the occipital and posterotemporal regions within a few seconds of eye closure and disappear on eye opening. It is unusual for hyperventilation or photic stimulation to influence the recording further.

Gastaut (1985) states that the typical visual seizures always cease during adolescence. On the other hand, Panayiotopoulos (1989) suggests that there are early and late-onset variants of this syndrome, with those children who have an onset in the first decade remitting by the age of 12 years, and those who present later more liable to continuing seizures. Thus for some girls who present with benign epilepsy with occipital paroxysms there is a possibility that the need for therapy will continue into the reproductive years.

Benign partial epilepsy with affective symptoms

The seizures in this syndrome are particularly distressing for the child. They consist of sudden fright or terror and may be very frequent over short periods of time. To the uninitiated they may appear primarily behavioural rather than epileptic in nature. In addition, their unpleasant manifestations can cause secondary difficulties with social interaction. Following the sudden onset of terror, chewing or swallowing movements, distressed laughter, arrest of speech with glottal noises, moans, salivation or autonomic phenomena may occur (Dalla Bernardina et al., 1985). The seizures last 1–2 minutes and although associated with some loss of awareness are not usually accompanied by complete loss of consciousness.

Affected children start to have seizures between 2 and 9 years and remission is likely during adolescence. Neurological and intellectual development are normal. Despite the affective symptomatology and its secondary effects during the period when seizures are present, Dalla Bernardina et al. (1985) report that behavioural difficulties do not persist after remission of seizures. Nevertheless personal experience suggests that the anxieties engendered both in the children and their parents when affective seizures are present are such that a study of the later social adjustment of those who have had this epileptic syndrome would be well justified.

The EEGs show normal background activity and sleep organization. Interictally slow spikes/slow waves, occurring in the frontotemporal or parietotemporal areas uni- or bilaterally, are activated by sleep. In ictal recordings the seizure discharges are clearly localized to the frontotemporal, centrotemporal or parietal areas.

One-third of children with benign partial epilepsy with affective symptoms have positive family histories for epilepsy, and one-fifth personal histories of febrile seizures (Dalla Bernardina *et al.*, 1985). Thus this syndrome belongs to the spectrum of genetically determined epilepsies.

Epilepsy with continuous spikes and waves during slow sleep (ESES)

The alternative title for this syndrome is electrical status epilepticus during slow sleep. The diagnosis is made on the basis of the EEG findings during sleep, when at least 85% of the period of slow wave sleep is associated with spike and wave discharges (Tassinari *et al.*, 1985b). It is probable that although comparatively rare, this condition is underdiagnosed. In patients described in the literature, a variety of clinically obvious seizure types have started in early childhood. These may be only rare motor, nocturnal attacks with remission in early adolescence, or motor with the development of absences, sometimes apparently typical, at the time of onset of ESES, and a tendency to (but not inevitable) remission before the age of 16 years. Alternatively, rare nocturnal seizures may be followed by atypical absences with clonic and atonic features appearing at the onset of ESES and remitting later in childhood or adolescence (Tassinari *et al.*, 1985b).

Although the outcome for ESES is itself good, other aspects of cerebral development fare less well. In the long term, severe problems with language, global retardation and behaviour difficulties are likely. Thus ESES is one of the epileptic syndromes of childhood with profound implications for adulthood. Information on the genetic input or implications is sparse and at present there is no reason to suspect that this is a syndrome associated with important genetic factors.

Epilepsy with generalized convulsive seizures

Epilepsy with primary generalized convulsive seizures alone is relatively rare in childhood (Oller-Daurella, 1985). Association of GTCS with absences or myoclonus is common and children with such seizure types in addition to GTCS of generalized onset should be classified as having syndromes other than epilepsy with generalized convulsive seizures. In this syndrome neurological findings and intellect are virtually always normal and there is a ready response to therapy, with a good prognosis. The EEG, when recorded interictally, shows normal background rhythms and may also contain generalized, bilateral, synchronous discharges of spike waves or polyspike waves.

A positive family history is obtained in 25% of cases. No other aetiological factor has been proposed, although from the pathological point of view there is evidence that microdysgenesis can play a part in the substrate for this type of epilepsy (Meencke, 1987). It may be that the propensity to microdysgenesis is heritable.

Juvenile myoclonic epilepsy (JME)

JME is also considered a primary generalized epilepsy and is discussed in Chapter 6.

Epilepsies associated with conditions in which there is autosomal dominant or recessive inheritance

Of the autosomal dominant conditions in which epilepsy is an important factor, tuberose sclerosis (TS) is recognized most often. Seizures, which occur in 90% of patients, usually begin early in life and are the most frequent presenting symptom of TS in childhood (Gomez, 1987). Typically the onset is with infantile spasms starting in the first year, before the facial angiofibromata appear. However, TS can be strongly suspected if hypomelanotic macules can be seen either in ordinary or ultraviolet light. Tonic, atonic, atypical absence and complex partial seizures can all be symptomatic of TS. Resistance to therapy is usual, mental retardation is present in about half the patients and severe behaviour difficulties are common. Children whose epilepsy is secondary to TS have a high, but not invariable, risk of severe handicap as adults.

Neurofibromatosis 1 (NF1) is also inherited in an autosomal dominant manner. Café-au-lait spots, plexiform neurofibromata, axillary freckling, iris hamartomata (Lisch nodules) and other rarer problems such as optic nerve gliomata, astrocytomata and cranioverteberal dysplasias occur. Epilepsy is present in about 10% of patients with NF1 (Carey *et al.*, 1979) and may be secondary to intracranial tumours. Clearly children with symptoms secondary to intracranial pathology associated with NF1 are likely to continue to have seizures throughout adulthood.

A large number of inborn errors of metabolism of infancy and childhood with autosomal recessive inheritance in which sex distribution is equal can present or be associated with seizures. The seizures are usually myoclonic and the underlying conditions progressive, with only a few amenable to biochemically orientated therapy. These disorders have been considered in detail by Berkovic and Andermann (1986) and, where possible, specific characteristics of their epileptic manifestations summarized by Aicardi (1985b).

SYNDROMES LESS COMMON IN FEMALES

Benign idiopathic neonatal convulsions ('fifth day fits') (Plouin, 1985)

There may be some difficulties in separating this syndrome from benign familial neonatal convulsions unless there is very good access to a detailed family history. Of the 139 infants reported in the literature, 38% are girls. Eighty per cent of infants have the seizures between days 4 and 6, and 95% between days

3 and 7. Thus the onset is rather later than in the familial condition. In addition, the interictal EEG is likely to have a characteristic appearance, with sharp theta waves which can be alternating or discontinuous, are unreactive and are frequently synchronous between the hemispheres. During seizures the EEG shows rhythmic spikes or slow waves. The seizures are clonic, usually partial and may be so frequent as to constitute status. There is a poor response to antiepileptic drugs and seizures appear to remit spontaneously, often within 24 hours. Although referred to as benign, the long-term outlook for this condition has not been well delineated and some children are known to have persisting EEG abnormalities or to go on to have other types of seizures.

Febrile seizures

Seizures which are precipitated by febrile illnesses occur less frequently in females, in a ratio of approximately 1:1.5. The influences of sex on many aspects of this special syndrome have been investigated in more detail than for any other type of seizure disorder. This is particularly so in relation to age at onset and hemispheric involvement when seizures are lateralized (Taylor, 1969; Taylor and Ounsted, 1971; Wallace, 1988). Overall, females have a more sharply defined period of vulnerability to febrile seizures, and the peak age at incidence is earlier than for males (Wallace, 1988). In addition febrile seizures with right hemisphere involvement in males tend to occur at later ages than those in females, with resulting possibly greater vulnerability to seizure damage in females who have earlier seizures. Genetic factors also appear to differ according to sex. In a broad family study, affected relatives of the child with febrile seizures were more likely to be paternal than maternal, and relatives of the father were at greater risk if male than female (Frantzen et al., 1970). When first-degree relatives only were considered, both parents and siblings of female probands were significantly less likely than those of male probands to have seizure disorders (Wallace, 1988). In addition, a positive family history of seizures appears to carry a more serious prognosis in females (Taylor and Ounsted, 1971). As possible predisposing factors to febrile seizures, previous parental subfertility and fetal distress have been found to be significantly more common in males, but not in females (Wallace, 1988). Both male and female cohorts have excesses of children whose birth weights are low for gestational age, and females are particularly likely to have weights less than the fifth centile when corrected for gestation, maternal height and birth order. Girls with later febrile seizures, unlike boys, do not have an increased likelihood of neonatal feeding difficulties.

Prior to febrile seizures, in contrast to males, females have no tendency to be late in starting to walk. However, there is possibly a tendency for females with febrile seizures to be later with talking in sentences than girls as a whole.

The sex distribution was equal in late talkers in a population of children with febrile seizures, in contrast to the usual excess of males in those with delay in speech and language development (Wallace, 1988). The initial seizure is more likely in girls than boys to be prolonged, lateralized or recurring in the same episode (Chevrie and Aicardi, 1975; Herlitz, 1941; Verity *et al.*, 1985). Young females are particularly likely to have severe febrile seizures (Wolf *et al.*, 1977; Taylor and Ounsted, 1971). In girls who develop acute, usually transient, hemipareses in association with febrile seizures, there is a tendency for left-sided weakness (right hemisphere abnormality) to occur at a younger age (Wallace, 1988). Persisting hemiparesis is commoner in girls than boys (Aicardi and Chevrie, 1976).

Virtually all studies of recurrence of febrile seizures and the development later of non-febrile seizures and epilepsy suggest that males and females are overall equally vulnerable (Wallace, 1988). However, girls who have subsequent complex partial seizures of left hemisphere origin belong to a significantly different and, on average, younger population than those whose prolonged, lateralized febrile seizures are not followed by epilepsy with complex partial seizures (Wallace, 1982).

In assessments during the two years immediately following the initial febrile seizures the overall developmental scores and results of specific tests of language function were higher in girls than boys (Aldridge Smith, 1984). The cognitive abilities of children tested eight to ten years later are apparently unrelated to sex when taken as a whole. However, when the initial seizures have been prolonged and lateralized, girls are more likely to be globally retarded and have, when compared with boys, significantly reduced verbal abilities (Wallace, 1982; Wallace and Cull, 1979). On the Wechsler Intelligence Scale for Children girls whose seizures started between the ages of 13 and 18 months have been found to have lower performance quotients than those with younger or older ages of onset (Cull, 1975). Girls with later global retardation are very likely to have had their first seizures before the age of 18 months but retardation is by no means invariable for those with such a young age of onset.

In summary, febrile seizures are less common in girls than in boys, but the implications are more serious for girls particularly if complex seizures occur at a relatively young age.

Early onset infantile epileptic encephalopathy

In 1976 Ohtahara and his colleagues first described, in Japanese, early infantile epileptic encephalopathy. Subsequent papers (Ohtahara *et al.*, 1987; Clarke *et al.*, 1987) have emphasized the specific characteristics of this condition, differentiating it, in particular, from early myoclonic encephalopathy (Aicardi, 1985a). Girls are affected somewhat less often than boys. The onset is very early in life, usually within one month of birth and often within the first 24 hours. The seizures always include tonic spasms which often occur in series. Partial motor or hemiconvulsions may also occur. The EEG is very characteristic, with an invariable periodic suppression–burst pattern occurring during sleep and waking. The bursts consist of irregular high-voltage slow waves with intermingled spikes. The underlying pathologies for this syndrome are very diverse. It has been described as symptomatic of disorders of neuronal migration, such as agenesis of the corpus callosum, of non-ketotic hyperglycinaemia and following asphyxia. In some cases, no cause is found. There is no obvious reason for the relative infrequency in females. The outlook is very poor. Death commonly occurs within the first year of life and all survivors are severely mentally and physically handicapped. Progression to West and the Lennox–Gastaut syndromes is common in those surviving. No sex-related trends have been reported for individual characteristics of this syndrome.

West syndrome

West (1841) described the clinical components of the syndrome now attributed to him. The EEG characteristics were described first by Gibbs and Gibbs (1952) and more fully by the same authors two years later (Gibbs *et al.*, 1954). Infantile spasms, mental retardation or deterioration and a hypsarrhythmic EEG are the cardinal features. West syndrome is commoner in males, particularly when an underlying aetiology can be defined (Lombroso, 1983). In a review of the neuropathological findings five groups could be identified: embryo-fetal lesions such as those secondary to disorders of neuronal migration or to metabolic disorders; peri-natal and post-natal encephalopathies; combined embryo-fetal and peri- and post-natal brain lesions, e.g. dysgenetic areas with additional evidence of anoxia; acute vascular and inflammatory disorders; and infants in whom no definable lesion was identified (Jellinger, 1987). The relative male and female proportions were not detailed for each group. However, Aicardi syndrome, one of the disorders of neuronal migration, occurs only in girls. Most of the inborn errors of metabolism described are inherited in an autosomal recessive manner, but Jellinger (1987) recorded three boys from unrelated families in whom infantile spasms were associated with hypotonia, microcephaly, GTCS and death before the age of 18 months, suggesting that there may be X-linked disorders with which West syndrome is associated. Should such disorders be identified, genetic counselling for, in particular, the mother is of great importance. The roles of influences of sex in determining embryo-fetal disorders and vulnerability to adverse peri-natal events could be relevant to the overall male preponderance in West syndrome, but an exact explanation for this is so far lacking.

West syndrome has a benign outcome in, at the most, 5% of cases. Thus for those who survive to adulthood, mental retardation, epilepsy and, frequently, behaviour disorders are continuing problems. Few children whose seizures start with infantile spasms are sufficiently socially competent for reproduction.

Benign myoclonic epilepsy in infants

This is a rare syndrome, reported in fewer than 20 patients when reviewed by Dravet *et al.* (1985a). Females are affected relatively infrequently. In otherwise normal children, brief bouts of generalized myoclonus commence between 4 months and 2½ years. Initially the attacks may be so brief that they are almost unnoticed, but later they become more prominent and may cause the child who is learning to stand and walk to fall frequently. EEGs recorded during attacks showed discharges of generalized spike–waves or polyspike–waves which occur in rapid succession and are of the same duration as the seizures. Photosensitivity may be present. During waking the inter-ictal EEG is usually normal for age, but drowsiness and the early stages of sleep lead to an increase in spike–wave discharges with accompanying myoclonus, both of which tend to disappear during slow wave and REM sleep. The seizures are responsive to sodium valproate, but some of the children are developmentally slow, with a need for specialized education, and for some followed to adolescence GTCS occur later. Thus the presentation of this syndrome in infancy can presage a need for sodium valproate therapy continuing into the reproductive years.

Severe myoclonic epilepsy in infants

As its name implies, this syndrome has important implications for the long-term neurodevelopmental status. Although Dalla Bernardina *et al.* (1982) in one of the first publications on this syndrome recorded males affected three times as commonly as females, on the whole there is only a small sex difference in incidence (Dravet *et al.*, 1985b). The children are initially normal and present in the first year of life with prolonged clonic seizures which may be generalized or lateralized and are usually associated with febrile illnesses. The seizures recur initially with fever but soon with no obvious provocation. During the second year of life generalized myoclonic attacks become prominent. These may be mild or sufficiently severe to make the child fall, and are likely to be precipitated by changes in light intensity. Partial seizures may start at much the same time as the myoclonias. EEGs are normal initially, but once the myoclonic seizures appear, paroxysmal rapid, generalized spike–waves or polyspike–waves which eventually become predominantly lateralized are recorded and photosensitivity is almost invariable. Cerebellar ataxia develops and cognitive development begins to slow down. Children with this syndrome tend to have, in particular, severe delay in language skills. The long-term outlook is for continued seizures, mental retardation and ataxia.

Myoclonic astatic epilepsy

Doose *et al.* (1970) have differentiated this syndrome from the Lennox–Gestaut syndrome. In myoclonic astatic epilepsy there is a sex ratio of 2 boys to 1 girl. Prior neurodevelopmental status is normal in most cases. A high prevalence of seizures is found in family members and this is greater in relatives of female than of male probands (Doose, 1985). Seizures start in the first 5 years of life. Bilateral myoclonic jerking, astatic attacks with abrupt loss of muscle tone, a combination of myoclonic and astatic components and atypical absences with irregular myoclonias are characteristic. Generalized tonic-clonic seizures may occur as the initial seizure type. Neither partial nor tonic seizures are typically present, but can appear in cases with unfavourable progression. The EEG shows changes such as those found in primary generalized epilepsies, i.e. bilaterally synchronous irregular spike and wave, prominent 4–7 c/s rhythms and photosensitivity. Although the syndrome is recognized as an entity there is a wide range of possible long-term outcomes. In some children there is complete resolution of symptomatology, in others the seizures persist and there is poor cognitive development with the appearance of ataxia, other problems with control of movement and difficulties with speech and language. There is no analysis in the literature of the relative outcomes for boys and girls.

Lennox–Gastaut syndrome

The onset of seizures is always before the age of 8 years. Tonic attacks are the hallmark, but atypical absence, atonic and sometimes myoclonic seizures also occur (Beaumanoir, 1985a; Aicardi and Gomes, 1988). Characteristically the EEG shows, during waking, diffuse slow (1.5–2 Hz) spike–wave, and during sleep, bursts of rapid (10 Hz) rhythms. The seizures appear to be just one aspect of an encephalopathy in which neurological, cognitive and behavioural disturbances are further problems. There is no ready explanation for the tendency for males to be affected rather more often than females, but sex has not been reported to be of importance in the outcome, which is usually bleak from the seizure, neurological and cognitive viewpoints.

Epilepsy with myoclonic absences

In this syndrome, in which absences are associated with symmetrical bilateral myoclonic jerking, sometimes with loss of posture, there is a male preponderance of 65% (Tassinari and Bureau, 1985). The EEG findings during the absences are indistinguishable from those of childhood absence epilepsy, showing bilateral synchronous and symmetrical 3-Hz spike and wave. In addition to the prominent myoclonic jerking and the preponderance of males, a further distinguishing feature from childhood absence epilepsy is the relative resistance to treatment with both sodium valproate and/or ethosuximide. Infrequent GTCS also occur. Affected children become progressively intellectually impaired, with a failure to gain new skills rather than loss of attainments, so that persistence of problems into adulthood is the rule.

Benign partial epilepsy with centrotemporal spikes (BECT)

Approximately 15–20% of all children with epilepsy have BECT (Lerman, 1985). Males are somewhat more likely to be affected (Loiseau et al., 1988). Children with BECT are almost invariably of normal neurological and intellectual status. The seizures may occur only during sleep, or during sleep and waking, and in 20% or less of cases in the waking state only. They start often as the child wakes from sleep, with unilateral paraesthesias involving the tongue, lips, gums and inner cheeks, with progression to unilateral tonic, clonic, or tonic–clonic convulsions which involve the face, lips, tongue and pharyngeal and laryngeal muscles, leading to anarthria and drooling. Consciousness is preserved. The nocturnal seizures can become generalized, and, if the partial onset is missed, this disorder may be incorrectly labelled as primary GTCS. The seizures tend to remit at puberty.

In a long-term follow-up, Loiseau et al. (1988) found sex to be an unimportant factor in prognosis, as were the type and timing of the seizures, but young age at onset and long duration of 'active' BECT predicted a less favourable outcome.

Benign partial epilepsy with extreme somatosensory evoked potentials

This syndrome seems to have been discovered as though by accident. It was found that between the ages of 2 and 5 years tapping the soles or heels of the feet would produce extremely high-voltage somatosensory potentials in a very small minority of children, who, when followed up, would next develop spontaneous focal EEG abnormalities during sleep, then during waking and finally partial motor seizures with head and body version (Tassinari and de Marco, 1985.) Males predominate in a ratio of 3:1. There is a good prognosis for the seizures, which remit within a year, but the EEG abnormalities persist for longer. The neurological and intellectual status of the children is normal.

Juvenile absence epilepsy

The absences in this syndrome, which commences in the second decade, are comparable in clinical expression to those of childhood absence epilepsy, but tend to be much less frequent and are more often associated with GTCS. The ictal EEG shows generalized, symmetrical, synchronous spike–wave at 3.5–4

Hz (i.e. faster than that of childhood absence epilepsy). Photosensitivity is relatively rare. There is only a slight male preponderance (Wolf and Inoue, 1984), but this is at variance with the consistent tendency for childhood absence epilepsy to be found more often in girls. Complete control of seizures can be problematical, and girls who have juvenile absence epilepsy are likely to enter their reproductive years while still receiving antiepileptic drug therapy.

Epilepsy with grand mal on awakening

The predisposition to epilepsy with GTCS on awakening is only marginally greater in males than females (Wolf, 1985). Onset is usually in the first part of the second decade but may be as early as 6 years. In addition to GTCS, absences and myoclonic jerks are often present and this syndrome can overlap with juvenile myoclonic and juvenile absence epilepsies. The neurological and intellectual findings are usually normal. In the EEG there is a generalized increase in background slow activity and generalized spike–wave activity is frequently, but not invariably, recorded inter-ictally. Photosensitivity is found in 9% of males and 17% of females (Wolf, 1985). Other precipitating factors are sleep deprivation, excessive alcohol intake and sudden external arousal; and, in older girls seizures are most likely before and during menstruation.

Benign partial seizures of adolescence

Only 30% of adolescents who present with the onset of benign partial seizures are female. The seizures are, at onset, simple or complex partial with motor or sensory symptomatology and may evolve to secondary generalization (Loiseau and Louiset, 1985). They may be isolated or occur in flurries over a period of hours, with subsequent long-term remission. The neurological, intellectual and inter-ictal EEG findings are all normal. Girls who present with this syndrome can look forward to a seizure-free adulthood.

Complex partial seizures secondary to defined lesions

Figures for the sex incidence of complex partial seizures other than those secondary to temporal lobe lesions are lacking. In a very clearly delineated group of 30 patients with complex partial seizures of childhood onset, the male:female ratio was 1.3:1 (Kotagal et al., 1987), but a much higher male:female ratio, 10.5:1, was reported by Ounsted et al. (1987). This latter study certainly included at least one child with benign epilepsy with centrotemporal spikes, but this cannot explain the very marked male predominance. The comparatively common history of febrile seizures, which had occurred in 9 of the 30 cases of Kotagal et al. (1987), has already been discussed. In the detailed study of Ounsted *et al.* (1987) of the long-term outcome of those presenting in childhood with temporal lobe epilepsy, equal numbers of men and women who survived into adulthood had IQs of less than 50, but an associated and socially debilitating hyperkinetic syndrome occurred twice as commonly in boys. In the same study, rage outbursts were equally common in males and females with temporal lobe epilepsy, but the girls affected had seizure onset at 9 months, compared with 16 months in affected boys. Associated aggression was found in girls only in those with severe retardation, and in boys throughout the range of cognitive abilities. The proportions of each sex considered so severely handicapped as to be unmarriageable were comparable in the group as a whole, but the likelihood of marriage in those less handicapped was significantly much higher in females than males. Remission by the age of 12 years occurred more often in girls than boys, but not significantly so. Thus, not only is the female sex less often represented in cohorts with temporal lobe epilepsy, but serious complications other than severe generalized handicap seem proportionately less common in the affected girls.

Landau–Kleffner syndrome

Clinical expression of epilepsy is not invariably present in the Landau–Kleffner syndrome, but abnormalities of the EEG are always recorded. These consist of repetitive spikes and spike–wave of high amplitude which are organized into foci, variable in time and space, but mainly located in the temporal or parieto-occipital regions (Beaumanoir, 1985b' Nakano *et al.*, 1989). Acquired aphasia is invariable. It starts with an auditory verbal agnosia and the early reduction in spontaneous verbal expression accompanied by stereotypies, perseveration and paraphrasias. Expressive language may be completely lost. There is a strong male predominance. The separate outcomes for males and females have not been examined. The outlook for recovery of language abilities is variable and it is probable that some deficits remain even in those with the most favourable outcomes.

Epilepsies associated with X-linked disorders

The fragile-X syndrome is associated primarily with non-progressive mental retardation, but large ears, hypo- or hypertonia and testicular enlargement are additional findings. Epilepsy is a further complication in 20–42% of cases (Wiesniewski *et al.*, 1985; Herbst, 1980). Female carriers may be mentally dull, but none of the three assessed by Wiesniewski *et al.* (1985) had epilepsy.

Menkes' disease occurs only in males (Menkes *et al.*, 1962). In the neonatal period feeding difficulties, vomiting and poor weight gain predominate, but by 8 weeks seizures, which become increasingly difficult to control, hypotonia, hypothermia and stiff kinky hair characterize the clinical picture. The serum copper and caeruloplasmin levels and the liver copper content are very low, but there is increased copper in duodenal mucosa and in cultured skin fibroblasts. Menkes' disease is usually fatal in the first year.

CONCLUSIONS

The two epileptic syndromes which are consistently more often found in females—absence epilepsy of childhood and photosensitivity—are both benign. The former is usually self-remitting and the latter readily treatable. On the other hand two conditions which occur exclusively in females—Rett and Aicardi syndromes—are characterized by severe epilepsy and mental retardation.

When an insult such as a prolonged lateralized febrile seizure occurs in early life, girls seem more vulnerable to severe effects than boys.

Most epileptic syndromes are commoner in boys, which strongly suggests that they are to some extent neurodevelopmentally rather than entirely genetically determined. For most epilepsies the long-term outcomes have not been examined separately for the sexes.

REFERENCES

Aicardi, J. (1985a) Early myoclonic encephalopathy. In: *Epileptic Syndromes in Infancy, Childhood and Adolescence* (eds J. Roger, C. Dravet, M. Bureau, F.E. Dreifuss and P. Wolf), pp. 12–22. John Libbey, London.

Aicardi, J. (1985b) Epileptic seizures in inborn errors of metabolism. In: *Epileptic Syndromes of Infancy, Childhood and Adolescence* (eds J. Roger, C. Dravet, M. Bureau, F.E. Dreifuss and P. Wolf), pp. 75–77. John Libbey, London.

Aicardi, J. (1986) *Epilepsy in Children*. Raven Press, New York.

Aicardi, J. and Chevrie, J.–J. (1976) Febrile convulsions: Neurological sequelae and mental retardation. In: *Brain Dysfunction in Infantile Febrile Convulsions* (eds M.A.B. Brazier and F. Coceani), pp. 247–257. Raven Press, New York.

Aicardi, J. and Gomes, A.L. (1988) The Lennox–Gastaut syndrome: Clinical and electroencephalographic features. In *The Lennox–Gastaut Syndrome* (eds E. Niedermeyer and R. Degen), pp. 25–46. Alan R. Liss, New York.

Aicardi, J., Chevrie, J.–J. and Rousellie, F. (1969) Le syndrome agénésic calleuse, spasmes en flexion, lacunes choriorétiniennes. *Arch. Fr. Pediatr.*, **26**, 1103–1120.

Aldridge Smith, J. (1984) *Cognitive Functioning and Febrile Convulsions*. PhD thesis, University of Wales.

Annotation (1990) Epilepsy and disorders of neuronal migration. *Lancet*, **336**, 1035.

Bader, G.G., Witt-Engerstrom, I. and Hagberg, B. (1989) Neurophysiological findings in the Rett syndrome. 1: EMG, conduction velocity, EEG and somatosensory evoked potential studies. *Brain Dev.*, **11**, 102–109.

Beaumanoir, A. (1985a) The Lennox–Gastaut syndrome. In *Epileptic Syndromes in Infancy, Childhood and Adolescence* (eds J. Roger, C. Dravet, M. Bureau, F.E. Dreifuss and P. Wolf), pp. 89–99. John Libbey, London.

Beaumanoir, A. (1985b) The Landau–Kleffner syndrome. In *Epileptic Syndromes in Infancy, Childhood and Adolescence* (eds J. Roger, C. Dravet, M. Bureau, F.E. Dreifuss and P. Wolf), pp. 181–191. John Libbey, London.

Berkovic, S.F. and Andermann, F. (1986) The progressive myoclonus epilepsies. In: *Recent Advances in Epilepsy 3* (eds T.A. Pedley and B.S. Meldrum), pp. 157–188. Churchill Livingstone, Edinburgh.

Buffery, A.W.H. (1976) Sex differences in the neuropsychological development of verbal and spatial skills. In: *The Neuropsychology of Learning Disorders* (eds R.M. Knights and D.J. Bakker), pp. 187–205. University Park Press, Baltimore.

Carey, J.C., Lamb, J.M. and Hall, B.D. (1979) Penetrance and variability in neuro-fibromatosis: A genetic study of 60 families. *Birth Defects*, Original Articles series 15 (5B), 271–281.

Cavazzuti, G.B. (1980) Epidemiology of different types of epilepsy in school-age children of Modena, Italy. *Epilepsia*, **21**, 57–62.

Chevrie, J.–J. and Aicardi, J. (1975) Duration and lateralisation of febrile convulsions: Relations with aetiological factors. *Epilepsia*, **16**, 781–789.

Chevrie, J.–J. and Aicardi, J. (1986) The Aicardi syndrome. In *Recent Advances in Epilepsy 3* (eds T.A. Pedley and B.S. Meldrum), pp. 189–210. Churchill Livingstone, Edinburgh.

Clarke, M., Gill, J., Noronha, M. and McKinlay, I. (1987) Early infantile epileptic encephalopathy with suppression burst: Ohtahara syndrome. *Dev. Med. Child Neurol.*, **29**, 520–528.

Cull, A. (1975) *Some Psychological Aspects of Febrile Convulsions*. MPhil thesis, University of Edinburgh.

Dalla Bernardina, B., Capovilla, G., Gattoni, M.B., Colamaria, V., Bondavalli, S. and Bureau, M. (1982) Epilepsie myoclonique grave de la première année. *Rev. EEG Neurophysiol.*, **12**, 21–25.

Dalla Bernardina, B., Chiamenti, C., Capovilla, C., Trevisan, E. and Tassinari, C.A. (1985) Benign partial epilepsy with affective symptoms. In: *Epileptic Syndromes in Infancy, Childhood and Adolescence* (eds J. Roger, C. Dravet, M. Bureau, F.E. Dreifuss and P. Wolf), pp. 171–175. John Libbey, London.

Delgado-Escueta, A.V., Greenberg, D.A., Treiman, L., Liu, A., Sparkes, R.S., Barbetti, A., Park, M.S. and Terasaki, P.I. (1989) Mapping the gene for juvenile myoclonic epilepsy. *Epilepsia*, **30** (Suppl. 4), S8–S18.

Donnenfeld, A.E., Packer, R.J., Zackai, E.H., Chee, C.M., Sellinger, B. and Emanuel, B.S. (1989) Clinical, cytogenetic and pedigree findings in 18 cases of Aicardi syndrome. *Ann. J. Med. Genet.*, **32**, 461–467.

Doose, H. (1985) Myoclonic astatic epilepsy of early childhood. In: *Epileptic Syndromes in Infancy, Childhood and Adolescence* (eds J. Roger, C. Dravet, M. Bureau, F.E. Dreifuss and P. Wolf), pp. 78–88. John Libbey, London.

Doose, H., Gerken, H., Leonhardt, R., Volzke, E. and Volz, Ch. (1970) Centren-cephalic myoclonic-astatic petit mal. *Neuropadiatrie*, **2**, 59–78.

Dravet, C., Bureau, M. and Roger, J. (1985a) Benign myoclonic epilepsy in infants. In: *Epileptic Syndromes in Infancy, Childhood and Adolescence* (eds J. Roger, C. Dravet, M. Bureau, F.E. Dreifuss and P. Wolf), pp. 51–57. John Libbey, London.

Dravet, C., Bureau, M. and Roger, J. (1985b) Severe myoclonic epilepsy in infants. In: *Epileptic Syndromes in Infancy, Childhood and Adolescence* (eds J. Roger, C. Dravet, M. Bureau, F.E. Dreifuss and P. Wolf), pp. 58–67. John Libbey, London.

Fois, A., Malandrini, F. and Mostardini, R. (1987) Clinical experiences of petit mal. *Brain Dev.*, **9**, 54–59.

Frantzen, E., Lennox-Buchthal, M.A. and Nygaard, E. (1970) A genetic study of febrile convulsions. *Neurology*, **20**, 909–917.

Gastaut, H.H. (1985) Benign epilepsy of childhood with occipital paroxysms. In *Epileptic Syndromes in Infancy, Childhood and Adolescence* (eds J. Roger, C. Dravet, M. Bureau, F.E. Dreifuss and P. Wolf), pp. 159–170. John Libbey, London.

Geschwind, N. and Galaburda, A.M. (1985) Cerebral lateralisation: Biological mechanisms, associations and pathology: I. A hypothesis and a program for research. *Arch. Neurol.*, **42**, 428–459.

Gibbs, F.A. and Gibbs, E.L. (1952) *Atlas of Encephalography, Vol. II: Epilepsy.* Addison-Wesley, Cambridge, MA.

Gibbs, F.A., Gibbs, E.L. and Fleming, M.M. (1954) Diagnosis and prognosis of hypsarrhythmia and infantile spasms. *Pediatrics*, **13**, 66–73.

Gomez, M.R. (1987) Tuberous sclerosis. In: *Neurocutaneous Diseases: A Practical Approach* (ed. M.R. Gomez), pp. 30–52. Butterworths, Boston.

Herbst, D.S. (1980) Non-specific X-linked mental retardation. 1. A review with information from 24 new families. *Am. J. Med. Genet.*, **7**, 443–460.

Herlitz, G. (1941) Studien uber die sog: Fieberkrampfe bei Kindern. *Acta Paediatr.*, **29**, Suppl. 1.

Jeavons, P.M. and Harding, G.F.A. (1975) *Photosensitive Epilepsy.* Heinemann, London.

Jellinger, K. (1987) Neuropathological aspects of infantile spasms. *Brain Dev.*, **9**, 349–357.

Kotagal, P., Rothner, A.D., Erenberg, G., Cruse, R.P. and Wyllie, E. (1987) Complex partial seizures of childhood onset. *Arch. Neurol.*, **44**, 1177–1180.

Leppert, M., Anderson, V.E., Quattlebaum, T., Stauffer, D., O'Connell, P., Nakamura, Y., Lolonel, J.–M., and White, R. (1989) Benign familial convulsions linked to genetic markers on chromosome 20. *Nature*, **337**, 647–648.

Lerman, P. (1985) Benign partial epilepsy with centro-temporal spikes. In: *Epileptic Syndromes in Infancy, Childhood and Adolescence* (eds J. Roger, C. Dravet, M. Bureau, F.E. Dreifuss and P. Wolf), pp. 150–158. John Libbey, London.

Loiseau, P. (1985) Childhood absence epilepsy. In: *Epileptic Syndromes in Infancy, Childhood and Adolescence* (eds J. Roger, C. Dravet, M. Bureau, F.E. Dreifuss and P. Wolf), pp. 106–120. John Libbey, London.

Loiseau, P. and Louiset, P. (1985) Benign partial seizures of adolescence. In: *Epileptic Syndromes in Infancy, Childhood and Adolescence* (eds J. Roger, C. Dravet, M. Bureau, F.E. Dreifuss and P. Wolf), pp. 274–277. John Libbey, London.

Loiseau, P., Duche, B., Cordova, S., Dartigues, J.F. and Cohadon, S. (1988) Prognosis of benign childhood epilepsy with centro-temporal spikes: A follow-up study of 168 patients. *Epilepsia*, **29**, 229–235.

Lombroso, C.T. (1983) A prospective study of infantile spasms: Clinical and therapeutic correlations. *Epilepsia*, **24**, 135–138.

Meencke, H.J. (1987) Neuropathology of generalised primary epilepsy. In: *Advances in Epileptology: XVIth Epilepsy International Symposium* (eds P. Wolf, M. Dam, D. Janz and F.E. Dreifuss), pp. 1–8. Raven Press, New York.

Menkes, J.H., Alter, M., Steigleder, G.K., Weakley, D.R. and Sung, J.H. (1962). A sex-linked recessive disorder with retardation of growth, peculiar hair and cerebral and cerebellar degeneration. *Pediatrics*, **29**, 764.

Nakano, S., Okuno, T. and Mikawa, H. (1989) Landau–Kleffner syndrome, EEG topographic studies. *Brain Dev.*, **11**, 43–50.

Neidich, J.A., Nussbaum, R.L., Packer, R.J., Emanuel, B.S. and Puck, J.M. (1990) Heterogeneity of clinical severity and molecular lesions in Aicardi syndrome. *J. Pediatr.*, **116**, 911–917.

Newton, R.W. and Aicardi, J. (1983) Clinical findings in children with occipital spike–wave complexes suppressed by eye-opening. *Neurology*, **33**, 1526–1529.

Niedermeyer, E. and Naidu, S. (1990) Further EEG observations in children with Rett syndrome. *Brain Dev.*, **12**, 53–54.

Ohtahara, S., Ohtsuka, Y., Yamatogi, Y. and Oka, E. (1987) The early infantile epileptic encephalopathy with suppression–burst: Developmental aspects. *Brain Dev.*, **9**, 371–376.

Oller-Daurella, L. (1985) Epilepsy with generalised convulsive seizures in childhood. In: *Epileptic Syndromes in Infancy, Childhood and Adolescence* (eds J. Roger, C. Dravet, M. Bureau, F.E. Dreifuss and P. Wolf), pp. 130–136. John Libbey, London.

Oller-Daurella, L. and Sanchez, M.E. (1981) Evolucion de las ausencias tipicas. *Rev. Neurol. (Barcelona)*, **9**, 81–102.

Ounsted, C., Lindsay, J. and Richards, P. (1987) *Temporal Lobe Epilepsy: A Biographical Study 1948–1986.* MacKeith Press, Oxford.

Panayiotopoulos, C.P. (1989) Benign childhood epilepsy with occipital paroxysms: A 15-year prospective study. *Ann. Neurol.*, **26**, 51–56.

Panayiotopoulos, C.P., Obeid, T. and Waheed, G. (1989) Differentiation of typical absence seizures in epileptic syndromes: A video EEG study of 224 seizures in 20 patients. *Brain*, **112**, 1039–1056.

Penry, J.K., Porter, R.J. and Dreifuss, F.E. (1975) Simultaneous recording of absence seizures with video tape and electroencephalography: A study of 374 seizures in 48 patients. *Brain*, **98**, 427–440.

Plouin, P. (1985) Benign neonatal convulsions (familial and non-familial). In: *Epileptic Syndromes in Infancy, Childhood and Adolescence* (eds J. Roger, C. Dravet, M. Bureau, F.E. Dreifuss and P. Wolf), pp. 2–11. John Libbey, London.

Rett, A. (1966) Uber ein eigenartiges hirnatrophisches Syndrom bei Hyperammonamie im Kindesalter. *Wien Med. Wochenschr.*, **116**, 723–726.

Robb, S.A., Harden, A. and Boyd, S.G. (1989) Rett syndrome: An EEG study in 52 girls. *Neuropediatrics*, **20**, 192–195.

Sato, S., Dreifuss, F.E., Penry, J.K., Kirby, D.D. and Palesch, Y. (1983) Long-term follow-up of absence seizures. *Neurology*, **33**, 1590–1595.

Tassinari, C.A. and Bureau, M. (1985) Epilepsy with myoclonic absences. In: *Epileptic Syndromes in Infancy, Childhood and Adolescence* (eds J. Roger, C. Dravet, M. Bureau, F.E. Dreifuss and P. Wolf), pp. 121–129. John Libbey, London.

Tassinari, C.A. and De Marco, P. (1985) Benign partial epilepsy with extreme somatosensory evoked potentials. In: *Epileptic Syndromes in Infancy, Childhood and Adolescence* (eds J. Roger, C. Dravet, M. Bureau, F.E. Dreifuss and P. Wolf), pp. 176–180. John Libbey, London.

Tassinari, C.A., Bureau, M., Dravet, C., Dalla Bernardina, B. and Roger, J. (1985) Epilepsy with continuous spikes and waves during slow sleep. In: *Epileptic Syndromes in Infancy, Childhood and Adolescence* (eds J. Roger, C. Dravet, M. Bureau, F.E. Dreifuss and P. Wolf), pp. 194–204. John Libbey, London.

Taylor, D.C. (1969) Differential rates of cerebral maturation between sexes and between hemispheres: Evidence from epilepsy. *Lancet*, **ii**, 140–142.

Taylor, D.C. and Ounsted, C. (1971) Biological mechanisms influencing the outcome of seizures in response to fever. *Epilepsia*, **12**, 33–45.

Verity, C.M., Butler, N.R. and Golding, J. (1985) Febrile convulsions in a national cohort followed-up from birth. I. Prevalence and recurrence in the first five years of life. *Br. Med. J.*, **290**, 1307–1310.

Wallace, S.J. (1982) Prognosis after prolonged unilateral febrile convulsions. In: *Advances in Epileptology, XIIIth Epilepsy International Symposium* (eds H. Akimoto, H. Kazamatsuri, M. Seino *et al.*), pp. 97–100. Raven Press, New York.

Wallace, S.J. (1988) *The Child with Febrile Seizures*. Wright, London.

Wallace, S.J. and Cull, A.M. (1979) Long-term psychological outlook for children whose first fit occurs with fever. *Dev. Med. Child Neurol.*, **21**, 28–40.

Wiesniewski, K.E., French, J.H., Fernando, S., Brown, W.T., Jenkins, E.C., Friedman, E., Hill, A.L. and Miezejeski, C.M. (1985) Fragile X syndrome: Associated neurological abnormalities and developmental disabilities. *Ann. Neurol.*, **18**, 665–669.

West, W.J. (1841) On a peculiar form of infantile convulsions. *Lancet*, **i**, 724–725.

Wolf, P. (1985) Epilepsy with grand mal on awakening. In: *Epileptic Syndromes in Infancy, Childhood and Adolescence* (eds J. Roger, C. Dravet, M. Bureau, F.E. Dreifuss and P. Wolf), pp. 259–270. John Libbey, London.

Wolf, P. and Gooses, R. (1986) Relationship of photosensitivity to epileptic syndromes. *J. Neurol. Neurosurg. Psychiatry*, **49**, 1386–1391.

Wolf, P. and Inoue, Y. (1984) Therapeutic response of absence seizures in patients of an epilepsy clinic for adolescents and adults. *J. Neurol.*, **231**, 225–229.

Wolf, S.M., Carr, A., Davis, D.C. *et al.* (1977) The value of phenobarbital in the child who has had a single febrile seizure: A controlled prospective study. *Pediatrics*, **59**, 378–385.

Discussion session 2

Professor Ross: From the national study, women with epilepsy tended to marry early but there are a lot of divorces.

Z. Kurz: Our population showed a marked increase of unmarried mothers.

Professor Ross: It was marrying and then divorcing that we were finding.

Z. Kurz: I think probably the numbers in the study are not quite big enough to compare with national rates in a rigorous way.

Dr Hockaday: Just for the record, I had a 4-year-old girl referred earlier this year with intractable seizures who was mentally retarded and she has fragile X syndrome.

Professor Ross: Yes, it can be difficult. I saw a child who I thought had fragile X recently, with all the features. The child turned out to have Klinefelter's syndrome.

Professor C.P. Panayiotopoulos: Dr Wallace, with regard to occipital paroxysms, in my opinion and in the long follow up I have with these patients, it is more common in females than in males. I think the differing results in relation to males and females in the benign epilepsies is because very few people discriminate between the child with epilepsy with centro-temporal spikes than the ones with the occipital spikes. Second is that the syndrome is not, in our opinion as strict as the authorities present it. As a matter of fact the most common clinical manifestation is of a girl, who, during sleep wakes up with vomiting and tonic deviation of the eyes. This may last for hours. This may or may not end in a generalised seizure.

Dr Wallace: I agree it's perhaps artificial to put these benign epilepsies, which we think are genetically determined, into categories as being more common in males or females. People mostly have been working with very small numbers. However, I think that most people have actually found that there have been rather more males than females in the occipital epilepsies. Your paper perhaps has more patients in it and that was one of the ones that suggested that there were more females with this condition.

Dr Verity: Professor Taylor, I am interested to hear what you have got to say about temporal lobe epilepsy and outcome in relation to early febrile seizures. In the child health and education study there are only a couple of children out of about 14000 followed for ten years who had prolonged focal seizures in infancy, and who then went on to develop partial seizure disorders.

Professor Taylor: Yes, I think we need to remember that these biologically important messages were delivered a generation ago, at a time when incidence was different and handling was different. Today, the speed at which febrile seizures can be arrested is very much different and the general health of the population is very much better.

Dr Verity: If I could just come back on that to endorse it. Both of the children that had these prolonged seizures, and we were talking about seizures probably over an hour, for them it was the first seizure that they had. So, in terms of the debate about whether prophylactic drugs would have prevented prolonged seizures and prevented later temporal lobe attacks, they would not have been very useful. The children actually presented with their prolonged seizures, they did not have one short one and then go on and have a prolonged one.

Dr Warr: What proportion of children with epilepsy can be allocated to the defined epileptic syndromes that Dr Wallace discussed?

Dr Wallace: This is a problem that several people have been addressing and a lot of paediatricians and paediatric neurologists say that it is just too difficult to use this classification of syndromes. I do not think that is really so. I think that probably one can fit at least 60 or 70% of children into one of these categories fairly easily.

Dr Pellock: In our twin study of febrile seizures we noticed that it is the female twin with febrile fits who transfers it much more commonly to her offspring than the male.

Dr Wallace: Yes, one should not ignore the possibility that there is a maternally inherited factor which is very important in the genetic epilepsies.

Section III

8

Anticonvulsant drugs, hormones and seizure threshold

PHILIP N. PATSALOS
University Department of Clinical Neurology, Institute of Neurology, London, UK

INTRODUCTION

The interrelationship between anticonvulsant drugs, hormones and seizures is very complex. To facilitate an understanding of the many interactions the following will be discussed:

1. The hypothalamic–pituitary–gonadal axis.
2. Sexual function in epileptic patients.
3. Hormones and seizure threshold.
4. Anticonvulsant drug effects.

THE HYPOTHALAMIC–PITUITARY–GONADAL AXIS

Figure 1 shows schematically the hypothalamic–pituitary–gonadal axis and the feedback loops that control the synthesis and circulating blood concentrations of steroid sex hormones. Although hypothalamic function is affected by several mechanisms, including neuronal input from other brain areas, the direct feedback loop is perhaps the most important. The loop works as follows: gonadotropin-releasing hormone (GNRH) is released from the preoptic and mesial basal nuclei (located in the mesial basal hypothalamus) in response to low circulating sex hormones (oestrogen, progesterone and testosterone). The GNRH moves along the nerve fibre to the median eminence at the base of the hypothalamus. Via the hypothalamic–pituitary portal system, GNRH travels to the anterior pituitary and promotes the production and secretion of follicle-stimulating hormone (FSH) and luteinizing hormone (LH).

Women and Epilepsy. Edited by M.R. Trimble
© 1991 John Wiley & Sons Ltd

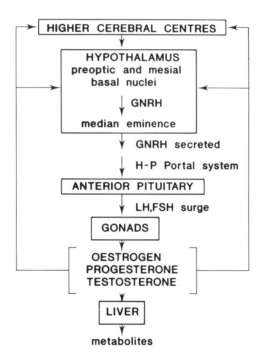

Figure 1.   The hypothalamic–pituitary–gonadal axis

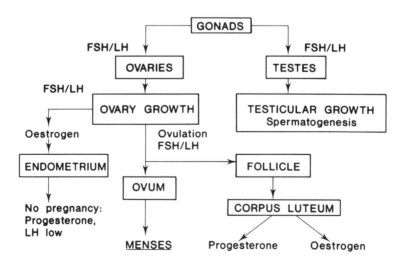

Figure 2.   Interrelationship of gonadal hormones

Figure 2 shows the interrelationship between the gonadal hormones. In men FSH and LH stimulate testicular growth and spermatogenesis. The feedback loop is fairly simple, with low testosterone increasing GNRH production and subsequent release of LH. LH acts on Leydig cells of the testes to increase testosterone production. In women, a surge in release of LH and FSH from the pituitary precipitates ovulation. The follicle develops into the corpus luteum, which in turn produces progesterone and oestrogen. Progesterone inhibits GNRH and consequently LH. In the absence of pregnancy and low LH, atresia of the corpus luteum occurs and the resulting fall in oestrogen and progesterone cause loss of endometrium and thus menses occurs. In normal circumstances this feedback regulatory system works efficiently and effectively. The metabolic precision of this cycle suggests that nature anticipated procreative success as the norm for every egg. Sex steroid hormones are inactivated primarily in the liver.

SEXUAL FUNCTION IN EPILEPTIC PATIENTS

Many studies have been undertaken to investigate the sexual function of patients with epilepsy (Toone, 1986; Ndegwa et al., 1986; Fenwick et al. 1985; Brodie, 1989) and all have reported a reduction in sexual interest, awareness and activity. Hyposexuality is particularly evident in patients with temporal lobe seizures. Although only a few studies have involved women, hyposexuality in this population also seems likely. Prevalence data on sexual impairment in the epileptic population are scarce; in one institution, 44% of male patients claimed never to have had an orgasm and an additional 20% having not had one in the last year (Fenwick et al., 1985).

Several explanations for the hyposexuality have been proposed:

1. Compromised psychological and social development; particularly evident in patients with early onset (before puberty) epilepsy (Webber et al., 1986).
2. Anticonvulsant drug-induced changes in testosterone levels; female sexual drive is thought to correlate highly with free testosterone levels in mid-cycle and anticonvulsant drugs have been observed to reduce free testosterone levels (Backstrom and Sodergard, 1977). Male sexual drive also relates to free testosterone levels (Brodie, 1989; Isojarvi et al., 1990).
3. Limbic structure disturbances in temporal lobes; disease or seizures which commonly arise from the hippocampus and other limbic structures might well affect hypothalamic function. This would occur through the stria terminalis, fornix and median forebrain bundle, which interconnect extensively with the limbic system and the hypothalamus. This has been noted experimentally in limbic stimulation studies (Trimble et al., 1984; Ellendorff et al., 1973).

4. Seizure-induced transient surges of pituitary hormones; tonic–clonic and partial seizures have been associated with marked changes in pituitary output (Trimble, 1978; Sperling *et al.*, 1986; Herzog *et al.*, 1986). A consistent observation is a marked rise in prolactin within the first 20 minutes post-ictally. FSH and LH may also rise. Although prolactin can inhibit GNRH and cause anovulatory cycles, constant modest rises in prolactin are considered more effective in inhibiting ovulation.

HORMONES AND SEIZURE THRESHOLD

Sex hormones

That cyclic changes in seizure frequency were possibly related to specific times in the menstrual cycle was first suggested by Locock (1857). In a series of 50 patients, Laidlaw (1956) observed a reduction in seizure frequency during the luteal phase and an increase peri-menstrually. He concluded that the cyclical pattern, as in catamenial epilepsy, was the effect of hormones and that progesterone had an anticonvulsant effect. A rapid fall in progesterone levels as occurs at or immediately prior to menses was considered to facilitate seizures (Laidlaw, 1956). Subsequently, Logothetis *et al.* (1959) gave conjugated oestrogens intravenously to 16 epileptic women with catamenial epilepsy and observed an electroencephalographic exacerbation of paroxysmal abnormalities in 11 of the women, four of which had clinical seizures. Backstrom (1976) investigated seizure frequency, oestrogen and progesterone levels during nine menstrual cycles in seven women with partial epilepsy. He demonstrated that seizure frequency was lowest during the luteal phase (when progesterone levels are high) and highest in the follicular phase (when oestrogen levels are high). However, the oestrogen/progesterone ratio was considered a better index of seizure susceptibility (Backstrom, 1976; Rosciszewska *et al.*, 1986).

Today manoeuvres to lower the oestrogen/progesterone ratio form the basis of the hormonal treatment of seizures. Groff (1962) gave norethynodrel to a patient with catamenial seizure exacerbation to suppress menses, and the seizures stopped. Hall (1977) successfully treated a woman who suffered from catamenial generalized tonic–clonic seizures with an oral contraceptive, norethisterone, containing a synthetic progestin. Another successful case was reported by Zimmerman *et al.* (1973) using oral methoxyprogesterone acetate. Two larger series support the above case reports; however, not all patients respond favourably to this treatment approach. Mattson *et al.* (1984) studied 14 women prescribed 20–40 mg methoxyprogesterone acetate per day for 3–24 months (mean 12 months). Of 11 who developed amenorrhea, seven had an average of 52% fewer seizures. Herzog *et al.* (1986) in their series of eight women evaluated the use of progesterone suppositories given either pre-menstrually or during the luteal phase. Overall, monthly seizure frequency dropped by 68% during three months of treatment in six patients.

The mechanism of action of sex hormones on seizure threshold is unknown. In experimental models and in man, both oestrogen and progesterone exhibit a rapid onset of action, suggesting a direct effect on neuronal membranes (Pfaff and McEwen, 1983). Other possible indirect mechanisms include changes in water retention (Ansell and Clarke, 1956) and alteration of anti-convulsant drug pharmacokinetics (Rosciszewska et al., 1986).

During pregnancy a modest increase in seizure frequency may occur. However, a hormonal effect is not considered to be the cause since, although oestrogen levels rise, a concomitant increase in progesterone also occurs and therefore the oestrogen/progesterone ratio remains constant. Possible mechanisms include changes in anticonvulsant drug pharmacokinetics (e.g. clearance, volume of distribution and plasma protein binding), non-compliance and sleep deprivation (Schmidt et al. 1984; Philbert et al., 1984). Some of these issues are discussed further in Chapter 9. Eclamptic seizures in non-epileptic pregnant women in part may be related to abnormal progesterone metabolism.

Oral contraceptives

Early animal studies indicated that oestrogen administration lowered seizure threshold and elicited epileptiform spikes in the electroencephalogram when topically applied to the brain (Logothetis et al., 1959; Wooley and Timiras, 1962). Further, intravenous administration of conjugated oestrogens to women with epilepsy was observed to increase epileptiform activity (Logothetis and Harner, 1960). Thus, when oral contraceptives were first introduced for clinical use they were contraindicated for use by women with epilepsy.

These early studies have now been refuted and it is generally considered that oral contraceptives are not epileptogenic in women. A number of placebo-controlled trials of oral contraceptives in epileptic women confirm that the use of pills containing oestrogen and progesterone do not cause a worsening of their epilepsy if seizures are already well controlled (Espir et al., 1969; Dana-Haeri and Richens, 1983).

ANTICONVULSANT DRUG EFFECTS

Epilepsy was believed by some to be related to excessive sexuality, and the introduction of bromides in the treatment of epilepsy was based on the observation that bromide salts produced impotence (Locock, 1857). Indeed, in Victorian times, surgical castration was not unusual for women and men as a 'treatment' for epilepsy. More recently, there was a vogue for hysterectomies and some women still request this 'treatment'.

Very little information is available concerning the direct effects of anticonvulsant drugs on the function of the hypothalamus and other brain areas that influence sexual behaviour. However, secondary effects on the hypothalamic–pituitary–gonadal axis, consequent to anticonvulsant drugs changing the metabolism of hormones and alternating circulating blood levels, are well documented.

Indirect effects

Hormone metabolism

Due to the lack of substrate specificity of the hepatic microsomal mixed function oxidases, drug interactions at the metabolic level are frequent (Patsalos and Lascelles, 1983; Pitlick, 1989). Four of the six commonly prescribed anticonvulsant drugs (carbamazepine, phenobarbitone, phenytoin and primidone) are among the most powerful of known inducers of hepatic microsomal enzymes and consequently the association between anticonvulsant drugs and hormones may be the result of interactions at these common metabolic pathways (Richens, 1984).

Kenyon (1972) was the first to report on an unplanned pregnancy in a woman with epilepsy. It was postulated that the pregnancy was the result of low hormone levels due to enzyme induction by anticonvulsant drugs. The same mechanism was suspected in three further cases of contraceptive failure (Janz and Schmidt, 1974). Oral contraceptive failure with accompanying breakthrough bleeding and an increased risk of pregnancy is now widely documented (Coulam and Annegers, 1979; Back et al., 1988).

The data from the Committee on Safety of Medicine show that during 1973–1984 a total of 43 cases of contraceptive failure were reported (Back et al., 1988). Phenytoin accounted for 25 of those cases, phenobarbitone for 20 and carbamazepine, primidone, ethosuximide and sodium valproate for 6, 7, 4 and 1, respectively. The difference among drugs may simply be a reflection of the frequency of use and the fact that ethosuximide and sodium valproate have minimal, if any, enzyme-inducing effects (Orme et al., 1989; Chapter 9). An additional consideration is that ethosuximide and sodium valproate were invariably part of polytherapy regimes (Back et al., 1988).

Insufficient synthetic steroid (oestrogen and progesterone levels) to block ovulation is considered the most common cause of contraceptive failure (Mattson et al., 1985). The most likely explanation for the lower levels is increased metabolism of the synthetic steroids as a consequence of hepatic microsomal enzyme induction by anticonvulsant drugs. The lower synthetic hormone levels may disinhibit the hypothalamus, resulting in GNRH release and the cascade of events leading to ovulation (Figures 1 and 2). This concept is further supported by the findings of Dana-Haeri and Richens (1983), who observed that patients receiving multiple anticonvulsant drug therapy had higher LH levels than patients on single drug therapy, suggesting dose-related induction. The LH release was due to low hormone levels.

Synthesis of sex hormone-binding globulin (SHBG)

An additional mechanism of action may be by an effect on SHBG, which is involved in the binding of sex steroids (including some synthetic steroids) in plasma. Detailed studies by Sodergard et al. (1982) indicate that only 2% of sex steroids circulate in the free, pharmacologically active form and therefore are available for hypothalamic monitoring in the feedback loop. Phenytoin, carbamazepine and phenobarbitone have been shown to increase the concentration of SHBG (Back et al., 1980; Isojarvi et al., 1990) and consequently decrease the pharmacologically active free fraction of circulating hormones, contributing to failure to block ovulation.

The reduction in plasma levels of oestrogens by anticonvulsant drugs, leading to breakthrough bleeding and contraceptive failure, is, however, rather unpredictable. There is a large inter-individual variability in anticonvulsant effects and therefore it is difficult to select with confidence the dose of oral contraceptive needed to compensate for the 'anticipated effect'. This difficulty may be remedied in the future by monitoring hormone plasma concentrations.

Direct effects

In animals, phenytoin has been demonstrated to block ovulation (Quinn, 1965). However, in man the evidence for a direct effect of anticonvulsant drugs on the hypothalamic–pituitary–gonadal axis is circumstantial. For example, decreased libido and potency are more commonly associated with phenobarbitone and primidone treatment than with carbamazepine or phenytoin, even though all four drugs are potent hepatic enzyme inducers (Mattson et al., 1985). Switching drugs or discontinuation of treatment often but not always corrects the problem (Dana-Haeri et al., 1984). The possibility therefore remains that anticonvulsant drugs directly depress the axis and prevent total reversal of the abnormality.

CONCLUSION

Our understanding of the human reproductive/endocrine system has increased significantly during the past two decades. However, the interrelationship between anticonvulsant drugs, sex hormones and seizure suppression/exacerbation is complex and far from clear; in some patients, progesterone may provide effective seizure control. Women with catamenial epilepsy as a patient group, if studied more extensively with frequent measurements of gonadotropins, hormones and anticonvulsant drug concentrations, may very well provide more information on the interrelationship.

The mechanism by which anticonvulsant drugs affect hormones can be attributed principally to their potent hepatic enzyme induction characteristics. The primary effects are a faster metabolism of hormones and an increased synthesis of SHBG. The secondary effects are the lowering of free (pharmacologically active) hormone concentrations which in turn increase gonadotropin concentrations. Circumstantial evidence suggests that anticonvulsant drugs may also directly affect the hypothalamic–pituitary–gonadal-axis.

ACKNOWLEDGEMENT

My thanks to Miss Carolyn Cowey for her excellent secretarial assistance.

REFERENCES

Ansell, B. and Clarke, E. (1956) Epilepsy and menstruation: The role of water retention. *Lancet*, **ii**, 1232–1235.

Back, D.J., Breckenridge, A.M., Crawford, F.E., MacIver, M., Orme, M.L.E., Perucca, E., Richens, A., Rowe, P.H. and Smith, E. (1980) The effect of oral contraceptive steroids and enzymic inducing drugs on sex hormone binding globulin capacity in women. *Br. J. Clin. Pharmacol.*, **9**, 115.

Back, D.J., Grimmer, S.F.M., Orme, M.L.E., Proudlove, C., Mann, R.D. and Breckenridge, A.M. (1988) Evaluation of Committee on Safety of Medicines Yellow Card reports on oral contraceptive-drug interactions with anticonvulsants and antibiotics. *Br. J. Clin. Pharmacol.*, **25**, 527–532.

Backstrom, T. (1976) Epileptic seizures in women related to plasma estrogen and progesterone during the menstrual cycle. *Acta Neurol. Scand.*, **54**, 321–347.

Backstrom, T. and Sodergard, R. (1977) The influence of antiepileptic drugs on steroid plasma levels and binding during the menstrual cycle. *Acta Endocrinol.*, **212** (Suppl. 85), 42.

Brodie, M.J. (1989) Anticonvulsants and sexual function. In: *Fourth International Symposium on Sodium Valproate and Epilepsy* (ed. D. Chadwick), pp. 228–235. Royal Society of Medicine Series, London.

Coulam, C.B. and Annegers, J.F. (1979) Do anticonvulsants reduce the efficacy of oral contraceptives? *Epilepsia*, **20**, 519–525.

Dana-Haeri, J. and Richens, A. (1983) Effects of norethesterone on seizures associated with menstruation. *Epilepsia*, **24**, 377–381.

Dana-Haeri, J., Oxley, J. and Richens, A. (1984) Pituitary responsiveness to gonadotropin-releasing and thyrotrophin-releasing hormones in epileptic patients receiving carbamazepine or phenytoin. *Clin. Endocrinol.*, **20**, 163–168.

Ellendorff, F., Colombo, J.A., Blake, C.A., Whitmoyer, D.I. and Sawer, C.H. (1973) Effect of electrical stimulation of the amygdala on gonadotropin release and ovulation in the rat. *Proc. Soc. Exp. Biol. Med.*, **142**, 417–420.

Espir, M., Walker, M.E. and Lawson, J.B. (1969) Epilepsy and oral contraception. *Br. Med. J.*, **1**, 294–295.

Fenwick, P.B.C., Toone, B.K., Wheeler, M.J., Nanjee, M.N., Grant, R. and Brown, D. (1985) Sexual behaviour in a centre for epilepsy. *Acta Neurol. Scand.*, **7**, 428–435.

Groff, D.N. (1962) Suggestion for control of epilepsy. *NY State J. Med.*, **63**, 3017.

Hall, S.M. (1977) Treatment of menstrual epilepsy with progesterone-only oral contraceptive. *Epilepsia*, **18**, 235–236.

Herzog, A.G., Seibel, M.M., Schomer, D.L., Vaitukaitis, J.L. and Geschwind, N. (1986) Reproductive disorders in women with partial seizures of temporal lobe origin. *Arch. Neurol.*, **43**, 341–346.

Isojarvi, J.I.T., Parkarinen, A.J., Ylipalosaari, P.J. and Myllyla, V.V. (1990) Serum hormones in male epileptic patients receiving anticonvulsant medications. *Arch. Neurol.*, **47**, 670–676.

Janz, D. and Schmidt, D. (1974) Antiepileptic drugs and failure of oral contraceptives. *Lancet*, **i**, 1113.

Kenyon, I.E. (1972) Unplanned pregnancy in an epileptic. *Br. Med. J.*, **1**, 686–687.

Laidlaw, J. (1956) Catamenial epilepsy. *Lancet*, **ii**, 1235–1237.

Locock, C. (1857) Discussion of paper by E.H. Sieveking: Analysis of 52 cases of epilepsy observed by the author. *Lancet*, **i**, 528.

Logothetis, J. and Harner, R. (1960) Electrocortical activation by estrogens. *Arch. Neurol.*, **3**, 290–297.

Logothetis, J., Harner, R., Morrell, F. and Torres, F. (1959) The role of estrogens in catamenial exacerbation of epilepsy. *Neurology*, **9**, 352–360.

Mattson, R.H., Cramer, J.A., Caldwell, B.V. and Siconolfi, B.C. (1984) Treatment of seizures with methoxyprogesterone acetate: Preliminary report. *Neurology*, **34**, 1255–1258.

Mattson, R.H., Cramer, J.A., Darney, P.D. and Naftolin, F. (1985) Use of oral contraceptives by women with epilepsy. *JAMA*, **256**, 238–240.

Ndegwa, D., Rust, J., Golombok, S. and Fenwick, P. (1986) Sexual problems in epileptic women. *Sex Marit. Ther.*, **1**, 175–177.

Orme, M., Back, D.J., Crawford, P., Bowden, A., Cleland, P., Chadwick, D.J., Tjia, J. and Martin. C. (1989) Oral contraceptive steroid therapy in patients taking anticonvulsant drugs. In: *Fourth International Symposium on Sodium Valproate and Epilepsy* (ed. D. Chadwick), pp. 236–240. Royal Society of Medicine Series, London.

Patsalos, P.N. and Lascelles, P.T. (1983) Biochemical pharmacology of anticonvulsant drug interaction. In: *Research Progress in Epilepsy* (ed. F. Clifford Rose), pp. 445–461. Pitman Press, London.

Pfaff, D.W. and McEwen, B.S. (1983) Actions of estrogens and progestins on nerve cells. *Science*, **219**, 808–814.

Philbert, A., Anderson, J., Rasmussen, S.N., Flachs, H. and Dam, M. (1984) Disposition of phenytoin during pregnancy: A pharmacokinetic study. In: *Advances in Epileptology: XVth Epilepsy International Symposium* (eds R.J. Porter, A.A. Ward, R.H. Mattson and M. Dam), pp. 251–258. Raven Press, New York.

Pitlick, W.H. (1989) *Antiepileptic Drug Interactions*. Demos Publications, New York.

Quinn, D.L. (1965) Influence of diphenylhydantoin on spontaneous release of ovulating hormone in the adult rat. *Proc. Soc. Exp. Biol. Med.*, **119**, 982–985.

Richens, A. (1984) Enzyme induction and sex hormones. In: *Advances in Epileptology: XVth Epilepsy International Symposium* (eds R.J. Porter, A.A. Ward, R.H. Mattson and M. Dam), pp. 215–219. Raven Press, New York.

Rosciszewska, D., Buntner, B., Guz, I. and Zawisza, L. (1986) Ovarian hormones, anticonvulsant drugs, and seizures during the menstrual cycle in women with epilepsy. *J. Neurol. Neurosurg. Psychiatry*, **49**, 47–51.

Schmidt, D., Canger, R., Carnaggia, C., Avanzini, G., Battino, D., Cusi, C., Beck-Mannegetta, G., Koch, S., Rating, D. and Janz, D. (1984) Seizure frequency during pregnancy and puerperium: The role of noncompliance and sleep deprivation. In: *Advances in Epileptology: XVth Epilepsy International Symposium* (eds R.J. Porter, A.A. Ward, R.H. Mattson and M. Dam), pp. 221–225. Raven Press, New York.

Sodergard, R., Backstrom, T., Shanbhag, V. and Carstensen, H. (1982) Calculation of free and bound fractions of testosterone and estradial-17β to human plasma proteins at body temperature. *J. Steriod Biochem.*, **16**, 801–810.

Sperling, M.R., Pritchard, P.B., Engel, J., Daniel, C. and Sagal, J. (1986) Prolactin in partial epilepsy: An indicator of limbic seizures. *Ann. Neurol.*, **20**, 716–722.

Toone, B.K. (1986) Sexual disorders in epilepsy. In: *Recent Advances in Epilepsy 3* (eds T.A. Pedley and B.S. Meldrum), pp. 233–260. Churchill Livingstone, Edinburgh.

Trimble, M.R. (1978) Serum prolactin in epilepsy and hysteria. *Br. Med. J.*, **2**, 1982.

Trimble, M.R., Dana-Haeri, J., Oxley, J. and Baylis, P.H. (1984) Some neuroendocrine consequences of seizures. In: *Advances in Epileptology: XVth Epilepsy International Symposium* (eds R.J. Porter, A.A. Ward, R.H. Mattson and M. Dam), pp. 201–208. Raven Press, New York.

Webber, M.P., Hauser, W.A., Ottman, R. and Annegers, J.F. (1986) Fertility in persons with epilepsy: 1935–1974. *Epilepsia*, **27**, 746–752.

Wooley, D.E. and Timiras, P.S. (1962) The gonad–brain relationship: Effects of female sex hormones on electroshock convulsion in the rat. *Endocrinology*, **70**, 196–209.

Zimmerman, A.W., Holden, K.R., Reiter, E.O. and Dekaban, A.S. (1973) Metroxyprogesterone acetate in the treatment of seizures associated with menstruation. *J. Pediatr.*, **83**, 961–963.

9

Contraception, epilepsy and pharmacokinetics

M. ORME, P. CRAWFORD AND D. BACK
New Medical School and Walton Hospital, Liverpool, UK

INTRODUCTION

Anticonvulsant drugs such as phenobarbitone and diphenylhydantoin have been in regular clinical use for more than 50 years. In contrast, the development of oral contraceptive steroid (OCS) preparations has been a much more recent activity. It is now 25 years since OCS were first used clinically on a regular basis, and we have learnt a lot. However, it is only in the last ten years that we have understood much about their kinetics. In the early years of contraceptive use, the dose of drugs was excessive and, because of the development of thrombotic complications directly related to the dose of ethinyloestradiol (EE_2), the dose of that oestrogen was reduced from 100 µg/day to 50µg/day. This resulted in a reduction in the incidence of deep vein thrombosis and pulmonary embolism (Royal College of General Practitioners Oral Contraceptive Study, 1977). Since that dose reduction was made, the daily dose has been further reduced to 30–35 µg EE_2. Although some women have adequate contraception with daily doses as low as 20 µg EE_2, on average 30–35 µg EE_2/day is the optimum. This dose is coupled with an effective progestogen, often in a triphasic preparation which mimics the normal cyclical pattern of hormone production in women.

Patients with epilepsy have, as far as is known, normal fertility and therefore are in as much need of adequate contraceptive as their healthy counterparts. However, it was discovered in the early days of reduced (i.e. 50 µg) dose administration with EE_2 that breakthrough bleeding occurred more frequently in women taking anticonvulsant drugs. Breakthrough bleeding is bleeding occurring in the middle of the cycle of contraceptive use and is usually due to relative oestrogen lack. It is usually taken as a sign of incipient failure of contraception. This was first described by Kenyon (1972) but further

Women and Epilepsy. Edited by M.R. Trimble

cases of breakthrough bleeding or contraceptive failure were described by Hempel *et al.* (1973), and other case reports followed (Janz and Schmidt, 1974, 1975; Gagnaire *et al.*, 1975; Belaisch *et al.*, 1976). Coulam and Annegers (1979) reviewed the literature at that time and provided four new cases of contraceptive failure with anticonvulsant drugs. The drugs implicated included phenobarbitone, methylphenobarbitone, phenytoin, primidone, carbamazepine and ethosuximide. Further cases have been reported by Diamond *et al.* (1985). Phenytoin appears to be the anticonvulsant most commonly implicated in causing contraceptive failure in women taking long-term OCS. This is borne out by recent data from the Committee on Safety of Medicines (CSM). Back *et al.* (1988) showed that a total of 43 cases of contraceptive failure had been reported to the CSM on yellow cards over the years 1973–1984 in women taking anticonvulsants with their OCS therapy. Phenytoin and phenobarbitone accounted for most of the cases. It should be borne in mind that the yellow card system is considerably under-used and Lumley *et al.* (1986) suggested that less than 10% of adverse reactions to drugs are reported to the CSM.

The anticonvulsant drugs phenytoin, phenobarbitone, primidone and carbamazepine are known to be potent inducers of the hepatic microsomal drug-metabolizing enzymes in man (Park and Breckenridge, 1981). In animal studies, a much wider range of compounds are known to induce these enzymes (Conney, 1967) and many studies have been done in animals to clarify the situation in man. However, because of the more limited list of enzyme-inducing agents in man, it is often difficult to extrapolate directly from animals to man. Nevertheless, Back *et al.* (1980a) have shown that phenobarbitone pre-treatment of rats and rabbits led to a significant reduction in the amount of norethisterone in the circulation after an oral dose of norethisterone.

In addition to the process of enzyme induction, the other mechanism that may contribute to the interaction of anticonvulsants and oral contraceptive steroids relates to high-affinity binding of the progestogens norethisterone and levonorgestrel to sex hormone-binding globulin (SHBG). Oestrogens do not bind to SHBG but will induce formation of more SHBG. Drugs like phenobarbitone will increase the capacity of SHBG to bind progestogens (Backström and Sodergaard, 1977; Victor *et al.*, 1976). This rise in SHBG will have the effect of reducing the free concentration of drug in the plasma.

CONTRACEPTION

As noted earlier, the OCS have undergone considerable changes since their first introduction. There is little doubt that combined OCS are the most effective form of contraception available. Efficacy is measured as the Pearl Index, which is the number of pregnancies per 100 women years of use. The figure for the efficacy of the modern low-dose preparations is about 0.5–0.3

pregnancies per 100 women years. In contrast, a standard barrier method (e.g. condom + spermicide) would give a figure of about 3 pregnancies per 100 women years. The combined OCS work by a feedback suppression on the pituitary gland to inhibit the secretion of follicle-stimulating hormone (FSH) and luteinizing hormone (LH). As a result of this inhibition the ovarian follicle does not develop, no egg is released and no corpus luteum is produced. Table 1 shows those steroids that are in common use as contraceptive agents. EE_2 is the main oestrogen present in virtually all preparations. Mestranol is still used occasionally and is essentially a pro-drug for EE_2, being metabolized by demethylation in the liver to produce EE_2.

There is a greater variety of progestogens (see Table 1) although this is not an exhaustive list. Both levonorgestrel and norethisterone have been in use for many years. While they are both very effective, they both have some androgenic effects (particularly levonorgestrel) and this may cause greasy skin, acne and hirsutism. In addition, the androgenic effects may lead to a fall in high-density lipoprotein (HDL) and a rise in low-density lipoprotein (LDL). Since these lipid changes are known to encourage the development of atheroma, concern has been expressed about the use of these drugs although there is little or no evidence that they cause atheroma in women. Ethynodiol diacetate and lynoestrenol are essentially pro-drugs for norethisterone. Desogestrel and gestodene are newer progestogens that are not androgenic and have no net effects on lipid patterns in women. If anything, HDL levels are increased by these two progestogens. Desogestrel is not active per se and needs to be metabolized in the liver to its active metabolite 3-keto-desogestrel in order to have a therapeutic effect.

Progestogens can be used on their own as contraceptive agents, but at least in younger women (under age 30) they are less effective than the combined OCS. They are known colloquially as the 'mini pill' and although ovulation is suppressed in some women they work by keeping the cervical mucus thick and hostile to spermatozoa and by preventing nidation of a fertilized ovum. The mini pill needs to be taken very regularly and is at maximum efficacy when taken about 4 hours prior to sexual intercourse, so compliance with therapy is very important. Women taking the mini pill often complain of

Table 1.   Steroids in common use as contraceptives

Oestrogens	Progestogens
Ethinyloestradiol	Levonorgestrel
Mestranol	Norethisterone
	Ethynodiol diacetate
	Lynoestrenol
	Desogestrel
	Gestodene

continuous spotting of blood per vaginum and this needs to be considered when using this form of contraception. In this chapter we will be dealing primarily with the combined OCS although it is assumed that factors affecting the progestogens when taken with oestrogens (as in the combined OCS) will also affect progestogens when taken on their own.

PHARMACOKINETICS

The term pharmacokinetics describes in essence what the body does to a drug and includes the processes of absorption, distribution, metabolism and excretion of the drug. This is in contrast to the term pharmacodynamics which describes the effects the drug has on the body. This is not the place to go into any great detail concerning pharmacokinetics but it may be helpful to explain a few terms. If we consider a drug taken by mouth (e.g. a standard OCS preparation), once the tablet has broken up in the stomach, and is in solution in the contents of the gastrointestinal tract, it is absorbed across the wall of the jejunum and ileum and enters the hepatic portal venous system. The drug then has to pass through the liver to reach the systemic circulation. During this phase all of the drug has to pass along this route and may be exposed to 'pre-systemic metabolism', also known as first-pass metabolism.

The progestogens are all well absorbed and pass virtually unchanged into the systemic circulation (Back et $al.$, 1978) (desogestrel apart, which as we have noted is converted almost quantitatively in the liver into its active metabolite). In contrast, EE_2 is extensively metabolized in the first pass such that on average only about 40% of EE_2 passes unchanged into the systemic circulation (Back et $al.$, 1979). In the case of EE_2 most of this pre-systemic metabolism occurs in the gut wall, where the drug is conjugated with sulphate (Back et $al.$, 1982). Figure 1 shows the plasma concentration versus time curve for both norethisterone as a typical progestogen and for EE_2. The concentrations of both drugs are measured specifically and sensitively by radioimmunoassays and are plotted on a logarithmic scale. The units in the case of norethisterone are nanograms per millilitre while for EE_2 the units are picograms per millilitre. A picogram is a million millionth part of a gram (or alternatively a millionth part of a microgram). The difference in units is partly accounted for by the difference in dose size: the standard dose of norethisterone is 1 mg while that for EE_2 is about 30–35 µg. Figure 1 shows the plasma concentration profiles for each drug after both oral and i.v. administration. While the two curves are very similar for norethisterone, the difference between the i.v. and oral curves for EE_2 shows the degree of first-pass metabolism. Examination of Figure 1 also shows a rapid absorption of the drug into plasma followed by a two-phase decay. This is more obvious for norethisterone than for EE_2. The initial phase of decay is due to distribution of the drug into tissues, while the second phase is due to elimination of the drug from the body.

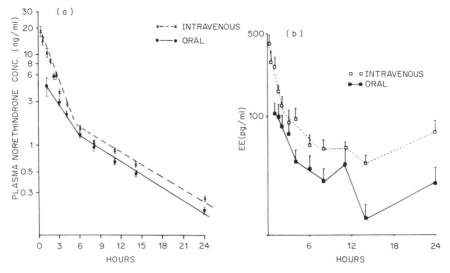

Figure 1. (a) Plasma concentrations of norethisterone (norethindrone) after an oral dose of 1 mg norethisterone acetate (● — ●) and after an identical intravenous dose (×- - -×) in six women. (Reproduced from Back *et al.*, 1978, by permission of the editor of *Clinical Pharmacology and Therapeutics*.) (b) Plasma concentrations of ethinyloestradiol after an oral dose of 30 μg (■ — ■) and after an identical intravenous dose (□ — □) in six women. Mean ± SD. (Reproduced from Back *et al.*, 1979, by permission of the editor of *Contraception*.)

The amount of drug absorbed into the systemic circulation is usually measured by the area under the plasma concentration versus time curve (AUC) and this is calculated by the trapezoidal rule. The AUC is calculated from the time of administration of the drug ($t = 0$) to the time of the last data point, usually 24 hours with contraceptive steroids. The terminal phase of the log–linear decay of the plasma concentration versus time curve is usually used to calculate the half-life of the drug ($t_{1/2}$). The half-life of any drug in plasma is given by the time it takes for the plasma concentration to fall by 50%. A look at Figure 1 shows that both norethisterone and EE_2 have relatively rapid decay rates in plasma, with half-lives of 5–15 hours. It is clear from Figure 1 that there is a considerable inter-individual variation in the plasma concentration of contraceptive steroids, and this is particularly true for EE_2. During long-term therapy, the plasma concentration of EE_2 10–12 hours after dosing varies between 10 and 160 pg/ml (Orme *et al.*, 1983). The reason for choosing 10–12 hours as the sampling point is seen in Figure 1, since plasma concentrations of EE_2 may rise at 24 hours, compared to 10–12 hours due to an enterohepatic circulation of EE_2. However, it is not felt that the enterohepatic recirculation of EE_2 contributes very much to overall blood levels of the drug.

The contraceptive steroids are bound in plasma to albumin, and as we have seen the progestogens bind to SHBG. On average at least 95% of the drug in plasma is bound to albumin. Since the free (unbound) concentrations are those that diffuse into tissues and are responsible for the therapeutic effects of the drugs, it can be seen that these levels are very low indeed. It is not possible to measure the free plasma concentrations of EE_2 with current methodology—the expected levels would be 50–1000 fg/ml (1 femtogram = 10^{-15}g).

EFFECT OF ANTICONVULSANTS ON PHARMACOKINETICS OF ORAL CONTRACEPTIVE STEROIDS

Studies with phenobarbitone

The anecdotal evidence described earlier gives fairly strong grounds for supposing that many anticonvulsant drugs reduce the efficacy of OCS. It has been said therefore that women taking long-term anticonvulsants should use alternative methods of contraception and should not rely on OCS. This is a major step to take and for many women the alternative barrier methods are not acceptable on social grounds. We need therefore to look more closely at the interaction between anticonvulsants and oral contraceptive steroids to see how we can take action to minimize the problem. Initial investigations were aimed at measuring blood levels of EE_2 in women taking long-term anticonvulsant therapy. In a group of five women aged 23–34 living in a long-term epileptic centre, blood levels were measured 10–12 hours after taking their regular OCS preparation, which contained 50 µg EE_2 and 250 µg levonorgestrel. All five women were taking at least two anticonvulsants, including carbamazepine, phenytoin or primidone. The plasma concentration of EE_2 was 11.1 ± 4.5 pg/ml, while the plasma levonorgestrel concentration was 0.83 ± 0.19 ng/ml (mean ± SD). For each steroid the blood levels are very much at the lower end of the normal range, particularly considering the relatively large daily dose of steroids used. It is, however, difficult to say much more about those plasma concentrations because of a lack of controls.

The studies therefore went on to examine four women (aged 18–25) over a three-month period of contraceptive use (Back et al., 1980b). Each woman initially presented with at least one episode of tonic–clonic seizures, and a decision to treat them with phenobarbitone 30 mg b.d. was taken. All four women were on long-term OCS therapy with a preparation containing 50 µg EE_2. Three women took Minovlar also containing 1 mg norethisterone acetate and one woman took Ovran (also containing 250 µg levonorgestrel). The women were studied over one cycle of OCS therapy before starting phenobarbitone and for two cycles after starting the anticonvulsant. Blood samples were taken 10–12 hours after OCS dosing on days 11, 14, 16, 18 and 21 of all three contraceptive cycles, and concentrations of EE_2, SHBG and norethisterone were measured.

The results of this study are shown in Table 2. In the group as a whole there was no significant change in the plasma concentration of EE_2 or norethisterone. However, in two women there were significant falls in their EE_2 concentrations from (patient 2) 104.8 ± 13.4 pg/ml to 47.7 ± 13.9 pg/ml and from (patient 3) 125.6 ± 23.8 pg/ml to 50.3 ± 4.7 pg/ml ($p < 0.05$). Figure 2 shows the plasma concentration of EE_2 and norethisterone in patient 2 during the study. The significant fall in EE_2 concentrations on starting phenobarbitone therapy is clear and this was accompanied by breakthrough bleeding. There were no significant changes in the plasma concentration of norethisterone but there were significant increases in the SHBG capacity in all four women. The plasma concentrations of phenobarbitone were just below the usually accepted therapeutic range (10–30 µg/ml) but this is not surprising given the low dose of phenobarbitone used. The low dose of phenobarbitone may also explain the variability of the data since only two of the women showed falls in EE_2 and none showed a fall in norethisterone concentration.

To try to ascertain if any long-term pharmacodynamic effects were occurring we measured plarma concentrations of FSH, which would be expected to rise if the OCS was losing its effect. No such rise was seen. We also measured plasma concentrations of progesterone on days 19, 20 and 21 of the contraceptive cycle, since a rise in progesterone concentration on these days is a good index of ovulation. No such rise was seen in these women, indicating that ovulation was still suppressed by their OCS. Thus phenobarbitone in low dosage was found to be capable of lowering plasma EE_2 concentrations in some women but we felt we needed to look at the kinetics in more detail in order to come to clearer conclusions.

Table 2. Plasma concentrations of ethinyloestradiol (EE_2), norethisterone, SHBG and phenobarbitone in four women taking phenobarbitone 30 mg twice daily together with their OCS preparation

Patient number	1	2	3	4	Mean ± SD
Plasma EE_2 conc.					
(pg/ml)　Cycle 1	43.4 ± 6.4	104.8 ± 13.4	125.6 ± 23.8	71.7 ± 2.8	86.4 ± 18.1
Cycle 2	52.0 ± 13.7	47.7 ± 13.9*	50.3 ± 4.7*	69.0 ± 9.6	54.7 ± 4.8
Plasma norethisterone conc.					
(ng/ml)　Cycle 1	2.0 ± 0.4	6.6 ± 0.6	4.6 ± 0.2	–	4.4 ± 1.3
Cycle 2	1.2 ± 0.1	7.1 ± 0.2	4.4 ± 0.7	–	4.2 ± 1.7
SHBG nmol/1					
Cycle 1	156.8 ± 12.6	285.4 ± 18.3	320.2 ± 4.3	100.7 ± 5.8	
Cycle 2	234.0 ± 6.7*	363.9 ± 11.6*	369.2 ± 14.3*	133.3 ± 1.2*	
Plasma phenobarbitone conc.					
(µg/ml)　Cycle 3	8.0	6.5	6	8.5	7.25 ± 0.6

* $p < 0.05$ compared to cycle 1.
Reproduced from Back *et al.* (1980b) by permission of the editor of *Contraception*.

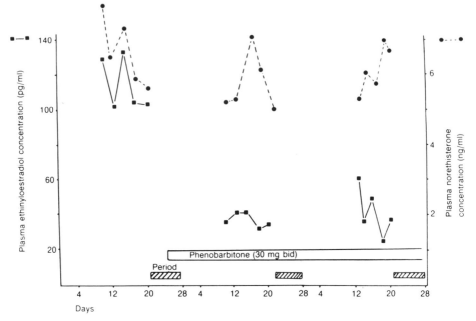

Figure 2. Plasma ethinyloestradiol (■ — ■) and norethisterone (● - - - ●) concentrations in a patient during a control cycle and two subsequent cycles when receiving phenobarbitone 30 mg twice daily. (Reproduced from Back *et al.*, 1980b, by permission of the editor of *Contraception*.)

Studies with phenytoin and carbamazepine

Phenytoin and carbamazepine are potent enzyme-inducing drugs and in reports to the CSM these two drugs figure highly (Back *et al.*, 1988). Studies were therefore conducted with both drugs, but instead of conducting studies in long-term users of OCS we chose instead to look at the kinetics of single doses of OCS in women before starting and again while taking either phenytoin or carbamazepine. In this type of study dynamic measurements are not possible but we felt that in the current climate it was not ethical to delay starting phenytoin or carbamazepine by the one month that would be needed to obtain control pharmacodynamic data.

Studies were performed in ten female patients aged between 16 and 37 years of age. All patients had presented with tonic–clonic seizures but were otherwise in good health as judged by clinical and laboratory examination. No patient had received OCS in the previous three months. Full details of these studies are given elsewhere (Crawford *et al.*, 1990). Prior to starting anticonvulsant therapy each woman took a single dose of Eugynon 50 by mouth at 09.00 after an overnight fast. Eugynon 50 contains 50 μg EE$_2$ and 250 μg levonorgestrel. Blood samples were taken at regular intervals up to 24 hours and the plasma concentrations of EE_2 and levonorgestrel were measured by radioimmunoassay. The AUC was calculated as described earlier.

Six patients were then treated with phenytoin (200–300 mg/day) and four patients were treated with carbamazepine (300–600 mg/day). All patients had their seizures controlled by the initial dose of anticonvulsant chosen. The single-dose study with Eugynon 50 was repeated in each patient 8–12 weeks after starting anticonvulsant therapy and the morning dose of anticonvulsant was given 2 hours after the dose of Eugynon 50. The values for the AUC measurements are shown in Table 3. Phenytoin causes a significant reduction in the AUC of both EE_2 and levonorgestrel, on average there being a 50% fall in the amount of steroid in plasma during phenytoin therapy. However, not all patients showed such a fall and it is noticeable that patient 4 with EE_2 and patient 3 with levonorgestrel actually showed an increase in steroid levels during phenytoin therapy. The explanation for this is not clear but is probably due to biological variation. However, it is noticeable that the blood levels of

Table 3.   Area under the plasma concentration versus time curve for ethinyloestradiol and levonorgestrel in patients taking phenytoin or carbamazepine

Patient	Daily phenytoin dose (mg)	Plasma phenytoin concentration (µg/ml)	Ethinyloestradiol AUC (pg/ml × h)		Levonorgestrel AUC (ng/ml × h)	
			Control	Treatment	Control	Treatment
1	250	1.0	641	303	41.8	22.6
2	200	3.5	956	326	23.1	17.2
3	200	7.0	944	234	10.5	13.7
4	200	3.0	785	1060	18.9	5.9
5	300	11.5	770	332	46.7	25.4
6	300	23.0	740	208	60.8	32.2
Mean ± SD			806 ± 132*	411 ± 132*	33.6 ± 7.8	19.5 ± 3.8*

Patient	Daily carbamaze-pine dose (mg)	Plasma carbamaze-pine concentration (µg/ml)	Ethinyloestradiol AUC (pg/ml × h)		Levonorgestrel AUC (ng/ml × h)	
			Control	Treatment	Control	Treatment
1	400	8.0	1833	630	14.9	10.5
2	300	3.5	1024	960	20.2	8.7
3	600	8.0	750	451	20.1	14.3
4	600	4.5	1047	648	36.6	21.9
Mean ± SD			1163 ± 466	672 ± 211*	22.9 ± 9.4	13.8 ± 5.8*

* $p < 0.05$ paired t test compared to control.
Reproduced from Crawford *et al.* (1990) by permission of the editor of the *British Journal of Clinical Pharmacology*.

phenytoin were low in these patients and below the usually accepted therapeutic range in plasma (10–20 µg/ml).

In contrast, the four patients given carbamazepine all showed a fall in the
plasma concentrations of EE_2 and levonorgestrel when carbamazepine was
given. Again the mean fall was about 50% and was statistically significant ($p <$
0.05). However, the range of fall in plasma concentration of steroid was
considerable and for EE_2 the fall varied between 6% and 66%. The plasma
concentrations of carbamazepine were mostly within the accepted therapeutic
range (4–8 µg/ml) and this may account for the more obvious effects of
carbamazepine compared to phenytoin. The half-lives of the OCS were not
calculated in these patients mainly because of difficulties in defining the terminal log–linear decay of the plasma concentration. However, in Figure 3 it
can be clearly seen that in this patient the rate of elimination of EE_2 is much

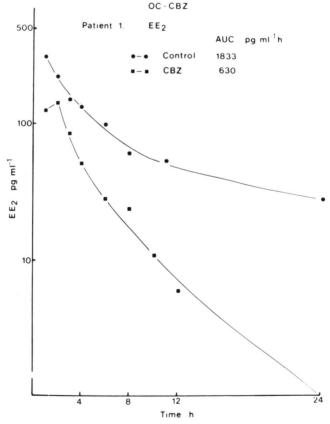

Figure 3.   Plasma concentrations of ethinyloestradiol over 24 hours after a single dose
of 50 µg in one woman before (● — ●) and during (■ — ■) treatment with carbamazepine 400 mg daily

more rapid during the carbamazepine phase compared to the control period. This strongly suggests that the explanation for the fall in steroid level is due to enzyme induction rather than to any alternative explanation such as reduced absorption from the gut.

Studies with sodium valproate

Although sodium valproate has been implicated in causing contraceptive failure in women taking oral contraceptive steroids (Coulam and Annegers, 1979; Back *et al.*, 1988), this drug is not known to be an enzyme-inducing agent (Gugler and Unruh, 1980; Park and Breckenridge, 1981). However, since sodium valproate is a known teratogen (Gugler and Unruh, 1980) it was clearly important to see whether this anticonvulsant affected the kinetics of oral contraceptive steroids.

Six women aged 16–37 years of age who presented to an epilepsy clinic with tonic–clonic seizures were chosen for study. The full details of the study are given elsewhere (Crawford *et al.*, 1986) but the design was very similar to that used for the phenytoin and carbamazepine studies. All women received a single oral dose of Eugynon 50 (containing 50 μg EE_2 and 250 μg levonorgestrel) at 09.00 after an overnight fast both before starting sodium valproate and again 8–12 weeks after starting sodium valproate in a dose of 200 mg twice daily. Blood samples were taken for analysis of the plasma concentration of EE_2 and levonorgestrel both before the dose of Eugynon 50 and at 1.0, 2.0, 3.0, 4.0, 6.0, 8.0, 11.0, 14.0 and 24 hours after Eugynon 50. The AUC for EE_2 and levonorgestrel was calculated as described earlier.

All six women completed the study without any ill effects and their tonic–clonic seizures were controlled by this relatively small dose of sodium valproate. The kinetics of EE_2 and levonorgestrel are shown in Table 4. Essentially there were no significant differences between the kinetics of the OCS during sodium valproate as compared to the control data before sodium valproate was started. Peak concentrations of EE_2 were significantly higher during sodium valproate therapy at 130.0 ± 17.5 pg/ml compared to the control period (85.2 ± 7.5 pg/ml). The explanation for this is not clear but it seems unlikely that it would have much clinical significance. If anything it would make the OCS more effective during valproate therapy. Concentrations of sodium valproate were always detectable in plasma and were between 4 and 45 μg/ml.

CONCLUSIONS

It is clear therefore that phenytoin, phenobarbitone and carbamazepine as well probably as primidone (since it is metabolized to phenobarbitone) lower concentrations of OCS in plasma and this will account for the contraceptive failures reported. The mechanism responsible for this effect cannot be proven

Table 4. Kinetics of ethinyloestradiol and levonorgestrel before and during sodium valproate therapy, mean ± SD

	Control	Sodium valproate
Ethinyloestradiol		
$AUC_{0-24\ h}$ (pg/ml × h)	880 ± 109	977 ± 130
Peak conc. (pg/ml)	85.2 ± 7.5	130.0 ± 17.5*
Trough conc. (pg/ml)	20.1 ± 4.1	21.1 ± 2.3
Levonorgestrel		
$AUC_{0-24\ h}$ (ng/ml × h)	29.1 ± 2.9	29.2 ± 1.9
Peak conc. (ng/ml)	4.15 ± 0.7	5.4 ± 0.2
Trough conc. (ng/ml)	0.39 ± 0.12	0.49 ± 0.15

* $p < 0.01$.
Reproduced from Crawford *et al.* (1986) by permission of the editor of *Contraception*.

from these studies but it is likely to be due to induction of the hepatic micro-somal enzymes that metabolize the contraceptive steroids. Sodium valproate is not an enzyme inducer in man and does not reduce the blood levels of the OCS.

The major pathway of metabolism of EE_2 involves 2-hydroxylation by cytochrome P450. Guengerich (1988) has argued that the specific isozyme responsible for EE_2 2-hydroxylation is $P450_{NF}$ (or P450IIIA4). It is known that phenobarbitone and other anticonvulsants induce this cytochrome P450. Ball *et al.* (1989) examined 16 human livers for their ability to hydroxylate EE_2 among other substrates. The highest EE_2 hydroxylase activity was seen in the liver of a patient who had been treated with phenytoin and phenobarbitone for many years. The main metabolites of both EE_2 and the progestogens have no pharmacological activity apart from desogestrel referred to earlier.

Thus the effect of phenytoin, phenobarbitone and carbamazepine on OCS can be overcome by using a larger dose of the OCS than is usual. Instead of starting with 30–35 µg EE_2 we start such patients on a 50 µg EE_2 preparation and only Ovran is still available in the UK for this purpose. If breakthrough bleeding occurs into the second cycle of contraceptive use then we increase the dose of EE_2 to 80 µg daily by giving one Ovran and one Ovranette tablet daily. In many women this dose is adequate but a few will need to be given 100 µg EE_2 daily to achieve good cycle control and contraceptive efficacy.

ACKNOWLEDGEMENTS

We acknowledge the help of a number of neurologists and laboratory technicians over the years in which these studies were performed. Financial support was provided by the Medical Research Council. The World Health Organization, the British Epilepsy Association, the Mersey Regional Health Authority, Ciba-Geigy Pharmaceuticals, Labaz Pharmaceuticals, Parke Davies & Co. Ltd and Schering AG.

REFERENCES

Back, D.J., Breckenridge, A.M., Crawford, F.E., MacIver, M., Orme, M.L'E., Rowe, P.H. and Smith, E. (1978) Pharmacokinetics of norethindrone in women. (2) Single dose kinetics. *Clin. Pharmacol. Ther.*, **24**, 447–454.

Back, D.J., Breckenridge, A.M., Crawford, F.E., MacIver, M., Orme, M.L'E., Rowe, P.H. and Watts, M. (1979) An investigation of the pharmacokinetics of ethinyloestradiol in women using radioimmunoassay. *Contraception*, **20**, 263–273.

Back, D.J., Breckenridge, A.M., Crawford, F.E., Orme, M.L'E. and Rowe, P.H. (1980a) Phenobarbitone interaction with oral contraceptive steroids in the rabbit and rat. *Br. J. Pharmacol.*, **69**, 441–452.

Back, D.J., Bates, M., Bowden, A., Breckenridge, A.M., Hall, M.J., Jones, H., MacIver, M., Orme, M.L'E., Perucca, A., Richens, A., Rowe, P.H. and Smith, E. (1980b) The interaction of phenobarbital and other anticonvulsants with oral contraceptive therapy. *Contraception*, **22**, 495–503.

Back, D.J., Breckenridge, A.M., MacIver, M., Orme, M.L'E., Purba, H., Rowe, P.H. and Taylor, I. (1982) The gut wall metabolism of ethinyloestradiol and its contribution to the presystemic metabolism of ethinyloestradiol in humans. *Br. J. Clin. Pharmacol.*, **13**, 325–330.

Back, D.J., Grimmer, S.F.M., Orme, M.L'E., Proudlove, C., Mann, R.D. and Breckenridge, A.M. (1988) Evaluation of Committee on Safety of Medicines Yellow Card reports on oral contraceptive–drug interactions. *Br. J. Clin. Pharmacol.*, **25**, 527–532.

Backström, T. and Sodergård, R. (1977) The influence of antiepileptic drugs on steroid plasma levels and binding during the menstrual cycle. *Acta Endocrinol. Suppl.*, **212**, 42.

Ball, S.E., Forrester, L.M., Wolf, C.R. and Back, D.J. (1989) Differences in the cytochrome P450 isozymes involved in the 2-hydroxylation of estradiol and 17-α-ethinyloestradiol: Relative activities of rat and human liver enzymes. *Biochem. J.*, **267**, 221–226.

Belaisch, J., Driguez, P. and Janaud, A. (1976) Influence de certains medicaments sur l'action des pillules contraceptifs. *Nouv. Presse Med.*, **5**, 1645–1646.

Conney, A.H. (1967). Pharmacological implications of enzyme induction. *Pharmacol. Rev.*, **19**, 317–366.

Coulam, C.B. and Annegers, J.F. (1979) Do anticonvulsants reduce the efficacy of oral contraceptives? *Epilepsia*, **20**, 519–526.

Crawford, P., Chadwick, D., Cleland, P., Tjia, J., Cowie, A., Back, D.J. and Orme, M.L'E. (1986) The lack of effect of sodium valproate on the pharmacokinetics of oral contraceptive steroids. *Contraception*, **33**, 23–29.

Crawford, P., Chadwick, D.J., Martin, C., Tjia, J., Back, D.J. and Orme, M.L'E. (1990) The interaction of phenytoin and carbamazepine with combined oral contraceptive steroids. *Br. J. Clin. Pharmacol.*, **30**, 892–896.

Diamond, M.P., Greene, J.W., Thompson, J.M., Vanttooydonk, J.E. and Wentz, A. (1985) Interaction of anticonvulsants and oral contraceptives in epileptic adolescents. *Contraception*, **31**, 623–632.

Gagnaire, J.C., Tchertchian, J., Revol, A. and Rochet, Y. (1975) Grossesses sous contraceptifs oraux chez les patients recevant des barbituriques. *Nouv. Presse Med.*, **4**, 3008.

Guengerich, F.R. (1988) Oxidation of 17-α-ethynylestradiol by human liver cytochrome P-450. *Mol. Pharmacol.*, **33**, 500–508.

Gugler, R. and Unruh, G.E. von (1980) Clinical pharmacokinetics of valproic acid. *Clin. Pharmacokinet.*, **5**, 67–83.

Hempel, Von E., Bohm, W., Carol, W. and Klinger, W. (1973) Medikamentose enzyminduktion und Hormonale Kontrazeption. *Zentrabl. Gynakol.*, **95**, 1451–1457.

Janz, D. and Schmidt, D. (1974) Antiepileptic drugs and failure of oral contraceptives. *Lancet*, **i**, 113.

Janz, D. and Schmidt, D. (1975) Antiepileptika und die Sicherheit oraler Kontrazeptiva. *Bibl. Psychiatr.*, **151**, 82–84.

Kenyon, T.E. (1972) Unplanned pregnancy in an epileptic. *Br. Med. J.*, **1**, 686–687.

Lumley, C.E., Walker, S.R., Hall, G.C., Staunton, N. and Grob, P.R. (1986) The under reporting of adverse drug reactions seen in general practice. *Pharm. Med.*, **1**, 205–212.

Orme, M.L'E., Back, D.J. and Breckenridge, A.M. (1983) The clinical pharmacokinetics of oral contraceptive steroids. *Clin. Pharmacokinet.*, **8**, 95–136.

Park, B.K. and Breckenridge, A.M. (1981) Clinical implications of enzyme induction and enzyme inhibition. *Clin. Pharmacokinet.*, **6**, 1–24.

Royal College of General Practitioners, Oral Contraceptive Study (1977) Mortality among oral contraceptive users. *Lancet*, **ii**, 727–733.

Victor, A., Weiner, E.L. and Johansson, E.D.B. (1976) Sex hormone binding globulin: The carrier protein for *d*-norgestrel. *J. Clin. Endocrinol. Metab.*, **43**, 244–247.

10

Catamenial seizures

PAMELA CRAWFORD
York District Hospital and Leeds General Infirmary, UK

INTRODUCTION

An increase in seizure frequency around the time of menstruation was first clinically documented in 1885 by Gowers, but cyclical variations in seizure frequency have been known about since antiquity and were initially attributed to the cycles of the moon (Temkin, 1971). No definitive definition exists for catamenial seizure exacerbations but the majority of reports refer to an increase in seizures around the time of the menses, either just before or during the first few days of menstruation. However, for seizures to be considered truly catamenial, there needs to be an increase in seizures in the majority of menstrual cycles.

CLINICAL STUDIES

Various studies have reported an increase in seizures (Table 1) around the menses but many are poorly documented and the women described are often unrepresentative of the female population with epilepsy. Although women with active epilepsy commonly report an increase in seizure frequency around the menses, when seizure diaries are kept, in only a minority will seizures be definitely catamenial. In a survey undertaken at Atkinson Morley's Hospital, in less than 10% of women with drug-resistant seizures was there a relationship with the menstrual cycle.

Cyclical fluctuations in seizures are not confined to women. In one study 29% of men had a cyclical increase in tonic–clonic seizures at between eight and 46 days (Almqvist, 1955) whilst ten prepubertal girls have been reported with recurrent monthly seizure exacerbations until puberty, when the seizures became catamenial (Livingston, 1972).

Women and Epilepsy. Edited by M.R. Trimble
© 1991 John Wiley & Sons Ltd

Table 1.   Incidence of catamenial epilepsy

Author	n	No. with catamenial seizures	Comments
Gowers (1885)	82	32 (39%)	
Healey (1928)	73	45 (62%)	
Dickerson (1941)	269	27 (10%)	
Almqvist (1955)[a]	84	17 (20%)	Tonic–clonic seizures
Laidlaw (1956)[a]	50	36 (72%)	Tonic–clonic seizures
Lennox and Lennox (1960)	686	333 (49%)	Questionnaire
Rosciszewska et al. (1986)	64	37 (58%)	
Atkinson Morley's Hospital	69	6 (9%)	Drug-resistant epilepsy

[a] Indicates studies involving in-patients in institutions.

ANIMAL STUDIES

Animal experiments suggest that catamenial seizure exacerbations may be related to the changing sex hormone concentrations during the menstrual cycle. In a wide variety of seizure models, oestrogens appear to be epileptogenic. They lower the seizure threshold in the hippocampus and amygdala and, when directly applied to the cortex, elicit seizure activity (Mattson and Cramer, 1985; see also Chapter 8).

Conversely, progestins appear to have anticonvulsant properties. However, their antiepileptic efficacy is unrelated to hormonal potency in animals or humans and appears, because of speed of action, to be related to a direct action on neural membranes. Treatment with various progestins decreases seizure susceptibility in animal models for electroshock and pentylenetetrazol thresholds, audiogenic seizures and kindling (Mattson and Cramer, 1985). An endogenous progesterone metabolite, 3α-hydroxy-5α-dihydroprogesterone, significantly potentiates γ-aminobutyric acid (GABA)-induced membrane hyperpolarization in cultured rat hippocampus and may act on the barbiturate binding site as a modulator of GABA-mediated inhibition (Majewska et al., 1986).

Therefore, experimental evidence from animal studies suggests that the change in seizure frequency during the menstrual cycle may be related to the relative oestrogen and progesterone concentrations. Human data tend to support this hypothesis, although there appear to be no clear differences in hormonal changes in women with and without catamenial seizures.

HUMAN STUDIES

The EEG in women without epilepsy tends to show minor fluctuations in background rhythms during the menstrual cycle with some slowing and a decrease in amplitude during menstruation (Newmark and Penry, 1980). Few studies have looked at EEG changes during the menstrual cycle in women with epilepsy but there appears to be an alteration in photosensitivity (Jeavons and Harding, 1975) and an increase in paroxysmal discharges (Newmark and Penry, 1980) around the time of the menses.

An increase in seizure frequency has been reported during the follicular phase, when highest oestrogen concentrations are found (Backstrom, 1976). Anovulatory cycles tend to be associated with higher seizure frequencies, in particular during times of peak oestrogen concentrations (Mattson *et al.*, 1981). Oestrogens, given pre-menstrually to women with catamenial seizures, appeared to exacerbate seizures in a small proportion of women and increase focal spikes and other paroxysmal EEG discharges (Logothetis *et al.*, 1959).

Intravenous infusions of progesterone in women with epilepsy decrease epileptiform spikes in some but not all women (Backstrom *et al.*, 1984). Studies have suggested an association between seizure susceptibility and the oestrogen/progesterone ratio and have shown that there is a decreased number of seizures during the luteal phase, when progesterone concentrations are highest (Backstrom, 1976). Laidlaw (1956) found a consistent decrease in seizures in the mid-luteal phase and suggested that high progesterone concentrations during this time had a protective effect, whilst the rapid fall in progesterone concentrations pre-menstrually resulted in an increase in seizures.

Although this evidence does seem to support the hypothesis that relative oestrogen and progesterone concentrations are of importance in catamenial seizures, other factors may have a role. Changes in anticonvulsant pharmacokinetics may be of importance. Variations in serum phenytoin concentrations were reported to be greater in women with catamenial seizures, with a marked fall in anticonvulsant concentrations on days 27 and 28 of the menstrual cycle, corresponding to an increase in seizure frequency. No such fall was found in women without catamenial seizures (Rosciszewska *et al.*, 1986). However, another study did not support these findings as no significant differences were found in phenytoin, phenobarbitone or carbamazepine concentrations throughout the menstrual cycle (Backstrom and Jorpes, 1979).

Another factor which needs to be taken into consideration is the relationship of catamenial exacerbation of seizures to pre-menstrual tension and menstrually related mood changes. Pre-menstrual tension is an ill-defined syndrome but commonly includes irritability, depression, tension and anxiety, feelings of bloatedness and weight gain, sleep disturbances and changes in appetite. The symptoms are restricted to the luteal phase of the menstrual cycle and reach their peak shortly before menstruation. Interestingly, it has been suggested that the syndrome may be caused by high oestrogen and low progesterone concentrations, but some authors disagree (Gath and Iles,1988). Stress and anxiety are well-recognized seizure precipitants and the mood changes which can occur pre-menstrually may be in part, or wholly, responsible for the change in seizure frequency. An increased incidence of pre-menstrual tension has been reported amongst women with catamenial seizures (75%) compared to other women with epilepsy (43%) (Rosciszewska et al., 1986).

Little recent attention has been paid to the role of fluid retention in catamenial seizures. One case report demonstrated an increase in seizure frequency within three days of the appearance of a positive water balance in a 14-year-old girl (McQuarrie, 1932). However, a study by Ansell and Clarke (1956a) of 14 women with epilepsy, five of whom had catamenial seizures, failed to show a significant difference between the two groups.

TREATMENT

Over the last century, many therapeutic agents have been tried, with varying degrees of success. Bromides were introduced by Locock in 1857 for the treatment of catamenial and hysterical epilepsies. By the turn of the century, it had been noted that seizure frequency occasionally decreased at the menopause or after ovariectomy (Newmark and Penry, 1980). In the 1950s came the introduction of acetazolamide, which, although advocated for the treatment of catamenial seizures, appears relatively ineffective (Ansell and Clarke, 1956b; Livingston, 1972).

Over the last decade, newer therapies have been introduced, based on our greater understanding of the aetiology of catamenial seizures. One of the main areas of therapeutic research has been in hormonal manipulation, trying either to increase relative progesterone concentrations or convert anovulatory to ovulatory cycles. It has been reported that about 50% of women with complex partial seizures have abnormal menstrual cycles (Herzog et al., 1986) and many women with epilepsy have anovulatory cycles (Mattson et al., 1981). Herzog (1986) described eight women with complex partial seizures with either anovulatory cycles or an inadequate luteal phase treated with progesterone suppositories in the appropriate phase of the menstrual cycle, resulting in a reduction in seizures by 68% in six of the eight women. In another study, clomiphene, an oestrogen analogue which stimulates the hypothalamic–pituitary axis to release gonadotrophins and hence induces ovulation, was used to treat 12 women with complex partial seizures and menstrual disorders. Ten of the group improved, all of whom developed normal ovulatory cycles (Herzog, 1988). Treatment with methoxyprogesterone acetate, a synthetic progesterone, has also been evaluated in 14 women with drug-resistant epilepsy. Of the 11 women who developed amenorrhoea, seven reported fewer seizures, with an overall seizure reduction of 30% (Mattson et al., 1984). However, it has to be appreciated that these are all open add-on studies in women with drug-resistant seizure disorders and not specifically studies of treatment for catamenial exacerbations of seizures.

An alternative approach has been intermittent anticonvulsant therapy around the time of menstruation. Many of the problems of tolerance, in particular those of benzodiazepines, can be overcome using this treatment model (Feely and Gibson, 1984). In a double-blind cross-over study of 20 mg clobazam versus placebo over a predetermined ten-day period in each menstrual cycle, clobazam was found to be superior to placebo in 14 (78%) women and completely prevented catamenial seizures in the majority (Feely *et al.*, 1982).

CONCLUSIONS

Reviewing the studies of catamenial epilepsy has demonstrated the large number of fundamental questions that still need to be answered. We still have no clear idea as to the incidence of catamenial seizures. The majority of studies relate either to institutional or hospital-based populations, which are unrepresentative of women with epilepsy. Studies have often examined only a few menstrual cycles or relied on self-reporting (Newmark and Penry, 1980; Lennox and Lennox, 1960).

A second important question relates to the seizures themselves. The majority of studies report catamenial seizures in women with complex partial seizures, although there are documented patients with generalized epilepsies. This probably reflects the relative resistance of partial seizures to anticonvulsant therapy and their over-representation in epilepsy clinics and institutions. Seizure frequency is also a factor which may be of relevance but is rarely stated.

How do women with catamenial seizures differ from other women with epilepsy? Do they have a higher incidence of anovulatory cycles, menstrual irregularities or pre-menstrual tension? Again, the literature is not clear.

The choice of anticonvulsant drug may be important. The majority of studies are pre-1970 and patients were treated with predominantly phenytoin or phenobarbitone, usually in combination. Both these anticonvulsants are potent hepatic microsomal enzyme inducers, as are carbamazepine, progesterone and oestrogen. The metabolism of all these compounds is interrelated. Studies looking at the incidence of catamenial seizures amongst women treated with sodium valproate might therefore be of interest as sodium valproate is not an enzyme inducer, nor is its metabolism affected by contraceptive steroids (Crawford *et al.*, 1986). Protein binding might also be of importance as changes in anticonvulsant binding occur throughout the menstrual cycle.

REFERENCES

Almqvist, R. (1955) The rhythm of epileptic attacks and its relationship to the menstrual cycle. *Acta Psychiatr. Scand. Neurol.* (Suppl. 105), 1–116.

Ansell, B. and Clarke, E. (1956a) Epilepsy and menstruation: The role of water retention. *Lancet*, **ii**, 1232–1235.

Ansell, B. and Clarke, E. (1956b) Acetazolamide in the treatment of epilepsy. *Br. Med. J.*, **1**, 650–654.

Backstrom, T. (1976) Epileptic seizures in women related to plasma estrogen and progesterone during the menstrual cycle. *Acta Neurol. Scand.*, **54**, 321–347.

Backstrom, T. and Jorpes, P. (1979) Serum phenytoin, phenobarbital, carbamazepine, albumin and plasma estradiol, progesterone concentrations during the menstrual cycle in women with epilepsy. *Acta Neurol. Scand.*, **59**, 63–71.

Backstrom, T., Zetterland, B., Blom, S. and Romano, M. (1984) Effects of intravenous progesterone infusions on the epileptic discharge frequency in women with partial epilepsy. *Acta Neurol. Scand.*, **69**, 240–248.

Crawford, P.M., Chadwick, D. and Cleland, P. *et al.* (1986) The lack of effect of sodium valproate on the pharmacokinetics of oral contraceptives. *Contraceptive*, **33**, 23–29.

Dickerson, W.W. (1941) The effect of menstruation on seizure incidence. *J. Nerv. Ment. Dis.*, **94**, 160–169.

Feely, M. and Gibson, J. (1984) Intermittent clobazam for catamenial epilepsy: Tolerance avoided. *J. Neurol. Neurosurg. Psychiatry*, **47**, 1279–1282.

Feely, M., Calvert, R. and Gibson, J. (1982) Clobazam in catamenial epilepsy: A model for evaluating anticonvulsants. *Lancet*, **2**, 71–73.

Gath, D. and Iles, S. (1988) Treating the premenstrual syndrome. *Br. Med. J.*, **297**, 237–238.

Gowers, W.R. (1885) *Epilepsy and Other Chronic Convulsive Diseases: Their Causes, Symptoms and Treatment.* William Wood, New York.

Healey, F.H. (1928) Menstruation in relation to mental disorders. *J. Ment. Sci.*, **74**, 488–492.

Herzog, A.G. (1986) Intermittent progesterone therapy and frequency of complex partial seizures in women with menstrual disorders. *Neurology*, **36**, 1607–1610.

Herzog, A.G. (1988) Clomiphene therapy in epileptic women with menstrual disorders. *Neurology*, **38**, 432–434.

Herzog, A.G., Seibel, M.M., Schomer, D.L. *et al.* (1986) Reproductive endocrine disorders in women with partial seizures of temporal lobe origin. *Arch. Neurol.*, **43**, 341–346.

Jeavons, P.M. and Harding, G.F.A. (1975) *Photosensitive Epilepsy: A Review of the Literature and a Study of 450 Patients.* Heinemann, London.

Laidlaw, J. (1956) Catamenial epilepsy. *Lancet*, **271**, 1235–1237.

Lennox, W.G. and Lennox, M.A. (1960) *Epilepsy and Related Disorders* (Vol 2). Little Brown, Boston.

Livingston, S. (1972) *Comprehensive Management of Epilepsy in Infancy, Childhood and Adolescence.* Thomas, Springfield, IL.

Locock, C. (1857) Discussion of Sieveking EH: Analysis of 52 cases of epilepsy observed by the author. *Lancet*, **i**, 527–528.

Logothetis, J., Harner, R., Morrell, F. and Torres, F. (1959) The role of estrogens in catamenial exacerbations of epilepsy. *Neurology (Minneapolis)*, **9**, 352–360.

Majewska, M.D., Harrison, N.L., Schwartz, R.D. *et al.* (1986) Steroid hormone metabolites are barbiturate-like modulators of the GABA receptor. *Science*, **232**, 1004–1007.

Mattson, R.H. and Cramer, J.A. (1985) Epilepsy, sex hormones and antiepileptic drugs. *Epilepsia*, **26** (Suppl. 1), S40–S51.

Mattson, R.H., Kamer, J.A., Caldwell, B.V. and Cramer, J.A. (1981) Seizure frequency and the menstrual cycle: A clinical study. *Epilepsia*, **22**, 242.

Mattson, R.H., Cramer, J.A., Caldwell, B.V. and Siconolfi, B.C. (1984) Treatment of seizures with medroxyprogesterone acetate: Preliminary report. *Neurology (Cleveland)*, **34**, 1255–1258.

McQuarrie, I. (1932) Some recent observations regarding the nature of epilepsy. *Ann. Intern. Med.*, **6**, 497–505.

Newmark, M.E. and Penry, J.K. (1980) Catamenial Epilepsy: A review. *Epilepsia*, **21**, 281–300.

Rosciszewska, D., Buntner, B., Guz, I. and Zawisza, L. (1986) Ovarian hormones, anticonvulsant drugs and seizures during the menstrual cycle in women with epilepsy. *J. Neurol. Neurosurg. Psychiatry*, **49**, 47–51.

Temkin, O. (1971) *The Falling Sickness* (2nd edn). Johns Hopkins Press, Baltimore.

11

Pregnancy and teratogenesis

MARK S. YERBY
Oregon Health Sciences University, Portland, Oregon, USA

INTRODUCTION

Epilepsy is a common neurological condition affecting 0.6–1% of the general population. Approximately 40% of this group are women of child-bearing age. Although there are an estimated 800 000 women with epilepsy in the USA who are potential parents, it has only been within the last 20 years that any significant attention has been directed at the problems or risks of childbearing for women with epilepsy. Prior to this, persons with epilepsy were frequently ostracized, isolated and institutionalized. The prospect of child-rearing for such a person was considered unwise at best. Greater understanding of the biology of epilepsy has paralleled a more enlightened social attitude toward persons with this disorder and, consequently, has made marriage and family planning an acceptable option.

Despite medical and social advances, women with epilepsy are considered high-risk pregnancies. This is because they are at greater risk for an increase in seizures during pregnancy (Bardy, 1987; Gjerde *et al.*, 1988; Knight and Rhind, 1975; Otani, 1985; Sabin and Oxorn, 1956; Schmidt *et al.*, 1983). Antiepileptic drugs (AED) undergo significant changes in metabolism and plasma concentrations, making the management of seizures more difficult (Dam *et al.*, 1979; Janz, 1982; Nau *et al.*, 1981; Yerby *et al.*, 1990a; Bardy *et al.*, 1990). In addition, women with epilepsy are at greater risk for complications of pregnancy, labor and delivery, and their offspring are at greater risk for adverse pregnancy outcomes (Bjerkedal and Bahna, 1973; Fedrick, 1983; Bethenod and Frederich, 1975; Yerby *et al.*, 1985; Kallen, 1986a).

EFFECT OF PREGNANCY ON MATERNAL SEIZURES

While most women with epilepsy will have no significant change in their seizure frequency during pregnancy, there is a group of such patients, 25–33%, who will have increased seizures.

Women and Epilepsy. Edited by M.R. Trimble
© 1991 John Wiley & Sons Ltd

It is difficult to predict these patients, since this phenomenon does not appear to be related to seizure type or duration of epilepsy. The experience in a previous pregnancy is not even a reliable indicator of what to expect in subsequent pregnancies. Generalized convulsive or tonic–clonic seizures are of particular concern because of the risk to the mother and fetus of injuries from falls. Intracranial hemorrhage in a fetus has been reported following a generalized seizure at 19 weeks of gestation (Minkoff et al., 1985). Suppression of fetal heart rate has been described following generalized seizures during labor (Teramo et al., 1979; Yerby, 1987). Though uncommon, miscarriages have been reported following a single generalized convulsion (Higgins and Comerford, 1974; Beaussant-Defaye et al., 1985). Partial seizures which do not generalize do not appear to have the same adverse effect on pregnancy. It is difficult, however, to predict whether partial seizures will generalize, therefore most neurologists attempt to maintain as effective control of seizures during pregnancy as they do during the non-pregnant state.

Most women with an increase in seizure frequency are found to have subtherapeutic AED levels. A significant proportion will have been deliberately non-compliant due to concerns about the risks of medications for their children (Otani, 1985; Schmidt et al., 1983; Bossi et al., 1980). Even in the face of constant and, in some cases, increased dosages of medication, anticonvulsant concentrations decline as pregnancy progresses (Mygind et al., 1976; Dam et al., 1979; Perucca and Crema, 1982; Eadie et al., 1977; Lander et al., 1977).

A variety of theories have been developed to explain this phenomenon. A single case of a woman with epilepsy with malabsorption of phenytoin during her pregnancy has been well described but never replicated, indicating that malabsorption must be an extremely rare complication of pregnancy (Ramsay et al., 1978). Plasma volume increases by one-third by the third trimester, hence a dilutional effect has been proposed as a mechanism. However, the timing and rate of decline of anticonvulsant concentration is different for different AED. The decline is fairly steady for valproate (Koerner et al., 1989). Eighty per cent of the decline in phenytoin occurs in the first trimester: a similar proportionate decline occurs in the first trimester for phenobarbital. Carbamazepine has its greatest decline in the third trimester (Yerby et al., 1990a; Otani, 1985). Increased plasma volume cannot therefore explain the fall in concentration seen with these compounds (Yerby et al., 1990a). Increased clearance has also been postulated as a mechanism. Antipyrine, a marker for the clearance of medications, has an increased rate of clearance from the first to the third trimester. The clearance rates are less, however, in pregnant than in non-pregnant persons (Dam et al., 1977; Nau et al., 1981). The clearance of some AED, carbamazepine and phenobarbital, does not change, and that of others, phenytoin and primidone, changes only during the third trimester (Otani, 1985).

The variability of the changes in AED concentration requires careful and regular monitoring at monthly intervals. Most epileptologists recommend maintaining the concentration within the therapeutic range.

ADVERSE OUTCOMES OF PREGNANCY

The children of mothers with epilepsy are at greater risk for a variety of adverse outcomes of pregnancy. Babies born to mothers with epilepsy have been found to be at increased risk for prematurity, with rates ranging from 4% to 11% of live births (Speidel and Meadow, 1972; Bjerkdal and Banha, 1973; Fedrick, 1983; Hill and Tennyson, 1982). Low birthweight—less than 2500 g—has been described in 7–10% of infants of mothers with epilepsy (Speidel and Meadow, 1972; Bjerkdal and Bahna, 1973, Hiilesmaa *et al.*, 1981; Nelson and Ellenberg, 1982; Yerby *et al.*, 1985). Microcephaly has been demonstrated in infants exposed to any anticonvulsant in utero (Nelson and Ellenberg, 1982; Neri *et al.*, 1983). Low Apgar scores have been reported to occur more commonly in these children (Speidel and Meadow, 1972; Bjerkdal and Bahna, 1973; Hiilesmaa *et al.*, 1981; Yerby *et al.*, 1985). Stillbirth rates, neonatal and perinatal death rates are also significantly higher in infants of mothers with epilepsy (Speidel and Meadow, 1972; Fedrick, 1983; Knight and Rhind, 1975; Nakane *et al.*, 1980; Nelson and Ellenberg, 1982; Beaussart-Defaye *et al.*, 1985).

Children of mothers with epilepsy have a threefold increased risk for developing seizures themselves (Annegers *et al.*, 1978). Paternal epilepsy appears to have little impact on the development of seizures in children. The presence of maternal seizures during pregnancy, but not AED use, has been associated with an increased relative risk of seizures of 2.4 in the offspring (Ottman *et al.*, 1988).

Mental retardation rates have been reported to be higher in infants of mothers with epilepsy (Speidel and Meadow, 1972; Hill *et al.*, 1974; Nelson and Ellenberg, 1982). None of these studies controlled for parental intelligence. When the IQ scores of children exposed to phenytoin in utero were compared with those of control children at 7 years of age, the full-scale IQ (FSIQ) scores of the exposed children were lower (FSIQ = 91.7 versus 96.8 for controls) (Nelson and Ellenberg, 1982). A five-point difference in IQ scores is not clinically significant. Jones *et al.* (1989) used a single standard deviation from the mean to classify 20% of children exposed to carbamazepine in utero as developmentally delayed. A more conventional classification using 2 standard deviations would have resulted in a more modest 3% rate of developmental delay. Clearly, children born to persons with mental deficiency are at greater risk for developing mental retardation. The majority of persons with epilepsy are, however, intellectually normal. When developmental outcome is evaluated more carefully (prospectively, controlling for socio-economic status, with blinded examiners), only slight differences are found between infants of mothers with epilepsy and controls (Gaily *et al.*, 1988a). Mental retardation does not appear to be associated with in utero exposure to AED concentrations below those likely to result in clinical toxicity or to brief maternal seizures.

Congenital malformations comprise the most dramatic and widely reported adverse outcome of pregnancy. Major malformations are defined as defects of medical, surgical or cosmetic importance. Minor physical defects are not well defined (Leppig *et al.*, 1987). Infants of mothers with epilepsy exposed to AED in utero are twice as likely to develop birth defects as infants not exposed to these drugs (Speidel and Meadow, 1972; Fedrick, 1983).

MAJOR MALFORMATIONS AND AED

The first report of a malformation associated with AED exposure in utero was with mephenytoin. The child had microcephaly, cleft palate, malrotation of the intestine, a speech defect and an IQ of 60 (Muller-Kuppers, 1963).

As a result of this report, Janz and Fuchs (1964) performed a retrospective survey to evaluate the problem of AED-associated malformations. Four hundred and twenty-six pregnancies in 246 mothers with epilepsy were studied. These patients had increased rates of miscarriages and stillbirths, but the malformation rate was only 2.2%—not significantly different from that of the general population of West Germany. The authors concluded that AED were not associated with an increased risk of malformations.

Other case reports describing malformations in children exposed to AED in utero followed. Pantarotto (1965) described a neonate with aplasia of the bone marrow after phenytoin exposure in utero. Centra and Rasore-Quartino (1965) reported the first case of congenital heart disease with in utero exposure to phenytoin and phenobarbital. Melchior *et al.* (1967) described orofacial clefts with exposure to primidone or phenobarbital.

Meadow (1968) reported six cases of children exposed to AED in utero with orofacial clefts, four of whom had additional abnormalities of the heart and dysmorphic facial features. He noted that similar abnormalities had been reported following the unsuccessful use of abortifactant folic acid antagonists. Since some antiepileptic drugs act as folic acid antagonists, Meadow postulated that this might account for antiepileptic drug teratogenicity.

The first report linking malformations with a specific AED exposure was published in 1970 by German *et al.* Trimethadione was implicated as a teratogen in eight of 14 pregnancies in which it was taken in the first trimester.

The first clear increase in the risk of congenital malformation for infants of mothers with epilepsy was demonstrated in a retrospective survey of 427 pregnancies by Speidel and Meadow (1972). The authors concluded that: (1) congenital malformations are twice as common in infants of mothers with epilepsy exposed to antiepileptic drugs; (2) no single abnormality was specific for antiepileptic drug exposure; (3) a group of these children would have a characteristic pattern of anomalies which at its fullest expression consisted of trigonocephaly, microcephaly, hypertelorism, low-set ears, short neck, transverse palmar creases and minor skeletal abnormalities.

Congenital malformations remain the most commonly reported adverse outcome in the pregnancies of mothers with epilepsy. Malformation rates in the general population range from 2% to 3% (Kalter and Warkany, 1983; Kelly, 1984a). Reports of malformation rates in various populations of infants of mothers with epilepsy range from 1.25% to 11.5% (Nakane *et al.*, 1980;

Table 1. Malformation rates in the offspring of epileptic and control mothers

Authors	Control Malformation rate (%)	No of pregnancies	Epileptic mothers Malformation rate (%)	No. of pregnancies
Sabin and Oxorn (1956)			5.4	56
Janz and Fuchs (1964)			2.3	225
German *et al.* (1970)			5.3	243
Elshove and Van Eck (1971)	1.9	12 051	15.0	65
Speidel and Meadow (1972)	1.6	483	5.2	427
South (1972)	2.4	7 892	6.4	31
Spellacy (1972)		50	5.8	51
Bjerkedal and Bahna (1973)	2.2	12 530	4.5	311
Fedrick (1973)	5.6	649	13.8	217
Koppe *et al.* (1973)	2.9	12 455	6.6	197
Kuenssber and Knox (1973)	3.0	14 668	10.0	48
Lowe (1973)	2.7	31 877	5.0	245
Meyer (1973)	2.7	110	18.6	593
Millar and Nevin (1973)	3.8	32 227	6.4	110
Monson *et al.* (1973)	2.4	50 591	4.7	306
Niswander and Werteleck (1973)	2.7	347 097	4.1	413
Biale *et al.* (1975)			16.0	56
Knight and Rhind (1975)	3.65	69 000	4.3	140
Starreveld-Zimmerman (1975)			7.0	372
Visser *et al.* (1976)	2.3	9 869	3.7	54
Weber (1977)	2.2	5 011	4.0	731
Annegers *et al.* (1978)	3.5	748	8.1	259
Seino and Miyokosh (1979)			13.7	272
Dieterich *et al.* (1980)				37
Majewski *et al.* (1980)			16.0	111
Nakane *et al* (1980)			11.5	700
Hiilesmaa *et al.* (1981)	2.0	5 613	7.7	4795
Stanley *et al.* (1985)	3.4	62 265	3.7	244
Beaussart-Defaye *et al.* (1985)			7.8	295
Rating *et al.* (1987)	3.7	162	5.3	150

Meadow, 1968; Philbert and Dam, 1982). These combined estimates yield a risk of malformations in an individual epileptic pregnancy of 4–6%. Table 1 reviews the various studies which compare malformation rates in the offspring of mothers with and without epilepsy.

CURRENT CONCEPTS OF MAJOR MALFORMATIONS

The increased rate of malformations in the offspring of mothers with epilepsy appears to be related to antiepileptic drug exposure in utero. Evidence to support this association comes from four observations. (1) Comparisons of the malformation rates in the offspring of mothers with epilepsy treated with antiepileptic drugs as opposed to those with no antiepileptic drug treatment reveal consistently higher rates in the children of the treated group (Nakane et al., 1980; Speidel and Meadow, 1972; Monson et al., 1973; Annegers et al., 1978; Lowe, 1973; South, 1972). (2) Mean plasma AED are higher in mothers with malformed infants than in mothers with healthy children (Dansky et al., 1980). (3) Infants of mothers taking multiple AED have higher malformation rates than those exposed to monotherapy (Nakane, 1979; Lindhout et al., 1984). (4) Maternal seizures during pregnancy do not appear to increase the risk of congenital malformations (Fedrick, 1983). Though Majewski et al. (1980) described increased malformation rates and central nervous system injury in infants of mothers with epilepsy exposed to maternal seizures, the majority of other investigators have found that maternal seizures during pregnancy had no impact on the frequency of malformations, development of epilepsy or febrile convulsions (Nakane et al., 1980; Annegers et al., 1978).

Virtually every type of congenital malformation has been reported in children of epileptic mothers, and every anticonvulsant medication has been implicated in their development. Cleft lip and/or palate and congenital heart disease account for a majority of the reported malformations (Annegers et al., 1978; Elshove and Van Eck, 1971; Anderson, 1976).

Orofacial clefts account for 30% of the excess of congenital malformations in infants of mothers with epilepsy. These are relatively common, occurring with a frequency of 1.5 per 1000 live births in the general population. Infants of mothers with epilepsy have a rate of orofacial clefting of 13.8 per 1000—a ninefold increase in risk (Kelly, 1984a; Kallen, 1986a). Studies of the prevalence of facial clefts in the siblings and children of 2072 persons with epilepsy found that observed/expected ratios increased only for maternal epilepsy. The risk was greater if AED were taken during pregnancy (4.7) than if no AED treatment was used (2.7). The authors concluded that there was no evidence that epilepsy itself contributed to the development of orofacial clefts (Friis et al., 1986). Israeli researchers have found that children with cleft lip/palate are four times as likely to have a mother with epilepsy as the general population, and mothers with epilepsy are six times as likely to bear a child with an orofacial cleft as non-epileptic women (Gatoh *et al.*, 1987).

Congenital heart defects are the second most frequently reported teratogenic abnormality associated with antiepileptic drugs. Infants of mothers with epilepsy have a 1.5–2% prevalence of congenital heart disease, a relative risk that is threefold greater than the general population (Kallen, 1986a). Anderson (1976) prospectively studied maternal epilepsy and AED use in 3000 children with heart defects at the University of Minnesota. Eighteen infants of mothers with epilepsy were identified. Twelve of these had ventricular septal defects, and nine of the 18 children had additional non-cardiac defects, eight of which were orofacial clefts.

No AED can be considered absolutely safe in pregnancy, but for the vast majority of drugs no specific pattern of major malformations has been identified (Kallen, 1986a). This lack of a particular or characteristic pattern of defects has been cited as evidence that antiepileptic drugs are not teratogenic. When phenobarbital is given during pregnancy for conditions other than epilepsy no increase in malformation rates has been demonstrated (Shapiro *et al.*, 1976).

Some investigators have found increased malformation rates in the infants of fathers with epilepsy and suggest that epilepsy per se is associated with birth defects and not AED exposure (Dieterich *et al.*, 1980; Friis and Hauge, 1985). Others have failed to demonstrate an increased malformation rate in infants of fathers with epilepsy (Grosse *et al.*, 1972). These studies were retrospective and the accuracy of case ascertainment uncertain. The weight of the evidence, however, tends to support some teratogenic effect of AEDs, for in addition to major malformations a variety of syndromes of minor anomalies associated with exposure have been described (Kallen, 1986a).

SYNDROMES OF MINOR ANOMALIES

In distinction to major malformations, minor anomalies are abnormalities of structure which, while varying from the norm, do not constitute a threat to health and are by definition rare, occurring in less than 4% of the population (Marden *et al.*, 1964). Patterns of anomalies in infants of mothers with epilepsy have been noted with specific AED exposure. Six clinical syndromes have been proposed: fetal trimethadione syndrome, fetal hydantoin syndrome, a fetal phenobarbital syndrome, a primidone embryopathy, fetal valproate syndrome and a fetal carbamazepine syndrome. The clinical features of these suggested syndromes are outlined in Table 2.

Fetal trimethadione syndrome

In 1970, German *et al.* described a case of a woman with epilepsy treated with trimethadione who had had four unsuccessful pregnancies. After

Table 2.   Syndromes of minor anomalies associated with anticonvulsants

Fetal trimethadione syndrome (German *et al.*, 1970)
    Development delay
    V-shaped eyebrows
    Low-set ears
    Intrauterine growth retardation
    Cardiac anomalies
    Speech difficulties
    Epicanthal folds
    Irregular teeth
    Microcephaly
    Inguinal hernia
    Simian creases
	Primidone embryopathy (Rudd and Freedom, 1979)
	    Hirsute forehead
	    Thick nasal root
	    Distal digital hypoplasia
	    Antiverted nostrils
	    Long philtrum
	    Straight thin upper lip
	    Psychomotor retardation

Fetal hydantoin syndrome (Hansen and Smith, 1975)
    Craniofacial anomalies
    Broad nasal bridge
    Short upturned nose
    Low-set ears
    Prominent lips
    Epicanthal folds
    Hypertelorism
    Wide mouth
    Ptosis or strabismus
    Distal digital hypoplasia
    IUGR
    Mental deficiency
	Fetal carbamazepine syndrome (Jones *et al.*, 1989)
	    Upslanting palpebral fissures
	    Epicanthal folds
	    Short nose
	    Long philtrum
	    Hypoplastic nails
	    Microcephaly
	    Developmental delay

Fetal valproate syndrome (DiLiberti *et al.*, 1984)
    Craniofacial anomalies
    Epicanthal folds inferiorly
    Small antiverted nose
    Shallow philtrum
    Flat nasal bridge
    Long upper lip
    Downturned mouth
    Thin vermilion border
	Fetal phenobarbital syndrome (Seip, 1976)
	    Developmental delay
	    Short nose
	    Low nasal bridge
	    Hypertelorism
	    Epicanthal folds
	    Ptosis
	    Low-set ears
	    Wide mouth
	    Protruding lips
	    Prognathism
	    Distal digital hypoplasia

trimethadione was discontinued, she delivered two healthy children. This prompted a survey of trimethadione-exposed infants delivered at New York Hospital between 1946 and 1968. The records of 278 women with epilepsy were reviewed, and of these 14 had taken trimethadione during pregnancy. Only two of these 14 children were normal. One had multiple hernias and diabetes; eight had developmental defects; three were spontaneously aborted; and only three of the 14 actually survived infancy.

The peculiar facial characteristics of these children were delineated by

Zachai *et al.* (1975), who noted that not only were these children short in stature and suffered from microcephaly; also they had V-shaped eyebrows, epicanthal folds, low-set ears, anteriorly folded helices and irregular teeth. In addition they frequently had other abnormalities: inguinal hernias, hypospadias and simian creases. Feldman *et al.* (1977) reviewed 53 pregnancies in which trimethadione was used. In 46 of these (87%) there was fetal loss or the development of a congenital malformation. Follow-up studies of the surviving children have reported significant rates of mental retardation (Goldman *et al.*, 1986).

Fetal hydantoin syndrome

The most controversial of the dysmorphic syndromes associated with AED is the fetal hydantoin syndrome (FHS). It was first reported by Loughnan *et al.* (1973), who described seven infants exposed to hydantoin in combination with a barbiturate, in utero, with hypoplasia and irregular ossification of the distal phalanges. In 1974 Barr *et al.* reported distal digital hypoplasia in eight children exposed to phenytoin and phenobarbital. The syndrome was named by Hanson and Smith (1975), who described five infants with multiple systemic abnormalities of the face, cranium, distal digital hypoplasia, intrauterine growth retardation, and mental deficiency who had been exposed to hydantoin in utero. Only one of the five was exposed to phenytoin monotherapy. Of the others, one was also exposed to phenobarbital, one to mephobarbital, one to phenobarbital and primidone, and one to a combination of phenobarbital, phensuximide and mephenytoin. Despite the multiplicity of exposures, and the authors' admitted resemblance of these children's features to the fetal alcohol syndrome, they stated that the abnormalities were due solely to hydantoin exposure and dubbed it the fetal hydantoin syndrome.

Subsequent work by Hanson's group found that approximately 11% of infants exposed to hydantoin in utero demonstrated the complete syndrome, and an additional 30% would have some anomalous components (Hanson *et al*;., 1976). Many of the features of the syndrome appear to be subjective, but some investigators believe that distal digital hypoplasia is a unique and relatively constant feature (Kelly, 1984b).

The prevalence and significance of the dysmorphic features of FHS remain unclear. Researchers at the University of Virginia followed 98 women with epilepsy who took phenytoin during pregnancy and found that 30% of their offspring had distal digital hypoplasia, with no other features of FHS (Kelly *et al.*, 1984c). Gaily *et al.* (1988) reported a prospective study of 121 children of mothers with epilepsy at the University of Helsinki, 82 of whom were exposed to phenytoin. None of the children had FHS. Hypertelorism and distal digital hypoplasia were the only dysmorphic features associated with phenytoin exposure. In our own experience following 64 infants of mothers with epilepsy no children with FHS were seen. Dysmorphic features could be seen with any drug exposure as well as in controls (Yerby *et al.*, 1990b).

The contention that FHS results in abnormal performance or mental deficiency is not supported by research. Of 103 infants of mothers with epilepsy exposed to phenytoin, only 1.4% displayed mental deficiency on the Wechsler Preschool and Primary Scale of Intelligence or Leiter International Performance Scale, not significantly different from the general population (Gaily *et al.*, 1988b).

Gaily's work suggests that there is a genetic component which permits expression of FHS. Children of mothers with epilepsy who are not exposed to antiepileptic drugs in utero have frequencies of dysmorphic abnormalities intermediate to those children exposed to AED and controls. Dizygotic twins exposed to hydantoins in utero have been shown to display discordant dysmorphism (Phelan *et al.*, 1982; Buehler, 1985). If the first child in a family has FHS, the chance of a second such child is 90%, compared to the 2% chance of having a second child with FHS if the first is normal (Van Dyke *et al.*, 1988). Observations such as these suggest that hydantoin exposure may be a necessary but not sufficient cause of infant dysmorphism.

In an unusual case report, Krauss *et al.* (1984) have described four siblings with craniofacial features of FHS. The first two were exposed to both phenytoin and primidone in utero. In an attempt to prevent further fetal injury Krauss discontinued the phenytoin and the patient was treated with primidone monotherapy. The two subsequent pregnancies resulted in children with similar dysmorphic features to their elder siblings.

Primidone embryopathy

Five years before Krauss' report, Rudd and Freedom (1979) had described craniofacial abnormalities in children exposed to primidone in utero. These children had hirsute foreheads, thick nasal roots, anteverted nostrils, long philtrum, straight thin upper lips, and hypoplastic nails. These children were also likely to be small for their gestational age and have psychomotor retardation and heart defects (Gustavson and Chen, 1985).

Fetal phenobarbital syndrome

Two children exposed to phenobarbital and primidone in utero have been described as having facial dysmorphism, pre- and post-natal growth deficiency, developmental delay and minor anomalies. The specific dysmorphic features of short nose, broad nasal bridge, hypertelorism, epicanthal folds, ptosis, low-set ears and wide mouth with protruding lips were noted by the author to be similar to those described in children having the fetal hydantoin and fetal alcohol syndrome (Sepi, 1976). Given the similarities, Seip suggested that describing these features as syndromic should be avoided. The author also noted that both phenytoin and phenobarbital as well as alcohol use could result in folate deficiency and queried if this could be a posible teratogenic mechanism.

The American Academy of Obstetrics and Gynecology has recommended phenobarbital as the drug of choice for pregnant women with epilepsy. Unfortunately there is little evidence to suggest that phenobarbital is safer than any other antiepileptic drug.

All of the cases in Loughnan's and four of five in Hanson and Smith's original series describing an FHS had also been exposed to phenobarbital or mephobarbital. Rates of cleft lip/palate in mice exposed to phenobarbital in utero range from 0.6% to 3.9%, compared to a 0.3% rate for controls (Sullivan and McElhatton, 1975). Phenobarbital suppresses development of hippocampal dendrites when given to pregnant rats (Jacobsen et al., 1988).

Fetal valproate syndrome

Reports of dysmorphic children exposed to valproate in utero had previously been made by other investigators (Dalens et al., 1980; Clay et al., 1981), but it was DiLiberti et al. (1984) who described a specific syndrome. They reported seven infants exposed to valproic acid in utero who had facial abnormalities characterized by inferior epicanthal folds, a flat nasal bridge, an upturned nose, a long upper lip, a thin vermilion border, a shallow philtrum and downturned mouth. These children also had abnormalities of their distal digits, and they tended to have long, thin overlapping fingers and toes, and hyper-convex nails.

The prevalence of this syndrome has not yet been established. Jager-Roman et al. (1986) described it in five of 14 children exposed to valproate monotherapy. In this same group, 43% of the children suffered distress during labor, and 28% had low Apgar scores. High doses of valproate were associated with hypotonia, and motor and language delay. In a review of 344 women who took valproate during the first trimester of pregnancy, Jeavons (1984) described a 19.8% rate of abnormal deliveries, but no evidence of a dose–response effect with valproate exposure.

Felding and Rane (1984) described an infant with severe congenital liver disease after in utero exposure to valproic acid and phenytoin. Ardinger et al. (1988) reported craniofacial dysmorphism in 19 children exposed to valproate in utero and confirmed the features described by DiLiberti. They also found that a large proportion of these infants had post-natal growth deficiency and microcephaly, particularly if the children were exposed to polytherapy.

Carbamazepine syndrome

The most recently described syndrome of minor anomalies associated with antiepileptic drug exposure is the carbamazepine syndrome. A single group of investigators has described craniofacial defects (upslanting palpebral fissures, epicanthal folds, short nose, long philtrum), hypoplastic nails and microcephaly, in 37 infants of mothers with epilepsy exposed to carbamazepine monotherapy (Jones *et al.*, 1989). The authors used the Bayley Scale of Infant Development, the Stanford–Binet IV and the Wechsler Scale of Preschool and Primary Intelligence in their evaluations, and found a 20% rate of developmental delay in 25 children of mothers taking carbamazepine monotherapy but, as mentioned previously, one standard deviation from the mean was used as the definition of abnormal instead of the generally accepted two standard deviations.

A case of distal digital hypoplasia in an infant of a mother who had been exposed to carbamazepine monotherapy had been described earlier (Niesen and Froscher, 1985), but that child was otherwise normal. Low birthweight has been reported with in utero exposure to carbamazepine monotherapy (Kallen, 1986a). A reduction in fetal head circumference was reported in children of women exposed to carbamazepine (Hiilesmaa *et al.*, 1981). While smaller than in control children, the head sizes were still within the normal range. Subsequent studies on the same clinical population failed to find differences in head circumference as the children matured (Granstrom, 1987).

Current concepts of minor anomalies

Clinical and laboratory evidence clearly support the association of certain anticonvulsants with teratogenic effects, especially facial and distal digital anomalies. However, the existence of drug-specific syndromes is doubtful. Facial dysmorphism is difficult to quantify and is clearly not drug specific. Infants of mothers with epilepsy with similar dysmorphic features have been described in the pre-anticonvulsant era (Philbert and Dam, 1982; Baptisti, 1938; Paskind and Brown, 1932). Follow-up of these infants into adult life has yet to be accomplished, and therefore the significance of these anomalies is unclear. Gaily *et al.* (1988) followed a cohort of children to 5½ years of age. These children had more minor anomalies characteristic of FHS than control children, but so did their mothers. Only hypertelorism and digital hypoplasia were associated with phenytoin exposure. Certain anomalies, particularly epicanthal folds, appeared to be associated with maternal epilepsy, not to AED exposure.

The hypothesized association of dysmorphic features with mental retardation (Kelly *et al.*, 1984) has not been confirmed (Granstrom, 1982; Hutch *et al.*, 1975). In the few cases which have been followed into early childhood, the dysmorphic features tend to disappear as the child grows older (Janz, 1982). Mental deficiency was found in only 1.4% of children of mothers with epilepsy followed to 5½ years of age (Gaily *et al.*, 1988). No association between features of fetal hydantoin syndrome and mental retardation could be demonstrated.

The primary abnormalities in these syndromes involve the mid-face and distal digits. A retrospective study spanning ten years of deliveries in Israel found hypertelorism to be the only anomaly seen more often in infants of epileptic mothers than in controls (Neri *et al.*, 1983). This was associated with all AED except primidone. A prospective study of 172 infants born to mothers with epilepsy evaluated eight specific AED and other potential confounding factors. No dose-dependent increase in the incidence of malformations was found to be associated with any individual antiepileptic drug. Furthermore, no specific defect could be associated with individual antiepileptic drug exposure (Kaneko *et al.*, 1988).

Since a variety of similar anomalies of the mid-face and distal digits are seen in a small proportion of children exposed to anticonvulsants in utero, it has been suggested that a more accurate term for these abnormalities would be fetal anticonvulsant syndrome or antiepileptic drug embryopathy (Dieterich *et al.*, 1980; Vorhees, 1986; Huot *et al.*, 1987).

MECHANISMS OF TERATOGENICITY

Over the last ten years a body of evidence has accumulated supporting the hypotheses that:

1. An arene oxide or epoxide metabolite of AEDs is the cause of their teratogenicity.
2. A genetic defect in epoxide hydrolase (arene oxide, or epoxide detoxifying enzyme system) increases the risk of fetal toxicity.

Or alternatively:

3. Free radicals are produced by AED metabolism and are cytotoxic.
4. A genetic defect in free radical scavenging enzyme activity (FRSEA) increases the risk of fetal toxicity.

Epoxides

A large number of drugs and chemicals can be converted into epoxides via reactions which are catalyzed by the microsomal monoxygenase system (Jerina and Daly, 1974; Sims and Grover, 1974). Arene oxides are unstable epoxides formed by aromatic compounds. Various epoxides are electrophilic and may elicit carcinogenic, mutagenic and other toxic effects by covalent binding to cell macromolecules (Nebert and Jensen, 1979; Shum *et al.*, 1979).

Epoxides are detoxified by two types of processes: (1) conversion to dihydrodiols catalyzed by epoxide hydrolase in the cytoplasm; or (2) conjugation with glutathione in the microsomes (spontaneously or mediated by glutathione transferase). Epoxide hydrolase activity in fetal livers is much lower than that of adults (Pacifici *et al.*, 1983). One-third to one-half of fetal circulation bypasses the liver, resulting in higher direct exposure of extrahepatic fetal organs to potential toxic metabolites (Pacifici and Rane, 1982).

Arene oxides are obligatory intermediates in the metabolism of aromatic compounds to *trans*-dihydrodiols. Phenytoin forms a *trans*-dihydrodiol metabolite (Chang *et al.*, 1970). This metabolite is also formed by neonates exposed to phenytoin in utero (Horning *et al.*, 1974). In vitro studies have shown that an oxidative metabolite of phenytoin binds irreversibly to rat liver (Martz *et al.*, 1977). This binding is increased by inhibiting epoxide hydrolase (with trichloroponene oxide, TCPO) and decreased by glutathione (Martz *et al.*, 1977; Pantarotto *et al.*, 1982; Wells and Harbison, 1985). In addition there was a correlation between the teratogenic effect and the amount of covalently bound material in fetal tissue. Using mouse hepatic microsomes to produce phenytoin metabolites, and human lymphocytes to assess cellular defense against toxicity, Spielberg *et al.* (1981) showed that cytotoxicity was enhanced by inhibiting epoxide hydrolase.

Strickler *et al.* (1985) examined lymphocytes from children exposed to phenytoin in utero as well as lymphocytes from their family members. The lymphocytes were incubated with phenytoin in a mouse microsomal system. A positive response was defined as an increase in cell death over baseline. Cells from 15 of 24 children gave a positive response. Each positive child had a positive parent (as many mothers as fathers). A positive response was highly correlated with major birth defects. The authors concluded that a genetic defect in arene oxide detoxification appears to increase the risk of major congenital malformations (Strickler *et al.*, 1985). However, no measurement of epoxide hydrolase activity was included in this study.

In 1985, Buehler reported epoxide hydrolase activity in skin fibroblasts of a pair of dizygotic twins exposed to phenytoin in utero. The infant who had more features of the fetal hydantoin syndrome showed lower epoxide hydrolase activity.

When epoxide hydrolase activity is measured in maternal amniocytes it is found to have a trimodal distribution. Four of 19 women with epilepsy on phenytoin monotherapy were found to have low epoxide hydrolase activity. All four of their offspring had clinical features consistent with fetal hydantoin syndrome (Buehler *et al.*, 1990). This suggests that deficiencies of epoxide hydrolase may increase the risk of teratogenicity, and that prenatal diagnosis may become possible. Two of the four children were hypotonic and had developmental delay, but none had any major malformations.

The evidence that epoxide metabolites of phenytoin are teratogenic can be summarized as follows. Phenytoin has an epoxide metabolite which binds to tissues. Inhibition of the detoxifying enzyme epoxide hydrolase increases the rate of orofacial clefts in experimental animals, lymphocyte cytotoxicity, and the binding of epoxide metabolite to liver microsomes.

These facts cannot completely explain the teratogenicity seen with phenytoin or other AEDs. The lymphocyte cytotoxicity seen with epoxide metabolites correlates with major but not minor malformations (Dansky *et al.*, 1987). Dysmorphic abnormalities have been described in siblings exposed to ethotoin in utero. Ethotoin is not metabolized through an arene oxide intermediate (Finnell and Diliberti, 1983). Embryopathies have also been described with exposure to mephenytoin, which does not form an arene oxide intermediate (Wells and Harbison, 1985). Trimethadione is clearly teratogenic, but has no phenyl rings, and thus cannot form an arene oxide metabolite. Therefore an alternative mechanism must exist.

Free radical intermediates of AED and teratogenicity

Some drugs are metabolized or bioactivated by co-oxidation during the synthesis of prostaglandins. Such drugs serve as electron donors to peroxidases, resulting in an electron-deficient drug molecule which by definition is called a free radical. In the search for additional electrons to complete their outer ring, free radicals can covalently bind to cell macromolecules, including nucleic acids (DNA, RNA), proteins, cell membranes and lipoproteins to produce cytotoxicity.

Phenytoin is co-oxidized by prostaglandin synthetase (PGS), thyroid peroxidase and horseradish peroxidase, producing reactive free radical intermediates which bind to proteins (Kubow and Wells, 1989). Phenytoin teratogenicity can be reduced by substances which reduce the formation of its free radicals. Acetylsalicylic acid irreversibly inhibits PGS, while caffeic acid is an antioxidant, and α-phenyl-*N-t*-butylnitrone (PBN) is a free radical spin trapping agent. Pre-treatment of pregnant mice with any of these compounds reduces the number of cleft lip/palates secondary to phenytoin in their offspring (Wells *et al.*, 1984).

Glutathione is believed to detoxify free radical intermediates. BCNU, a drug used in the management of cancer, inhibits glutathione reductase, an enzyme necessary to maintain adequate cellular glutathione concentrations, and increases phenytoin embryopathy at doses at which BCNU alone has no embryopathic effect (Wong and Wells, 1989). The metabolic production by phenytoin or other AEDs of free radical intermediates may be responsible for the teratogenicity seen in infants of mothers with epilepsy.

OTHER POTENTIAL MECHANISMS OF AED TERATOGENICITY

It has been proposed that the glucocorticoid receptor mediates the teratogenicity of phenytoin. Arachidonic acid reverses clefting induced by glucocorticoids in rats. Phospholipase inhibitory proteins (PLIPs) inhibit arachidonic acid release. Glucocorticoid receptors mediate the induction of PLIPs. Infants of mothers with epilepsy exposed to phenytoin with the stigmata of FHS have increased levels of glucocorticoid receptors, hence less arachidonic acid (Goldman *et al.*, 1987). Clefting, however, is not a feature of the FHS.

Deficiencies in folate have been implicated in the development of birth defects. Certain AEDs interfere with folate metabolism. Dansky *et al.* (1987) found significantly lower blood folate concentrations in women with epilepsy with abnormal pregnancy outcomes. Co-treatment of mice with folic acid, with or without vitamins and amino acids, reduced malformation rates and increased fetal weight and length in mice pups exposed to phenytoin in utero (Zhu and Zhou, 1989). Biale and Lewenthal (1984) reported a 15% malformation rate in infants of mothers with epilepsy with no folate supplementation, while none of 33 folate-supplemented children had congenital abnormalities.

VALPROIC ACID TERATOGENICITY

One of the factors necessary for classifying a substance as a teratogen is an increase in a specific adverse outcome associated with exposure. Phocomelia associated with exposure to thalidomide is one such example. Though orofacial clefts are the most commonly reported malformations associated with antiepileptic drug exposure, they are clearly not the majority of malformations associated with these drugs, which have led some investigators to contend that true teratogenicity is not associated with AED.

The introduction of valproic acid to the anticonvulsant armamentarium has modified our thinking in this regard. Dysmorphism has been associated with in utero exposure to valproic acid. The first such case was reported by Dalens *et al.* (1980), who described an infant exposed to valproic acid in utero who was born with low birthweight, hypoplastic nose and fronto-orbital ridges, and levocardia. The baby died at 19 days of life. Subsequent reports of dysmorphism were followed by Clay *et al.* (1981) and a child with lumbosacral meningocele was described by Gomez (1981). Kaneko *et al.* (1988) found valproic acid to result in the highest malformation rate of any AED utilized in 172 pregnancies. As already noted, a fetal valproate syndrome has been described (DiLiberti *et al.*, 1984) and several additional cases reported (Jeavons, 1984; Tein and MacGregor, 1985).

The first reported association of an AED with a specific malformation was with valproic acid and neural tube defects. The Institute European de Gen-omutations in Lyons, France, registered 145 cases of spina bifida between 1976 and 1982. They noted that of infants of mothers with epilepsy exposed to valproic acid, 34% had malformations, and five of nine exposed to valproic acid monotherapy had spina bifida at a rate 20 times that expected (MMWR, 1982).

Robert et al. (1984) sent questionnaires to 646 women with epilepsy, aged 15–45 years. Of 280 responses (43%), they collected data on 74 deliveries to which they added 74 additional cases collected from women delivering in Lyon, France. The malformation rate of the entire group was 13%, with a higher than expected rate of neural tube defects in children exposed to valproic acid.

Stanley and Chambers (1982) reported an infant exposed to valproic acid in utero with spina bifida whose two normal siblings were not exposed to the drug. Lindhout and Schmidt (1986) surveyed 18 epilepsy groups and collected 12 cases of infants and epileptic mothers with neural tube defects. A higher rate was seen in children exposed to valproic acid monotherapy (2.5%) than polytherapy (1.5%). The increased risk appeared to be limited to spina bifida rather than other neural tube defects, with an overall risk of an infant exposed to valproic acid in utero of 1.5%.

The actual mechanism of valproic acid teratogenicity is unknown. A combination of valpromide and carbamazepine results in an increase in carbamazepine 10,11-epoxide (Pacifici et al., 1985). Valpromide and valproate inhibit epoxide hydrolase (Kerr and Levy, 1984). Epoxides have been implicated as teratogens, but carbamazepine epoxide is quite stable and there appears to be a greater risk of spina bifida with valproic acid monotherapy than polytherapy.

Valproic acid appears to be embryotoxic to cultured rat embryos, but none of the hydroxlyated metabolites have exhibited any significant embryotoxicity (Rettie et al., 1986). This implies a direct teratogenic effect of the parent drug.

Weak acids are frequently teratogenic. The intracellular pH of mouse and rat embryos is higher than maternal plasma. Valproate and its 4-en metabolite accumulate in embryonic tissue. Nau and Scott (1986) have suggested that alterations in intracellular pH may explain the teratogenicity of valproic acid. Lindhout (1989, 1990) has proposed different mechanisms, such as interference with lipid metabolism, alterations in zinc concentrations, or disruption of folate utilization.

CONCLUSIONS

Infants of epileptic mothers exposed to anticonvulsants in utero have a greater risk of developing congenital malformations than non-exposed infants, or infants of mothers without epilepsy. The overall risk of a birth defect is between 4% and 6%. In addition, a subgroup of exposed children will have characteristic dysmorphic features of the mid-face and distal digits which are of uncertain long-term significance. The prevalence of this anticonvulsant syndrome is unclear; 5–45% of infants of mothers with epilepsy may have some minor anomalies (Kallen, 1986a).

All commonly used AED cross the placenta and are present in the fetal circulation. All commonly used AED have been associated with congenital malformations, and while many different types have been described orofacial clefts are the most common, accounting for approximately 30% of the excess of malformations seen (Friis *et al.*, 1986). Specific major malformations associated with AED have been described only for valproic acid, which causes a 1–2% risk of spina bifida in exposed infants. AED share many of the features of classic teratogens but generally do not produce a consistent pattern of major malformations. Hence the factors contributing to birth defects in children exposed to these drugs must be, in part, multifactorial.

Generalized convulsions pose clear risks for maternal injury and miscarriage (Higgins and Comerford, 1974; Stumpf and Frost, 1978; Burnett, 1946). For most women, anticonvulsant therapy needs to be continued during pregnancy. In our experience, risks of adverse outcome can be reduced by careful pre-natal care, good seizure control and maintenance of high serum folate levels.

Monotherapy has empirical and theoretical advantages over polytherapy and should be used whenever possible. Once a woman is pregnant, halting or changing her AED will not reduce the risk of major malformations, because most fetal organ systems will already be well established by the eighth week of gestation. Halting or changing from an AED which effectively controls a woman's seizures will place her at risk for an increase in seizure frequency and its attendant hazards. The best AED for a pregnant woman is the one which controls her seizures with the least amount of toxicity. Free AED concentrations should be monitored regularly if available through pregnancy and the post-partum period.

Multivitamins with folate may reduce the risk of malformations or minor anomalies. We suggest placing all women with epilepsy of child-bearing age on multivitamins, for if they are to be effective one must have good concentrations at the time of conception. Supplementary vitamin K_1 should be given to the mother during the last week of pregnancy.

Women taking valproic acid should be informed of the additional risks of spina bifida. The unique nature of this defect permits detection in the pre-natal period. A combination of real-time ultrasonography and amniocentesis for α-fetoprotein concentration between 16 and 18 weeks gestation will detect over 95% of all cases of spina bifida. The risk of spina bifida must be weighed against the risk of an amniocentesis. Serum α-fetoprotein determinations have a 20% false-negative rate and are therefore less useful.

This chapter has concentrated on adverse outcomes of pregnancy for women with epilepsy. While these patients have an increased risk for complications, the proportion of affected persons is small. Over 90% of women with epilepsy will deliver healthy children, free of congenital malformations.

REFERENCES

Anderson, R.C. (1976) Cardiac defects in children of mothers receiving anticonvulsant therapy during pregnancy. *J. Pediatr.*, **89**, 318–319.

Annegers, J.F., Hauser, W.A., Elveback, L.R., Anderson, V.E. and Kurland, L.T. (1978) Congenital malformations and seizure disorders in the offspring of parents with epilepsy. *Int. J. Epidemiol.*, **7**, 241–247.

Baptisti, A. (1938). Epilepsy and pregnancy. *Am. J. Obstet. Gynecol.*, **35**, 818–824.

Bardy, A.H. (1987) Incidence of seizures during pregnancy, labor, and puerperium in epileptic women: A prospective study. *Acta Neurol. Scand.*, **75**, 356–360.

Bardy, A.H., Hiilesmaa, V.K., Teramo, K. and Neuvonen, P.J. (1990) Protein binding of antiepileptic drugs during pregnancy, labor, and puerperium. *Ther. Drug Monit.*, **12**, 40–46.

Barr, M., Pozanski, A.K. and Schmickel, R.D. (1974) Digital hypoplasia and anticonvulsant during gestation: A teratogenic syndrome? *J. Pediatr.*, **84**, 254–256.

Beaussart-Defaye, J., Basten, N., Demarca, C. and Beaussart, M. (1985) *Epilepsies and Reproduction. Nord Epilepsy Research and Information Group* (Vol. II). Grine Lille, France.

Bethenod, M. and Frederich, A. (1975) Les enfants des antiepileptiques. *Pediatrie*, **30**, 227–248.

Biale, Y. and Lewenthal, H. (1984) Effect of folic acid supplementation on congenital malformations due to anticonvulsant drugs. *Eur. J. Obstet. Gynecol. Reprod. Biol.*, **18**, 211–216.

Bjerkedal, T. and Bahna, S.L. (1973) The course and outcome of pregnancy in women with epilepsy. *Acta Obstet. Gynecol. Scand.*, **52**, 245–248.

Bossi, L., Assrel, B.M., Avanzini, G. *et al.* (1980) Plasma levels and clinical effects of antiepileptic drugs in pregnant epileptic patients and their newborns. In: *Antiepileptic Therapy: Advances in Drug Monitoring* (eds S.I. Johannessen *et al.*), pp. 9–14. Raven Press, New York.

Buehler, B.A. (1985) Epoxide hydrolase activity and the fetal hydantoin syndrome. *Clin. Res.*, **33**, A129.

Buehler, B.A., Delimont, D., VanWass, M. and Finnell, R.H. (1990) Prenatal prediction of risk of the fetal hydantoin syndrome. *N. Engl. J. Med.*, **322**, 1567–1572.

Burnett, C.W.F. (1946) A survey of the relation between epilepsy and pregnancy. *J. Obstet. Gynecol.*, **53**, 539–556

Centra, E. and Rasore-Quartino, A. (1965) La sindrome malformatine 'digitocardiaca' forme genetsche e fenocopie. *Probabile Azione Teratogena dei Farmaci Antiepileptici Pathol.*, **57**, 227–232.

Chang, T., Savory, A. and Glazko, A.J. (1970) A new metabolite of 5,5-diphenylhydantoin. *Biochem. Res. Commun.*, **38**, 444–449.

Clay, S.A., McVie, R. and Chen, H.C. (1981) Possible teratogenic effect of valproic acid. *J. Pediatr.*, **98**, 828.

Dalens, B., Raynaud, E.J. and Gaulme, J. (1980) Teratogenicity of valproic acid. *J. Pediatr.*, **97**, 332–333.

Dam, M., Christiansen, J. and Munck, O. (1977) Antiepileptic drugs: Metabolism in pregnancy. *Clin. Pharmacokinet.*, **2**, 427–436.

Dam, M., Christiansen, J., Munck, O. and Mygind, K.I. (1979) Antiepileptic drugs: Metabolism in pregnancy. *Clin. Pharmacokinet.*, **4**, 53–62.

Dansky, L.V., Andermann, E., Rosenblatt, D., Sherwin, A.L. and Andermann, F. (1987) Anticonvulsants, folate levels, and pregnancy outcomes: A prospective study. *Ann. Neurol.*, **21**, 176–182.

Dansky, L.V., Andermann, E., Sherwin, A.L., Andermann, F. and Kinch, R.A. (1980) Maternal epilepsy and congenital malformations: A prospective study with monitoring of plasma anticonvulsant levels during pregnancy. *Neurology*, **3**, 15.

Dansky, L.V., Strickler, S.M., Andermann, E., Miller, M.A., Seni, M.H. and Spielberg, S.P. (1987) Pharmacogenetic susceptibility to phenytoin teratogenesis. In: *Advances in Epileptology* (eds P. Wolf, M. Dam, D. Janz and F. Dreifuss), Vol. 16, pp. 555–559. Raven Press, New York.

Dieterich, E., Steveling, A., Lukas, A., Seyfeddinipur, N. and Spranger, J. (1980) Congenital anomalies in children of epileptic mothers and fathers. *Neuropediatrics*, **11**, 274–283.

DiLiberti, J.H., Farndon, P.A., Dennis, N.R. and Curry C.J.R. (1984) The fetal valproate syndrome. *Am. J. Med. Genet.*, **19**, 473–481.

Eadie, M.J., Lander, C.M. and Tyner, J.H. (1977) Plasma drug level monitoring in pregnancy. *Clin. Pharmacokinet.*, **2**, 427–436.

Elshove, J. and Van Eck, J.H.M. (1971) Aangeboren misvorminge, met name gespleten lip met zonder gespleten verhemelte, bij kinderen van moders met epilepsie. *Ned. Tijdschr. Geneesk.*, **115**, 1371–1375.

Fedrick, J. (1983) Epilepsy and pregnancy: A report from the Oxford record linkage study. *Br. Med. J.*, **2**, 442–448.

Felding, I. and Rane, A. (1984) Congenital liver damage after treatment of mother with valproic acid and phenytoin? *Acta Pediatr. Scand.*, **73**, 565–568.

Feldman, G.L., Weaver, D.D. and Lovrien, E.W. (1977) The fetal trimethadione syndrome: Report of an additional family and further delineation of this syndrome. *Am. J. Dis. Child.*, **131**, 89–92.

Finnell, R.H. and Diliberti, J.H. (1983) Hydantoin induced teratogenesis: Are arene oxide intermediates really responsible? *Helv. Paediatr. Acta*, **38**, 171–177.

Finnell, R.H., Mohl, V.K., Bennett, G.P. and Taylor, S.M. (1986) Failure of epoxide formation to influence carbamazepine-induced teratogenesis in a mouse model. *Teratogenesis Carcinog. Mutagen.*, **6**, 393.

Friis, M.L. and Hauge, M. (1985) Congenital heart defects in live born children of epileptic parents. *Arch. Neurol.*, **42**, 374–376.

Friis, M.L., Breng-Nielsen, B., Sindrup, E.H. Lund, M., Gogh-Andersen, P. and Hauge, M. (1981) Facial clefts among epileptic patients. *Arch. Neurol.*, **38**, 227–229.

Friis, M.L., Holm, N.V., Sindrup, E.H., Fogh-Andersen, P. and Hauge, M. (1986) Facial clefts in sibs and children of epileptic patients. *Neurology*, **38**, 346–350.

Gaily, E., Granstrom, M.L., Hiilesmaa, V. and Bandy, A. (1988a) Minor anomalies in offspring of epileptic mothers. *J. Pediatr.*, **112**, 520–529.

Gaily, E., Kantula-Sorsa, E. and Granstrom, M.L. (1988b) Intelligence of children of epileptic mothers. *J. Pediatr.*, **113**, 677–684.

Gatoh, N., Millo, Y., Taube, E. and Bechar, M. (1987) Epilepsy among parents of children with cleft lip and palate. *Brain Dev.*, **9**, 296–299.

German, J., Kowal, A. and Ehlers, K.H. (1970) Trimethadione and human teratogenesis. *Teratology*, **3**, 349–362.

Gjerde, I.O., Strandjord, R.E. and Ulstein, H. (1988) The course of epilepsy during pregnancy. *Acta Neurol. Scand.*, **78**, 198–205.

Goldman, A.S., Zachai, E.H. and Yaffe, S.J. (1986) Environmentally induced birth defect risks. In: *Teratogen Update* (eds J.L. Sever and R.L. Brent), pp. 35–38. Liss, New York.

Goldman, A.S., Van Dyke, D.C., Gupta, C. and Katsumata, M. (1987) Elevated glucocorticoid receptor levels in lymphocytes of children with the fetal hydantoin syndrome. *Am. J. Med. Genet.*, **28**, 607–618.

Gomez, M.R. (1981) Possible teratogenicity of valproic acid. *J. Pediatr.*, **9**, 508.

Granstrom, M.L. (1982) Development of the children of epileptic mothers: Preliminary results from the prospective Helsinki study. In: *Epilepsy, Pregnancy and the Child* (eds D. Janz, M. Dam, A. Richens, L. Bossi, H. Helge and D. Schmidt), pp. 403–408. Raven Press, New York.

Granstrom, M.L. (1987) Early postnatal growth of the children of epileptic mothers. In: *Advances in Epileptology* (eds P. Wolf, M. Dam, D. Janz and F. Dreifuss), Vol. 16, pp. 573–577. Raven Press, New York.

Grosse, K.P., Schwanitz, G., Rott, H.D. and Wissmuler, H.F. (1972) Chromosomenuntersuchungen bei behandlung mit anticonvulsiva. *Humangenetik*, **16**, 209–216.

Gustavson, E.E. and Chen, H. (1985) Goldenhar syndrome: Enterloencephalocele and aqueductal stenosis following fetal primidone exposure. *Teratology*, **32**, 13–17.

Hanson, J.W. and Smith, D.W. (1975) The fetal hydantoin syndrome. *J. Pediatr.*, **87**, 285–290.

Hanson, J.W., Myrianthopoulos, N.C., Sedgwich, M.A. and Smith, D.W. (1976) Risks to the offspring of women treated with hydantoin anticonvulsants with emphasis on the fetal hydantoin syndrome. *J. Pediatr.*, **89**, 662–668.

Higgins, T.A. and Comerford, J.B. (1974) Epilepsy in pregnancy. *J. Irish Med. Assoc.*, **67**, 317–320.

Hiilesmaa, V.K., Teramo, K., Granstrom, M.L. and Bardy, A.H. (1981) Fetal head growth retardation associated with maternal antiepileptic drugs. *Lancet*, ii, 165–167.

Hill, R.M. and Tennyson, L. (1982) Premature delivery, gestational age, complications of delivery, vital data at birth on newborn infants of epileptic mothers: Review of the literature. In: *Epilepsy Pregnancy and the Child* (ed. D. Janz), pp. 167–174. Raven Press, New York.

Hill, R.M. and Tennyson, L.M. (1986) Maternal drug therapy: Effect on fetal and neonatal growth and neurobehavior. *Neurotoxicology*, **7**, 121–140.

Hill, R.M., Berniaum, W.M., Morning, M.G. *et al.* (1974) Infants exposed in utero to antiepileptic drugs. *Am. J. Dis. Child.*, **127**, 645–652.

Horning, M.G., Stratton, C., Wilson, A., Horning, E.C. and Hill, R.M. (1974) Detection of 5-(3,4)-dephenylhydantoin in the newborn human. *Anal. Letters*, **4**, 537–582.

Huot, C., Gauthier, M., Lebel, M., and Larbisseau, A. (1987) Congenital malformations associated with maternal use of valproic acid. *Can. J. Neurol. Sci.*, **14**, 290–293.

Hutch, H.C., Steinhouse, H.C. and Helge, H. (1975) Mental development in children of epileptic parents. In: *Epidemiology of epilepsy in Rochester, Minnesota, 1935 through 1967* (eds W.A. Hauser and L.T. Kurland), *Epilepsia*, **16**, 1–66.

Jacobson, C.D., Autolick, C.L. Scholey, R. and Vemura, E. (1988) The influence of prenatal phenobarbital exposure on the growth of dendrites in the rat hippocampus. *Dev. Brain Res.*, **44**, 233–239.

Jager-Roman, E., Deichl, A., Jakob, S. *et al.* (1986) Fetal growth major malformations and minor anomalies in infants born to women receiving valproic acid. *J. Pediatr.*, **108**, 997–1004.

Janz, D. (1982) Antiepileptic drugs and pregnancy: Altered utilization patterns and teratogenesis. *Epilepsia*, **23**, 553–563.

Janz, D. and Fuchs, U. (1964) Are antiepileptic drugs harmful when given during pregnancy? *German Med. Monthly*, **9**, 20–22.

Jeavons, P.M. (1984) Non dose related side effects of valproate. *Epilepsia*, **25** (Suppl. 1), 550–555.

Jerina, D.M. and Daly, J.W. (1974) Arene oxides: A new aspect of drug metabolism. *Science*, **197**, 185–573.

Jones, K.L., Lacro, R.V., Johnson, K.A. and Adams, J. (1989) Pattern of malformations in the children of women treated with carbamazepine during pregnancy. *N. Engl. J. Med.*, **320**, 1661–1666.

Kallen, B. (1986a) A register study of maternal epilepsy and delivery outcome with special reference to drug use. *Acta Neurol. Scand.*, **73**, 253–259.

Kallen, B. (1986b) Maternal epilepsy, antiepileptic drugs and birth defects. *Pathologica*, **78**, 757–768.

Kalter, H., and Warkany, J. (1983) Congenital malformations. *N. Engl. J. Med.*, **308**, 491–497.

Kaneko, S., Otani, K., Fukushima, Y., Ogawa, Y., Nomura, Y., Ono, T., Nakane, Y., Teranishi, T. and Goto, M. (1988) Teratogenicity of antiepileptic drugs: Analysis of possible risk factors. *Epilepsia*, **29**, 459–467.

Kelly, T.E. (1984a) Teratogenicity of anticonvulsant drugs 1: Review of literature. *Am. J. Med. Genet.*, **19**, 413–434.

Kelly, T.E. (1984b) Teratogenicity of anticonvulsants III: Radiographic hand analysis of children exposed in utero to diphenylhydantoin. *Am. J. Med. Genet.*, **19**, 445–450.

Kelly, T.E., Edwards, P., Rein, M., Miller, J.Q. and Dreifuss, F.E. (1984c) Teratogenicity of anticonvulsant drugs II: A prospective study. *Am. J. Med. Genet.*, **19**, 435–443.

Kerr, B.M. and Levy, R.H. (1984) Inhibition of epoxide hydrolase by anticonvulsants and risk of teratogenicity. *Lancet*, **i**, 610–611.

Knight, A.H. and Rhind, E.G. (1975) Epilepsy and pregnancy: A study of 153 pregnancies in 59 patients. *Epilepsia*, **16**, 99–110.

Koerner, M., Yerby, M.S., Friel, P.N. and McCormick, K.B. (1989) Valproic acid disposition and the protein binding in pregnancy. *Ther. Drug Monit.*, **11**, 228–230.

Koppe, J.G., Bosmon, W., Oppers, V.M. *et al.* (1973) Epilepsie en aangeborn afwijkingen. *Ned. Tijdsch. Geneesk.* **117**, 220–224.

Krauss, C.M., Holmes, L.B., Van Lang, Q.C. and Keith, D.A. (1984) Four siblings with similar malformations after exposure to phenytoin and primidone. *J. Pediatr.*, **105**, 750–755.

Kubow, S. and Wells, P.G. (1989) In vitro bioactivation of phenytoin to a reactive free radical intermediate by prostaglandin synthetase, horseradish peroxidase, and thyroid peroxidase. *Mol. Pharmacol.*, **35**, 504–511.

Kuenssberg, E.V. and Knox, J.D.E. (1973) Teratogenic effect of anticonvulsants. *Lancet*, **i**, 198.

Laegreid, L., Olegard, R., Wahlstrom, J. and Conradi, N. (1987) Abnormalities in children exposed to benzodiazepines in utero. *Lancet*, **i**, 108–109.

Lander, C.M., Edward, V.E., Eadie, M.J. and Tyner, J.H. (1977) Plasma anticonvulsant concentrations during pregnancy. *Neurology*, **27**, 128–131.

Leppig, K.A., Werler, M.M., Cann, C.I., Cook, C.A. and Holmes, L.B. (1987) Predictive value of minor anomalies 1. Association with major malformations. *J. Pediatr.*, **110**, 530–537.

Levy, R.H. and Yerby, M.S. (1985) Effects of pregnancy on antiepileptic drug utilization. *Epilepsia*, **26** (Suppl. 1), 525–557.

Lindhout, D. (1989) Commission reviews teratogenesis and genetics in epilepsy. *World Neurol.*, **4**, 3–7.

Lindhout, D. (1990) Joint European Study on Pregnancy and the Child. Presented at: *An International Symposium on Pregnancy, Teratogenesis and Genetics in Epilepsy.* Santa Monica, California.

Lindhout, D. and Schmidt, D. (1986) In utero exposure to valproate and neural tube defects. *Lancet*, **i**, 1392–1393.

Lindhout, D., Rene, J.E. Hoppener, A. and Meinardi, H. (1984) Teratogenicity of antiepileptic drug combinations with special emphasis on epoxidation (of carbamazepine). *Epilepsia*, **25**, 77–83.

Loughnan, P.M., Gold, H. and Vance, J.C. (1973) Phenytoin teratogenicity in man. *Lancet*, **i**, 70–72.

Lowe, C.R. (1973) Congenital malformations among infants born to epileptic women. *Lancet*, **i**, 9–10.

Majewski, F., Raft, W., Fischer, P., Huenges, R. and Petruch, F. (1980) Zur Tertogenitat von Anticonvulsiva. *Deutsche Med. Wochenschr.*, **105**, 719–723.

Marden, P.M., Smith, D.W. and McDonald, M.J. (1964) Congenital anomalies in the newborn infant, including minor variations. *J. Pediatr.*, **64**, 357.

Martz, F., Failinger, C. and Blake, D.A. (1977) Phenytoin teratogenesis: Correlation between embryopathic effect and covalent binding of putative arene oxide metabolite to gestational tissue. *J. Pharmacol. Exp. Ther.*, **203**, 231–239.

Meadow, S.R. (1968) Anticonvulsant drugs and congenital abnormalities. *Lancet*, **ii**, 1296.

Melchior, I.C., Svensmark, O. and Trolle, D. (1967) Placental transfer of phenobarbitone in women and elimination in newborns. *Lancet*, **ii**, 860–861.

Meyer, J.G. (1973) The teratological effects of anticonvulsants and the effects of pregnancy and birth. *Eur. Neurol.*, **10**, 179–180.

Millar, J.H.D. and Nevin, N.C. (1973) Congenital malformations and anticonvulsant drugs. *Lances*, **ii**, 328.

Minkoff, H., Schaffer, R.M., Delke, I. and Grunebaum, A.N. (1985) Diagnosis of intracranial hemorrhage in utero after a maternal seizure. *Obstet. Gynecol.*, **65** (Suppl. 3), 225–243.

MMWR (1982) Valproic acid and spinal bifida: a preliminary report. *Morbid. Mortal. Weekly Rep.*, **31**, 565–566.

Monson, R.R., Rosenberg, L. and Hartz, S.C. (1973) Diphenyhydantoin and selected congenital malformations. *N. Engl. J. Med.*, **289**, 1049–1052.

Muller-Kuppers, von M. (1963) Embryopathy during pregnancy caused by taking anticonvulsants. *Acta Paedopsychiat.*, **30**, 401–405.

Mygind, K.I., Dam, M. and Christiansen, J. (1976) Phenytoin and phenobarbitone plasma clearance during pregnancy. *Acta Neurol. Scand.*, **54**, 160–166.

Nakane, Y. (1979) Congenital malformations among infants of epileptic mothers treated during pregnancy. *Folia Psychiat. Neurol. Jpn.*, **33**, 363–369.

Nakane, Y., Oltuma, T., Takahashi, R. *et al.* (1980) Multi-institutional study on the teratogenicity and fetal toxicity of anticonvulsants: A report of a collaborative study group in Japan. *Epilepsia*, **21**, 663–680.

Nau, H. and Scott, W.J. (1986) Weak acids may act as teratogens by accumulating in the basic milieu of the early mammalian embryo. *Nature*, **323**, 276–278.

Nau, H., Kuhnz, W., Egger, H.J., Rating, D. and Helge, H. (1981) Anticonvulsants during pregnancy and lactation: Transplacental, maternal and neonatal pharmacokinetics. *Clin. Pharmacokinet.*, **7**, 508–543.

Nebert, D.W. and Jensen, N.M. (1979) The Ah locus: Genetic regulation of the metabolism of carcinogens, drugs, and other environmental chemicals by cytochrome P-450 mediated mono-oxygenases. *CRC Crit. Rev. Biochem.*, **6**, 401–437.

Nelson, K.B. and Ellenberg, J.H. (1982) Maternal seizure disorder outcomes of pregnancy and neurologic abnormalities in the children. *Neurology*, **32**, 1247–1254.

Neri, A., Heifetz, L., Nitke, S. *et al.* (1983) Neonatal outcomes in infants of epileptic mothers. *Eur. J. Obstet. Gynecol. Reprod. Biol.*, **16**, 263–268.

Niesen, M. and Froscher, W. (1985) Finger and toenail hypoplasia after carbamazepine monotherapy in late pregnancy. *Neuropediatrics*, **16**, 167–168.

Niswander, J.D. and Werteleck, W. (1973) Congenital malformation among offspring of epileptic women. *Lancet*, **i**, 1062.

Otani, K. (1985) Risk factors for the increased seizure frequency during pregnancy and puerperium. *Folia Psychiatr. Neurol. Jpn.*, **39**, 33–44.

Ottman, R., Annegers, J.F., Hauser, W.A. and Kurland, L.T. (1988) Higher risk of seizures in offspring of mothers than fathers with epilepsy. *Am. J. Hum. Genet.*, **43**, 357–364.

Pacifici, G.M. and Rane, A. (1982) Metabolism of styrene oxide in different human fetal tissues. *Drug Metab. Dispos.*, **10**, 302–305.

Pacifici, G.M., Colizzi, C., Giuliani, L. and Rane, A. (1983) Cytosolic epoxide hydrolase in fetal and adult human liver. *Arch. Toxicol.*, **54**, 331.

Pacifici, G.M., Tomson, T., Beatilsson, L. and Rane, A. (1985) Valpromide/carbamazepine and the risk of teratogenicity. *Lancet*, **i**, 397–398.

Pantarotto, C., Arboix, M., Sezzano, P. and Abbruzzo, R. (1982) Studies on 5,5-dephenylhydantoin irreversible binding to rat liver microsomal proteins. *Biochem. Pharmacol.*, **31**, 1501–1507.

Pantarotto, M.F. (1965) A case of bone marrow aplasia in a newborn attributable to anticonvulsant drugs used by the mother during pregnancy. *Quat. Clin. Obstet. Gynecol.*, **67**, 343–338.

Paskind, H.A. and Brown, M. (1932) Constitutional differences between deteriorated and non deteriorated patients with epilepsy. *Arch. Neurol. Psychiatry*, 1037–1044.

Perucca, E. and Crema, A. (1982) Plasma protein binding of drugs in pregnancy. *Clin. Pharmacokinet.*, **7**, 336–352.

Phelan, M.C., Pellock, J.M. and Wance, W.E. (1982) Discordant expression of fetal hydantoin syndrome in heteropaternal dizygotic twins. *N. Engl. J. Med.*, **307**, 99–101.

Philbert, A. and Dam, M. (1982) The epileptic mother and her child. *Epilepsia*, **23**, 85–99.

Ramsay, R.E., Strauss, R.G., Wilder, B.J. and Willmore, L.J. (1978) Status epilepticus in pregnancy: Effect of phenytoin malabsorption on seizure control. *Neurology*, **28**, 85–89.

Rating, D., Jäger-Roman, E., Koch, S., Jakob, S., Deichl, A., Helge, H. and Nau, H. (1987) Major malformations and minor anomalies in infants exposed to different antiepileptic drugs during pregnancy. In: *Advances in Epileptology* (eds P. Wolf, M. Dam, D. Janz and F.E. Dreifuss), Vol. 16, pp. 561–565. Raven Press, New York.

Rettie, A.E., Rettenmeir, A.W., Beyer, B.K., Baile, T.A. and Jachau, M.R. (1986) Valproate hydroxylation by human fetal tissues and embryotoxicity of metabolites. *Clin. Pharmacol. Ther.*, **40**, 172–177.

Robert, E., Lofkvist, E. and Maugiere, F. (1984) Valproate and spina bifida. *Lancet*, **i**, 1392.

Rudd, N.L. and Freedom, R.M. (1979) A possible primidone embryopathy. *J. Pediatr.*, **94**, 835–837.

Sabin, M. and Oxorn, H. (1956) Epilepsy and pregnancy. *Obstet. Gynecol.*, **7**, 175–199.

Schmidt, D., Canger, R., Avanzini, G. *et al.* (1983) Change of seizure frequency in pregnant epileptic women. *J. Neurol. Neurosurg. Psychiatry*, **46**, 751–755.

Seino, M. and Miyakoshi, M. (1979) Teratogenic risks of antiepileptic drugs in respect to the type of epilepsy. *Folia Psychiatr. Neurol. Jap.* **33**, 379–385.

Seip, M. (1976) Growth retardation, dysmorphic facies and minor malformations following massive exposure to phenobarbital in utero. *Acta Paediatr. Scand.*, **65**, 617–621.

Shapiro, S., Slone, D., Hartz, S.C., Rosenberg, L., Siskind, V., Monson, R.R., Mitchell, A.A., Heinonen, O.P., Idanmpaan-Heikkila, J., Haro, S., Saxen, L. *et al.* (1976) Anticonvulsant and parental epilepsy in the development of birth defects. *Lancet*, **i**, 272–275.

Shum, S., Jensen, N.M. and Nebert, D.W. (1979) The Ah locus: in utero toxicity and teratogenesis associated with genetic differences in B(a)P metabolism. *Teratology*, **20**, 365–376.

Sims, P. and Grover, P.L. (1974) Epoxides in polycyclic aromatic hydrocarbon metabolism and carcinogenesis. *Adv. Cancer Res.*, **20**, 165.

South, J. (1972) Teratogenic effects of anticonvulsants. *Lancet*, **i**, 1154.

Speidel, B.D. and Meadow, S.R. (1972) Maternal epilepsy and abnormalities of the fetus and newborn. *Lancet*, **ii**, 839–843.

Spellacy, W.N. (1972) Maternal epilepsy and abnormalities of the fetus and newborn. *Lancet.*

Spielberg, S.P., Gordon, G.B., Blake, D.A., Mellits, E.D. and Bross, D.S. (1981) Anticonvulsant toxicity in vitro: Possible role of arene oxides. *J. Pharmacol. Exp. Ther.*, **217**, 386–389.

Stanley, O.H. and Chambers, T.L. (1982) Sodium valproate and neural tube defects. *Lancet*, 1282–1283.

Starreveld-Zimmerman, A.A.E., Van Der Kolk, W.J., Meinardi, H. (1973) Are anticonvulsants teratogenic? *Lancet*, **ii**, 48–49.

Strickler, S.M., Dansky, L.V., Miller, M.A., Seni, M.H., Andermann, E., and Spielberg, S.P. (1985) Genetic predisposition to phenytoin induced birth defects. *Lancet*, **i**, 746–749.

Stumpf, D.A. and Frost, M. (1978) Seizures, anticonvulsants, and pregnancy. *Am. J. Dis. Child.*, **132**, 746–748.

Sullivan, F.M. and McElhatton, P.R. (1975) Teratogenic activity of the antiepileptic drugs, phenobarbital, phenytoin, and primidone in mice. *Toxicol. Appl. Pharmacol.*, **34**, 271–282.

Tein, I. and MacGregor, D.L. (1985) Possible valproate toxicity. *Arch. Neurol.*, **42**, 291–293.

Teramo, K., Hiilesmaa, V., Bardy, A. and Saarihosk, S. (1979) Fetal heart rate during a maternal grand mal epileptic seizure. *J. Perinat. Med.*, **7**, 3–6.

Traggis, D.G., Mauz, D.L. and Baroudy, R. (1984) Hemorrhage in a neonate of a mother on anticonvulsant therapy. *J. Pediatr. Surg.*, **19**, 598–599.

Van Dyke, D.C., Hodge, S.E., Heide, F. and Hill, L.R. (1988) Family studies in fetal phenytoin exposure. *J. Pediatr.*, **113**, 301–306.

Visser, G.H., Huisjes, H.J. and Elshove, J. (1976) Anticonvulsants and fetal malformations. *Lancet*, **i**, 970.

Vorhees, C.V. (1986) Developmental effects of anticonvulsants. *Neurotoxicology*, **7**, 235–244.

Weber, L.W.D. (1977) Benzodiazepines in pregnancy—academic debate or teratogenic risk? *Biol. Res. Preg.*, **6**, 151–167.

Wells, P.G. and Harbison, R.D. (1985) Significance of the phenytoin reactive arene oxide intermediate, its oxepintantomer, and clinical factors modifying their roles in phenytoin-induced teratology. In: *Phenytoin-induced Teratology and Gingival Pathology* (eds T.M. Hussell, M.C. Johnston and K.H. Dudley), pp. 83–112. Raven Press, New York.

Wells, P.G., Zubovits, J.T., Wong, S.T., Malinaro, L.M. and Ali, S. (1984) Modulation of phenytoin teratogenecity and embryonic covalent binding by acetylsalicylic acid, caffeic acid, and α-phenyl-N-E-butylnitrone: Implications for bioactivation by prostaglandin synthetase. *Toxicol. Appl. Pharmacol.*, **97**, 192–202.

Wong, M. and Wells, P.G. (1989) Modulation of embryonic glutathione reductase and phenytoin teratogenicity by 1,3-bis (2-chloroethyl)-1-nitrosourea (BCNU). *J. Pharmacol. Exp. Ther.*, **250**, 336–342.

Yerby, M.S. (1987) Problems in the management of the pregnant woman with epilepsy. *Epilepsia* (Suppl), **3**, 529–536.

Yerby, M.S., Koepsell, T. and Daling, J. (1985) Pregnancy complications and outcomes in a cohort of women with epilepsy. *Epilepsia*, **26**, 631–635.

Yerby, M.S., Friel, P.N., McCormick, K.B., Koerner, M., VanAllen, M., Leavitt, A.M., Sells, C.J. and Yerby, J.A. (1990a) Pharmacokinetics of anticonvulsants in pregnancy: Alterations in plasma protein binding. *Epilepsy Res.*, **5**, 223–228.

Yerby, M.S., Leavitt, A., Erickson, D., Lowenson, R.B., McCormick, K.B., Van Allen, M.I., Sells, C.J. and Benedetti, T.J. (1990b) Congenital anomalies in infants of epileptic mothers. *Neurology*, **40**, 188.

Zachai, E.H., Mellman, W.J. Neideren, B. and Hanson, J.W. (1975) The fetal trimethadione syndrome. *J. Pediatr.*, **87**, 280–284.

Zhu, M. and Zhou, S. (1989) Reduction of the teratogenic effects of phenytoin by folic acid and a mixture of folic acid, vitamins, and amino acids: A preliminary trial. *Epilepsia*, **30**, 246–251.

Discussion session 3

Dr Espir: Dr Patsalos said that since 1984 few or no cases of unwanted pregnancy related to anticonvulsant prescription have been reported to the CSM. I am sure these cases continue to occur. A lot of general practitioners still do not know that there is this interaction. I feel that there should not be any complacency because of those figures and that we should continue to emphasize this possible interaction.

Dr Patsalos: Those comments are very true. I looked at the prescribing recommendations in MIMS on oral contraceptives and there is absolutely no advice that the dose of oral contraceptive should be increased in patients who are taking anticonvulsant drugs.

Dr Hopkins: Pregnant girls are not being reported to the CSM but are actually reporting themselves to the Medical Protection Society and the Medical Defence Union. If you get pregnant and have not been told of the possibility by your family doctor, you are very likely to sue. There have been a number of cases settled. One girl said to me, 'It's in the package insert. If I know about it because it's in the package insert, surely the family doctor ought to know about it.'

Dr. Bradbury: I am in the habit of writing down 'advised about DVLC' and 'advised about contraception' in the notes, when I see the patient first of all and start them on treatment. I had a patient who thought she was pregnant who came into the clinic two weeks ago with a very angry husband. They were threatening to sue me on the grounds that I had not advised them about possible failure of contraception, when in fact it was documented in the notes. In these litigious times, we should write these things down.

Dr Besag: Patients and parents are often nervous about using a higher dosage of oral contraception, and I wondered if there was any way of reassuring them, perhaps even by measuring blood levels. Also, on the rate of onset of the enzyme induction and how quickly it goes away; if we change patients to a non-enzyme-inducing drug how long will the enzyme induction last?

Professor Orme: On your first question, I think the only way of getting the message over is really constant information. The only potential harm that we can ever conceive is obviously if you are using 100 µg of ethanol oestradiol you are generating more metabolites with the enzyme induction. If those metabolites would be active then you might be producing long-term harm, but all the studies that have been done show that metabolites both of oestrogen and progestogen are inactive in the toxological sense.

In terms of measuring blood levels, yes it would be nice, but measuring ethanol oestradiol levels is very difficult. It takes about a week's work to measure an ethanol oestradiol sample and so it is not routine. Even if it was, the range of what is so-called normal lies between 6 and 160, and you've not got the slightest idea what a random sample from the patient really means.

Your specific question in terms of onset and offset—it depends on the enzyme inducer, but with the anticonvulsant enzyme inducers the onset of enzyme induction occurs over a period of about a month to six weeks. You get an initial effect really quite quickly, within a week or two, and probably within a month the enzyme induction effect is maximal. There is obviously a dose–response relationship, so if you increase the dose of the drug you do get more enzyme induction. In terms of offset, it seems to depend primarily upon the dose and also upon the length of time that the patient has been on the enzyme inducer. There are obviously many patients who have been on anticonvulsants for years, and I reckon it's going to take three months. The longest we've seen is nine months for the enzyme induction to wear off, but I think that is exceptional. I would say three to six months is fairly common.

Dr Pellock: We participated in a study of converting people from one anti-epileptic drug to another, comparing the classic enzyme inducers to valproate. The interesting thing was we all had this feeling that by one or two months we would be through adjusting doses. However, four, five, even six months out we were still reducing doses of valproate because of the prolonged de-induction phase.

Dr Reynolds: Dr Yerby, what is the risk of teratogenicity in the offspring of epileptic fathers, and secondly with regard to the folate hypothesis of teratogenicity, are there studies of red cell folate in relation to outcome of pregnancy?

Dr Yerby: The first question is whether or not there is any increase in adverse pregnancy outcomes in which the fathers have epilepsy. Interestingly enough this has been rarely studied. The best report of this was done by Hauser and colleagues using the database at the Mayo Clinic. The outcomes which they examined in the infants of fathers with epilepsy were for major malformation and the development of a seizure disorder or epilepsy in the children. They did not find any increased risks for major malformations or for epilepsy in the children of fathers with epilepsy. So the best information we have to date seems to suggest that there is little impact of paternal epilepsy on at least major malformations and seizures.

In answer to the question of whether or not we measured red cell or serum folate—in our study we measured serum folate. In fact, in most of the studies it is serum folate, not red cell folate, that has been assessed.

Dr Allen: Dr Yerby, what was your control population?

Dr Yerby: Our control population for our prospective study were women without epilepsy who were attending the obstetrical clinics at the University of Washington. The people were chosen and matched for age and for parity and an attempt was made to match for socio-economic status by using the maximum number of years of education in both the woman and in her spouse.

Participant: Dr Yerby, when you speak of multi-vitamin supplements during pregnancy are you speaking just of water-soluble vitamins or are you including non-soluble vitamins in that supplementation, thinking particularly of K and E, which of course does have a scavenging effect in relation to free radicals?

Dr Yerby: The vitamins we are primarily speaking of are water-soluble vitamins; most of the vitamins in the general pre-natal vitamin supplements contain those. We give additional K, which is a fat-soluble vitamin, during that last portion of pregnancy. Some of my colleagues, because of issues of compliance, have chosen to use intramuscular K, giving the women an injection of intramuscular K during that last month of pregnancy, and that seems to be effective.

Dr Rowe: Is there catamenial cycling of pseudoseizures or hysterical fits.

Dr Crawford: There is no evidence on this.

Dr Trimble: Dr Yerby, with a female patient who wants to become pregnant who is on valproic acid, should I change her medication before she becomes pregnant? Also, what is your preferred monotherapy for patients who come to you saying they would like to get pregnant and they want to plan it all very carefully?

Dr Yerby: In most of the studies that we have to look at, while they show a general increase in risk of adverse outcomes and major malformations, the numbers are relatively small. Our ability to do comparisons of specific therapies and mono- or polytherapy is limited by the relatively small sample sizes, since the power is not terribly good. Having said that, especially knowing the issue of spina bifida and some of the theoretical mechanisms, there are drugs that we would rather avoid and if we could avoid valproic acid in pregnant patients I think it would be a good idea. In actual practice, however, I, and I am sure others, have patients for whom valproate appears to be their only truly effective medication in controlling their seizures; a classic example would be women with juvenile myoclonic epilepsy. In a patient like that who is controlled on monotherapy and with whom we are able to get control with reasonably modest doses, I do not recommend a change because the alternative of poor seizure control also places her at risk for an adverse outcome.

On the other hand, if we had a new patient who had not been treated yet and we felt that we had made the proper diagnosis and we felt that issues of efficacy and clinical toxicity for the individual patient were equivalent, which drug would appear to be safest? There is good theoretical evidence to suggest that carbamazepine has advantages. I have a preference for the use of that compound.

Dr Trimble: Could you comment on the potential cognitive and developmental effects of anticonvulsant drugs on the very young child of a mother who has been on anticonvulsants?

Dr Yerby: We are limited by the size of the studies that have been done and by the fact that most studies of these problems of pregnancy outcomes has stopped at delivery. Children have been examined at delivery or fairly soon afterwards, adverse outcomes have been recorded and that has been the end of it. Very few studies have gone on to follow children. One of the best is from the University of Helsinki. They followed children up to the age of 5 years. They found no significant difference in mental development in the children of mothers with epilepsy compared to the rates of children with intellectual problems generally. There are other studies, and probably the most famous of these was the collaborative peri-natal project of the NINCDS. This study followed some 50 000 women through their pregnancies in the United States and then their children were monitored until the age of 7. A subset of these women were on anticonvulsant drugs. When they looked at children who were exposed to phenytoin in utero, and compared their IQ at 7 years of age with controls, they found it to be statistically lower. It averaged 92 compared with the IQs of the control children, which was 97. The problem is that this was a statistically significant difference, because you have a good number of patients, but not a clinically significant one, because an IQ differential of 5 points is fairly small on a clinical basis.

Developmental delay unfortunately has been poorly evaluated in most studies. Our study at the age of 1 year has found a differential in the Bayley scores of children looking at the mental developmental index, compared with the physical developmental index. Only the mental developmental index scores are different and they are statistically significantly different, with scores for children with mothers with epilepsy being lower than controls. However, although the scores are lower, the children with mothers with epilepsy had a mean score of 103, which is still above the mean, which was 100. So that while the scores may be lower there still is not any clinical evidence that the children themselves have significant delay.

Dr Wallace: Could I ask Dr Yerby about this theory that there is a subset of patients with relative deficiencies of epoxide hydroxylates. Is there any way of identifying those patients and could you perhaps protect them from the drugs which might produce abnormal metabolites which might have adverse effects for the fetus?

Dr Yerby: Theoretically, yes. The measurement of these enzymes is, at the present time, fairly difficult. In order to measure the free radical scavenging enzymes you need plasma and you have to harvest it carefully. It cannot be frozen or you will destroy the enzyme activity, so it has to be refrigerated but not frozen and then processed very quickly. There was an interesting study published in the last year in which people looked at epoxide hydroxylase activity in amniocytes taken at amniocentesis and found that in a subset of women there was a significantly lower concentration, or activity level. In some of those patients their children tended to have more dysmorphism. This is not the same as having a major malformation, but again it does suggest that there are persons with enzyme activity that falls at the low end and their children are more likely to have developmental difficulties.

   However, note that trimethadione, which has to be the most teratogenic agent that we ever use as neurologists, has no epoxide so this is not the entire story.

Dr Trimble: Oxcarbazepine is a new drug that some of us are working with at the moment. It is suggested that this drug has fewer side effects than carbamazepine, and one of the features of oxcarbazepine is that it does not produce an epoxide. Another property of oxcarbazepine is that it has fewer enzyme induction characteristics than carbamazepine. Does Professor Orme have any experience with this drug and oral contraception?

Professor Orme: The answer to your question is no. In animal studies it appears to be less of an enzyme inducer, but I have not seen the details of human studies.

Patricia Knight: Dr Yerby noted the importance of patient education for women. I have just done some work to produce material for adolescents with epilepsy, and certainly one of the major concerns that young women had was about future parenting. When should such information be given to young women?

Dr Yerby: As soon as possible, although it is hard to say. I am always surprised with young people at the age at which they become sexually active. I try to do this early on in my patient's adolescence.

Section IV

12

Sex, sexual seizures and the female with epilepsy

B. TOONE
King's College Hospital, London, UK

INTRODUCTION

This chapter will encompass three related topics: sexual seizures, i.e. epileptic seizures, part of the phenomenology of which is of a sexual nature, relating either to the genitalia or to the sexual act; post-ictal sexual disinhibition; and the immediate temporal relationship between seizure activity and sexual behaviour.

SEXUAL SEIZURES

Sexual sensation or behaviour as a manifestation of epileptic activity is an uncommon occurrence and it is only in relatively recent years that it has been recognized and described (Bente and Kluge, 1953), although both Reynolds and Esquirol, reporting in an era before EEG confirmation had become available, provide accounts of orgasmic episodes believed to be epileptic. Most of these occurred in women (see Critchley, 1935). Our present understanding is far from complete and is derived for the most part from single case history studies with only occasional extended series (e.g. Remillard *et al.*, 1983). Sexual phenomena as part of the ictus would appear to be confined almost exclusively to seizures of focal onset. Sensations referred to the genitalia may form part or the whole of the aura or the latter may take the form of a poorly localized sense of sexual excitement. Orgasmic activity may ensue. Disinhibited sexual behaviour may also form part of an ictal automatism.

Three areas of the brain account for the great majority of cases described: the superior post-central gyrus and parietal parasagittal region; the frontal lobes; and the temporal lobes. Sexual seizures arising from the parietal area

Women and Epilepsy. Edited by M.R. Trimble

form a small but readily definable subgroup. Most of the remainder are associated with abnormalities related to the mediobasal temporal lobes, but a few appear to have a predominantly frontal pathology. Temporal and frontal subgroups are less clearly distinguishable from one another and may represent different patterns of limbic epilepsy.

Parietal seizures

Sexual seizures that arise from foci in the parietal cortex have certain distinguishing characteristics. The initial aura may consist of feelings of a sexual or non-sexual nature referred to the genitalia or to other erogenous areas of the body, or it may be represented by a diffuse sense of heightened sexual arousal. This may or may not progress to further sexual activity. In contrast to frontotemporal seizures, the subject is conscious and alert throughout and is able to recognize the sexual nature of the episodes while not necessarily finding them pleasurably erotic.

The first case was reported by Erickson (1945). A 54-year-old woman was admitted with a diagnosis of nymphomania:

> The patient described how, for the past 12 years, she had become increasingly 'passionate'. At night she would awake with a 'hot feeling' which would last for about 5 minutes and which felt as if she were having coitus. She explained, 'these spells are just the same as ordinary intercourse, but only on the left side. They are relieved for a while after intercourse, but I could have intercourse all the time without very much relief.' When pronounced she might gain relief by taking a luke-warm bath and packing her vagina with broken ice.
>
> Two years after onset she suddenly felt unable to speak during one of the 'hot spells' and had jerking movements of the left leg and left side of the abdomen. These attacks lasted for about 20 minutes. Subsequently, investigations revealed a haemangioma in the right parietal parasagittal area.

The ego-alien quality of some parietal lobe sexual seizures is stressed by Ruff (1980), who reported two cases, one a 43-year-old woman who

> developed paroxysmal episodes of orgasm. The episodes started with a sensation of clitoral warmth, breast engorgement, and tachycardia and escalated to climax within minutes. On two occasions the left leg jerked at the time of orgasm. She normally enjoyed sex, but these episodes were painful and frightening. The episodes were not triggered by normal sexual activity. A malignant glioma was removed from the superior right post-central gyrus.

A focal sensory aura referred to the genitalia may not always be experienced as erotic. York et al. (1979) described a 9-year-old boy who described testicular pain followed by left-sided clonic facial movements associated with right-sided EEG abnormalities.

In the case history reported by Ruff (1980) it may be concluded from the account of the episode that orgasm was a consequence of spreading seizure activity. In a recent case report (Calleja *et al.*, 1988) the epileptic nature of the orgasmic experience was confirmed during sleep polygraph recordings:

A 38-year-old woman developed frequent, brief nocturnal somatosensory seizures. The episodes usually awakened the patient after falling asleep and consisted of a sudden sensation of electrical discharge of the neck, which spread to the right leg and lasted a few seconds. The right leg jerked at the end of each seizure. Investigations were negative, but phenobarbitone was prescribed and she became seizure free. Treatment was withdrawn two years later and within five months her seizures reappeared, their pattern significantly altered. She was awakened by the electrical discharge described before, now with paresthesia in the right lateral abdominal and pubic regions and about her genitalia. A sensation of vaginal dilatation ensued immediately afterwards, which inevitably brought about either a pleasant or a painful orgasm. During these episodes there was no confusion or memory loss. Routine investigations remained negative, but a sleep EEG showed frequent left central parietal spikes and sharp waves spreading to the right. The seizure began with a paroxysm of central parietal spike and wave, orgasm corresponding with a generalization of paroxysmal activity.

The sensory representation of the genitalia lies in the paracentral lobule at the upper lip of the callosomarginal sulcus on the medial surface of the hemisphere (Erickson, 1945). Penfield recorded sensation on the opposite side of the penis following central fissure stimulation (Penfield and Boldrey, 1937) and the spreading of paraesthesia from the abdominogenital area to the ipsilateral nipple (Penfield and Rasmussen, 1950). These observations are consistent with a locus for one form of sexual seizure on the medial surface of the parietal lobe. Orgasm seems to occur in the context of spreading electrical stimulation and the relevant structures may be sited elsewhere.

Temporal and frontal lobe seizures

Sexual seizures associated with temporal lobe foci assume various forms. An eroticized aura may consist only of a diffuse sense of heightened arousal (Remillard *et al.*, 1983):

A 22-year-old right-handed secretary had her first seizure at age 12. The attacks were preceded by a 'fine feeling' identical to that brought about by masturbation.

More commonly, pleasurable sensations referred to the genitalia and to other erogenous areas are described:

> Another aura was a sudden libidinous feeling sometimes associated with a sense of familiarity. As this feeling increased, she became aware of pleasurable sensations in her sexual organs, occasionally feeling as if someone touched these sensuous areas of her body. If only this sensuous feeling and nothing more occurred, she felt as if she had suddenly been cut off from a sexual experience. 'There is no resolution . . .'

These experiences might proceed to orgasm. In other cases a sensation of impending orgasm might constitute the initial subjective experience followed by loss of consciousness and a tonic–clonic seizure. In all 12 of the cases reported by Remillard et al., the sexual components of the ictus are experienced in clear consciousness as genuinely erotic and identical to those achieved during normal sexual activity. Other cases are described (e.g. Currier et al., 1971) in which disinhibited sexual behaviour occurs during an altered state of consciousness which the subject subsequently cannot recollect. These have the characteristics of an epileptic automatism.

Drawing on their own experience and from the admittedly somewhat scanty literature, Remillard et al. (1983) reached a number of conclusions. They noted the preponderance of ictal erotic manifestations in women and the opposite state of affairs in men, and proposed a sexual dimorphism in cerebral function. Most published case histories are consistent with this hypothesis, but there are certainly exceptions (Ruff, 1987; Warneke, 1976). The same authors were also impressed by a possibility of a laterality affect. If all published material is taken into account there is a bias in favour of right-sided pathology over left in a ratio of approximately 2:1.

Another feature that characterized Remillard et al.'s (1983) group was late age of seizure onset (mean age 27 years). This is also true of cases reported by other authorities. When seizure onset precedes puberty, the erotic manifestations are delayed until pubertal onset. To quote Remillard et al. (1983) 'the hormonal priming of brain may be required for the ictal sexual manifestations'.

Sexual automatisms without preceding auras may arise from discharges in the temporal regions (see above); they may also have a frontal lobe onset. Spencer et al. (1983) describes four such cases, one of which was a woman:

> Some seizures were preceded by a strange feeling and evolved into bizarre motor activity; she would turn on her stomach and thrash and roll in bed, with shuffling movements of the legs and feet and pelvic thrusts, but with no convulsive activity in the EEG. At right frontal lobectomy a marble-sized mass buttressing on the anterior wall of the right lateral ventricle was removed.

Sexual automatisms arising from temporal and frontal lobe foci may be indistinguishable.

POST-ICTAL HYPERSEXUALITY

Sexual behaviour may also occur in the setting of a post-ictal confusional state. Gastaut and Collomb (1954) describe a 70-year-old woman who had since adolescence experienced seizures preceded by an epigastric aura. During the immediate post-ictal period she appeared confused and sexually aroused. She would often make obscene gestures of which she had no recall.

SEIZURES INDUCED BY SEXUAL ACTIVITY

Seizures may resemble or induce sexual activity. The reverse may also occur. Such cases are distinctly uncommon. Bancaud *et al.* (1971) described one such case, a 20-year-old patient who from the age of 4 had had seizures due to a right temporal lobe astrocytoma:

> The attacks, which were essentially paroxysmal sexual manifestations ending in orgasm, could be triggered by masturbation, and by fantasies in which the parental image appeared and by suggestion.

The authors stressed the significance of psychological and socio-cultural contributions.

The precise, sometimes exclusive, nature of the psychological precipitant is illustrated by a single case study reported by Hoenig and Hamilton (1960):

> A housewife began to have seizures at the age of 23. An epigastric aura was followed by loss of consciousness. On recovery she noticed a twitching of the left leg. After a period of freedom from attacks they returned, taking on a new pattern. Immediately following completion of the sexual act the patient became pale and then lost consciousness. After a minute, twitching of the left arm and left leg occurred and she regained consciousness. All investigations were normal. During a subsequent hospital admission she was hypnotized and it was suggested to her that she was having intercourse with her husband, whereupon she lost consciousness and a seizure ensued. An EEG recording showed a slow wave discharge over the right frontotemporal area corresponding to the approach of orgasm.

It is interesting to note that seizure activity only ensued if intercourse resulted in orgasm. Gautier-Smith (1980) has described a case in which seizures occurred as a consequence of coital hyperventilation, but this did not seem to be the case here.

CONCLUSIONS

Seizures and sexual activity are intertwined at several different levels. Seizures with a sexual aura, and seizures precipitated by coitus or orgasm, seem rare, although some authors have hinted at differences in such experiences between women and men. Post-ictal sexual arousal is reported rarely, but is probably more common. Studies of patients with such conditions may help unravel the neurology of sexual expression more precisely.

REFERENCES

Bancaud, J. *et al.* (1971) Paroxysmal sexual manifestations and temporal epilepsy. *Electroenceph. Clin. Neurophysiol.*, **30**, 368–374.

Bente, D. and Kluge, E. (1953) Sexuelle Reizzustande in Rahmen des Uncinatus Syndroms. *Arch. Psychol. (Frankfurt)*, **190**, 357–376.

Calleja, J., Carpixo, R. and Berciano, J. (1988) Orgasmic epilepsy. *Epilepsia*, **29**, 635–639.

Critchley, M. (1935) Uber Reflex-epilepsie. *Schweiz. Arch. Neurol. Psychiatry*, **35**, 256–270.

Currier, R.D. *et al.* (1971) Sexual seizures. *Arch. Neurol.* **25**, 260–264.

Erickson, T.C. (1945) Erotomania (nymphomania) as an expression of cortical epileptiform discharge. *Arch. Neurol. Psychiatry*, **53**, 226–231.

Gastaut, H. and Collomb, H. (1954) Etude du comportement sexuel chez les epileptiques psychomoteurs. *Ann. Med. Psychol.*, **112**, 657–696.

Gautier-Smith, P.C. (1980) Atteintes des fonctions cerebrales et troubles du comportement sexuel. *Rev. Neurol. (Paris)*, **136**, 311–319.

Hoenig, J. and Hamilton, C.N. (1960) Epilepsy and sexual orgasm. *Acta Psychiatr. Neurol. Scand.*, **35**, 448–456.

Penfield, W. and Boldrey, E. (1937) Somatic motor and sensory representation in the cerebral cortex of man as studied by electrical stimulation. *Brain*, **60**, 389–443.

Penfield, W.G. and Rasmussen, T.B. (1950) *The Cerebral Cortex of Man.* Macmillan, New York.

Remillard, G.N. *et al.* (1983) Sexual ictal manifestations predominate in women with temporal lobe epilepsy: A finding suggesting sexual dimorphism in the human brain. *Neurology*, **33**, 323–330.

Ruff, R.K. (1980) Orgasmic epilepsy. *Neurology*, **30**, 1252.

Spencer, S.F., Spencer, D.D., Williamson, T.D. and Mattson, R.H. (1983) Sexual automatisms in complex partial seizures. *Neurology*, **33**, 527–533.

Warneke, L.B. (1976) A case of temporal lobe epilepsy with an orgasmic component. *Can. Psychiatr. Assoc. J.*, **21**, 319–323.

York, G.K., Gabor, A.J. and Dreyfuss, P.M. (1979) Paroxysmal genital pain: An unusual manifestation of epilepsy. *Neurology*, **29**.

13

Cognitive differences between males and females with epilepsy

D. UPTON, P. THOMPSON AND R. CORCORAN
Chalfont Centre for Epilepsy, Gerrards Cross, and Institute of Neurology, London, UK

> All psychologists who have studied the intelligence of women as well as poets and novelists recognize today that they represent the most inferior forms of human evolution and that they are closer to children and savages than to adult civilized man.
>
> (Gustave le Bon 1879)

INTRODUCTION

For centuries questions have been raised about possible differences between the sexes in intellectual capacity. Most early accounts come down in favour of the superiority of the male intellect, with perhaps the most acrimonious debates on the subject arising in the nineteenth century; the opening quote is fairly representative of the conclusions drawn by male 'observers' at the time. The larger brain size and weight of the male *Homo sapiens*, as documented by phrenologists and surgeons, was taken as strong evidence of this superiority. Later, realization that females had smaller bodies and the brain size to body ratio did not differ significantly between the sexes did not always sway opinion. In 1914 the German psychologist Hugo Munsterberg wrote that the average female is 'capricious, over-suggestible, often inclined to exaggeration, is disinclined to abstract thought, unfit for mathematical reasoning, impulsive, over-emotional'.

There began, as we entered the twentieth century, a more enlightened view that females had specific abilities, although these were considered by some to be less important and less intellectually sound than males. Wooley (1914) wrote that females' abilities were rather limited and extended to only 'card dealing and clerical tasks'.

Women and Epilepsy. Edited by M.R. Trimble
© 1991 John Wiley & Sons Ltd

More recent investigations have focused on specific aspects of cognitive ability rather than the global concept of general intelligence. This broadening of research was, in part, stimulated by Maccoby and Jacklin's (1974) extensive review of more than 2000 studies. These authors concluded that much of the evidence on sex differences came from methodologically weak studies and few relatively reliable sex differences existed. Their review favoured differences in three areas: verbal ability, visuo-spatial ability and mathematical skills. Other commentators have suggested that further qualifications upon these conclusions are warranted (Block, 1976; Fairweather, 1976; Deaux, 1985).

Maccoby and Jacklin (1974) considered that the available evidence indicated a female superiority for certain verbal skills. Benton and Hamsher (1977) found females did consistently better on verbal tasks such as verbal fluency. McGee (1979) reported female superiority on verbal learning tasks. Heaton *et al.* (1986) reported female superiority on an aphasia screening test. Subsequent studies and analysis have suggested that the evidence for female superiority in the verbal domain is at best weak (Sherman, 1978; Hyde, 1981).

Male superiority in the area of spatial ability has received some support (Hyde, 1981; McGee, 1979; Cohen and Wilkie, 1979). The sex difference in spatial skills appears to emerge prior to adolescence and seems to be limited to particular types of skill. Specifically, males have been reported to be superior on measures of mental rotation and tests of horizontality and verticality, with no apparent differences in spatial visualization tasks requiring more analytic sequential strategies (Deaux, 1985). Furthermore, evidence exists that training can significantly alter the performance of both males and females on such tasks (Newcombe *et al.*, 1983).

Masculine excellence for mathematical skills is the area of cognition that has attracted most attention vis-à-vis sex differences. Maccoby and Jacklin (1974) concluded that males are better than females, but the differences occurred from the period of adolescence onwards. Other researchers, however, have suggested the difference exists prior to adolescence. Benbow and Stanley (1983) report a study involving testing of 19883 male and 19937 female seventh graders. The groups were equated for verbal skills, but the boys consistently did better on mathematical tasks. The authors wrote that 'the principal conclusion is that males dominate the highest ranges of mathematical reasoning ability before they enter adolescence'. Deaux (1985) cites an unpublished study where mathematical male superiority was confined to differences on algebraic tasks and was not seen on arithmetical or geometric problems.

A recent meta-analytical study of sex differences related to year of study covering a 20-year period has demonstrated that the differences between the sexes in favour of the male are diminishing (Rosenthal and Rubin, 1982).

CEREBRAL DAMAGE

Differential effects of cerebral damage related to sex have been reported. There is some evidence to support the hypothesis that females have more diffuse lateralization and localization of cognitive functions within the cerebral hemispheres, such that males are cognitively more vulnerable to unilateral brain damage than females (Kimura and Harshman, 1984; McGlone, 1977). A more recent study of more than 600 patients with unilateral cerebral lesions failed to demonstrate any differential influence of sex on cognitive sequelae of cerebral lesions (Warrington *et al.*, 1986). These authors propose that previous studies may have had biased patient samples.

More consistent findings of male cognitive vulnerability exists for children. Thus, evidence suggests the male dominant hemisphere has a longer maturation period and therefore is more susceptible to insult during early childhood. This is taken by some authors to explain why learning disability, dyslexia and autism in males outnumber females (Hynd and Cohen, 1983; Taylor, 1985; see also Chapter 5).

STUDIES OF EPILEPSY

In epilepsy, the evidence for cognitive differences between the sexes is sparse. Sex differences related to cognitive functioning have attracted most attention for children. Stores and Hart (1976) compared the reading skills of 17 children who had consistently generalized discharges on their EEG with 17 who had consistently focal discharges. For each study child, a control child without epilepsy was chosen from the school class. Significant differences were few, but boys with left focal epileptic discharges had poorer reading skills. Similarly, Stores *et al.* (1978) reported that boys, but not girls, with epilepsy were more inattentive than their peers without epilepsy. Bennett-Levy and Stores (1984) found that boys with epilepsy were judged lacking in concentration, to be more impaired in processing information and less alert than males without epilepsy. No differences were observed for females. However, the authors found that when matching included scholastic attainments such differences disappeared.

In a recent study, Seidenberg and colleagues (1986, 1989) assessed 182 children aged between 7 and 15 with a full-scale IQ greater than 70 on a number of areas, including word recognition, reading, comprehension and arithmetic. Seventy-two had generalized seizures and 50 partial seizures. Females performed significantly better than males on measures of word recognition and spelling.

For adults there is less evidence of sex differences; indeed, sex is often a variable controlled for in studies of cognitive functioning in epilepsy and given little consideration in reviews of the subject (e.g. Dodrill, 1988).

Kupke *et al.* (1979) specifically compared the neuropsychological profile of 137 male and 113 female patients with epilepsy. All were out-patients of a neurological clinic. Only 15% had strong evidence of lateralized cerebral lesions, 72% showing evidence of bilateral dysfunctioning on the EEG. The authors took electrophysiological data as evidence of diffuse cerebral dysfunction. The patients were matched for present IQ, age, seizure type, neuropathology, EEG focus and type of anticonvulsant medication. Thirty-three neuropsychological measures covering a range of functions were administered. Significant differences were obtained on 12 of the 33 measures. Pronounced sex differences, however, were largely limited to motor speed and strength in favour of the males. The authors note that the differences they observed 'simply seem to reflect premorbid differences between male and female patients rather than the differential effects of brain dysfunction on the sexes'.

Gross cognitive deterioration in epilepsy has been observed to occur in a small minority of cases (Thompson *et al.*, 1987). There is some suggestion that males may have greater susceptibility but also there may be different 'dementia' profiles, with females showing less marked deterioration in visuo-spatial areas (Brown and Vaughan, 1988). Investigations to date, however, have been methodologically inadequate, in particular having very small samples.

The differential impact of epilepsy surgery on the sexes has been commented upon in a few studies. Bennett-Levy *et al.* (1980) assessed self-perception of memory function in 58 patients who had undergone temporal lobectomies. Amongst their findings was a significant effect of side of operation and sex. More specifically, males who had undergone a right temporal lobectomy reported significantly poorer memories post-operatively. The authors proposed that for real life memory the integrity of the right hemisphere is as important as the left hemisphere, and if males have a greater degree of right hemisphere specialization they are at more of a disadvantage post-operatively. A more recent study reports a similar finding but offers an alternative explanation which is more in keeping with our own research data. Wands and McGlone (1989) followed 72 cases of post-temporal lobectomy. Post-operative cases perceived a positive change in their memory, with the exception of males undergoing a right temporal lobectomy. The authors argued that either males have a better, more realistic perception of their memory or the male sample were more depressed which had led them to underestimate their memory capacity. This is certainly in agreement with our own findings (Corcoran and Thompson, in preparation).

In an attempt to explore further the role of sex differences we have drawn on data from three different lines of investigation. First, neuropsychological profiles in intractable epilepsy; second, memory complaints in people with epilepsy, and finally, cognitive strategies employed by people with epilepsy.

Neuropsychological profiles

The National Hospitals Assessment Centre for Epilepsy provides a full medical evaluation for patients with intractable seizures. Individual assessment includes a neuropsychological evaluation aimed to assess strengths and weaknesses pertinent to rehabilitation needs. In a significant proportion of patients suitability for surgery is evaluated (Thompson and Shorvon, in press). For the purposes of this paper we have examined the neuropsychological profile of 65 males and 65 females in our database. For all patients the diagnosis of epilepsy was confirmed and all individuals had an IQ greater than 65. Details of the patient group are given in Table 1. Clearly these individuals are not representative of people with epilepsy and are biased to individuals with problematic seizures; however, this group are most at risk for problems of a neuropsychological nature (Trimble and Thompson, 1986).

Table 1. Medicodemographic details of the study group

	Males (n = 65)	Females (n = 65)
Age of onset (years)		
Mean	7.4	9.51
SD	4.87	7.48
Range	0–20	0–41
Age (years)		
Mean	27.45	26.85
SD	8.44	9.08
Range	16–55	16–53
Duration of epilepsy (years)		
Mean	20.09	17.31
SD	8.95	9.91
Range	6–41	1–42
Years active seizures (years)		
Mean	18.82	16.12
SD	9.39	10.1
Range	2–40	1–39
Seizures (%)		
Primary generalized	10.8	10.8
Complex partial	20.0	23.8
Secondary generalized	69.2	75.4
Seizure frequency (%)		
Daily or greater	49.2	43.1
Weekly	38.5	40.0
Monthly	7.7	10.8
Yearly or less	4.6	6.1

The sample are, for the most part, young with an early age of onset. Seizures are poorly controlled, with many individuals experiencing weekly attacks with no significant period of remission. The majority of cases have complex partial seizures with secondary generalization. Analysis revealed no significant differences at the 5% level between the sexes on any of the variables given.

The following measures were employed.

Intelligence

Performance on seven subtests of the Revised version of the Wechsler Adult Intelligence Scale (WAIS-R) provided a measure of current intellectual ability (Wechsler, 1981). The four verbal subtests were Vocabulary, Arithmetic, Digit Span and Similarities; and three performance subtests were Picture Completion, Block Design and Picture Arrangement.

Memory

Recognition memory tests for both verbal and non-verbal stimuli were employed, with the verbal stimuli consisting of printed words and non-verbal stimuli of photographs of unfamiliar faces (Warrington, 1984). In addition, a measure of verbal learning was administered which required patients to learn a list of 15 unrelated words over five successive presentations. Retention was also tested following a distracting list (Coughlan and Hollows, 1985). Recall of ten simple geometric designs was assessed via the Benton Visual Retention Test (Benton, 1974).

Language

A stringent word-naming test was employed to assess expressive functions (McKenna and Warrington, 1980). The test requires individuals to name pictures of objects graded for increasing difficulty. Language comprehension was screened using the De Renzi Token Test, which requires patients to follow commands of increasing complexity (De Renzi and Faglioni, 1978).

Mental flexibility

Verbal fluency was assessed by asking patients to generate as many words as they could beginning with the letter S and then as many animal names in one minute. Disturbance on such tests had been associated with dominant frontal lobe lesions (Kartsounis, 1990). In addition, patients also completed the Trail Making Test. This requires subjects to alternate between an alphabetical sequence and a numerical sequence, thereby necessitating rapid changes of mental set (Reitan, 1958). Information-processing speed was assessed using a number cancellation task (Coughlan and Hollows, 1985).

The results of the neuropsychological assessment are given in Table 2. On the Wechsler Scale males had a significantly higher verbal and full-scale IQ although the absolute difference is small. At the subtest level the only significant difference occurred on arithmetic, again a male superiority being noted. On the other 13 neuropsychological measures only one significant difference occurred, female scores being significantly lower than males on the naming test.

The impact of early seizure onset was explored by dividing the samples according to whether seizures occurred before or after the age of 5. If males were more vulnerable to early brain disturbance, then greater cognitive

Table 2.   Neuropsychological test scores of the male and female samples

Test	Males	Females	p level (t-test)
WAIS–R prorated IQs			
VIQ	86.82	82.87	0.05
PIQ	84.37	81.62	NS
FSIQ	84.98	81.62	0.04
WAIS–R subtests (scales scores)			
Digit span	7.26	6.96	NS
Vocabulary	7.86	7.04	NS
Similarity	7.78	6.98	NS
Arithmetic	6.86	5.95	0.04
Block Design	7.76	7.64	NS
Picture Arrangement	6.83	6.32	NS
Picture Completion	7.20	6.78	NS
Memory tests (Warrington, 1984)			
Recognition Words	42.72	42.49	NS
Recognition Faces	36.31	36.33	NS
List Learning A1–5	40.00	38.11	NS
Post-distractor A6	8.13	7.52	NS
Intrusions	4.53	4.00	NS
Benton	6.26	6.29	NS
Language			
DeRenzi	12.31	12.76	NS
Naming	13.76	10.39	0.006
Flexibility			
Fluency S	9.96	9.90	NS
Fluency Animal	11.71	12.82	NS
Trial A	34.91	26.82	NS
Trial B	58.58	54.82	NS
Information-processing speed			
Motor speed	40.07	43.65	NS

deficits, particularly in the verbal domain, would be expected for males rather than females with an early age of onset. Table 3 gives the results for males and females, divided according to epilepsy onset. Of the 23 comparisons made, only one significant difference emerged; males with a seizure onset after the age of 5 were more impaired on a naming task than males with an earlier seizure onset.

Overall, the results provide little support for male cognitive vulnerability in epilepsy. The first analysis suggested a male advantage in the verbal domain, most notably on the measure of expressive language skills. This is contrary to the profile differences noted earlier in non-brain-injured samples. The second

Table 3. Neuropsychological test scores of the male and female samples according to seizure onset

Test	Males		Females		Sig.
	Early < 5 yrs	Late > 5 yrs	Early < 5 yrs	Late > 5 yrs	
WAIS–R prorated IQ					
VIQ	85.31	87.82	80.73	83.97	NS
PIQ	82.84	85.38	81.91	81.46	NS
FSIQ	83.46	86.00	79.86	81.42	NS
WAIS–R subtests (scales scores)					
Digit Span	7.04	7.41	6.82	7.42	NS
Vocabulary	7.34	8.10	6.32	7.42	NS
Arithmetic	6.46	7.12	5.82	6.02	NS
Similarity	7.42	8.03	6.73	7.11	NS
Picture Completion	7.11	7.26	7.00	6.67	NS
Picture Arrangement	6.27	7.21	6.05	6.46	NS
Block Design	7.66	7.85	7.91	7.51	NS
Memory tests (Warrington, 1984)					
Recognition Faces	35.68	36.74	33.95	37.51	NS
Recognition Words	42.70	42.73	43.95	41.33	NS
List Learning A1–5	39.56	39.58	40.33	37.37	NS
Post-distractor A6	7.73	7.11	8.39	7.71	NS
Intrusions	4.05	4.00	4.87	4.00	NS
Benton	6.30	5.47	6.24	6.72	NS
Language					
DeRenzi	12.36	12.75	12.27	12.77	NS
Naming	14.21	8.47	13.37	11.30	0.025
Flexibility					
Fluency S	9.83	10.47	10.07	9.58	NS
Fluency Animal	12.13	13.22	11.36	12.59	NS
Trial A	25.55	25.27	32.71	27.60	NS
Trial B	52.50	46.87	63.87	58.80	NS
Information-processing speed					
Motor speed	37.86	41.65	49.06	40.78	NS

analysis yielded significantly inferior naming skills in association with late-onset epilepsy for males. This is contrary to the belief of a male vulnerability to early insult; however, it could be argued as in keeping with the male specialization hypothesis (e.g. McGlone, 1977).

Caution is needed in interpreting the results presented here. The sample is clearly biased toward the more intractable cases and to those with more limited intellectual abilities. With an intellectually more able sample, the neuropsychological differences between the sexes may be more apparent. The number of significant results was small; however, statistical analysis has been limited and to date no multivariate techniques have been employed. More importantly, many variables were not adequately controlled for in the analysis. Electrophysiological data pertaining to lateralization and localization were inadequate and for many individuals the result of a single routine EEG was the only available evidence. EEG recordings undertaken as part of the assessment procedure suggested no marked differences between the sexes regarding lateralization of cerebral disturbances. Past EEG reports, however, suggested the female sample was biased towards more left hemisphere dysfunctioning. Differences observed between the sexes, particularly in the verbal domain, may reflect greater dominant hemispheric disturbance in the female sample. Thus, side of epileptic discharges may be a stronger predictor of the difference observed than sex.

Memory complaints

Over a three-year period we have been researching into the nature of memory complaints made by people with epilepsy. The study arose because of the perceived high level of complaints in this patient group (Thompson, 1989). In particular we were interested in the frequency and type of everyday memory failures reported by people with epilepsy. In 1861, Russell Reynolds suggested women with epilepsy complained more of memory difficulties than men. For the purpose of this paper we have reconsidered some of our data in relation to differences between the sexes. In particular, we were interested in comparing male and female memory complaints, but it also seemed important in the light of previous studies to explore the role of laterality (Bennett-Levy et al., 1980; Wands and McGlone, 1989). Furthermore, previous research has demonstrated a relationship between memory complaints and mood (Kahn et al., 1975; Yesavage et al., 1982) which we had confirmed in our epilepsy sample (Corcoran and Thompson, in preparation). Accordingly, the role of mood in relation to complaints of memory was considered.

Over 900 people have participated in our memory survey. Of these 405 females and 355 males have epilepsy. Those with epilepsy range in severity from individuals under the supervision of their general practitioner who have infrequent or fully controlled seizures to individuals with problematic control requiring short-term in-patient evaluation.

All participants completed an 18-item everyday memory questionnaire adapted from a measure employed to assess memory complaints following head injury (Sunderland *et al.*, 1983). In addition, patients had to rate their memories according to a four-point nuisance rating scale from 'no nuisance at all' to 'a serious nuisance'. The Beck Depression Inventory and the Hospital Anxiety and Depression Scale were employed to obtain a measure of emotional state (Beck and Beamesdefer, 1974; Zigmund and Snaith, 1983).

Responses of the entire sample revealed no differences in terms of opinions about frequency of daily memory failures between women and men, either within the epilepsy group or the non-epilepsy group. Neither were significant differences uncovered when the nuisance ratings were considered.

A subsample was considered for further analysis where evidence existed concerning lateralization of epileptic discharges. Thirty-five males and 34 females were identified with predominantly right-sided foci and 50 males and 50 females with left-sided foci. A group of 16 males and 18 females with evidence of bilateral discharges were also identified. Analysis of the total number of memory failures and nuisance rating revealed no differences between the sexes (Figure 1). The trend was for males with evidence of left-sided disturbance to report more frequent everyday memory failures and to have higher memory nuisance ratings. Males and females in this sample did not differ in self-ratings of depression, although a significant difference was observed for ratings of anxiety with higher levels reported in the females ($p < 0.008$). Higher levels of depression and anxiety, however, were related to more reported memory failures and higher levels of complaint irrespective of sex ($p < 0.05$).

Thus, we failed to find any relationship between self-perception of memory failures and degree of memory nuisance between the sexes. Neither did we find a relationship between sex, laterality and perceived poor memory. Mood, as before, was a better predictor of memory complaint.

Cognitive strategies

Finally, we broadened the definition of cognition to consider cognitive strategies employed by people with epilepsy to deal with the stress arising from their condition. Increased rates of emotional problems have been reported in epilepsy (Dodrill *et al.*, 1980; Robertson and Trimble, 1983; Robertson *et al.*, 1987; Betts, 1988). Many studies focus on medication and neuroepileptic variables often to the exclusion of other psychosocial variables (Whitman and Hermann, 1989). We have recently completed a study which explored the relationship between coping strategies and emotional adjustment (Upton and Thompson, in preparation). In particular, we were interested to see whether different coping strategies contributed to poor adjustment in epilepsy.

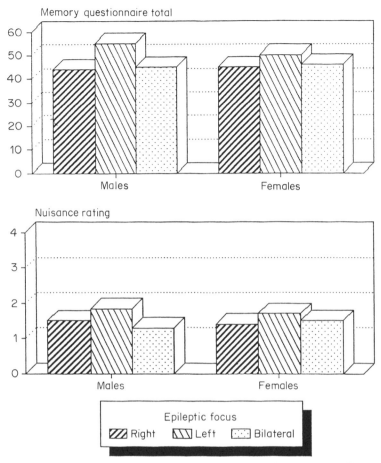

Figure 1. Memory questionnaire totals and nuisance ratings of the epilepsy group according to sex and laterality of epileptic discharges

Our study revealed that one coping strategy was associated with deleterious adjustment, namely 'wish-fulfilling fantasy', and another was associated with better emotional adjustment, namely 'cognitive restructuring'. The former involves an indulgence in pining for the illness to go away or be over with. It allows people to alleviate the distress by providing escape in fantasy, for example, 'hoping for a miracle to happen'. The second, 'cognitive restructuring', describes an individual's efforts to find positive aspects about the illness experience allowing cognitive reappraisal of the illness; for example, to concentrate on something good that may come out of the situation.

For the purpose of this chapter we examined our data to see if there were any differences between the sexes regarding the cognitive strategies adopted.

The data also allow comparison between the sexes regarding emotional adjustment. Other investigators have suggested that poorer emotional adjustment in females is associated with the employment of less adaptive coping strategies (Pearlin and Schooler, 1978; Kessler and McRae, 1981; Kessler and McRae, 1983). One hundred and thirty-nine people with epilepsy participated in the study—53 males and 86 females. The patient group had intractable epilepsy, with the majority having complex partial seizures with secondary generalization and 72% seizures occurring on a weekly basis. All participants completed the Hospital Anxiety and Depression Scale (Zigmund and Snaith, 1983), Self-Esteem Scale (Rosenberg, 1967) and the Ways of Coping Checklist (Folkman and Lazarus, 1980; Felton et al., 1984).

Females were assessed to be significantly more anxious ($p < 0.05$) and to have lower self-esteem ($p < 0.04$) than their male counterparts. Differences in coping strategies were observed although these were small in magnitude. Females reported using cognitive restructuring significantly less frequently ($p < 0.05$) and wish-fulfilling fantasy significantly more frequently ($p < 0.05$). The results are in keeping with other samples which suggest that adoption of less adaptive coping strategies by females may contribute to poorer emotional adjustment.

CONCLUSION

In general, cognitive differences between the sexes has attracted considerable comment and study. For epilepsy, in contrast, research work focusing on this demographic variable is sparse. Analysis of our own data yielded few significant cognitive differences between the sexes. Rather, available evidence suggests that when such differences exist other factors may be more pertinent. Neuropsychological differences observed may be more influenced by neuroepileptic variables such as site of focus, and memory complaints by psychosocial variables. In the area of coping strategies, sex differences were observed but these seem in keeping with findings in other chronic disorders. They nonetheless may have relevance for patient management. The three personal investigations reviewed here were not designed to assess hypotheses regarding sex differences and accordingly have many methodological weaknesses. A definitive study of cognitive differences between the sexes would be difficult to design and almost impossible to undertake. Our experience leads us to suggest gender as a weak predictor of cognitive functioning in epilepsy and rather that other neuroepileptic, medication and psychosocial factors have a more important role.

Dr Johnston, when asked who was the more intelligent—man or woman—replied, 'Which man, which woman?' In a similar vein, the novelist Ivy Compton Burnett wrote 'There are probably more differences within the sexes than between them.' In short, this is what we have found for cognitive functioning in our epilepsy samples.

REFERENCES

Beck, A.T. and Beamesderfer, A. (1974) Assessment of depression: The depression inventory. In: *Psychological Measurement in Psychopharmacology, Vol. 7* (ed. P. Pichot). Marger-Basel, Paris.

Benbow, C.P. and Stanley, J.C. (1983) Sex differences in mathematical reasoning: More facts. *Science*, **222**, 1029–1031.

Bennett-Levy, J. and Stores, G. (1984) The nature of cognitive dysfunction in school-children with epilepsy. *Acta Neurol. Scand.*, **69** (Suppl. 99), 79–82.

Bennett-Levy, J., Polkey, C.E. and Powell, G.E. (1980) Self-report of memory skills after temporal lobectomy: The effect of clinical variables. *Cortex*, **16**, 543–557.

Benton, A.L. (1974) *The Revised Visual Retention test*, 4th ed. Psychological Corporation, New York.

Benton, A.L. and Hamsher, K.D.E.S. (1977) *Multilingual Aphasia Examination.* University of Iowa, Iowa.

Betts, T.A. (1988) Epilepsy and behaviour. In: *A Textbook of Epilepsy, 3rd edn* (eds J. Laidlaw, A. Riches and J. Oxley), pp. 350–385. Churchill Livingstone, Edinburgh.

Block, J.M. (1976) Issues, problems and pitfalls in assessing sex differences: A critical review of the psychology of sex differences. *Merrill-Palmer Quarterly*, **22** (4), 283–308.

Brown, S.W. and Vaughan, M. (1988) Dementia in epileptic patients. In: *Epilepsy, Behaviour and Cognitive Function* (eds M.R. Trimble and E.H. Reynolds), pp. 177–188. Wiley, Chichester.

Cohen, D. and Wilkie, F. (1979) Sex related differences in cognition among the elderly. In: *Sex-related Differences in Cognitive Functioning* (eds M.A. Wittig and A.C. Petersen), pp. 145–159. Academic Press, New York.

Coughlan, A.K. and Hollows, S.E. (1985) The adult memory and information processing battery. *AMIPB Test Manual*, A.K. Coughlan, Leeds.

Deaux, K. (1985) Sex and gender. *Annu. Rev. Psychol.*, **36**, 49–81.

De Renzi, E. and Faglioni, P. (1978) Normative data and screening power of a shortened version of the token test. *Cortex*, **14**, 41–49.

Dodrill, C.B. (1988) Neuropsychology. In: *A Textbook of Epilepsy* (eds J. Laidlaw, A. Richens and J. Oxley), pp. 406–483. Churchill Livingstone, Edinburgh.

Dodrill, C.B., Batzel, L.W., Quiesser, H.R. and Temkin, N.R. (1980) An objective method for the assessment of psychological and social difficulties among epileptics. *Epilepsia*, **21**, 123–135.

Fairweather, H. (1976) Sex differences in cognition. *Cognition*, **4**, 231–280.

Felton, B.J., Revenson, T.A. and Hinrichsen, G.A. (1984) Stress and coping in the explanation of psychological adjustment among chronically ill adults. *Soc. Sci. Med.*, **18**, 889–898.

Fenwick, P. (1988) Epilepsy and anxiety. Paper presented at *Epilepsy and Psychiatry— New Departures*, Aston University, September 1988.

Folkman, S. and Lazarus, R.S. (1980) An analysis of coping in a middle-aged community sample. *J. Health Soc. Behav.*, **21**, 219–239.

Heaton, R.K. Grant, I. and Matthews, C.G. (1986) Differences in neuropsychological test performance associated with age, education and sex. In: *Neuropsychological Assessment of Neuropsychiatric Disorders* (eds I. Grant and K.M. Adams), pp. 100–120. Oxford University Press, New York.

Hyde, J.S. (1981) How large are cognitive gender differences? A meta analysis using w and d. *Am. Psychol.*, **36**, 892–901.

Hyde, J.S., Feinema, E. and Lanon, S.J. (1990) Gender differences in mathematic performance: A meta-analysis. *Psychol. Bull.*, **107**, 139–155.

Hynd, G. and Cohen, M. (1983) *Dyslexia: Neuropsychological Theory, Research and Clinical Differentiation*. Grune and Stratton, Orlando.

Kahn, R.L., Sarit, S.H., Bilbert, N.M. and Niederche, M.H. (1975) Memory complaint and impairment in the aged: The effects of depression and altered brain function. *Arch. Gen. Psychiatry*, **32**, 1569–1573.

Kartsounis, L. and Warrington, E.K. (1991) Neuropsychology. In: *Neurology in Clinical Practice* (eds W.G. Bradley, R.B. Daroff, G.M. Finichel and C.D. Marsden), pp. 469–492. Butterworths, Stoneham.

Kessler, R.C. and McRae, J.A. (1981) Trends in the relationship between sex and psychological distress 1957–76. *Am. Sociol. Rev.*, **46**, 443–452.

Kessler, R.C. and McRae, J.A. (1983) Trends in the relationship between sex and attempted suicide. *J. Health Soc. Behav.*, **24**, 98–110.

Kimura, D. and Harshman, R.A. (1984) Sex differences in brain organisation for verbal and non-verbal functions. *Prog. Brain Res.*, **61**, 423–441.

Kupke, T., Lewis, R. and Rennick, P. (1979) Sex differences in the neuropsychological functioning of epileptics. *J. Consult. Clin. Psychol.*, **47**, 1128–1130.

Maccoby, E.E. and Jacklin, C.N.J. (1974) *The Psychology of Sex Differences*. Stanford University Press, Stanford.

McGee, M.G. (1979) *Human Spatial Abilities*. Praeger, New York.

McGlone, J. (1977) Sex differences in the cerebral organisation of verbal function in patients with unilateral brain lesions. *Brain*, **100**, 775–793.

McKenna, P. and Warrington, E.K. (1980) Testing for nominal dysphasia. *J. Neurol. Neurosurg. Psychiatry*, **43**, 781–788.

Newcombe, N., Bandura, M.M. and Taylor, D.C. (1983) Sex differences in spatial ability and spatial activities. *Sex Roles*, **9**, 377–386.

Pearlin, L.I. and Schooler, C. (1978) The structure of coping. *J. Health Soc. Behav.*, **19**, 2–21.

Reitan, R.M. (1958) Validity of the trail making test as an indication of organic brain damage. *Percept. Mot. Skills*, **8**, 271–276.

Robertson, M. and Trimble, M.R. (1983) Depressive illness in patients with epilepsy: A review. *Epilepsia*, **24**, *(Suppl. 2)*, S109–S116.

Robertson, M.M., Trimble, M.R. and Townsend, H.R.A. (1987) The phenomenology of depression in epilepsy. *Epilepsia*, **28**, 364–372.

Rosenberg, M. (1967) *Society and the Adolescent Self-image*. Princetown University Press, Princetown.

Rosenthal, R. and Rubin, D.B. (1982) Further meta analytic procedures for assessing cognitive gender differences. *J. Educ. Psychol.*, **74**, 708–712.

Russell-Reynold, J. (1861) *Epilepsy: Its Symptoms, Treatment and Relation to Other Chronic Convulsive Disorders*. John Churchill, London.

Seidenberg, M. (1989) Academic achievement and school performance of children with epilepsy. In: *Childhood Epilepsies: Neurological, Psychosocial and Intervention Aspects* (eds B. Hermann and M. Seidenberg), pp. 105–118. Wiley, New York.

Seidenberg, M., Beck, N., Geisser, M., Giordani, B., Sackarelles, J.C., Berent, S., Dreifuss, F.E. and Boll, T.J. (1986) Academic achievement of children with epilepsy. *Epilepsia*, **27**, 753–759.

Sherman, J. (1978) *Sex Related Cognitive Differences*. Thomas, Springfield, IL.

Stores, G. and Hart, J. (1976) Reading skills of children with generalised or focal epilepsy attending ordinary school. *Devel. Med. Child Neurol.*, **18**, 705–716.

Stores, G., Hart, J. and Piran, M. (1978) Inattentiveness in schoolchildren with epilepsy. *Epilepsia*, **19**, 169–175.

Sunderland, A., Harris, J.E. and Baddeley, A.D. (1983) Do laboratory tests predict everyday memory? A neuropsychological study. *J. Verbal Learning Verbal Behav.*, **22**, 341–357.

Taylor, D.C. (1985) Mechanisms of sex differentiation: Evidence from disease. In: *Human Sexual Dimorphism* (eds J. Ghesquiere, R.D. Martin and F. Newcombe), pp. 169–189. Taylor and Francis, London.

Thompson, P.J. (1989) Epilepsy and memory. In: *Advances in Epileptology 17* (eds J. Manelis, B. Bental, J.N. Loeber and F.E. Dreifuss), pp. 404–406. Raven Press, New York.

Thompson, P.J. and Shorvon, S.D. (in press) The epilepsies. In: *Neurological Rehabilitation* (eds R.J. Greenwood, M.P. Barnes, T.M. McMillan and C.D. Ward). Churchill Livingstone, Edinburgh.

Thompson, P.J., Sander, J.W.A.S. and Oxley, J. (1987) Intellectual deterioration in severe epilepsy. *Advances in Epileptology: XVIth Epilepsy International Symposium* (eds P. Wolf, M. Dam, D. Janz and F.E. Dreifuss), pp. 611–614. Raven Press, New York.

Trimble, M.R. and Thompson, P.J. (1986) Neuropsychological aspects of epilepsy. In: *Neuropsychological Assessment of Neuropsychiatric Disorders* (eds I. Grant and K.M. Adams), pp. 321–356. Oxford University Press, New York.

Wands, K. and McGlone, J. (1989) *Memory Complaints in Temporal Lobe Epilepsy*. Paper presented at the INS meeting in Vancouver, February 1989.

Warrington, E.K. (1984) *Recognition Memory Test*. NFER, Windsor.

Warrington, E.K. and Taylor, A.M. (1973) The contribution of the right parietal lobe to object recognition. *Cortex*, **9**, 152–164.

Warrington, E.K., James, M. and Maciejewski, C. (1986) The WAIS as a lateralising and localising diagnostic instrument: A study of 656 patients with unilateral cerebral lesions. *Neuropsychologia*, **24**, 223–239.

Wechsler, D. (1981) *Wechsler Adult Intelligence Scale—Revised Manual*. Psychological Corporation, New York.

Whitman, S. and Hermann, B.P. (1989) The architecture of research in the epilepsy/psychopathology field. *Epilepsy Res.*, **3**, 93–99.

Wooley, H.T. (1914) The psychology of sex. *Psychol. Bull.*, **11**, 353–378.

Yesavage, J., Rose, T. and Spiegel, D. (1982) Relaxation training and memory impairment in elderly normals: Correlation of anxiety ratings and recall improvement. *Exp. Aging Res.*, **8**, 195–198.

Zigmund, A.S. and Snaith, R.P. (1983) The Hospital Anxiety and Depression Scale. *Acta Psychiat. Scand.*, **67**, 361–370.

14

Depression in epilepsy

MARY M. ROBERTSON
Middlesex Hospital, London, UK

INTRODUCTION

Despite the fact that depression is more common in women than in men (see below) examples of famous people who have been depressed are nearly always men. Thus the earliest mention of depression appears in the biblical story of King Saul (ca 1033 BC). Detailed clinical accounts of his life suggest an early 'psychopathic tendency' and that his prophecies occurred under 'strong emotional tension'. He then appears to have had a recurrent depression, some 'ecstatic seizures', homicidal attempts and finally committed suicide by falling on his sword (Robertson, 1983). Much later, in a fascinating manuscript, the lives and careers of men such as Newton, Beethoven, Dickens and Van Gogh are dissected by Lieb (1988), who examines the role of manic-depression in their creative lives. It is also well known that Sir Winston Churchill suffered from depression (Storr, 1990), and illustrations from the writings of the depressed poet William Cowper elegantly describe some of the emotions of a depressed person: 'Day and night I was upon the rack, lying down in horror and rising in despair . . . rising cheerless and distressed in the morning, and brightening a little as the day goes on' (Meyer and Meyer, 1987).

That depression is common in the context of epilepsy is well recognized, although only a few investigations have defined what exactly is meant by depression or have used recognized diagnostic criteria of depressive illness for entry into the studies. Nevertheless, there is an extensive literature on the relationship between the two disorders, as well as comprehensive reviews on the topic (Robertson, 1988a; Robertson, 1989). This chapter will attempt to give a brief overview of the subject, addressing in particular the topic of gender differences noted in studies, and thereafter some suggestions will be made as to the aetiology of the depression.

Women and Epilepsy. Edited by M.R. Trimble

Epidemiology of depression

The epidemiology of depression has been well documented, and two comprehensive reviews (Boyd and Weissman, 1982; Hirschfield and Cross, 1982) and a clear description of the course of affective illness (Angst, 1981) will be summarized. It is generally agreed that depression is more common in women. Thus the point prevalence (that proportion of the population which has a disorder at a given point in time) of non-bipolar depression in industrialized nations is 3.2% of the adult male population, and 4.5%–9.3% of the adult female population. The incidence (number of new cases in the population per year) of non-bipolar depression is 82–201 per 100000 men per year, and 247–7800 per 100000 women per year. Risk factors for non-bipolar depression are: being female, particularly in the age group 35–45 years; having a family history of depression or alcoholism; having childhood experiences in a disruptive, hostile and generally negative environment in the home; having had recent negative life events; lacking an intimate confiding relationship; having had a baby in the preceding six months.

Non-bipolar depressive disorder has a later mean average age of onset (45 years) than does bipolar depressive disorder (35 years). The incidence of bipolar disorder for men is 9–15.2 new cases per 100 000 per year, and for women 7.4–32 new cases per 100 000 per year.

Genetic endowment has long been acknowledged a risk factor in depression, and in this context women appear to be more vulnerable. Thus many workers reporting a female preponderance of affective disorders (Slater and Cowie, 1971) have found an increase in affected female sibs of probands (Winokur and Clayton, 1967), affected offspring of bipolar probands (Reich *et al.*, 1969) as well as a female preponderance in unipolar illness (Winokur and Clayton, 1967; Bertelsen *et al.*, 1977).

Epidemiology of epilepsy

Sex differences in the epidemiology of epilepsy are not as well documented as those for depression and are discussed further in Chapter 4. Annual incidence rates for epilepsy are around 35–50 per 100 000 population and the prevalence of epilepsy is 5 per 1000 of the population (Hauser and Kurland, 1975; Pond, 1981). It has been suggested that there is probably some excess of the epilepsies among males (Neugebauer and Susser, 1979; Pond, 1981; Zielinski, 1982).

DEPRESSION IN THE CONTEXT OF EPILEPSY

A relationship between depression and epilepsy has been documented since the earliest medical writings. Hippocrates clearly considered that epilepsy and melancholia were closely related when he stated: 'melancholics ordinarily become epileptics and epileptics melancholics: of these two states, what deter-mines the preference is the direction the malady takes; if it bears upon the body, epilepsy, if upon the intelligence, melancholy' (Lewis, 1934). Somewhat later, the suggestion was made that Julius Caesar not only had epilepsy but also had peri-ictal depression (Robertson, 1988b). Temkin (1971) quotes Aretaeus as having said that epileptics were 'languid, spiritless and dejected', while several authors from Griesinger in the 1850s to White, Barham, Baugh and Jones in the early 1900s discussed melancholia specifically interlinked with epilepsy (for references refer to Robertson, 1988a).

In keeping with one of the standard classifications of psychiatric disorders in epilepsy, there are broadly two major types of depression: peri-ictal (those relating to the attacks); and inter-ictal, in which the disturbances are chronic and not directly related to the epileptic discharge. This chapter will focus on inter-ictal depression, the most common and clinically important syndrome.

Prevalence of inter-ictal depression

It is well known that epilepsy may compromise a person's quality of life (Scambler, 1987), rendering some individuals susceptible to psychiatric illness. Depression is a serious and probably the most common psychiatric illness associated with epilepsy, but there have been no epidemiological studies to determine the exact frequency. Nevertheless it has been suggested that some 20% of people with temporal lobe epilepsy (TLE) become depressed (Currie et al., 1971). Recently, Victoroff et al. (1990) documented that 62% of patients with medically intractable complex partial seizures had a history of depres-sion, of whom 38% met criteria for major depressive illness.

Only one investigation has set out to enquire as to whether depression occurs more frequently in individuals with epilepsy compared with other disabling conditions. Mendez et al. (1986) reported that the frequency of inter-ictal depression in community-based patients was greater, and prior attempted suicide more common, than in a control population with similar socio-economic backgrounds and levels of disability. They therefore sug-gested that depression in epilepsy is more than a non-specific reaction to a chronic disability, noting also that a significantly higher than expected number of patients with epilepsy were hospitalized for psychiatric care as a conse-quence of depression (Mendez et al., 1986).

The prevalence of inter-ictal depression in people with epilepsy can be further deduced from studies investigating psychopathology using standard-ized psychiatric rating scales. Many studies employing the Minnesota Multi-phasic Personality Inventory (MMPI) and instruments such as the Standard Psychiatric Interview have shown that depression is prominent in people with epilepsy and higher than controls, while several have reported higher MMPI depression scores for patients with psychomotor epilepsy or temporal lobe epilepsy (TLE) compared with those with generalized attacks (see Robertson, 1988a, 1989).

Other studies, using alternatives to the MMPI such as the Present State Examination, the Bear–Fedio Inventory, the Middlesex Hospital Questionnaire or Crown Crisp Experiential Index (CCEI) and the General Health Questionnaire, have also evaluated psychopathology in people with epilepsy. Adults with epilepsy have been compared with normal controls, patients from general practices, patients with locomotor disorders, general neurological problems and neuromuscular disorders. Those with epilepsy have been more depressed and anxious (Robertson, 1988a, 1989).

Whitman *et al.* (1984) conducted a literature search locating all published MMPI reports of patients with epilepsy, those with other neurological disorders and those with non-neurological chronic physical disorders. Results suggested those with epilepsy run a higher risk for psychopathology than members of the general population. No increase of psychopathology was found in patients with epilepsy compared with those with other chronic disorders, and no difference was found between patients with TLE and generalized epilepsy. Individuals with neurological conditions were demonstrated to be at significantly greater risk for psychopathology compared with people with epilepsy and other chronic illnesses (Whitman *et al.*, 1984). The question as to whether depressive illness occurs more commonly in people with epilepsy was not specifically asked, but half of the investigations which were included in the epilepsy group found that depression scores were increased in people with epilepsy (Klove and Doehring, 1962; Meier and French, 1965; Matthews and Klove, 1968; Mignone *et al.*, 1970; Glass and Matson, 1973).

Dodrill and Batzel (1986) undertook a similar project which included investigations evaluating inter-ictal behavioural features of patients with epilepsy using many objective measures, comparing the index group with patients with cerebral disorders other than epilepsy, chronic medical non-neurological problems, and normal volunteers. They concluded that those with epilepsy have more emotional and psychiatric problems than normal individuals, more difficulties than patients with non-neurological disorders, but have approximately the same incidence of these problems as persons with other neurological disorders. They also suggested that increased emotional and psychiatric problems were not reported in patients with TLE when compared with patients with other types of epilepsy and that the number of seizure types was far more relevant to emotional or psychiatric problems in epilepsy than was the particular seizure type. Patients with TLE often have more than one seizure type and thus as a consequence appear to be more maladjusted.

The CCEI and the Zung Depression Inventory were used by de Angelis and Vizioli (1983) to compare the depression ratings of two groups of patients with epilepsy with patients with syncopal attacks and another group with chronic non-neurological diseases. Results showed that the individuals with epilepsy scored no higher than the controls.

Several studies based on clinical judgement have also found that depression is a common symptom or illness in adults with epilepsy (Dominian *et al.*, 1963; Currie *et al.*, 1971; Dalby, 1971; Taylor, 1972; Betts, 1974; Serafetinides, 1975; Gunn, 1977; Toone and Driver, 1980), while others described that children with epilepsy were particularly prone to depression (Mellor *et al.*, 1974; Pazzangia and Frank-Pazzangia, 1976).

It is clear that more properly controlled studies should be performed to determine more precisely the prevalence of inter-ictal depression in epileptic populations compared with those with other chronic diseases. However, regardless of the source of referral, namely psychiatric, neurological or general practice, the majority of studies to date are remarkably consistent in highlighting the fact that depressive symptomatology is common in patients with epilepsy.

The complexity and difficulties encountered in the relationship between depression and epilepsy can be further illustrated by four case reports. Bacon and Benedek (1982) reported a 26-year-old male epileptic patient who developed a mild depressive illness (requiring psychotherapy) and 'spells' at the age of 24 years, and after two years he experienced typical grand mal seizures. His personality changed in that he showed unusual affect, lowered attentiveness and alternating lethargy and excitement. Following a latent period after a major seizure, he developed a psychosis during which he displayed bizarre emotions, a euphoric affect accompanied by anxiety, automatisms, and a grandiose delusional system which was characterized by religious and mystical ideas: an epileptic focus was identified in the right temporal lobe.

Maurice-Williams and Sinar (1984) reported a 62-year-old woman who had focal epilepsy (left frontotemporal) and an agitated depression. She had a previous history of depression which necessitated electroconvulsive therapy (ECT). Because of the severity and intractability of the depression and repeated suicidal attempts, a leucotomy was performed which led to a dramatic improvement in her depression, although her epilepsy remained unchanged. Twenty-three years later her seizures became worse and, on reinvestigation, a large left frontal meningioma was discovered and removed. One year after removal of the tumour she was reported as being well, with no seizures and no depression.

A 24-year-old male patient who reported a life-long history of temper outbursts and a changing pattern of moods consistent with bipolar disorder was discribed by Pellegrini *et al.* (1984). There was no clinical evidence of epilepsy but an EEG showed bilateral paroxysmal bursts of 5–6-Hz spikes and slow wave activity. Family history revealed epilepsy ($n = 2$), abnormal EEG ($n = 4$) and affective disturbance ($n = 4$) in seven members of the patient's nuclear family. A diagnosis of complex partial seizures was made, and all symptoms responded to treatment with phenytoin.

Rubin *et al.* (1985) reported a 38-year-old woman with a depression, meeting DSM-III criteria for melancholia with mood-congruent somatic delusions, involving alterations of body parts (e.g. that her eyes became sockets when she slept). She had no history of psychiatric or seizure disorder. She was unresponsive to the antidepressant buproprion combined with lithium carbonate, but following the occurrence of two grand mal seizures, probably precipitated by her medication, she experienced rapid improvement of both depression and psychotic symptoms.

Type and phenomenology of depression in epilepsy

Several investigations have examined specific aspects of inter-ictal depression found in people with epilepsy. Those based on clinical judgement have described the depression as being either 'reactive' (Mulder and Daly, 1952) or 'endogenous' (Betts, 1974). Palia and Harper (1986) and Robertson *et al.* (1987) using standardized psychiatric rating scales reported that most patients were rated as non-endogenous on the Levine–Pilowsky (LPD) and Newcastle scales. The severity of the depression is moderate (Palia and Harper, 1986; Robertson *et al.*, 1987), with accompanying anxiety, neuroticism, hostility, sadness, obsessionalism, dependence and altered sexual interest (Roy, 1979; Palia and Harper, 1986; Robertson *et al.*, 1987). In one cohort, 13 out of 66 (20%) were psychotic (Robertson *et al.*, 1987) while, in another study, depressed epileptic patients were characterized by paranoia, irritability, humourlessness, an abnormal affect and less self-pity, brooding, guilt, somatization, anxiety and hopelessness (Mendez *et al.*, 1986).

Depressed epileptic patients often have a significant past history of depressive illness, deliberate drug overdosage and self-harm (Roy, 1979; Palia and Harper, 1986; Robertson *et al.*, 1987) but no more so than a depressed group without epilepsy (Mendez *et al.*, 1986). In the study of Robertson *et al.* (1987) only two out of 66 (5%) had a history of bipolar disorder.

Aetiology of depression in people with epilepsy

Whybrow *et al.* (1984) in a comprehensive review have suggested that mood disorders and indeed depression can best be understood by integrating psychodynamic, biological, social and behavioural approaches. This is probably also true in the case of depression in the context of epilepsy.

Genetic predisposition

Genetic predisposition appears to be well recognized in bipolar illness and recurrent unipolar depressions (see Gurling, 1990). Hancock and Bevilacqua (1971) reported that one of four of their depressed epileptic patients had a family history of suicide. Mendez *et al.* (1986) reported that their cohort of 20 depressed epileptic patients had less family history of affective illness than their depressed controls, while Robertson *et al.* (1987) found that 25% of their 66 depressed epileptic patients had a family history of psychiatric disorder, of which the most common illness was depression. The exact contribution of genetic endowment to depression in individuals with epilepsy remains unclear.

Brent *et al.* (1987) reported that a differential prevalence of depression between anticonvulsant medication groups (phenobarbital (PB) and carbamazepine (CBZ), see below) in patients with epilepsy was only noted in those with a family history of major depressive disorder among first-degree relatives.

The effect of epilepsy and seizure variables

The temporal relationship between seizures and mood has been known for some time. Although not frequent, reports of peri-ictal depression have been documented, although not many would qualify as depressive illness. Having said that, the lowered mood often warranted treatment with antidepressant drugs which improved with therapy. One could therefore argue that in these instances the seizures (or increase thereof) contributed to the lowering of mood. (For a full discussion of peri-ictal depression see Robertson, 1988a, 1989.)

When one considers inter-ictal depression, several authors have noted a decrease in seizure frequency prior to the onset of the lowered mood (Flor-Henry, 1969; Betts, 1974; Standage and Fenton, 1975; Dongier, 1959/1960), whereas others found that depression was associated with an increase in seizures (Dodrill and Batzel, 1986; Fenton, 1986). Patients with intractable TLE were administered measures of depression and locus of control (a psychological term for where a person perceives their choices in life as coming from) both pre-operatively and post-operatively (anterior temporal lobectomy, ATL) by Hermann and Wyler (1989). There was a significant pre-operative relationship between depression and an external locus of control, but this relationship no longer existed post-operatively. Post-operative declines in depression were independent of any alterations in locus of control. Moreover, depression declined significantly only in patients rendered completely seizure free.

Many investigators have found depressive symptomatology not to be intimately related to neuro-epilepsy variables such as age of onset of epilepsy, the presence of an intracranial lesion, seizure frequency, type, site or side of lesion (Roy, 1979; Trimble and Perez, 1980a, 1980b; Mendez *et al.*, 1986; Fralin *et al.*, 1987; Kramer *et al.*, 1987; Robertson *et al.*, 1987; Hermann and Wyler, 1989). Mignone *et al.* (1970) found that the depression scores were higher for those patients with late-onset seizures.

Psychosocial contributions

Various psychosocial models of depression have been suggested and many of these models may apply to people with epilepsy. Many have reported on the stigma and social prejudice to which people with epilepsy are subject, while only a few patients suggest they do not feel stigmatized by their illness (Robertson, 1988a, 1989).

Danesi *et al.* (1981) interviewed adult/adolescent epileptic patients attending a neurological clinic about their social problems and found that a substantial number had school problems, lost income, friends or spouses and a few had withdrawn from social activities. It was concluded that most problems arose from poor seizure control, due to poor compliance with anticonvulsant medication. Danesi (1984) subsequently found that approximately one-third of patients, despite having seizures, were unable to accept a diagnosis of epilepsy, and of those who were prepared to accept the diagnosis two-thirds were not willing to disclose the fact to other people.

Beran and Read (1981) reported how patients with epilepsy attending a neurological clinic saw their condition, their role in society and society's expectations of them. The majority thought that people with epilepsy had more emotional problems and mood swings compared with those without, and there was a trend for people with epilepsy to consider themselves less well endowed with many positive attributes.

Dodrill and colleagues (1984a, 1984b) evaluated psychosocial problems among adults with epilepsy in a national study using the self-rating Washington Psychosocial Seizure Inventory (WPSI), and documented that emotional, interpersonal, vocational and financial concerns were commonly found, as well as problems coping with epileptic attacks.

Arntson *et al.* (1986) also investigated psychosocial consequences of having epilepsy and found that the epilepsy sample differed from controls. Anxiety was the most frequently reported problem (39% for epilepsy versus 9% norm) followed by depression (25% for epilepsy versus 9% norm). In addition, the stigma scale was significantly and positively related to perceived helplessness, depression, anxiety and somatic symptoms, and significantly negatively related to self-esteem and life satisfaction.

In Fenton's (1986) study depression in male epileptic patients was significantly related to unemployment. Patients who were depressed had experienced significantly more life events during the three months preceding the assessment (Fenton, 1986).

Hermann (1979) argued the case for epilepsy being a human analogue of the learned helplessness theory of depression suggested by Seligman and colleagues (Seligman, 1975; Abramson *et al.*, 1978). Hermann (1979) proposed that epilepsy is a high psychopathological risk disorder, as affected individuals are constantly exposed to unpredictable, uncontrollable, aversive events (seizures) which produce a pattern of emotional, motivational and cognitive disorders initially presenting as anxiety, but if prolonged, depression. Further, individuals with epilepsy suffer discrimination, a higher incidence of employment difficulties, social exclusion, lower marital rates and are predisposed to cognitive impairment due to cerebral damage and/or anti-epileptic medication (Robertson, 1988a, 1989). This is important when one considers that many of these problems, and the reactions of society to people with epilepsy, are usually unpredictable and not under the control of the person with epilepsy (Hermann, 1979).

Hermann and Whitman (1989) investigated a wide variety of psychosocial, neuro-epilepsy and medication variables and related them to self-reported depressive symptomatology in a sample of adults with epilepsy. Results revealed that the following variables were predictive of increased depression: increased stressful life events, poor adjustment to seizures, and financial stress. Others (Palia and Harper, 1986; Brent *et al.*, 1987) also found stressful life events and family discord to be instrumental in provoking depression in people with epilepsy.

Ictal fear and fear of seizures

Two other groups (besides Strauss *et al.*, 1982) have examined fear, both ictal and inter-ictal, and its relationship to psychopathology. Hermann *et al.* (1982) assessed patients with ictal fear, and controls using the MMPI, and results suggested that patients who have ictal fear run a higher risk of psychopathology, scoring higher on five subscales including depression. Mittan (1984) assessed patients' fears about their epilepsy and evaluated psychopathology. The 'high fear' group scored significantly higher on many of the depression-related psychiatric rating scales than did the 'low fear' group. By contrast, the 'low fear' group scored within normal limits when compared to test norms. Mittan (1984) therefore suggested that the level of patients' fears may be a strong predictor of the presence of psychopathology.

The laterality hypothesis

Flor-Henry in 1969 suggested that when patients had a combination of TLE and psychosis, a dominant-side pathology (usually left-sided) and was more likely to be related to a schizophreniform presentation, while a non-dominant abnormality (usually right-sided) was associated with a manic-depressive psychosis. While the former suggestion has been reaffirmed by several authors, the association of affective illness and the non-dominant hemisphere has been noted by only a few authors (for review see Trimble and Robertson, 1987).

Several epilepsy studies have subsequently addressed the laterality hypothesis and found that, contrary to the original suggestion, the left side is more implicated in depression (Nielsen and Kristensen, 1981; Perini and Mendius, 1984; Perini *et al.*, 1983; Palia and Harper, 1986; Robertson *et al.*, 1987) while others have found no left–right differences (Camfield *et al.*, 1984; Brandt *et al.*, 1985). Mendez *et al.* (1986) suggested that the left temporal lobe was specifically associated with depression, a finding which has been recently been reaffirmed by others (Victoroff *et al.*, 1990; Altshuler *et al.*, 1990). The latter group documented that these left-sided TLE patients scored significantly higher than the others on self-ratings for depression and which could not be accounted for by factors such as duration of epilepsy, employment status, education, age of onset of seizures, or antiepileptic medication. No significant difference in the level of anxiety was found among the groups.

Anticonvulsants and mood

Carbamazepine (CBZ) was first noted to have a psychotropic effect in patients with epilepsy by Dalby as early as 1971. Since then there have been many investigations showing the psychotropic action of CBZ in this population, including studies from independent centres which have documented significant associations between levels of CBZ or its breakdown product in blood and/or cerebrospinal fluid (CSF) and a positive psychotropic action (Robertson, 1988a, 1989).

Robertson *et al.* (1987) reported that patients receiving phenobarbitone (PB) were more depressed than those not receiving the drug, while patients on CBZ were less depressed and had lower trait anxiety. Smith and Collins (1987) evaluated the mood and behaviour of patients with epilepsy on a variety of antiepileptic drugs and found that CBZ did not affect mood adversely, in contrast to phenytoin, PB and primidone, with PB and primidone being the worst offenders. Recently Victoroff *et al.* (1990) documented that barbiturates were a possible aetiological factor in depressive illness.

Brent *et al.* (1987) compared the prevalence and severity of psychopathology in 15 epileptic patients treated with PB and 24 patients treated with CBZ. The groups were similar across a wide range of demographic, seizure-related and family–environmental variables. Patients treated with PB, when compared with those treated with CBZ, showed a significantly higher prevalence of major depressive disorder and suicidal ideation, as determined by semi-structured interviews. The differential prevalence of depression between medication groups was only noted in those with a family history of major depressive disorder among first-degree relatives. Family discord and number of stressful life events were also associated with depression in this cohort.

Other anticonvulsant drugs have been noted to alter mood. Ring and Reynolds (1990) reported depression as an unwanted side effect of vigabatrin, while valproic acid has been shown to be a useful adjunct in treatment of manic-depressive illness, depression and mania (Emrich *et al.*, 1984). Clonazepam has been reported as antimanic (Chouinard, 1983).

GENDER

Depression in the general population is well documented as being more common in women than men (see above) and in depressed epileptic populations this has also been shown to be the case in some (Palia and Harper, 1986; Robertson *et al.*, 1987; Hermann and Whitman, 1989) but not other studies. (Fenton, 1986; Mendez *et al.*, 1986; Altschuler *et al.*, 1990). No sex differences for the occurrence of depression in epileptic patients were reported by Victoroff *et al.* (1990). As this is important, these studies will be discussed in detail below.

The effects of seizures and epilepsy variables: studies which have reported a sex difference

Strauss *et al.* (1982) reported that ictal fear (the most common ictal emotion) was associated equally with left and right temporal lobe foci. With respect to inter-ictal fear, however, patients with left and right foci feared different things, and men with foci on the right side had less fear than those on the left.

Fenton (1986) assessed 182 patients with epilepsy in a general practice population using the CCEI. They were compared with a control sample of non-epileptic patients from the same practices, matched for age, sex and social class. The male epileptic patients scored significantly higher on the depression, free-floating anxiety and obsessionalism subscales than did the control patients, while the scores of the female patients with epilepsy showed insignificant differences on all subscales when compared with controls. The scores of the index group were then compared with those from a neurotic out-patient population taken from the scores from the CCEI manual, and similar results were obtained; namely, that the male epileptic patients scored significantly higher on the depression, free-floating anxiety and obsessionalism subscales. The gender difference was found to be significantly related to seizure frequency (increased seizures, more psychopathology) but not to anticonvulsant polytherapy, high plasma anticonvulsant levels, or the type of epilepsy. The type of neurotic symptoms differed with age in that younger patients exhibited anxiety, while older patients reported more depression.

Palia and Harper (1986) assessed 53 psychiatric in- and out-patients with epilepsy. Eighty-eight per cent of the group were female and the mean age was 42.5 years. The depressed patients (the index group) were compared with those who were not depressed. The type of epilepsy amongst the depressed group was generalized in six and partial in 11 patients. Serum folate levels were lower in the epileptic group with psychiatric disorders than a group without psychiatric disorders, but there was no significant difference between the depressed and non-depressed group.

Mendez *et al.* (1986) compared 20 depressed epileptic patients (mean HDRS (Hamilton depression rating scale) 21.7) with 20 depressed patients without epilepsy (mean HDRS 24.7), all of whom satisfied DSM-III criteria for major depression. Both groups were in-patients in a psychiatric hospital and were comparable with respect to personal and socio-economic factors, the control subjects having no complicating medical or neurological illnesses. Control patients without epilepsy were significantly older (47.5 years as compared to 40.3 years), but analysis of variance revealed no statistically significant age effects. Male patients predominated in both groups (index = 15; control = 19), the majority of patients were right-handed (index = 18; control = 17) and equal numbers of patients (*n* = 15) in both groups had made previous suicide attempts. Significant differences between the two groups were that more control patients (*n* = 11) than index patients (*n* = 3) had a family history of depression, while more index patients (*n* = 14) than control patients (*n* = 6) had psychotic features, such as persecutory auditory hallucinations, delusions and paranoid ideation. These acute agitated peri-ictal psychoses were associated with an increase in seizure frequency, usually as a result of non-compliance with medication or alcohol abuse. Among the 20 patients with a combined diagnosis of depression and epilepsy, 16 had complex partial seizures, 15 proceeding to secondary generalization. No associations were found between depression and seizure frequency or the duration of depression and serum anticonvulsant dosages or levels. Neither did the aetiology of the epilepsy or the presence of an aura bear any relationship to the depression.

Robertson and colleagues (1987) screened 80 consecutive adult patients referred to a neuropsychiatric department with a clinical diagnosis of both epilepsy and depression, and 66 who fulfilled epilepsy criteria, the Research Diagnostic Criteria for major depressive disorder, and who scored over 12 on the HDRS were included in their investigation. Of these, 46 were female, 59 right-handed, and their mean age was 38 years (18–67). Twenty-five patients had complex partial secondary generalized seizures, 20 had complex partial seizures, nine had secondary generalized seizures, eight had primary generalized seizures, three had partial simple seizures and one was unclassified due to insufficient information. The duration of epilepsy correlated significantly with the severity of the depression, and an association was found between complex partial seizures and a past history of depression. No other significant relationships emerged between depression and epilepsy variables. Thus, the type, severity and features of depression were not influenced by gender, the age of onset of epilepsy, the type of epilepsy, the site of a focal lesion, the seizure frequency or the red blood cell or serum folic acid.

Hermann and Whitman (1989) assessed a wide variety of psychosocial, neuro-epilepsy and medication variables and related them to self-reported depressive symptomatology in a sample of 102 adults with epilepsy. The results of multiple regression analysis revealed that four variables were predictive of increased depression: increased stressful life events, poor adjustment to seizures, financial stress and female gender.

The association between anxiety, depression and lateralization of an epileptogenic focus was explored by Altshuler *et al.* (1990) in 18 adult neurological epileptic patients with a left temporal lobe focus, 21 with a right focus, 20 with bilateral foci and 16 individuals with absence seizures. Results showed that patients with left-sided temporal lobe epilepsy scored significantly higher than the other groups on self-ratings for depression. This could not be accounted for by factors such as duration of epilepsy, employment status, education, age of onset of seizures or anticonvulsant medication. The left temporal lobe epilepsy group had a non-significantly larger number of males and left-handed subjects. No significant difference in the level of anxiety was found among the groups.

Victoroff *et al.* (1990) evaluated 47 patients with medically intractable complex partial seizures using electrophysiological techniques (EEG and positron emission tomography (PET) scan) and a recognized standardized psychiatric interview (Structured Clinical Interview for DSM-III-R Epilepsy Version (SCID–Epilepsy)). Twenty-nine (62%) had a history of interictal depressive disorders of whom 18 (38%) met DSM-III-R criteria for one or more major depressive disorders. All depressions occurred with or following the onset of epilepsy. There were no differences in depressive frequency by age, sex or age at seizure onset.

With respect to the relationship of gender with depression, it seems well established that depression is more commonly found in women. Epilepsy is encountered more in men. However, in the depressed epileptic population three studies had more females (Palia and Harper, 1986; Robertson *et al.*, 1987; Hermann and Wyler, 1989), but only one found depression and female gender to be significantly related (Hermann and Wyler, 1989). One study had no sex effects (Victoroff *et al.*, 1990) while three studies had male gender not only over-represented, but significantly related to variables such as increased seizures, life events, unemployment (Fenton, 1986) and a left-sided lesion (Mendez *et al.*, 1986; Altschuler *et al.*, 1990). In one study, males with left-sided foci had more inter-ictal fear (Strauss *et al.*, 1982).

As the findings are inconsistent and the methods of the studies vary enormously, no firm conclusions can be drawn. However, there seems to be no clear-cut preponderance of females in the depressed epileptic group and it is thus tempting to suggest that men in this particular instance may possibly be more vulnerable to depression. This may be due to several factors. Firstly, from the social perspective, women with epilepsy may well be able to fulfil their role as a mother, whereas males may be unemployed (on the open market) and subject to more stigma as far as work/role fulfilment is concerned, which may render them susceptible to depression. From the biological aspect, the left side of the brain appears to be more implicated. Whether this is specific, as suggested by Mendez *et al.* (1986), or because damage of the left hemisphere and frontotemporal areas seem particularly associated with psychopathology, as evidenced by studies on head injury (Lishman, 1968; Robinson and Szetla, 1981), stroke patients (Robinson *et al.*, 1984), and patients with epilepsy (Bingley, 1958; Taylor, 1972; Stores, 1978; Pritchard, *et al.*, 1980), is unclear. Since, in some series, focal abnormalities are found more commonly on the left (Scott, 1985), selection bias needs to be excluded. In this context it is interesting to note that developmental studies suggest that left-sided lesions and male patients are particularly vulnerable to psychopathology (see Chapter 5).

Hormonal factors may also affect the differential susceptibility to depression in the epileptic population. Investigations reviewed in Chapter 8 have shown that alterations of serum luteinizing hormone, sex hormone-binding globulin and free testosterone occur (Dani-Haeri, 1982; Toone *et al.*, 1980). In some studies baseline prolactin levels are raised (Toone *et al.*, 1980). There is a complex relationship between the biogenic amines and prolactin, and adrenocorticotrophic hormone (ACTH) has been reported to be anticonvulsant (Robertson, 1983). Thus, the delicate balance between hormones and monoamines in a person with epilepsy may be upset and predispose to depression.

SUICIDE AND ATTEMPTED SUICIDE

The importance of suicide when discussing depression in the setting of epilepsy cannot be overstressed. According to figures from the Registrar General, the crude suicide rate for men in England and Wales is approximately 9.7 per 100000 and for women 6.2 per 100000 (averages for 1974–1978) (Kreitman, 1983). Patients with affective illness are particularly at risk, as those treated by psychiatrists for manic-depressive psychosis and reactive depression have approximately 30 times the risk of death by suicide compared with the general population. In people with epilepsy, suicide and attempted suicide are also over-represented.

Thus there is a general consensus that the risk of suicide in people with epilepsy is four to five times greater than that of the general population (Barraclough, 1981; Matthews and Barabas, 1981; Wannamaker, 1983) while those with TLE have an increased risk of approximately 25 times that expected (Barraclough, 1981). Several investigations have reported a 5–7% increase in self-poisoning (parasuicide) in people with epilepsy, finding that repeated attempts were common, with barbiturates being implicated in particular (Mackay, 1979; Hawton *et al.*, 1980; Brent *et al.*, 1987). People with epilepsy make more attempts (15.8 times more frequent than one would expect, given the prevalence of epilepsy in school-age children), make medically more serious suicide attempts, show more premeditation, and have higher suicidal intent than do non-epileptic attempters (Brent, 1986).

CONCLUSIONS

Inter-ictal depression occurs frequently in individuals with epilepsy. Several investigations using standardized psychiatric rating scales have found the depression scores to range from moderate to severe and to compare favourably with studies on depressed patients without epilepsy (Robertson, 1983). Many of these would therefore qualify as having a depressive illness.

A number of variables have been suggested with regard to the pathogenesis of the depression, and predisposing factors include genetic diathesis, social stigma, unemployment, adverse life events, patients' fears, and a past history of depressive illness. The phenomenology of the depression does not in the main seem intimately linked with neuro-epilepsy variables (such as age at onset of epilepsy, seizure frequency and presence of an intracranial lesion), with some exceptions. Thus, antiepileptic drugs can affect the mental state, and the longer the duration of epilepsy the more severe the depression. The laterality hypothesis of depression in this population has not been upheld, although several studies have shown the left hemisphere to be implicated, with some emphasis on TLE/complex partial seizure patients. Whether this is specific, as suggested by some authors, or because the left hemisphere and frontotemporal areas seem particularly vulnerable to be associated with psychopathology is as yet uncertain. The effect of gender is not clear but the predominance of females, noted in primary affective disorder, is not clear in epileptic populations.

An attractive model which could be suggested in this context of gender, depression and epilepsy is that originally proposed by Akiskal and McKinney (1975), who view depressive illness as a 'psychobiological final common pathway' and the culmination of various processes which converge on those areas of the diencephalon that modulate arousal, mood, motivation and psychomotor function. They take the view that the specific form that the depressive illness will take in a given individual depends on the interaction of several factors which has relevance to this review and topic: (1) genetic vulnerability (as suggested by some studies); (2) developmental events (and their disruption by epileptic seizures); (3) psychosocial events (such as unemployment and stigma); (4) physiological stressors (again, for example, a seizure), which impinge on diencephalic function; and (5) personality traits. In several studies of depression in epilepsy, trait anxiety, obsessionality, neuroticism and hostility were much higher when compared with other populations.

REFERENCES

Abramson, L.Y., Seligman, M.E.P. and Teasdale, J.D. (1978) Learned helplessness in humans: Critique and reformulation. *J. Abnormal Psychol.*, **87**, 49–74.

Akiskal, H.S. and McKinney, W.T. Jr (1975) Overview of recent research in depression. *Arch. Gen. Psychiatry*, **32**, 285–305.

Altschuler, L.L., Devinsky, O., Post, R.M. and Theodore, W. (1990) Depression, anxiety, and temporal lobe epilepsy: Laterality of focus and symptoms. *Arch. Neurol.*, **47**, 284–288.

Angelis, G. de and Vizioli, R. (1983) Epilepsy and depression. In: *Advances in Epileptology: XIVth Epilepsy International Symposium* (eds M. Parsonage, R.H.E. Grant, A. Craig and A.A.J. Ward Jr), pp. 203–206. Raven Press, New York.

Angst, J. (1981) Clinical indications for a prophylactic treatment of depression. *Adv. Biol. Psychiatry*, **7**, 218–229.

Arntson, P., Droge, D., Norton, R. and Murray, E. (1986) The perceived psychosocial consequences of having epilepsy. In: *Psychopathology in Epilepsy: Social Dimensions* (eds S. Whitman and B. Hermann), pp. 143–161. Oxford University Press, Oxford.

Bacon, P.D. and Benedek, E.P. (1982) Epileptic psychosis and insanity: Case study and review. *Bull. AAPL*, **10**, 203–210.

Barraclough, B. (1981) Suicide and epilepsy. In: *Epilepsy and Psychiatry*, (eds E.H. Reynolds and M.R. Trimble), pp. 72–76. Churchill Livingstone, Edinburgh.

Beran, R.G. and Read, T. (1981) Patient perspectives of epilepsy. *Clin. Exp. Neurol.*, **17**, 56–69.

Bertelsen, A., Harvald, B. and Hauge, M. (1977) A Danish twin study of manic depressive disorders. *Br. J. Psychiatry*, **130**, 330–351.

Betts, T.A. (1974) A follow-up study of a cohort of patients with epilepsy admitted to psychiatric care in an English city. In: *Epilepsy: Proceedings of the Hans Berger Centenary Symposium* (eds P. Harris and C. Mawdsley), pp. 326–338. Churchill Livingstone, Edinburgh.

Betts, T.A. (1981) Depression, anxiety and epilepsy. In: *Epilepsy and Psychiatry*, (eds E.H. Reynolds and M.R. Trimble), pp. 60–71. Churchill Livingstone, Edinburgh.

Bingley, T. (1958) Mental symptoms in temporal lobe epilepsy and temporal lobe gliomas. *Acta Psychiat. Neurol. Scand.*, **33** (Suppl. 120), 1–151.

Boyd, J.H. and Weissman, M.M. (1982) Epidemiology. In: *Handbook of Affective Disorders* (ed. E.S. Paykel), pp. 109–125. Churchill Livingstone, Edinburgh.

Brandt, J., Seidman, L.J. and Kohl, D. (1985) Personality characteristics of epileptic patients: A controlled study of generalised and temporal lobe cases. *J. Clin. Exp. Neuropsychol.*, **7**, 25–38.

Brent, D.A. (1986) Overrepresentation of epileptics in a consecutive series of suicide attempters seen at a children's hospital, 1978–1983. *J. Am. Acad. Child Psychiatry*, **25**, 242–246.

Brent, D.A., Crumrine, P.K., Varma, R.R., Allan, M. and Allman, C. (1987) Phenobarbital treatment and major depressive disorder in children with epilepsy. *Pediatrics*, **80**, 909–917.

Camfield, P.R., Gates, R., Ronen, G., Camfield, C., Ferguson, A. and MacDonald G.W. (1984) Comparison of cognitive ability, personality profile, and school success in epileptic children with pure right versus left temporal lobe EEG foci. *Ann. Neurol.*, **15**, 122–126.

Chouinard, G. (1983) Antimanic effects of clonazepam. *Psychosomatics*, **26**, 7–12.

Currie, S., Heathfield, K.W.G., Henson, R.A. and Scott, D.F. (1971) Clinical course and prognosis of temporal lobe epilepsy: A survey of 666 patients. *Brain*, **94**, 173–190.

Dalby, M.A. (1971) Antiepileptic and psychotropic effect of carbamazepine (Tegretol) in the treatment of psychomotor epilepsy. *Epilepsia*, **12**, 325–334.

Dana-Haeri, J. (1982) *Hypothalamic–Pituitary Axis in Epilepsy*. PhD thesis, University of London.

Danesi, M.A. (1984) Patient perspectives on epilepsy in a developing country. *Epilepsia*, **25**, 184–190.

Danesi, M.A., Odusote, K.A., Roberts, O.O. and Adu, E.O. (1981) Social problems of adolescent and adult epileptics in a developing country, as seen in Lagos, Nigeria. *Epilepsia*, **22**, 689–696.

Dodrill, C.B. and Batzel, L.W. (1986) Inter-ictal behavioural features of patients with epilepsy. *Epilepsia*, **27** (Suppl. 2), S64–S76.

Dodrill, C.B., Breyer, D.N., Diamond, M.B., Dubinsky, B.L. and Geary, B.B. (1984a) Psychosocial problems among adults with epilepsy. *Epilepsia*, **25**, 168–175.

Dodrill, C.B., Beier, R., Kasparick, M., Tacke, I., Tacke, U. and Tan, S.Y. (1984b) Psychosocial problems in adults with epilepsy: Comparison of findings from four countries. *Epilepsia*, **25**, 176–183.

Dominian, J., Serafitinides, E.A. and Dewhurst, M. (1963) A follow-up study of late onset epilepsy. 11: psychiatric and social findings. *Br. Med. J.*, **1**, 431–435.

Dongier, S. (1959/1960) Statistical study of clinical and electroencephalographic manifestations of 536 psychotic episodes occurring in 516 epileptics between clinical seizures. *Epilepsia*, **1**, 117–142.

Emrich, H.M., Dose, M. and von Zerssen, D. (1984) Action of sodium valproate and of oxcarbazepine in patients with affective disorders. In: *Anticonvulsants in affective disorders* (eds H.M. Emrich, T. Okuma and A.A. Muller), pp. 45–55. Excerpta Medica, Amsterdam.

Fenton, G.W. (1986) *Minor Psychiatric Morbidity in People with Epilepsy: Evidence for a Gender Difference*. Presented at the Annual Meeting of the Royal College of Psychiatrists, 8–10 July 1986, Southampton.

Flor-Henry, P. (1969) Psychosis and temporal lobe epilepsy: A controlled investigation. *Epilepsia*, **10**, 363–395.

Fralin, C., Kramer, L.D., Berman, N.G. and Locke, G.E. (1987) Interictal depression in urban minority epileptics. *Epilepsia*, **28**, 598.

Glass, D.H. and Mattson, R.H. (1973) Psychopathology and emotional precipitation of seizures in temporal lobe and non-temporal lobe epileptics. *Proc. 81st Ann. Conv. Am. Psychol. Assoc.*, **8**, 425–426.

Gunn, J. (1977) *Epileptics in Prison*. Academic Press, London.

Gurling, H.M.D. (1990) Recent advances in the genetics of psychiatric disorder. *1990 Human Genetic Information: Science, Law and Ethics*, pp. 48–62. Wiley, Chichester.

Hancock, J.C. and Bevilacqua, A.R. (1971) Temporal lobe dysrhythmia and impulsive or suicidal behaviour: Preliminary report. *Southern Med. J.*, **64**, 1189–1193.

Hauser, W.A. and Kurland, L.T. (1975) The epidemiology of epilepsy in Rochester, Minnesota, 1935 through 1967. *Epilepsia*, **16**, 1–66.

Hawton, K., Fagg, J. and Marsack, P. (1980) Association between epilepsy and attempted suicide. *J. Neurol. Neurosurg. Psychiatry*, **43**, 168–170.

Hermann, B.P. (1979) Psychopathology in epilepsy and learned helplessness. *Med. Hypotheses*, **5**, 723–729.

Hermann, B.P. and Whitman, S. (1989) Psychosocial predictors of interictal depression. *J. Epilepsy*, **2**, 231–237.

Hermann, B.P. and Wyler, A.R. (1989) Depression, locus of control, and the effects of epilepsy surgery. *Epilepsia*, **30**, 332–338.

Hermann, B.P., Dikmen, S., Schwartz, M.S. and Karnes, W.E. (1982) Inter-ictal psychopathology in patients with ictal fear: A quantitative investigation. *Neurology*, **32**, 7–11.

Hirschfield, R.M.A. and Cross, C.K. (1982) Epidemiology of affective disorders. *Arch. Gen. Psychiatry*, **39**, 35–46.

Klove, H. and Doehring, D.G. (1962) MMPI in epileptic groups with differential etiology. *J. Clin. Psychol.*, **18**, 149–153.

Kramer, L.D., Fralin, C., Berman, N.G. Locke, G.E. (1987) Relationship of seizure frequency and interictal depression. *Epilepsia*, **28**, 629.

Kreitman, N. (1983) Suicide and parasuicide. In: *Companion to Psychiatric Studies*, 3rd edn (eds R.E. Kendell and A.K. Zealley), pp. 396–411. Churchill Livingstone, Edinburgh.

Lewis, A.J. (1934) Melancholia: A historical review. *J. Ment. Sci.*, **80**, 1–42.

Lieb, J. (1988) *The Key to Genius: Manic Depression and the creative life*. Prometheus Books, Buffalo, NY.

Lishman, W.A. (1968) Brain damage in relation to psychiatric disability after head injury. *Br. J. Psychiatry*, **114**, 373–410.

Mackay, A. (1979) Self-poisoning: A complication of epilepsy. *Br. J. Psychiatry*, **134**, 277–282.

Matthews, C.H.G. and Klove, H. (1968) MMPI performances in major motor, psychomotor and mixed seizure classifications of known and unknown etiology. *Epilepsia*, **9**, 43–53.

Matthews, W.S. and Barabas, G. (1981) Suicide and epilepsy: A review of the literature. *Psychosomatics*, **22**, 515–524.

Maurice-Williams, R.S. and Sinar, E.J. (1984) Depression caused by an intracranial meningioma relieved by leucotomy prior to diagnosis of the tumour. *J. Neurol. Neurosurg. Psychiatry*, **47**, 884–887.

Meier, M.J. and French, L.A. (1965) Some personality correlates of unilateral and bilateral EEG abnormalities in psychomotor epilepsy. *J. Clin. Psychol.*, **1**, 3–9.

Mellor, D.H., Lowit, I. and Hall, D.J. (1974) Are epileptic children behaviourally different from other children? In: *Epilepsy: Proceedings of the Hans Burger Centenary Symposium* (eds P. Harris and C. Mawdsley), pp. 313–316. Churchill Livingstone, Edinburgh.

Mendez, M.F., Cummings, J.L. and Benson, D.F. (1986) Depression in epilepsy. *Arch. Neurol.*, **43**, 766–770.

Meyer, J.E. and Meyer, R. (1987) Self portrayal by a depressed poet: A contribution to the clinical biography of William Cowper. *Am. J. Psychiatry*, **114**, 127–132.

Mignone, R.J., Donnelly, E.F. and Sadowsky, D. (1970) Psychological and neurological comparisons of psychomotor and non-psychomotor epileptic patients. *Epilepsia*, **11**, 345–359.

Mittan, R.J. (1984) Patient's fears about seizures may predict presence and absence of psychopathology. *Epilepsia*, **25**, 648.

Mulder, D.W. and Daly, D. (1952) Psychiatric symptoms associated with lesions of the temporal lobe. *JAMA*, **150**, 173–176.

Neugebauer, R. and Susser, M. (1979) Some epidemiological aspects of epilepsy. *Psychol. Med.*, **9**, 207–215.

Nielsen, H. and Kristensen, O. (1981) Personality correlates of sphenoidal EEG-foci in temporal lobe epilepsy. *Acta Neurol. Scand.*, **64**, 289–300.

Palia, S.S. and Harper, M.A. (1986) *Mood Disorders in Epilepsy: A Survey of Psychiatric Patients*. Presented at the Annual Meeting of the Royal College of Psychiatrists, University of Southampton, 8–10 July 1986.

Pazzangia, P. and Frank-Pazzangia, L. (1976) Record in grade school in pupils with epilepsy: An epidemiological study. *Epilepsia*, **17**, 361–366.

Pellegrini, A., Lippman, S.B., Crump, G. and Manshadi, M. (1984) Psychiatric aspects of complex partial seizures. *J. Nerv. Ment. Dis.*, **172**, 287–290.

Perini, G. and Mendius, R. (1984) Depression and anxiety in complex partial seizures. *J. Nerv. Ment. Dis*, **172**, 287–290.

Perini, G., Suny, M.D. and Mendius, R. (1983) Interictal emotions and behavioural profiles in left and right temporal lobe epileptics. *Psychosom. Med.*, **45**, 83.

Pond, D. (1981) Epidemiology of the psychiatric disorders of epilepsy. In: *Epilepsy and Psychiatry* (eds E.H. Reynolds and M.R. Trimble), pp. 27–32. Churchill Livingstone, Edinburgh.

Pritchard, P.B., Lombroso, C.T. and McIntyre, M. (1980) Psychological complications of temporal lobe epilepsy. *Neurology*, **30**, 227–232.

Reich, T., Clayton, P.J. and Winokur, G. (1969) Family history studies: v. The genetics of mania. *Am. J. Psychiatry*, **125**, 1358–1369.

Ring, H.A. and Reynolds, E.H. (1990) Vigabatrin and behaviour disturbance. *Lancet*, **335**, 970.

Robertson, M.M. (1983) *Depression in Patients with Epilepsy*. MD thesis, University of Cape Town, South Africa.

Robertson, M.M. (1988a) Depression in patients with epilepsy reconsidered. *Recent Advances in Epilepsy*, vol 4 (eds T.A. Pedley and B.S. Meldrum), pp. 205–240. Churchill Livingstone, Edinburgh.

Robertson, M.M. (1988b) Epilepsy and mood. In: *Epilepsy Behaviour and Cognitive Function* (eds M.R. Trimble and E.H. Reynolds), pp. 145–157. Wiley, Chichester.

Robertson, M.M. (1989) The organic contribution to depressive illness in patients with epilepsy. *J. Epilepsy*, **2**, 189–230.

Robertson, M.M., Trimble, M.R. and Townsend, H.R.A. (1987) The phenomenology of depression in epilepsy. *Epilepsia*, **28**, 364–372.

Robinson, R.G. and Szetla, B. (1981) Mood change after left hemispheric brain injury. *Ann. Neurol.*, **9**, 447–453.

Robinson, R.G., Kubos, K.L., Starr, L.B., Rao, K. and Price, T.R. (1984) Mood disorders in stroke patients. *Brain*, **107**, 81 93.

Roy, A. (1979) Some determinants of affective symptoms in epileptics. *Can. J. Psychiatry*, **24**, 554–556.

Rubin, A.L., Charney, D.S., Price, L.H. and Heninger, G.R. (1985) Rapid improvement of delusional depression following drug induced seizures: Case report. *J. Clin. Psychiatry*, **46**, 146–147.

Scambler, G. (1987) Sociological aspects of epilepsy. In: *Epilepsy* (ed. A. Hopkins), Demos Publications, New York.

Scott, D.F. (1985) Left and right cerebral hemisphere differences in the occurrence of epilepsy. *Br. J. Med. Psychol.*, **58**, 189–192.

Seligman, M.E.P. (1975) *Helplessness: On Depression, Development and Death*. Freeman, San Francisco.

Serafetinides, E.A. (1975) Psychosocial aspects of neurosurgical management of epilepsy. In: *Advances in Neurology*, Vol. 8 (eds D.P. Purpura and U.K. Penry), p. 323. Raven Press, New York.

Slater, E. and Cowie, V. (1971) *The Genetics of Mental Disorders*. Oxford University Press, London.

Smith, D.B. and Collins, J.B. (1987) Behavioral effects of carbamezepine, pheno-barbital, phenytoin and primidone. *Epilepsia*, **28**, 598.

Standage, K.F. and Fenton, G.W. (1975) Psychiatric symptom profiles of patients with epilepsy: A controlled investigation. *Psychol. Med.*, **5**, 152–160.

Stores, G. (1978) School children with epilepsy at risk for learning and behavioural problems. *Dev. Med. Child Neurol.*, **20**, 502–508.

Storr, A. (1990) *Churchill's Black Dog*. Fontana, Glasgow.

Strauss, E., Risser, A. and Jones, M.W. (1982) Fear responses in patients with epilepsy. *Arch. Neurol.*, **39**, 626–630.

Taylor, D.C. (1972) Mental state and temporal lobe epilepsy: A correlative account of 100 patients treated surgically. *Epilepsia*, **13**, 727–765.

Temkin, O. (1971) *The Falling Sickness*. Johns Hopkins Press, Baltimore.

Toone, B.K. and Driver, M.V. (1980) Psychosis and epilepsy. *Res. Clin. Forums*, **2**, 121–127.

Toone, B.K., Wheeler, M. and Fenwick, P.B.C. (1980) Sex hormone changes in male epileptics. *Clin. Endocrinol.*, **12**, 391–395.

Trimble, M.R. and Perez, M.M. (1980a) Quantification of psychopathology in adult patients with epilepsy. In: *Epilepsy and Behaviour '79 and Proceedings of WOPSASSEPY I 1980* (eds B.M. Kulig, H. Meinardi and G. Stores), pp. 118–126. Swets and Zeitlinger, Lisse.

Trimble, M.R. and Perez, M.M. (1980b) The phenomenology of the chronic psychoses of epilepsy. *Adv. Biol. Psychiatry*, **8**, 98–105.

Trimble, M.R. and Robertson, M.M. (1987) Laterality and psychopathology: Recent findings in epilepsy. In: *Cerebral Dynamics, Laterality and Psychopathology*, Vol. 3 (eds P. Flor-Henry and J. Gruzelier), pp. 359–369. Elsevier, North-Holland.

Victoroff, J.I., Benson, D.F., Engel, J. Jr. Grafton, S. and Mazziotta, J.C. (1990) Interictal depression in patients with medically intractable complex partial seizures: Electroencephalography and cerebral metabolic correlates. *Ann. Neurol.*, **28**, 221.

Wannamaker, B.B. (1983) *Unexplained Mortality in Epilepsy. A Perspective on Death of Persons with Epilepsy*. Presented at the 15th Epilepsy International Symposium, Washington DC, September 1983.

Whitman, S., Hermann, B.P. and Gordon, A.C. (1984) Psychopathology in epilepsy: How great is the risk? *Biol. Psychiatry*, **19**, 213–236.

Whybrow, P.C., Akiskal, H.S. and McKinney, W.T. (1984) *Mood Disorders: Towards a New Psychobiology*. Plenum Press, New York.

Winokur, G. and Clayton, P. (1967) Family history studies: Two types of affective disorders separated according to genetic and clinical factors. *Recent Adv. Biol. Psychiatry*, **9**, 35–50.

Zielinski, J.J. (1982) Epidemiology. In: *A Textbook of Epilepsy*, 2nd edn (eds J. Laidlaw and A. Richens), pp. 16–33. Churchill Livingstone, Edinburgh.

15

Pseudoseizures (non-epileptic attack disorder)

TIM BETTS AND SARAH BODEN
Queen Elizabeth Hospital, Birmingham, UK

> If a woman suddenly becomes voiceless . . . and if you then palpate the uterus it is not in the proper place: her heart palpitates, she gnashes her teeth, there is copious sweat, and all the other features characteristic of those who suffer from the sacred disease.
>
> (Hippocrates)

> Toujours c'est la chose sexuelle.
>
> (attributed to Charcot)

INTRODUCTION

Pseudoseizure is an unfortunate term. Pseudoseizures are as real as epileptic seizures and only very rarely is the person who has the pseudoseizure trying to deceive. Most pseudoseizures are mistaken for epilepsy and labelled as such by professionals and not by the patient. We prefer the term non-epileptic attack disorder (NEAD). This is less pejorative and implies the true definition of a pseudoseizure: a sudden disruptive change in a person's behaviour, which is usually time limited, and which resembles, or is mistaken for, epilepsy but which does not have the characteristic electrophysiological changes in the brain detectable by electroencephalography which accompanies a true epileptic seizure.

In specialist epilepsy practice non-epileptic seizures are comparatively common. They may occur in up to 20% of the patients seen in a specialist clinic or in specialist facilities dedicated to the care of severe and intractable forms of epilepsy (Ramani, 1986). Thus their detection occupies a great deal of the time of the specialist in epilepsy. How common NEAD is in the general population is uncertain.

A recent study of newly diagnosed epileptic seizures in a general population (Sander *et al.*, 1990) showed that some 28% of patients suspected of

Women and Epilepsy. Edited by M.R. Trimble
© 1991 John Wiley & Sons Ltd

having epilepsy either did not have it (7%) or the diagnosis could not be substantiated, at least in the short term (21%). Some of these patients had other physiological causes for seizures resembling epilepsy (such as migraine) but some were labelled as having probable 'pseudoseizures'. This suggested that NEAD may well also be important in the general population. In a careful study like the one in question, non-epileptic seizures will be correctly identified (or the diagnosis of epilepsy delayed until the diagnosis is certain). In general medical practice this is unlikely and the above figures suggest NEAD becomes labelled as epilepsy. Once fixed, the label is difficult to remove, and the patient will be stigmatized as a 'known epileptic' and no one will look critically at the seizures again.

There is another factor: many people with epilepsy do not have the condition recognized and treated in the community (Betts, 1974), and this may also apply to people that have non-epileptic seizures, recognition and treatment depending on complex social factors, including how obtrusive or how much of a nuisance the seizure is to the general public and the population's cultural expectations of medical services. In some fundamentalist religious sects, for instance, NEAD, often induced by overbreathing, is culturally sanctioned and rewarded as in the voodoo cult of the West Indies.

CLASSIFICATION OF NON-EPILEPTIC ATTACK DISORDER

Non-epileptic seizures fall into three main groups (Table 1). Organic illness may cause seizure-like or convulsive behaviour which is non-epileptic but which may be mistaken for it (Sander *et al.*, 1990; Andermann, 1991). In our own series of over 100 patients with non-epileptic seizures (Betts *et al.*, 1991) such patients accounted for 5% of the population. Since such non-epileptic organic seizures will often respond to other treatment it is important to recognize them and to distinguish them from epilepsy. We have not included here

Table 1.   Types of non-epileptic attack disorders

Physical
    (a) Neurological, e.g. cataplexy, transient ischaemic attacks
    (b) Cardiovascular, e.g. Stokes Adams, aortic stenosis
    (c) Other, e.g. hypoglycaemia
Psychiatric disorder
    e.g. hyperventilation/panic, derealization
Emotional attack
    'Swoon'—cut-off behaviour
    'Tantrum'—frustration/rage
    'Abreactive'—symbolic attacks
    Deliberate simulation—conscious or unconscious
    Pseudo-status epilepticus—usually 'abreactive'

---

those patients who have epileptic seizures which are triggered off by other organic diseases such as cardiovascular disease.

Psychiatric conditions may present with sudden alterations in behaviour, often of a disruptive nature, which may be mistaken for epilepsy. In our personal series such cases accounted for 37% of the patients. The commonest psychiatric phenomenon mistaken for epilepsy is severe anxiety, particularly if it is accompanied by panic attacks. Some of the other symptoms of severe anxiety or depression, particularly depersonalization or derealization and odd temporal lobe-like symptoms (like changes in perception, heightened awareness of smells, taste, etc.; Silberman *et al.*, 1985), make confusion with partial seizures easy. Panic attacks accompanied by tingling extremities, tetanic spasms and then unconsciousness are very easily mistaken for major seizures. Vasovagal attacks, common in a psychiatric population, may also be easily mistaken for epilepsy, particularly if the victim is not allowed to lie flat, but remains upright and exhibits symptoms which, although common in fainting, are often not recognized as a concomitant part of a faint such as incontinence and muscle twitching.

Just over 50% of our own personal series of patients with NEAD had attacks which had been mistaken for epilepsy, with no organic basis, and which were not typical of recognized psychiatric attacks. They seemed to fall into four broad groups (using a classification of such sudden and disruptive behaviour proposed by Betts, 1990). They often were, of course, occurring in patients who had psychiatric illness, e.g. anxiety, depression, personality disorders or mental impairment. The classification is based on observation of a large number of non-epileptic seizures. Some authorities divide 'pseudoseizures' into two groups—'convulsive' and 'non-convulsive' (Savard and Andermann, 1990)— but we feel that convulsive and non-convulsive can be separated into four groups rather than two.

Emotional attacks

The first group consists of patients who exhibit abrupt 'cutting-off' behaviour (in the setting of sudden environmental stress or the intrusion into consciousness of unpleasant thoughts or ideas which cannot be tolerated by the patient). Characteristically a patient closes his eyes, sinks without injury to the floor and lies inert, flaccid and unresponsive for variable lengths of time, often with a peculiar flickering of the eyelids as he or she takes surreptitious peeps at the surroundings. Such behaviour (not uncommon and potentially charming in children) we have termed a '*swoon*'.

Some patients have sudden disruptive behaviour (often evoked by environmental challenge) which very much resembles a childish *tantrum*. The person will often emit a piercing scream and throw herself violently to the floor (or may suddenly drop) and then will thrash about kicking and screaming, often biting onlookers; there is a characteristic increase in struggle if the patient is restrained. The attack lasts for variable periods of time (but if restraint is applied may continue for a very long time—often several hours). Such behaviour is particularly likely to occur in the brain-damaged and the socially disadvantaged. Injury is common, caused by falling, head-banging or biting of the lips, the inside of the cheeks or the hands or arms; onlookers may also be bitten.

The third kind of non-epileptic seizure is what we have termed the '*abreactive*' attack. In our own series it accounted for 22% of the patients seen. Attacks often occur at night when the patient is in bed and *apparently* asleep, although they may occur in the day-time, in which case falling usually initiates the attack. If the patient is already lying down there is usually a period of overbreathing, followed by stiffening of the body with back-arching, followed by thrashing of the limbs and characteristic pelvic thrusting and gasping which sounds and looks a little like sexual activity. These attacks resemble those described by Charcot and others, although the dramatic 'arc de cercle' is not often seen (see Figure 1).

Simulation of an epileptic attack may also occur where the intention—conscious or unconscious—is to deceive. Usually the layman's idea of epilepsy is simulated with dramatic noise, thrashing of limbs and movement. Unconscious simulation usually occurs in patients who also have epilepsy and who receive 'reward' for it. Conscious simulation is rare and usually more accomplished (sometimes partial seizures are imitated: usually a friend or relative

Figure 1. A patient in the arc de cercle position. (From the series by Richer; editor's collection)

with genuine partial seizures is the model and the imitation is often extremely accurate, as one might expect. Imitating a tonic–clonic seizure is much more difficult and needs feedback and practice). The usual motive is to gain attention or phenobarbitone or a bed for the night. 'Pseudostatus epilepticus' may also occur; in our experience this is usually a prolonged 'abreactive' seizure. Intravenous benzodiazepines often make it worse.

Mixed forms and variants can occur. For instance, some patients, who appear to be showing cutting-off behaviour, do not sink slowly to the floor but drop suddenly, often with injury to the head, and then lie inert and unresponsive. Drop attacks are very difficult to diagnose and sometimes it can be impossible to tell what the aetiology is (particularly because a sudden fall with striking of the head makes interpretation of an ambulatory EEG record very difficult). It can be impossible to decide if one is dealing with epilepsy or a non-epileptic attack. In some 6% of our patients we were unable to make a definitive diagnosis between epilepsy and NEAD.

This difficulty is often compounded, because some 62% of our sample of patients with clear and proven non-epileptic seizures also had epilepsy, or had a clear previous history of it. Epilepsy brings with it such immense social disadvantage that it may seem surprising that patients with the condition will also imitate it; but some patients find that there are social rewards for seizure activity, particularly in terms of disrupting social situations or receiving care or concern. Patients may wish to exaggerate, enhance or continue their sick role long after the epilepsy itself has ceased. Eric Berne's description of the 'games', 'uproar' and 'wooden leg' apply to many patients with epilepsy. Patients may feel that their epileptic seizures are not being taken seriously enough, or panic after experiencing one. There is widespread disagreement in the literature about how common epilepsy is in populations of people who also have NEAD—figures from 10% to 90% have been quoted (Ramani, 1986). Our figure of 62% is high but includes patients who have both *present* epilepsy and NEAD plus those who no longer have epilepsy but have a clear history of it in the past.

The classification of NEAD given above can only be tentative and is of course based on our own personal experience. What is clear is that not all 'pseudoseizures' are the same and they do not have a single cause, although there is evidence that many people with NEAD have other psychiatric disabilities (Roy, 1979; Savard and Andermann, 1990). Affective disorder, personality disorder and somatization disorder, including Briquet's syndrome, are probably over-represented: a few patients are probably malingering (although this is rare in our experience). The prevalence of psychiatric disorder, especially anxiety and depression, is also high in people with epilepsy, usually related to the social and psychological effects of having seizures (Betts, 1991).

The majority of people who have non organic non-epileptic seizures are female. This is largely true for the specialist population of patients with seizure disorders in whom non-epileptic seizures seem to occur commonly but may also be true for the general population (Sander *et al.*, 1990). In a general population study of newly diagnosed epilepsy, the ratio between the sexes for proven epilepsy was even, but a greater proportion of female patients (59%) had 'possible epilepsy' and an even greater population (65%) were in the 'not epilepsy' category: both these categories contained patients with presumed 'pseudoseizures' (Sander *et al.*, 1990). Almost twice as many women as men consult their general practitioners about disorders of consciousness (Morrell *et al.*, 1971) although whether this is due to factors of age, increased awareness of lapses of consciousness in women or to a genuine increase is not entirely clear. Although most clinicians would agree that the majority of their non-epileptic seizure patients are female, this is not a universal experience. In the Maudsley Hospital clinic the sex ratio of patients with non-epileptic seizures is almost 1 : 1 (Fenwick, 1990, personal communication). In our own series of patients with non-epileptic seizures (Betts *et al.*, 1991), however, only 13% were male, 87% being female. Possible reasons for this general prepon-derance of women having non-epileptic seizures will be discussed later.

INVESTIGATION OF NON-EPILEPTIC ATTACK DISORDER

It has to be admitted that the recognition of NEAD is often not easy and we have to be prepared to accept a degree of uncertainty, particularly because to establish positive evidence of epilepsy occurring during a seizure may require intrusive electrical recording, which may be difficult to obtain and difficult to justify ethically (unless surgery is indicated). In our own series some 6% of the patients had seizures which were impossible to diagnose. In these patients seizure activity either eventually disappeared (suggesting that we had been seeing emotional seizures occurring during a period of stress) or their epilep-tic origin became apparent. We feel it better to say in certain circumstances that one does not know what the seizures are, rather than making a definitive diagnosis either way. All of us have had the experience of making a confident diagnosis of epilepsy, only to discover eventually that the patient had a NEAD; equally embarrassing, if not more so, is the experience of making a confident diagnosis of NEAD only to discover eventually that the patient has epilepsy. Frontal-based seizures in particular (Tinuper *et al.*, 1990), with their often very bizarre behaviour which looks 'hysterical' and which are often not very stereotyped, can easily be mistaken for pseudoseizures. Since epilepsy itself can be precipitated and maintained by emotional trauma including in-cest (Betts, 1991), emotional and traumatic events occurring at the time sei-zures started may also be misleading.

A careful history of the attack taken from witnesses is obviously manda-tory, although witnesses, who are often frightened during the attack, may exaggerate what happened or may give you a description more of what they think they should have seen rather than what they actually did see (it is sometimes helpful to show a witness a video-tape of a typical tonic–clonic seizure and ask him if what he saw was anything like what he is seeing on the screen). Careful description by a skilled witness of the attack is particularly helpful but skilled observers are hard to find, as even professional people, if they do not know what they are supposed to be looking for or are emotionally involved with the person having the attack, may not give a clear account of what happened. A video-tape recording of the attack in question is obviously extremely helpful, although such video-tapes are often of poor quality. As the wide variety of often apparently quite bizarre behaviour that epilepsy can produce is increasingly recognized it is important, if one is going to video-tape a patient's attacks, to video-tape several of them, as a stereotyped nature of the attack and its brevity are strong indicators of epilepsy.

To be able to diagnose NEAD confidently from the description given by others requires great skill in history taking, with a sound knowledge of the varieties and vagaries of epileptic experience and a little luck. If this is combined with personal observation of the attack then the chances of being right increase, but even personal observations can be misleading, and there are no absolute criteria for distinguishing NEAD from genuine epilepsy. If one has seen many NEADs (and been wrong a few times!) then a recently published list of criteria for differential diagnosis (Mulder, 1990) fills one with alarm; many of his differential diagnostic criteria for 'hysterical seizures' have been personally seen in epilepsy and would mislead the unexperienced. Possession of certain criteria may lead to the *suspicion* that the seizures are NEAD but are rarely, if ever, diagnostic.

Diagnostic accuracy is enhanced by recording EEG evidence of epileptic activity occurring during the attack. An inter-ictal EEG is unhelpful since many people with NEAD also have epilepsy (and a small proportion of people in the population who have never had an epileptic seizure in their lives will have epileptic activity in their EEG). A normal EEG recorded between seizures does not mean that the seizures in themselves are not epileptic (although a person having several major seizures a day who has an entirely normal EEG must be unusual). Post-ictal recording is useful, in that, particularly after a major seizure, characteristic post-ictal slowing or flattening of the EEG is usually seen, but even here exceptions occur. Recording during the actual ictus itself is therefore essential and this is usually achieved by ambulatory EEG monitoring or continual telemetered EEG recording, often combined with video-tape recording at the same time. This always supposes that the patient is having seizures sufficiently often that at least one will be recorded in the limited time available for recording.

Although a major tonic–clonic seizure will always show epileptic activity in an ictal EEG, the epileptic nature of simple and some complex partial seizures may not be reflected in scalp EEG recording. (Even if electrode placements cover the frontal area adequately, frontal seizures may still be missed by 16-channel ambulatory EEG recording.) Special electrode placements such as sphenoidal electrodes or foramen ovale electrodes may be necessary to demonstrate that epileptic activity does occur during the patient's seizure. Sphenoidal electrodes are unpleasant and foramen ovale electrodes can only be inserted by a neurosurgeon, thus limiting the centres that can use the technique: they are also not without risk, particularly if the patient has a violent seizure. Occasionally epileptic activity is only detected by electrodes lying directly on the cortex. In cases where great doubt exists and diagnostic certainty is important (particularly if surgery is indicated if the patients' attacks do turn out to be epilepsy) such extreme investigatory methods may be necessary. For most of us, who either do not have access to such facilities or for whom diagnostic certainty is not so important, investigations will finish at the ambulatory EEG recording level and we may be forced to make a clinical decision about the nature of the patient's attacks and be prepared to accept that we may be wrong.

Ambulatory EEG recording is very prone to artefacts which may at times look very like epileptic activity. Chewing, swallowing, lying on some of the electrodes, sweating under the electrodes, head-shaking and eye movement may all be misinterpreted as epilepsy: ambulatory EEG recording analysis needs a great deal of experience. Ambulatory recording also requires an accurate description of what the patient did during the seizure (a video-tape of the behaviour is very useful) and it is important if at all possible to record several of the patient's seizures. Ambulatory EEG recording is unlikely to be helpful in patients having infrequent seizures (say less than one a week) although some centres will withdraw a patient's medication whilst recording is being done to try to increase seizure frequency (although one has to be certain that these withdrawal seizures are similar to the basic seizure one is trying to diagnose).

Measurement of serum prolactin levels some 20 minutes to half an hour after a seizure may also be useful. Dramatic rises in serum prolactin occur after generalized tonic–clonic seizures and to a lesser but significant degree after complex partial seizures (but not after simple partial seizures). Providing the patient's baseline prolactin levels are known, changes in prolactin levels after a seizure may be of prognostic importance as they do not seem to occur after non-epileptic seizures (Rao et al., 1989).

MANAGEMENT OF NON-EPILEPTIC ATTACK DISORDER

Once a clinical diagnosis of non-epileptic seizures has been made, and it has been decided to treat the patient's seizures as non-epileptic (the clinician must recognize that he or she can never be 100% certain), it is usually best not to directly confront the patient with the diagnosis but to help the patient understand that although the seizure activity is 'real' it does not have an epileptic basis. Many patients are already aware of this and will accept it if gently told, particularly if the information is put in a positive way so that the patient understands that now the basis of the seizure is understood help will be available. It is important that the patient is not rejected: it is better to treat non-epileptic and epileptic seizures in the same clinic if at all possible. It is unwise to suddenly push the patient for the first time in the direction of a psychiatrist, paticularly as few psychiatrists unversed in epilepsy are comfortable with treating pseudoseizures. Any epilepsy clinic worth its salt should already have its own facilities for the behavioural and psychological management of epileptic seizures, which work equally well for non-epileptic seizures.

Exploration of the patient's needs for the seizures should be undertaken, looking particularly at the circumstance surrounding the time when the seizures first started. Abreactions, either hypnotic or chemical, may be helpful although often unnecessary. Many non-epileptic seizures (as, indeed, do epileptic seizures) start at a time of stress and then become reinforced by other factors. Obviously, although one needs to deal with the reinforcing factors, some understanding of what was happening to the patient at the time the seizures started is also very useful, particularly if the stresses and conflicts which were current at that time have not in themselves been resolved. It is useful often to see a NEAD as a form of non-verbal communication which needs to be acknowledged and understood.

It is also important to look at what reinforces the seizure activity, because a secondary gain may have become more important than the primary gain. Non-epileptic seizures are usually reinforced by the fuss and attention that the patient gets during and after the seizure (it is very important to make sure that onlookers, family, fellow patients on the ward and nurses learn to studiously ignore seizure activity even to the point of stepping over the convulsing patient so that reward is extinguished). Any reward should be applied to seizure-free intervals. Seizures often increase in frequency at first when this treatment is applied. Frequency rises to a crescendo and then suddenly stops. This is certainly our experience of applying behaviour therapy (operant conditioning) to NEAD in adults and also the experience of Aldenkamp and Van Rossum (1987) in children. Providing the family can be taught not to reinforce the behaviour when the patient goes home this may be very effective.

For many patients intensive anxiety management directed at recognizing when a seizure is about to start, and learning ways of controlling it, is very important. Cognitive therapy may also be important in terms of helping patients to correct negative thought patterns which tend to lead to seizures. It is important to emphasize that all this also applies to the psychological treatment of epilepsy. It also applies to those pseudoseizures which appear to occur in sleep, particularly as ambulatory monitoring has usually demonstrated that the patient was actually awake at the time the seizure started.

Family therapy may be essential, particularly to avoid the patient's becoming a scapegoat. (Many families are angry unless the situation is carefully explained as they feel they have been cheated or conned, often for many years, by the patient.) For some patients psychotherapy may be appropriate, particularly for those patients described in the last section of this chapter, whose seizures arise out of previous sexual abuse. Very occasionally, particularly for those patients who are depressed, chemotherapy may be appropriate.

The prognosis of non-epileptic seizures has been little discussed in the literature and quoted rates of improvement have varied widely, with very little long-term follow-up (Lesser, 1985). In our own series (Betts et al., 1991) the immediate prognosis is good. In nearly two-thirds of the patients pseudoseizures had stopped before discharge from hospital. Unfortunately relapses were common, perhaps because patients returned to the environment which was reinforcing the non-epileptic seizure activity in the first place: only a third of our patients remained seizure free at follow-up two years later. (In some patients, who had gained insight into their condition, seizure frequency was a great deal less, and was less socially obtrusive.) In those patients who are able to lose their seizures without also losing face, the prognosis appears to be better, as it also appears to be better in patients whose families appear able to accept the change in diagnosis without recrimination. It is extremely important in managing NEAD that the patient is allowed to save face, that it is made clear she is still valued as a human being, and that the attacks are seen as a form of communication and not as something amusing or needing punishment or rejection.

Mulder (1990) makes two important points about treatment with which we would agree. Some patients, after gentle confrontation, lose their NEAD without any other intervention being necessary (this is more likely to occur in patients without significant psychopathology). At times, particularly in patients with significant psychopathology, 'symptom substitution' may take place and must be guarded against.

NON-EPILEPTIC ATTACK DISORDER AND WOMEN

In most reports of series of patients with non-epileptic seizures (reviewed by Goodwin, 1989) the patients are female. This may not be true for all series; the sex ratio probably depends on the type of 'pseudoseizure' that a particular clinic or treatment facility engages with (see discussion above).

In our own series of over 100 patients admitted and assessed with non-epileptic seizures (Betts et al., 1991) 83% were female. In the few male patients the diagnosis was invariably one of anxiety, panic attacks or 'tantrums'; 'swoons' and 'abreactive' attacks were not seen. (We have subsequently seen one male patient with abreactive attacks who had been subjected to repeated forceful anal intercourse whilst in prison.)

There are scattered indications in the literature that there may be an association between previous sexual abuse and the later development of NEAD in the patient (Standage, 1975; Liske and Forster, 1964; Goodwin, 1989). However, although many clinicians experienced in investigating and managing NEAD acknowledge that previous sexual abuse may be a contributory factor in some of their patients, the literature contains surprisingly little reference to it; indeed, the latest two authoritative reviews (Savard and Andermann, 1990; Mulder, 1990) fail to mention it at all. This may be because, as we shall show, only certain types of NEAD are associated with previous sexual abuse and because it can be difficult to decide, without a great deal of experience and patience, whether a person has actually been previously abused.

The problems in deciding if previous sexual abuse or incest is a factor in the genesis of NEAD in women are that first one has to define the type of 'pseudoseizure' one is describing (Gross, 1979); secondly, one must define what one means by sexual abuse; and thirdly, one should have a knowledge of what the underlying prevalence of previous sexual abuse is in the general population. It also requires one to be able to believe the history recounted by the victim of the abuse. Incest victims have always suffered from the inability of other people to accept that the abuse happened. Freud, for instance, was presented with evidence of previous sexual abuse in many of the early patients he saw with hysteria. He initially believed it but then came to reject it, although almost certainly what his patients were telling him was the truth. Many abuse victims are silent about the abuse and do not reveal it at all, or only after they have developed a trusting relationship with the person to whom they eventually confide the details of what happened. One other point about abuse victims is important: that, as with rape victims, they often tell their story in a curious flat, unemotional and detached way so that the listener, who does not understand that this is a defence mechanism, interprets the patient's demeanour as meaning that the story is fabricated.

The background level of sexual abuse of all kinds in our society is not known with any certainty and published estimates vary widely. In community surveys disclosure may not be complete (Baker and Duncan, 1985). The best estimate is that a history of sexual abuse of all kinds and severity occurs in 10–20% of the population, whilst severe penetrative abuse in the female population occurs in perhaps 5–10%. Some victims seem to recover completely from the abuse but at least 20% of victims develop long-standing psychological complications as a result, particularly if the abuse occurred early and finished late, if abuse was by the father rather than some other perpetrator, and if physical sexual contact occurred, especially if there was force or multiple perpetrators (Hobbs, 1990).

In our own series of in-patients with non-epileptic seizures, the prevalence of *proven* previous sexual abuse did not differ significantly from patients with psychiatric disorders or epilepsy admitted to the same ward over a four-year period, *except* in patients who had the 'swoon' type of pseudoseizure and particularly in those who had the 'abreactive' type of seizure where there was a highly significant level of previous penetrative abuse. In the abreactive type 70% of the patients had a previous confirmed episode of abuse (Betts *et al.*, 1991). In this subgroup, seizure activity would only cease following intensive abuse counselling, if then. Follow-up suggests that seizures will often return at times of stress in the patient's life or if she is subsequently reminded of the abuse experience.

It should be emphasized that a proven abuse history does occur in some patients with epilepsy, often the proven abuse and proven epilepsy starting at the same time (Betts, 1991). Since epilepsy will often start in those with a low convulsive threshold at a time of stress this is perhaps not surprising. In several of these patients, however, the epilepsy only came under control when the abuse experience had been worked through and counselled. The epileptic experience often mirrored the abuse in a symbolic way, e.g. automatisms of thigh-brushing or an ictal sexual feeling.

TREATMENT OF THE ABUSE VICTIM

In our patients treatment was by abreaction, repetitive talking through of the experience and discharge of the accompanying emotion (shame, guilt and anger) using a female therapist to start with (often followed by a male/female co-therapy team) followed by group therapy of victims and a follow-up support group. Other possible treatment approaches include behavioural and cognitive therapy (reviewed by Hobbs, 1990). Treatment often has to be prolonged, is emotionally exhausting for the victim and for the therapists, but is often successful.

CONCLUSION

Non-epileptic seizures are not a single entity and need to be classified in the same way as epileptic seizures. Some types of non-epileptic seizure (particularly those we have classified as 'swoons' and 'abreactive' attacks) do seem to be significantly more common in women than in men and also seem (at least in our experience) to be significantly and directly related to a previous history of serious sexual abuse. Such a history is only likely to be obtained when the confidence of the patient has been gained or, as in our experience, in a setting where disclosure is encouraged and supported. It is important to realize that a previous abuse history may also occur in patients with epilepsy; it is important to distinguish the 'abreactive' kind of NEAD from frontal seizure discharge which can produce very similar phenomena (including back-arching and pelvic thrusting). A history of previous abuse is therefore not diagnostic of NEAD, but in many patients NEAD can be understood better if a history of abuse is disclosed. Certainly previous sexual abuse probably explains why certain types of non-epileptic disorder are commoner in women than in men.

APPENDIX: REPRESENTATIVE CASE HISTORIES

Anxiety attacks related to abuse

Maureen was a 40-year-old housewife who was admitted for investigation of the recent onset of attacks which had been diagnosed as epilepsy by her general practitioner. She would develop tingling in her hands and feet, accompanied by a rising feeling of tension which she described as arising in her abdomen, developed a feeling of intense derealization and then would collapse apparently unconscious, recovering a little dazed a few minutes later. Clinically these were thought to be panic attacks (and ambulatory EEG monitoring during several attacks revealed no abnormality). It transpired that there was a previous history of sexual abuse by an uncle. This had left her with permanent difficulties in sexual relationships (she was divorced). Her anxiety attacks began when her 14-year-old daughter was molested by the now elderly uncle and she was uncertain how to cope with the situation. The perpetrator was confronted and social services were involved (the uncle was too ill to be prosecuted) and the anxiety attacks stopped.

Anxiety attacks misdiagnosed as epilepsy for 20 years

Pauline was admitted following referral by a local general hospital where she had been admitted in 'status epilepticus'. There was a 20-year history of poorly controlled epilepsy. She was a 38-year-old housewife of limited intellect who was taking three anticonvulsants, which had given her severe osteomalacia.

Observation of her attacks in hospital revealed brisk hyperventilation followed by tetany of the hands, followed by general body stiffening, dilatation of the pupils, sialorrhoea and a gradual collapse on to the floor or a bed, where there was continuing bodily stiffness accompanied by generalized trembling: she would then moan in obvious distress. The stiffness and trembling would gradually subside (to return if she was disturbed, sometimes for several hours); if the attack was allowed to subside she would fall asleep to awake feeling stiff and with a headache.

Ambulatory monitoring did not reveal any EEG abnormality during these episodes (although inter-ictal EEG showed some bitemporal theta activity). The attacks tended to occur when Pauline was overwhelmed by domestic stress. She was treated with an intensive anxiety management programme and a slow but steady reduction in her anticonvulsants. Four years after the index admission she is seizure free and is no longer taking anticonvulsants.

Simulated partial epilepsy

Dymphna, a 30-year-old industrial nurse, was accidentally exposed to industrial solvent, some of which she inhaled. There seemed to be no sequelae to this exposure but shortly afterwards she began to get attacks in which she would stare, swallow repeatedly and then develop pouting of the lips followed by sniffing; stiffness and twitching of the right arm would then develop and the attack would go on for many hours. It never progressed and always responded promptly to intravenous diazepam. Numerous anticonvulsants were tried: all seemed to work initially but then attacks would return and she had numerous admissions to various hospitals with 'status epilepticus'. Her attacks generated much anxiety in both her relatives and medical attendants. EEGs during attacks were consistently normal but she strongly denied that the attacks were not epilepsy (at one point she threatened to sue a doctor who suggested that they were not). It was difficult to manage her locally as she was such a 'well-known epileptic' that intravenous diazepam was always given to her as soon as she crossed the threshold of her local hospital. Finally she was referred to a hospital 100 miles away, where the attacks were consistently ignored (and were not reinforced by family anxiety). They disappeared whilst she was in hospital and have not returned. It is not certain whether they were some form of post-traumatic event (she had been badly frightened by the exposure to the solvent) or whether they were a deliberate disability in an unsuccessful attempt to gain compensation, although the latter hypothesis is favoured.

Interestingly, during a separate family crisis, her 15-year-old niece developed drop attacks followed by prolonged unconsciousness; they were not epileptic.

Abreactive status epilepticus

Katherine, a 28-year-old woman, came to us via a local general hospital where she had been admitted and treated for protracted status epilepticus. Her attacks always started at night, but always whilst awake. She had been a 'known epileptic' for some 14 years and was taking (in rather haphazard dosage) three anticonvulsants. She had also had a history of frequent overdoses of her anticonvulsant drugs and episodes of wrist-slashing; she had worked as a prostitute. When admitted she was in a common law marriage with a man with an unstable personality who frequently beat her. Her two children were in care.

Her attacks invariably occurred at night and would often continue for several hours. They would start with an increase in respiratory rate followed by pelvic thrusting and rocking; shaking of the body would then occur, followed by flailing of the arms (often alternately). She would hold her breath and then gasp some air in. Intravenous diazepam seemed, if anything, to prolong her attacks and make them more vigorous. Intravenous Heminevrin would stop them but only when the infusion produced unconsciousness (she had had two previous respiratory arrests during treatment). Ambulatory EEG monitoring showed no abnormality and also revealed normal alpha rhythm (indicating wakefulness with closed eyes) just before the attack started. Wretching and spitting would terminate the attack.

The attacks were ignored and praise was given for seizure-free nights, and a slow but steady withdrawal of anticonvulsants started. In the 'women's group' on the ward she eventually reported multiple episodes of incest by a stepfather and uncles (abetted by her mother, who was afraid of losing the stepfather's support). The abuse had included forced fellatio (wretching or vomiting during a non-epileptic seizure is often suggestive of this). Confirmation of this history was obtained eventually from one of her sisters.

As counselling proceeded, the attacks gradually died away; in the last four years they have occasionally reappeared. If they do the patient now recognizes that she is being stressed by something and voluntarily seeks further counselling. She is off anticonvulsants and there have been no further overdoses or self-mutilation. She lives on her own with her two children.

ACKNOWLEDGEMENTS

We acknowledge with gratitude the help of several members of the team of the Top Floor ward of the Midland Nerve Hospital, which housed the Neuropsychiatry Unit for four years, including Diana Inskip, Diana Markman, Elizabeth Grace, Stuart Eastman, Dee Harris and Catherine Piggot. A particular debt of gratitude is owed to Davina Parker, who has continued to counsel many of the patients mentioned above.

REFERENCES

Aldenkamp, A. and Van Rossum, A. (1987) Effects of pedagogic strategies in the treatment of children with epilepsy. In: *Advances in Epileptology* (eds P. Wolf, M. Dam, D. Jantz and F. Dreifus), pp. 621–627. Raven Press, New York.

Andermann, F. (1991) Non epileptic paroxysmal neurological events. In: *The Dilemma of Non-epileptic (Pseudoepileptic) Seizures* (eds A. Rowan and J. Gates). Demos Publications, New York (in press).

Baker, A.W. and Duncan, S.P. (1985) Child sexual abuse: A study of prevalence in Great Britain. *Child Abuse Neglect,* **9**, 457–467.

Betts, T. (1974) A follow up study of a cohort of patients with epilepsy admitted to psychiatric care in an English City. In: *Epilepsy: Proceeding of the Hans Berger Centenary Symposium* (eds P. Harris and C. Maudsley), pp. 326–336. Churchill Livingstone, Edinburgh.

Betts, T. (1990) Pseudoseizures: Seizures that are not epilepsy. *Lancet,* **336,** 163–164.

Betts, T. (1991) Neuropsychiatry. In: *A Textbook of Epilepsy,* 4th edn (eds J. Laidlaw, A. Richens and D. Chadwick). Churchill Livingstone, Edinburgh (in press).

Betts, T., Boden, S. and Parker, D. (1991) A follow up study of a group of patients with non epileptic seizures: The role of previous sexual abuse (to be published).

Goodwin, J. (ed.) (1989) *Sexual Abuse: Incest Victims and Their Families,* 2nd edn. Mosby/Ycarbook, Chicago.

Gross, M. (1979) Incestuous rape: A cause for hysterical seizures in four adolescent girls. *Am. J. Orthopsychiatry,* **49,** 704–708.

Hobbs, M. (1990) Childhood sexual abuse: How can women be helped to overcome its long-term effects? In: *Dilemmas in the Management of Psychiatric Patients* (eds K. Hawkins and P. Cowen), pp. 183–196. Oxford University Press, Oxford.

Lesser, R. (1985) Psychogenic seizures. In: *Recent Advances in Epilepsy,* Vol. 2 (eds T. Pedley and B. Meldrum), pp. 273–296. Churchill Livingstone, Edinburgh.

Liske, E. and Forster, F.M. (1964) Pseudoseizures: A problem in the diagnosis and management of epileptic patients. *Neurology,* **14,** 41–49.

Morrell, D., Gage, H. and Robinson, N. (1971) Symptoms in general practice. *J. Roy. Coll. Gen. Pract.,* **21,** 32–43.

Mulder, O. (1990) Management of pseudo-epileptic seizures. In: *Comprehensive Epileptology* (eds M. Dam and L. Gram), pp. 495–504. Raven Press, New York.

Ramani, V. (1986) Intensive monitoring of psychogenic seizures, aggression and dyscontrol syndromes. In: *Advances in Neurology, Vol. 46, Intensive Neurodiagnostic Monitoring* (ed. R. Gumnit), pp. 203–217. Raven Press, New York.

Rao, M.L., Stephan, H. and Bauer, J. (1989) Epileptic but not psychogenic seizures are accompanied by simultaneous elevation of serum pituitary hormones and cortisol levels. *Neuroendocrinology,* **49,** 33–39.

Roy, A. (1979) Hysterical fits previously diagnosed as epilepsy. *Psychol. Med.,* **7,** 271–273.

Sander, J., Hart, Y., Johnson, A. and Shorvon, S. (1990) National general practice study of epilepsy: Newly diagnosed epileptic seizures in a general population. *Lancet,* **336,** 1267–1271.

Savard, G. and Andermann, G. (1990) Convulsive pseudoseizures: A review of current concepts. *Behav. Neurol.,* **3,** 133–141.

Silberman, E., Post, R., Nurnberger, J., Theodore, W. and Boulenger, J.-P. (1985) Transient sensory, cognitive and affective phenomena in affective illness: A comparison with complex partial epilepsy. *Br. J. Psychiatry,* **146,** 81–89.

Standage, K.F. (1975) The aetiology of hysterical seizures. *Can. Psychiat. Assoc. J.,* **20,** 67–73.

Tinuper, P., Cerullo, A., Cirignotta, F., Curtelli, P., Lugaresi, E. and Montagna, P. (1990) Nocturnal paroxysmal dystonia with short lasting attacks: Three cases with evidence for an epileptic frontal lobe origin of seizures. *Epilepsia,* **31,** 549–556.

Discussion session 4

Dr Wallace: Dr Betts, could I ask you about Munchausen by proxy, where the mothers actually produce children who they say are having seizures but they are not. Have you any evidence that this is also related to any sort of abuse in the mother?

Dr Betts: The work on this suggests that the mother usually has some kind of psychiatric disorder and has often been a victim of abuse herself.

Dr Trimble: Dr Betts, Freud said much the same. He said that women with hysteria had been sexually abused. Then of course it dawned on him that it was all in their imagination. One wonders, therefore, what kind of verification you have that the women in your series really were abused? People such as Masson have made a fair amount of political capital out of this, suggesting that Freud changed his mind simply to preserve psychoanalysis in the climate of Viennese medicine.

If these data are correct, are your swooners and your abreactors perhaps best labelled as true hysteria in the Freudian sense?

The third question is: have you had any problems of changing the diagnosis from epilepsy to non-epilepsy such that subsequently that person sues the neurologist who made the original diagnosis of epilepsy?

Dr Betts: I was at the pseudoseizure conference in the States earlier this year and I know that this legal problem is starting to happen there. It has not happened with us, I think, because I am so bumbling in my approach and I say: 'Well I am not certain, but let's treat it this way and see what happens.' I am not very authoritative, so maybe I am avoiding that kind of clash.

In our patients, there was independent confirmation from families, from sisters, mothers, from the police and from social workers that this abuse had actually taken place. We were not just relying on the girls' words, although I think that usually you can. The other thing which we do, which I think is fairly unique to us, is that part of the treatment is to try to get a confrontation between the girl and the perpetrator or offender. That is a very important part of the treatment package and it often works.

Dr Green: Do you see much of a problem with pseudoseizures in the mentally retarded?

Dr Betts: I think it is more likely that in the severely retarded the behaviour they show is just not labelled as epilepsy; it is recognized that this is just how a frustrated person of limited intellectual capacity will behave. It is of interest why this behaviour sometimes gets labelled as epilepsy and sometimes not.

Member of the audience: Dr Toone, I wonder how often we ask our patients, particularly those who are female, whether they have these sexual sensations. I think we can put the question to them very simply, that people can experience funny feelings in any part of their body and have they experienced these.

Dr Toone: I don't know whether it is necessarily an embarrassment on the part of the clinician. I think that a lot of patients are embarrassed to discuss these matters, but nevertheless obviously these are things we should be raising with them.

Member of the audience: There is a difference between genital feelings and feelings that have erotic content. You may have genital subjective sensations but erotic content is not necessarily a component of that. Do you think that different localization has any bearing on whether or not the content is erotic or whether or not this is more of a social phenomenon that is superimposed on subjective sensations?

Dr Toone: That, I think, is one of the more interesting points that comes out. I think that the parietal localized seizures simply produced sensation in the genital areas but without necessarily any erotic content. Limbic structure seizures seem to produce erotic experiences which were virtually indistinguishable from normal erotic experiences in the non-epileptic context.

Dr T. Betts: Perhaps the reason why in the literature women appear to have these events more often than men is that spontaneous sexual feeling in men is a normal phenomenon and perhaps therefore if a man gets it as part of an epileptic experience it is not so remarkable and he may not report it so often as a woman does.

The other point is that if we did ask more directly what patients mean by the expression 'funny feeling' they might tell us. I have been looking at a group of women who have true epilepsy which started at the time they were sexually abused. Many of them in fact do experience as part of the aura a sexual feeling, but they will not tell you that. So they start off at age 7 saying that it is an indescribable feeling; at the age of 15 they say it is a warm feeling, and at the age of 20 they say it is a sexual feeling. In other words it is the same feeling but at different ages they label the experience differently.

I think we should start picking up the cues that our patients are giving us and actually asking what they mean by a 'funny feeling' or 'a guilty feeling'. One or two of the patients have said to me, 'I get this unpleasant guilty feeling', and yet it is actually a sexual feeling they are describing. The other phenomenon I have noticed in this group of patients is that they often have an automatism like brushing the thighs or pushing something away, which again is related to sexuality.

Dr Toone: I think that is a very good way of putting it. The majority of the cases presented here were dominated by sexual phenomenology and when that happens there is a high chance that the clinician will pick it up. However, many partial complex seizures have sexual components which are not necessarily the most prominent and therefore are not remarked upon.

Member of the audience: I noticed that the cases you presented were mainly secondary to brain tumours.

Dr Toone: These are case reports, and people are inclined to be reticent to publish case reports unless they have a definite neuropathology. So there may be a bias in the direction of publishing cases which are cut and dried and one knows the exact localization of the seizure onset because a tumour has been demonstrated. Secondly, I was selective about the cases that I presented; I have chosen only women. My impression was that by no means all cases had a clear-cut demonstrative pathology.

Dr S. Kirk: I was wondering if patients who have had temporal lobectomies for complex partial seizures report any change in their normal orgasms?

Dr Toone: Yes, I think they do. Blumer and Walker describe hypersexuality occurring post temporal lobectomy, not related to confusional states.

16

Women and epilepsy: famous and not so famous

Institute of Neurology, London, UK

INTRODUCTION

Whenever famous personalities with epilepsy are written about or discussed, certain names crop up with regularity. These include rulers and leaders such as Julius Caesar and Alexander the Great, poets and novelists such as Byron, Flaubert and Lear, and visionaries such as Mohammed, Swedenborg and van Gogh (Lennox, 1941). One feature of all such names is that they are men, and the number of famous women with epilepsy quoted in the literature is remarkably few. In this paper some famous and other not so famous women with epilepsy are discussed.

ANCIENT TIMES

Since some of the earliest of medical writings were of Greek origin, it is germane to begin with a famous Greek female, namely the Oracle of Delphi. According to the *Encyclopaedia Brittanica* (1910/1971) the most sacred objects at Delphi were the omphalos or navel, allegedly the centre of the earth, and the tripod on which the Delphic priestess sat. It was believed that she delivered her oracles under the direct inspiration of God, possession working 'like an epileptic seizure'. According to one legend she chewed leaves of the sacred laurel, and then a vapour issued from a cleft in the floor of the adytum (holy of holies) where she was seated on the tripod. This intoxicated the priestess and she passed into a trance. She would then utter unintelligible words which were interpreted into relevance by a prophet.

If indeed we have an early case of seizures here, then there was a famous meeting of two people with seizure disorders recorded in early history. Thus,

Women and Epilepsy. Edited by M.R. Trimble
© 1991 John Wiley & Sons Ltd

Alexander the Great visited the oracle, but on a day when her inspiration would not take place, and he was told she would not prophesy. He took hold of her and dragged her to the tripod. She cried out 'My lad, you are invincible', and he took this as a good reply.

Hippocrates, in his famous text on epilepsy *On the Sacred Disease*, noted the various manifestations of epilepsy, and the gods responsible for various seizure types. One of these was Cybela, the Mother of the Gods, who was responsible for right-sided focal seizures (Adams, 1939).

RELIGION AND MYSTICISM

Perhaps the most famous woman to mention in the context of religiosity is Joan of Arc. She was born around the year 1410 in a hamlet of ancient Lorraine. At an early age she was distinguished by her passion for contemplation, her melancholy, and her love of devotions.

From the age of 13 she experienced frequent visual and auditory hallucinations, unknown voices resounding in her ears when she believed herself to be in perfect solitude. When older she thought herself visited by the Archangel Michael, by the Angel Gabriel, by Saint Catherine and Saint Margaret.

France was at war with the combined forces of England and Burgundy, and her visions ordered her in the name of God to deliver the city of Orleans. As an example of her experiences, she said: 'I heard this voice to my right towards the church; rarely do I hear it without its being accompanied also by a light. The light comes from the same side as the voice.'

She was eventually captured and imprisoned by the Burgundians, and subjected to humiliation. She was arraigned by a court on charges of witchcraft and heresy, but still insisted that the saints appeared to her and spoke to her. These were not the outpourings of an overactive imagination, she insisted, but were true heavenly voices. She was burned at the stake in Rouen when less than 20 years of age. It was reputed that her heart failed to burn. One explanation of this was that she had tuberculosis. Thus, a cerebral tuberculoma would explain the seizure disorder, and a tuberculous pericarditis the robustness of her heart (Ratnasuriya, 1986). Bayne and Foote-Smith (1991) have suggested that Joan of Arc may have suffered from musicogenic epilepsy, her seizures being provoked by the sound of church bells.

Other female mystics sometimes quoted in the context of epilepsy include St Catherine of Genoa (1447–1510), St Teresa of Avilla (1515–1582), St Catherine Dei Ricci (1522–1590), St Margaret Mary (1647–1690), Mme Guyon (1648–1717) and St Therese of Lisieux (1873–1897) (Dewhurst and Beard, 1970). These were mainly visionary saints. For example, St Margaret Mary, between 1673 and 1675 experienced four visions of Christ. These became known to other nuns of her order, some of whom recognized their delusionary nature. St Catherine of Genoa underwent a religious conversion in 1473, and from that time led an idiosyncratic religious life, for example attending communion every day when to do so would have been considered unusual.

St Teresa of Lisieux had a series of mystical states that began about age 9 years. She experienced terrifying visual hallucinations which later became celestial visions, and had strange and violent tremblings all over her body. St Catherine Dei Ricci also had visual hallucinations, and regularly lost consciousness at noon on Thursdays, recovering some 24 hours later.

St Teresa of Avilla had chronic headaches, visions and episodes of transient loss of consciousness. At the age of 24 she had a prolonged episode of coma lasting four days, and was given up for dead. When she recovered she had bitten her tongue and was badly bruised.

Another association with a saint, this time a male, creeps in with the drawing by Bruegel the Elder called 'The Epileptic Women of Molenbeek'. This supposedly illustrates St Vitus' dance (see Figure 1), a condition often confused with epilepsy. Thus, St Vitus became the patron saint of actors and dancers, and his name was bound up with the dancing manias which occurred in medieval Europe. Groups of people seemed to dance compulsively, often for hours on end. According to Temkin (1971), many of the dancers had epileptic seizures since 'their limbs jerked and they collapsed snorting, unconscious and frothing'. In Bruegel's drawing pilgrims, who must dance on St John's day at Molenbeek outside Brussels, are depicted. In the legend they have to jump over a bridge to be cured of their disease for a whole year.

There is one famous woman, who probably had epilepsy, who founded a religious sect. This was Ann Lee, founder of the Shakers. This extraordinary religious sect, of which there are at present nine living members, practised celibacy, and believed in the androgynous nature of Christ. The name derives from the strange rocking motions members make during worship. Ann Lee, daughter of an illiterate blacksmith who emigrated from Manchester in 1774, had ecstatic utterances, spoke in 72 different tongues, and had visions, but also had convulsions. She had a conversion experience in which Jesus stood before her and became one with her in form and spirit. During the convulsions it is said that 'her body was dreadfully distorted, and she would clench her hands until blood oozed through the pores of her skin. She continued so long in these fits that her flesh and strength wasted away, and she required to be fed and nursed like an infant' (quoted in Howden, 1873).

God revealed several mysteries directly to her, including the revelation that Jesus Christ was the chief Elder of the Shakers, and that she was the Head Eldress. After her death in 1794, her followers worshipped her as the second Christ and still await her parousia.

266

Figure 1. The drawing of 'The epileptic women of Molenbeek' by Bruegel.

EXAMPLES FROM NINETEENTH- AND TWENTIETH-CENTURY LITERATURE

Purdon Martin (1973) has analysed in careful detail Henry James' *Turn of the Screw*. Even the title may have been carefully chosen—the *double entendre* of the word 'turn'. The narrator is writing an account of her experience as a governess to two children, based on events that happened years before. Purdon Martin noted in the story several descriptions that resembled seizures. In the first, at the end of the day while walking in the grounds of the house in the country where the children and she were living, the governess describes visions:

> I stopped short on emerging from one of the plantations and coming in view of the house. What arrested me on the spot—and with a shock much greater than any vision had allowed for—was the sense that my imagination had, in a flash, turned real. He did stand there!—but high up, beyond the lawn and at the very top of the tower . . .
>
> It produced in me, this figure, in the clear twilight, I remember, two distinct gasps of emotion, which were, sharply, the shock of my first and second surprise. My second was a violent perception of the mistake of my first; the man who met my eyes was not the person I had precipitately supposed. There came to me thus a bewilderment of vision of which, after these years, there is no living view that I can hope to give . . . the figure that faced me . . . I had not seen it anywhere.

The experience, which lasts barely a minute, and in which the image was 'as definite as a picture in a frame', was accompanied by an intense hush, and 'all the rest of the scene had been stricken with death'. There is also a description of a post-ictal automatism for, after the above sequence, she describes:

> Agitation, in the interval (before I re-entered the house), certainly had held me and driven me, for I must, in circling about the place, have walked three miles.'

The second turn was on a Sunday evening when she was preparing to go to church. She became aware of:

> a person on the other side of the window and looking straight in . . . He remained but a few seconds—long enough to convince me he also saw and recognized; but it was as if I had been looking at him for years and had known him always.

She ran out of the house, and there:

> The terrace and the whole place, the lawn and the garden beyond it, all I could see of the park, were empty with a great emptiness.

In the third attack, the governess sees an image of her predecessor dressed in black across a lake, of which the other person with her—one of the children in her care—is unaware. There are other episodes in the story in which she sees the man or a female figure or in which she hears a loud shriek.

There is even an episode suggestive of a convulsion. Thus, she is with one of the children and another member of the household when she sees the female figure. The others do not see it, but the adult says to her 'What a dreadful turn, to be sure, Miss. Where on earth do you see anything?' The child is taken home, and the governess is left alone:

> Of what first happened when I was left alone, I had no subsequent memory . . . I must have thrown myself, on my face, on the ground . . . when I raised my head the day was almost done.

For those who have not read the story, I will not disclose its ending. Suffice to say, however, that it involves a further possible seizure and a death.

Purdon Martin noted the similarity of these episodes to the partial seizures that Hughlings Jackson had recently described, notably those with 'intellectual auras' which derived from the temporal lobes, or complex partial seizures in our current terminology. He noted that James was a friend of the publisher Frederick Macmillan, who published *Brain*, of which Hughlings Jackson was an editor and which contained many of his papers on epilepsy. Further, brother William was a noted professor of psychology who would have known Hughlings Jackson and quoted his works. Finally, it is known that Alice James, sister to both, was a notorious invalid who suffered from, amongst other ailments, fainting spells and visited many nerve specialists in both England and America.

There is one book and one play devoted entirely to the theme of a woman with epilepsy. The book, *A Ray of Darkness* by Margiad Evans, is an autobiographical account of her epilepsy, which she developed at the age of 41, although it seems she may have had partial seizures since about the age of 9, possibly as a result of a fall from a pony. For her, in the moment of unconsciousness one of two things was happening:

> Either the entities which had gained entrance into myself were saying they would divide me . . . or my incoherent conviction that it was possible to be where I was and be elsewhere at the same time was spiritually symbolical of the One which is everywhere and the everywhere which is one.

She remarkably outlines psychopathological features of epilepsy, which she herself recognizes, and some of which are present before her major seizures begin. Already a deeply spiritual person, she describes how, within two years of her first seizure, she was able to associate it with God. An intense religiosity permeates the whole of this remarkable book, and a seeking for the meaning of her attacks:

What a curious, persistent association this is—God with light! . . . Out of darkness came light, out of God came light, therefore God being the beginning, if not the end, God is darkness—a deep but dazzling darkness.

After experiencing her seizures and having the diagnosis confirmed, she asks: 'Is epilepsy a religious or a moral disease? Is it possible it is my fault?'

She also describes hypergraphia. 'And in my writing I, who had always written so thoughtfully and so slowly that words and phrases were like a birth, began to race over the pages without stopping.' She wrote more and better poetry with mystical and spiritual themes.

Sadly she describes the deleterious effects of her anticonvulsant drugs, phenobarbitone and phenytoin, on her creative processes.

In the text she gives eloquent descriptions of her attacks, and the effects of them on her personality. She notes how she had 'fallen through Time, Continuity and Being'. There is:

total blackness, a hole in the self . . . People who suffer from epilepsy must . . . cling to themselves more than normal people, for they are likely at any moment to become something else . . . They are bound to be reminded that their roots are in darkness . . . in a constant communion . . . with a general and dark source of being.

She describes the religious inturning thus:

So that an epileptic, if he is not born religious, is likely to become so out of his unconscious and profound excursions into infinity. He must find God, or the source which arbitrarily and often absorbs himself.

On theories of demonic possession she opined that they:

arose not from the onlookers of sufferers in fits but from the sufferers themselves. Because in the violent attacks one feels as though the body has been entered by a terrific alien power; and that that power is trying, after entrance, to push its way out again.

The play devoted to a woman with epilepsy is *Night, Mother* by Marsha Norman. This ran originally on Broadway in 1983, and won a Pulitzer prize. It is all about the last hours of a girl who determines to commit suicide, and her mother. Jessie, the girl, 'has never been communicative', but tonight she has 'peaceful energy . . . and . . . a sense of purpose'. The whole play takes place in the kitchen and living room of their house around 8.30 p.m. Jessie has determined to shoot herself, and declares this intention to her mother. Her immediate response is 'it must be time for your medicine'! Her potential incompetence to carry out this final act is declared:

You'll miss. You'll end up a vegetable. How would you like that? Shoot your ear off? You know what the doctor said about getting excited. You'll cock the pistol and have a fit.

As the time passes on, elements of her seizure history are revealed. She at one time had gum hypertrophy and memory problems, suggestive of phenytoin treatment which had been changed to barbiturates. Whether the latter had anything to do with her suicide is unclear, but it is known that this drug is particularly associated with suicide attempts and death (Brent *et al.*, 1986).

She is unable to get a job. Friends and neighbours will not visit the house if she is there because they 'can't take the chance it's catching', and her husband and child have left her. Her mother explains:

> Your fits made him sick and you know it.

She replies angrily:

> Say seizures, not fits. Seizures.

It is revealed that her father had a seizure disorder. Jessie asks what she is like when she has her attacks:

> You just . . . crumple, in a heap, like a puppet and somebody cut the strings all at once, or like the firing squad in some Mexican movie, you just slide down the wall . . . Your chest squeezes in and out, and you sound like you're gagging, sucking air in and out . . . it's awful sounding . . . Your mouth bites down and I have to get your tongue out of the way fast . . . and then you turn blue, and the jerks start up. Like I'm standing there poking you with a cattle prod or you're sticking your finger in a light socket as fast as you can.

Jessie interposes:

> Foaming like a mad dog the whole time.

Her mother replies:

> It's bubbling, Jess, not foam like the washer overflowed, for God's sake; it's bubbling like a baby spitting up. I go get a wet washcloth, that's all. And then the jerks slow down and you wet yourself and it's over.

Jessie had always been led to believe that her seizures started when she fell off a horse as an adolescent, but it is revealed that she had them as a small child. Why, she wonders, was she not told? The inevitable conclusion that Jessie spits to her mother is 'You were ashamed.' She describes her estrangement:

> *Mama:* You are my child.
>
> *Jessie:* I am what became of your child. I found an old baby picture of me. And it was somebody else, not me. It was somebody pink and fat who never heard of sick or lonely . . . It's somebody I lost . . . it's my own self. Who I never was . . . Somebody I waited for who never came. And never will.

WOMEN WITH EPILEPSY AS REPRESENTED IN OTHER MODERN NOVELS

There are scattered references to women with epilepsy in several other stories, including *The Andromeda Strain* by Michael Crichton, *Heat and Dust* by Ruth Prawer Jhabvala, and *History* by Elsa Morante.

In the original of *The Andromeda Strain*, five scientists are called on to crack the mystery of a strange infective particle that ravages communities by producing coagulation of the blood, especially in the brain. In the book, all five scientists are male, and one, Leavitt, has a seizure provoked by warning lights which are flashing at three cycles per second. The pejorative nature of the description of the attack is interesting, Leavitt 'crying, through his clenched teeth, like an animal'. Thus, in the film version, the part is transposed to that of a woman, and through the seizure a vital clue to the solution of the problem is missed. The female then becomes the weak link, notably through her epilepsy.

In *Heat and Dust*, an infant is described who has nocturnal seizures. She is the daughter of an Indian housekeeper, and immediately after the attack the mother scatters rice grains over her head.

History documents the life of Iduzza, an Italian teacher who from the age of 5 had seizures which came 'from some subterranean source'. In them, 'a brutal electrical current seemed to assail her little body'. She grows up ashamed of two stigma—being epileptic and having Jewish blood in her ancestry—themes which permeate the story. Interestingly, there is a description of her having a seizure provoked by rape, for which she is amnesic, but as a consequence of which she becomes pregnant.

Finally, in relationship to novels, the pejorative image that epilepsy often arouses is noted in William Peter Blatty's *The Exorcist*. The child, possessed and finally exorcised, makes a dramatic entrance to a dinner party that her parents are hosting by urinating on the dining room carpet. She develops attacks of shaking, and is taken to a neurologist. Her complaints, and those of her mother, are taken as evidence of epilepsy, especially the bad smells that the child experiences, and her amnesic episodes. Although her EEG is normal, a diagnosis of temporal lobe epilepsy is made, and retained for a while. In this book, ideas of possession are intermingled with those of epilepsy, schizophrenia and hysteria, and no resolution to the muddle emerges as the story progresses.

TWO IMPORTANT WOMEN WITH EPILEPSY

It is often noted that behind every famous man there is a female, and epileptologists are no exception. Hughlings Jackson married his cousin Elizabeth Dade Jackson when he was 30 years old. They had known each other from childhood, and had been engaged for seven years. Although so little is known about Hughlings Jackson's personal life, it is recorded that his wife developed cerebral thrombosis, and as a consequence of this illness she developed localized seizures. Hughlings Jackson thus witnessed these first hand, and it is suggested that this experience must have inspired and coloured his lifelong interest in epilepsy, and his descriptions of focal seizures.

His wife died at the age of 31 and thereafter Hughlings Jackson seems to have become somewhat of a social recluse, took little interest in hospital politics and travelled as little as possible.

The other great epileptologist whose work may have been inspired by a woman was William Lennox. He wanted to be a missionary in China, but was persuaded to obtain medical training. After this, he went to China with his wife and three children. Two of his daughters developed whooping cough, and one of them had frequent nocturnal convulsions. She was 5 at the time (1921), and the attacks continued for two years.

On return to the USA a paediatric neurologist diagnosed epilepsy, and suggested that the child should go to an institution. Lennox, whose preferred line of therapy was prayer and physical fitness (there were no substantive treatments for epilepsy at that time), was horrified, and his lifelong devotion to the understanding and management of epilepsy was born.

CONCLUSIONS

Epilepsy, in one form or another, and in one way or another, has inspired saints, mystics, philosophers, writers, physicians, health care workers and patients. The (on the whole) pejorative nature of so much that has been written about epilepsy contrasts with the trials, tribulations and achievements of so many who have suffered from or suffered its outrageous paroxysms of self-distortion and annihilation. The personalities reviewed here— all women who have had, or who are said to have had, epilepsy—are as much a part of the heritage of the disorder, as purely medical and technological achievements.

Some will feel that a number of the cases described had hysterical or pseudoseizures, especially some of the more flamboyant visionary mystics and martyred saints. Hagiography will take us no further, but even such events intertwine with the history of epilepsy itself and our current clinical practice. Indeed, a separate manuscript could be written on 'women and pseudoseizures', and include such characters as Tennyson's Elaine, Charlotte Brontë's Lucy in *Villette*, and some of the characters from the tales of Maupassant. For a marvellous example read *The Graveyard Sisterhood*.

The drama of seizures belongs to women as well as men; the urge to be famous belongs to all.

REFERENCES

Adams, F. (1939) *The Genuine Works of Hippocrates*. Williams and Wilkins, Baltimore.

Bayne, L. and Foot-Smith, E. (1991) Joan of Arc. *Epilepsia* (in press).

Brent, D.A. (1986) Overrepresentation of epileptics in a consecutive series of suicide attempters seen at a children's hospital, 1978–1983. *J. Am. Acad. Child. Psychiatry*, **25**, 242–246.

Dewhurst, K. and Beard, A.W. (1970) Sudden religious conversions in temporal lobe epilepsy. *Br. J. Psychiatry*, **117**, 497–508.

Howden, J.C. (1873) The religious sentiments of epileptics. *J. Ment. Sci.*, **18**, 482–497.

Lennox, W.G. (1941) *Science and Seizures*. Harper Brothers, New York.

Purdon Martin, J. (1973) Neurology in fiction: The turn of the screw. *Br. Med. J.*, **4**, 717–721.

Ratnasuriya, R.H. (1986) Joan of Arc, creative psychopath: Is there another explanation? *J. R. Soc. Med.*, **79**, 234–235.

Temkin, O. (1971) *The Falling Sickness*. Johns Hopkins, Baltimore.

Index